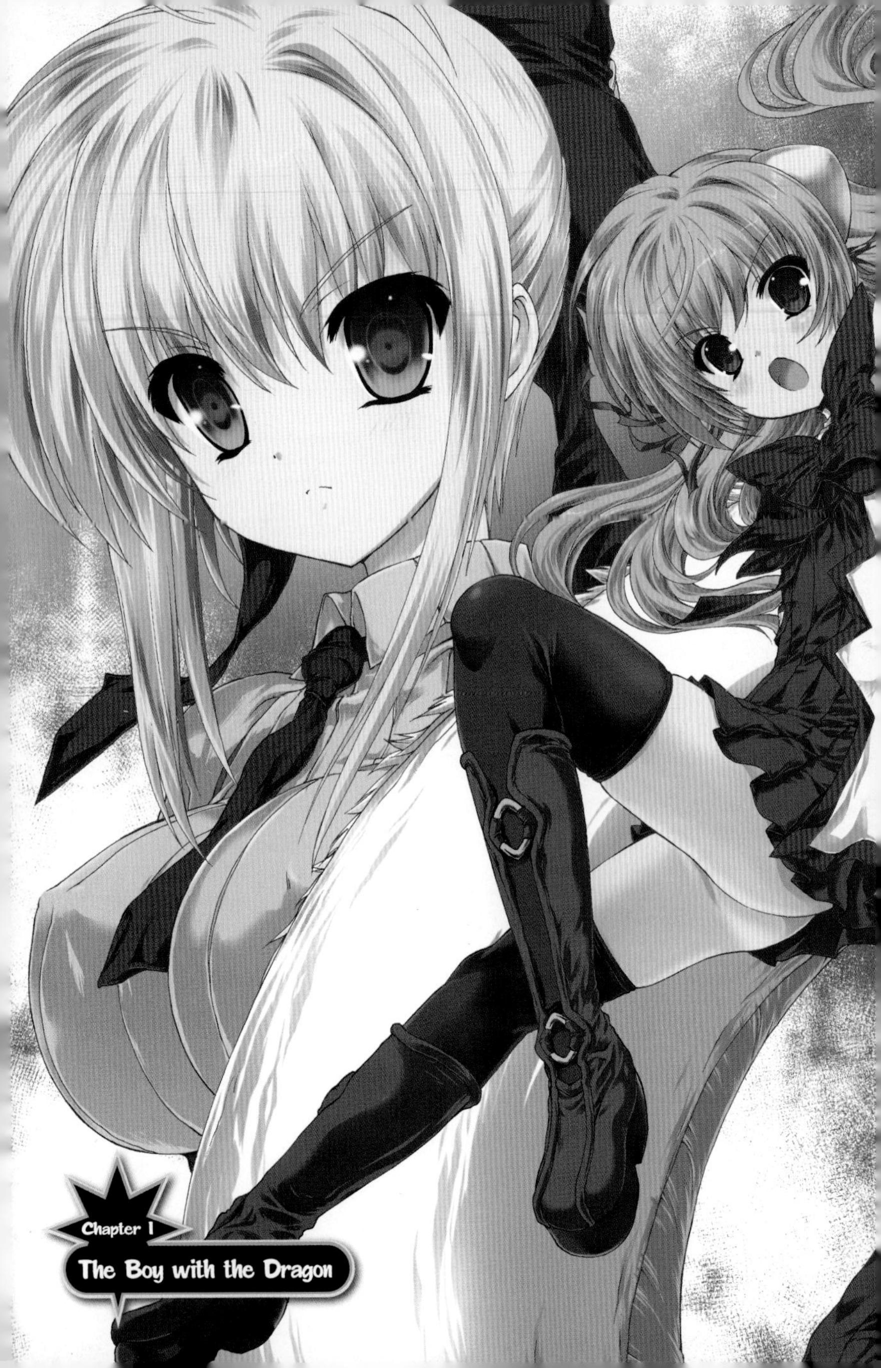
Chapter 1
The Boy with the Dragon

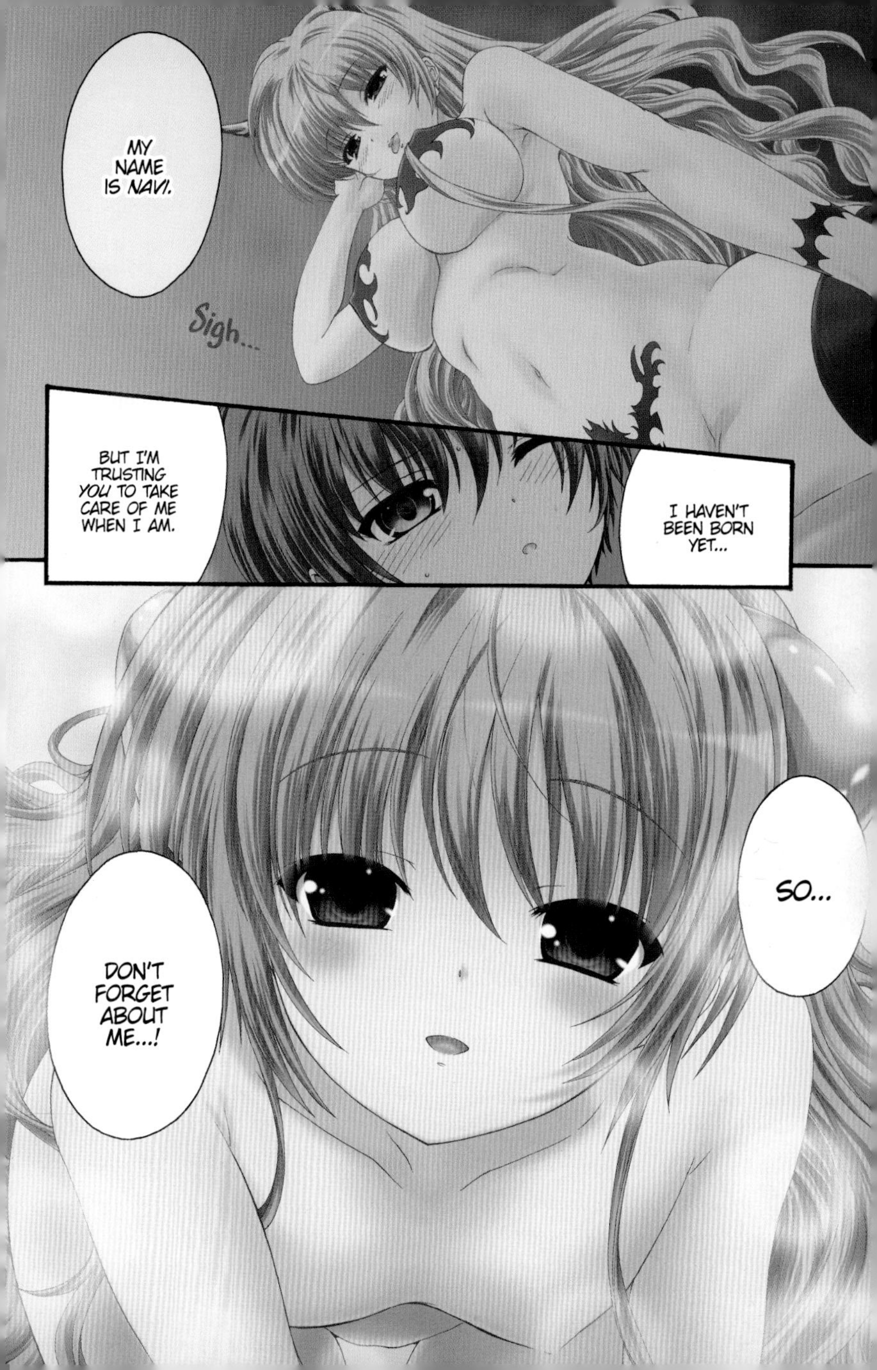
MY NAME IS NAVI.
Sigh...
I HAVEN'T BEEN BORN YET...
BUT I'M TRUSTING YOU TO TAKE CARE OF ME WHEN I AM.
SO...
DON'T FORGET ABOUT ME...!

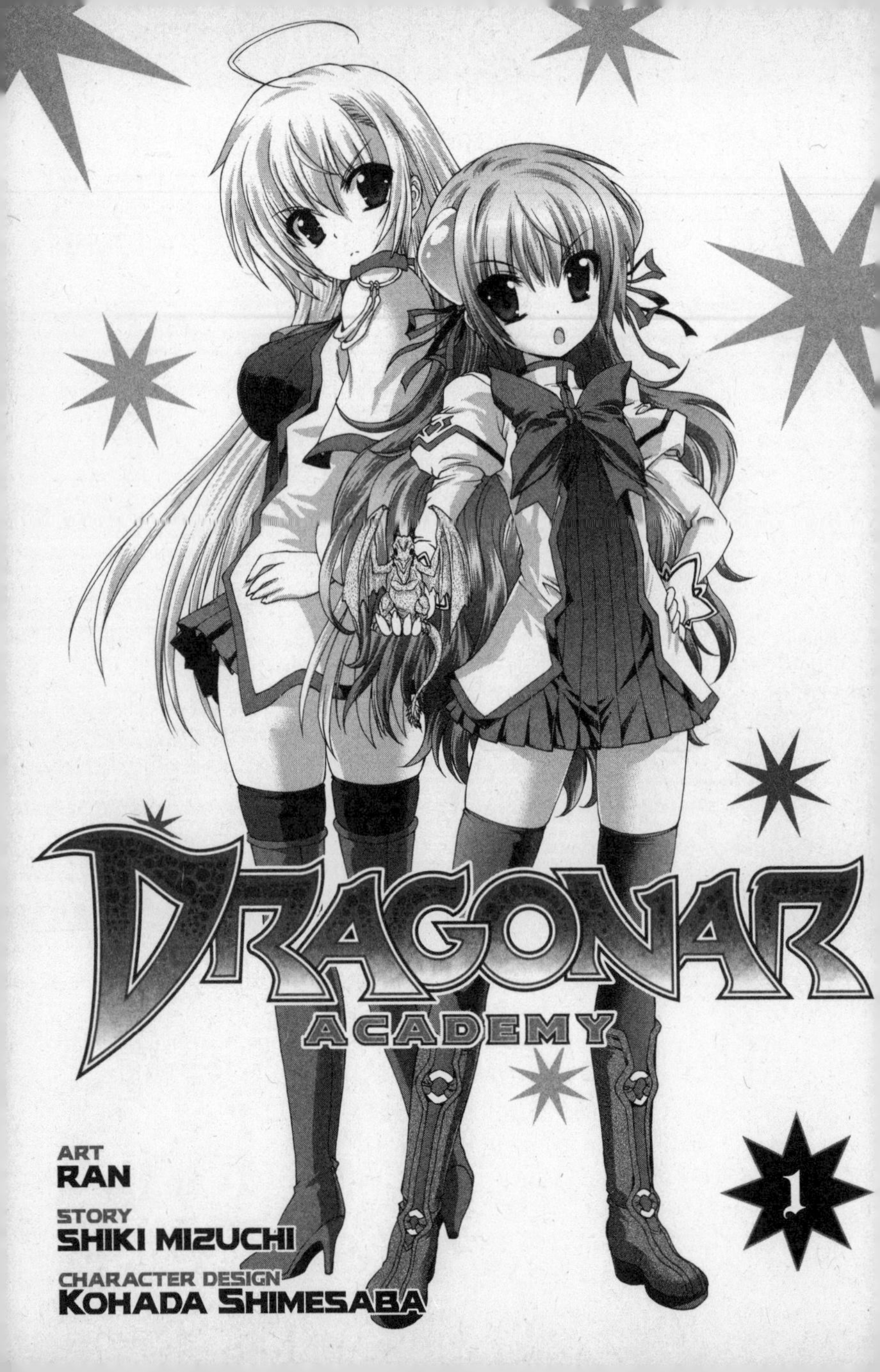
DRAGONAR
ACADEMY
1
ART
RAN
STORY
SHIKI MIZUCHI
CHARACTER DESIGN
KOHADA SHIMESABA

SEVEN SEAS ENTERTAINMENT PRESENTS

DRAGONAR ACADEMY

VOLUME 1

art by **RAN** / story by **SHIKI MIZUCHI** / Character Design by **KOHADA SHIMESABA**

TRANSLATION
Yuko Fukami

ADAPTATION
Libby Mitchell

LETTERING AND LAYOUT
Paweł Szczęszek

COVER DESIGN
Phil Balsman
Nicky Lim

PROOFREADER
Laura Hastings
Conner Crooks

MANAGING EDITOR
Adam Arnold

PUBLISHER
Jason DeAngelis

DRAGONAR ACADEMY VOL. 1
© Ran 2011, © Shiki Mizuchi 2011
Edited by MEDIA FACTORY.
First published in Japan in 2011 by KADOKAWA CORPORATION.
English translation rights reserved by Seven Seas Entertainment, LLC.
under the license from KADOKAWA CORPORATION, Tokyo.

Seven Seas books may be purchased in bulk for educational, business, or
promotional use. For information on bulk purchases, please contact Macmillan
Corporate & Premium Sales Department at 1-800-221-7945 (ext 5442)
or write specialmarkets@macmillan.com.

Seven Seas and the Seven Seas logo are trademarks of
Seven Seas Entertainment, LLC. All rights reserved.

ISBN: 978-1-626920-04-0

Printed in Canada

First Printing: February 2014

10 9 8 7 6 5 4 3 2 1

FOLLOW US ONLINE: *www.gomanga.com*

READING DIRECTIONS

This book reads from *right to left*, Japanese style.
If this is your first time reading manga, you start
reading from the top right panel on each page and
take it from there. If you get lost, just follow the
numbered diagram here. It may seem backwards at
first, but you'll get the hang of it! Have fun!!

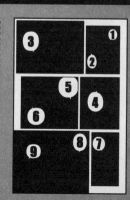

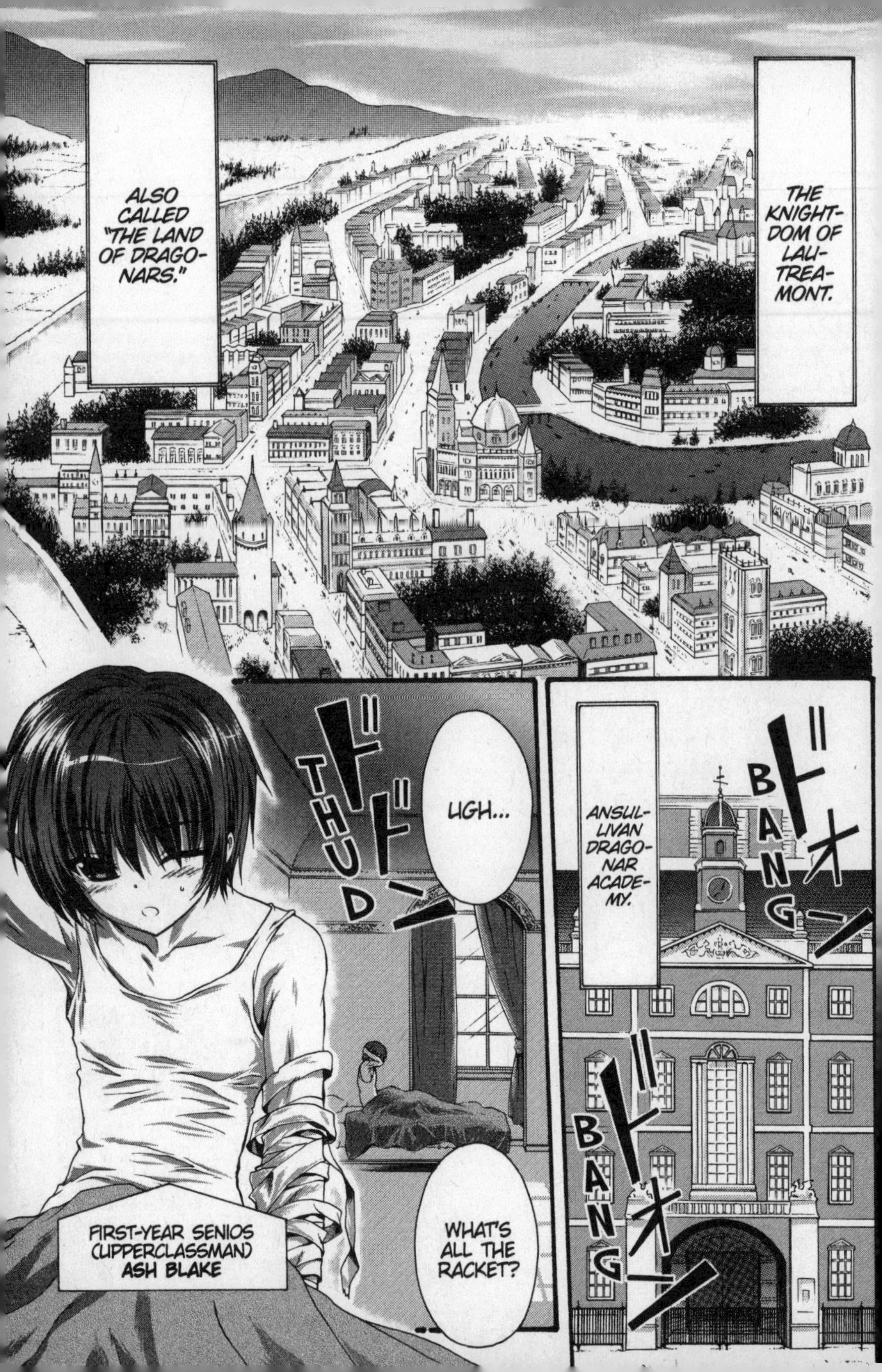
THE KNIGHTDOM OF LAUTREAMONT.
ALSO CALLED "THE LAND OF DRAGONARS."
ANSULLIVAN DRAGONAR ACADEMY.
BANG
BANG
THUD
UGH...
WHAT'S ALL THE RACKET?
FIRST-YEAR SENIOS (UPPERCLASSMAN) ASH BLAKE

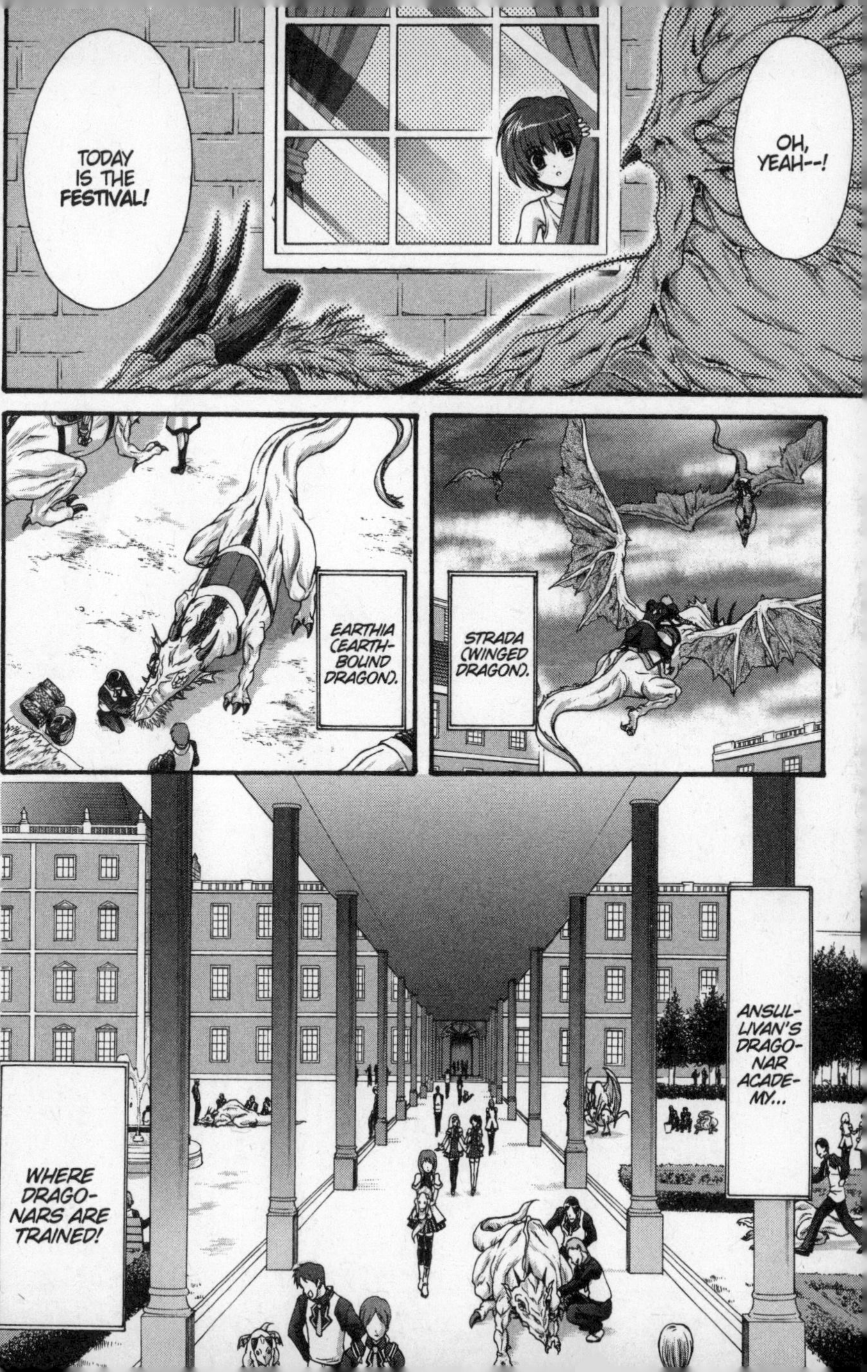
OH, YEAH--!
TODAY IS THE FESTIVAL!
STRADA (WINGED DRAGON).
EARTHIA (EARTH-BOUND DRAGON).
ANSULLIVAN'S DRAGONAR ACADEMY...
WHERE DRAGONARS ARE TRAINED!

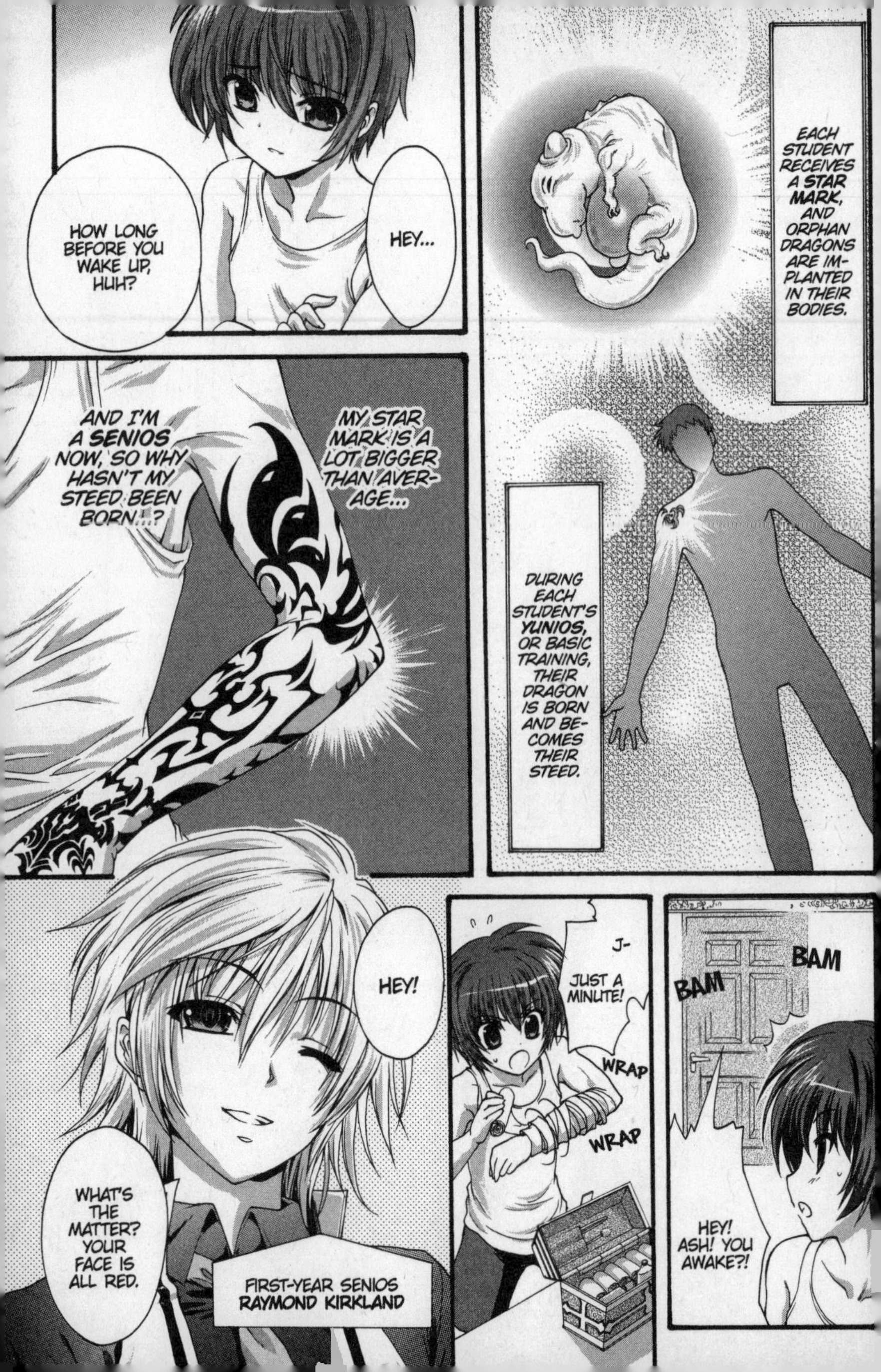
EACH STUDENT RECEIVES A STAR MARK, AND ORPHAN DRAGONS ARE IMPLANTED IN THEIR BODIES.
DURING EACH STUDENT'S YUNIOS, OR BASIC TRAINING, THEIR DRAGON IS BORN AND BECOMES THEIR STEED.
HEY...
HOW LONG BEFORE YOU WAKE UP, HUH?
MY STAR MARK IS A LOT BIGGER THAN AVERAGE...
AND I'M A SENIOS NOW, SO WHY HASN'T MY STEED BEEN BORN...?
BAM
BAM
HEY! ASH! YOU AWAKE?!
J-
JUST A MINUTE!
WRAP
WRAP
HEY!
WHAT'S THE MATTER? YOUR FACE IS ALL RED.
FIRST-YEAR SENIOS RAYMOND KIRKLAND

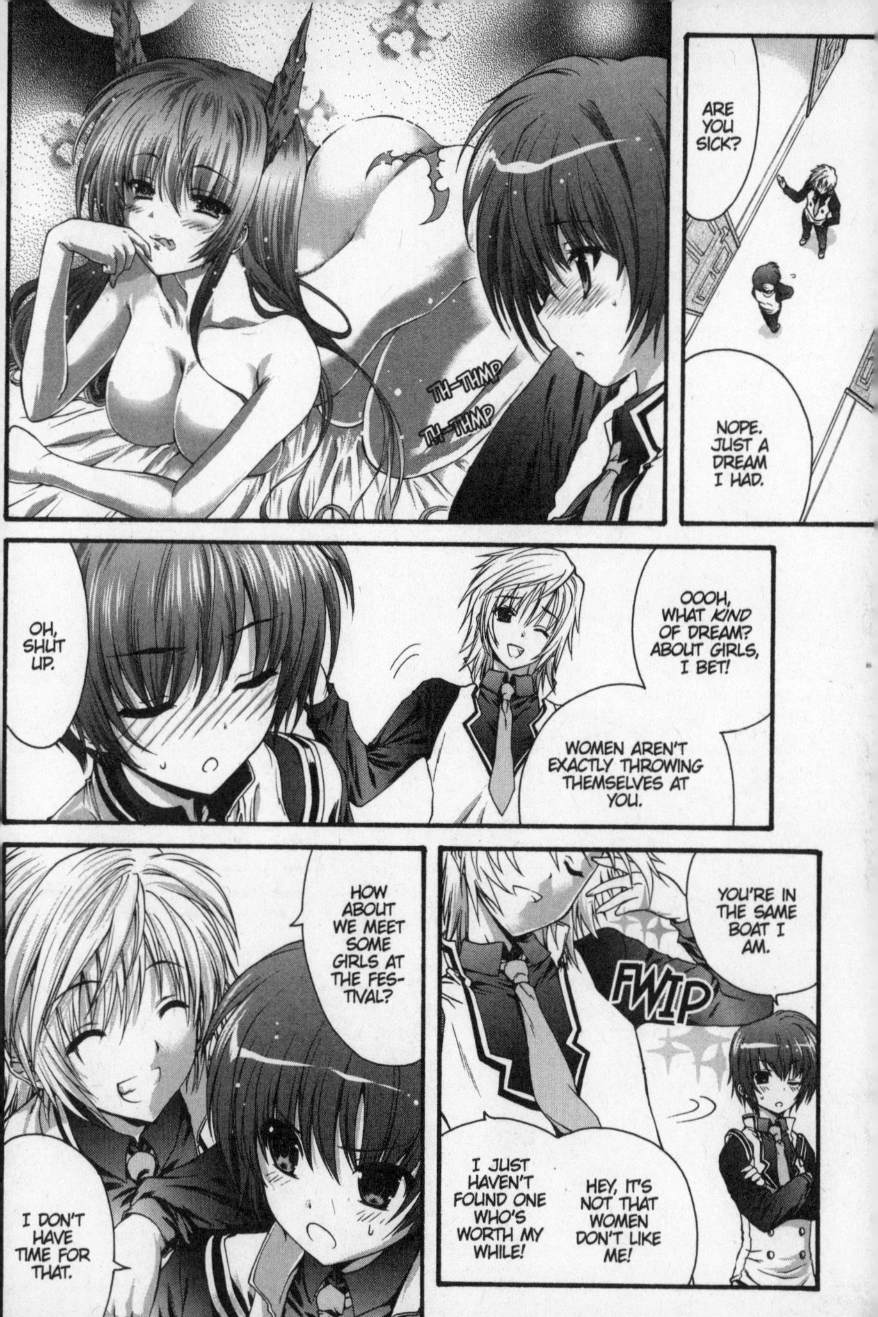
ARE YOU SICK?
NOPE. JUST A DREAM I HAD.
TH-THMP
TH-THMP
OOOH, WHAT *KIND* OF DREAM? ABOUT GIRLS, I BET!
WOMEN AREN'T EXACTLY THROWING THEMSELVES AT YOU.
OH, SHUT UP.
YOU'RE IN THE SAME BOAT I AM.
FWIP
HEY, IT'S NOT THAT WOMEN DON'T LIKE ME!
I JUST HAVEN'T FOUND ONE WHO'S WORTH MY WHILE!
HOW ABOUT WE MEET SOME GIRLS AT THE FES-TIVAL?
I DON'T HAVE TIME FOR THAT.

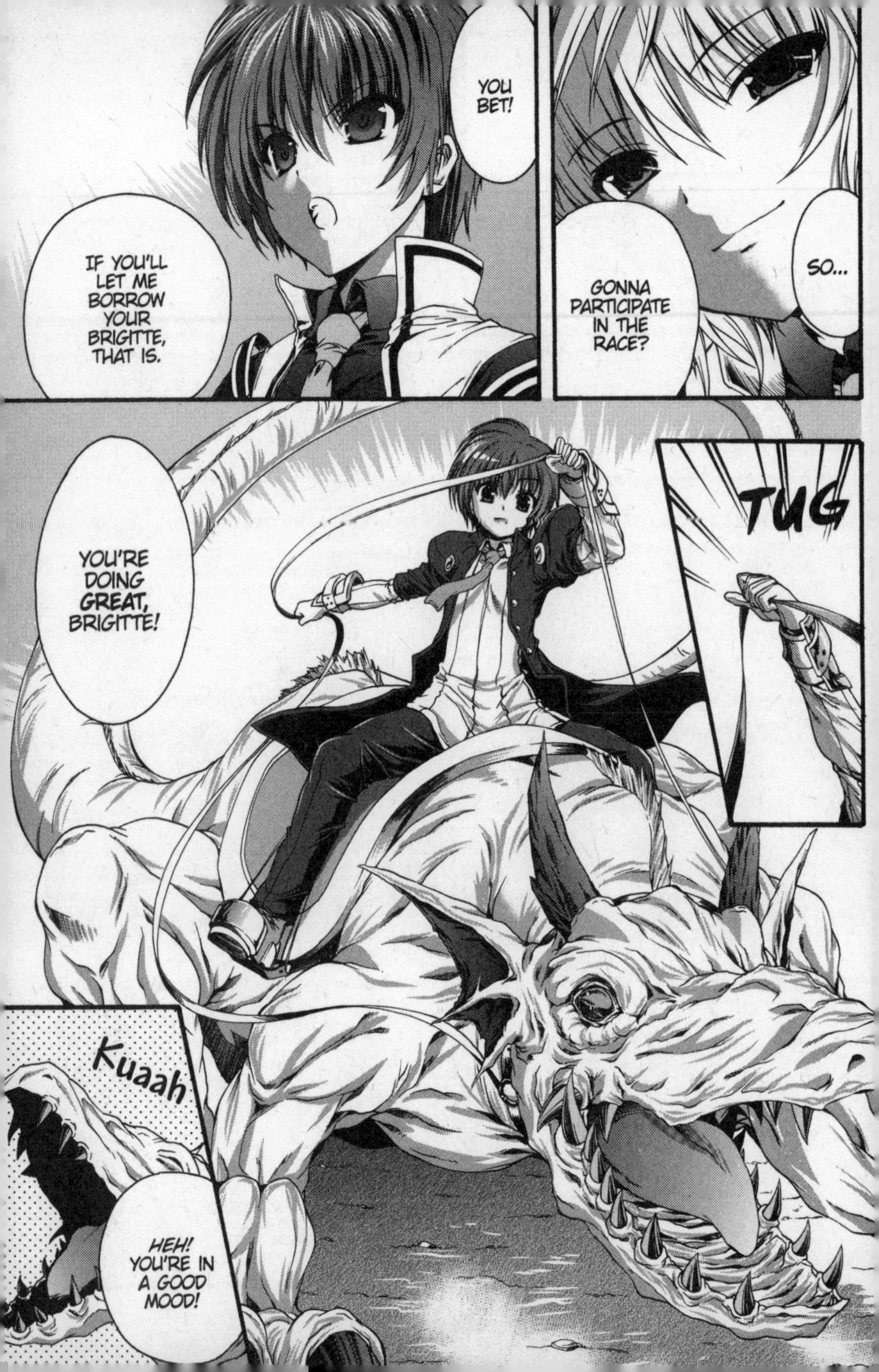
SO...
GONNA PARTICIPATE IN THE RACE?
YOU BET!
IF YOU'LL LET ME BORROW YOUR BRIGITTE, THAT IS.
TUG
YOU'RE DOING GREAT, BRIGITTE!
Kuaah
HEH! YOU'RE IN A GOOD MOOD!

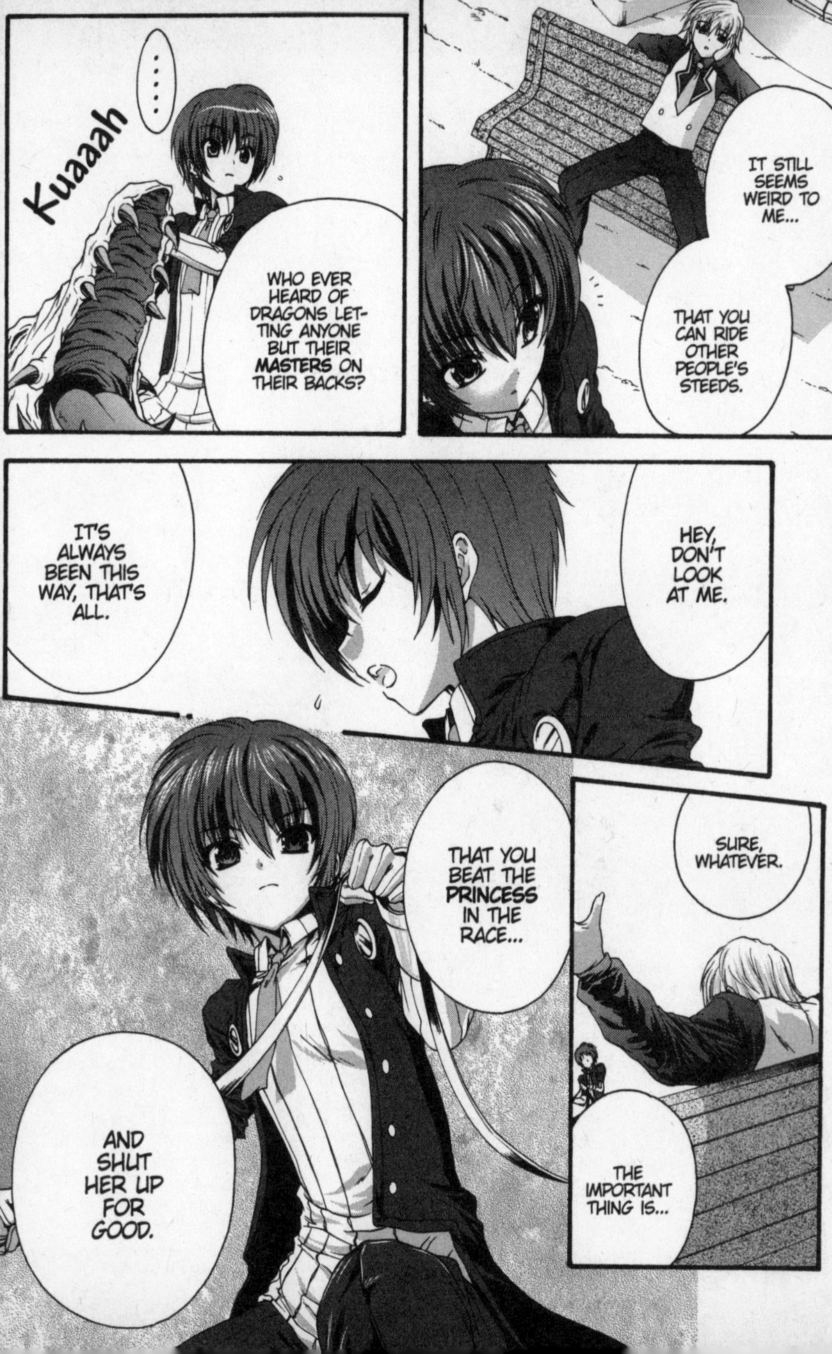
IT STILL SEEMS WEIRD TO ME...
THAT YOU CAN RIDE OTHER PEOPLE'S STEEDS.
......
Kuaaah
WHO EVER HEARD OF DRAGONS LET-TING ANYONE BUT THEIR MASTERS ON THEIR BACKS?
HEY, DON'T LOOK AT ME.
IT'S ALWAYS BEEN THIS WAY, THAT'S ALL.
SURE, WHATEVER.
THE IMPORTANT THING IS...
THAT YOU BEAT THE PRINCESS IN THE RACE...
AND SHUT HER UP FOR GOOD.

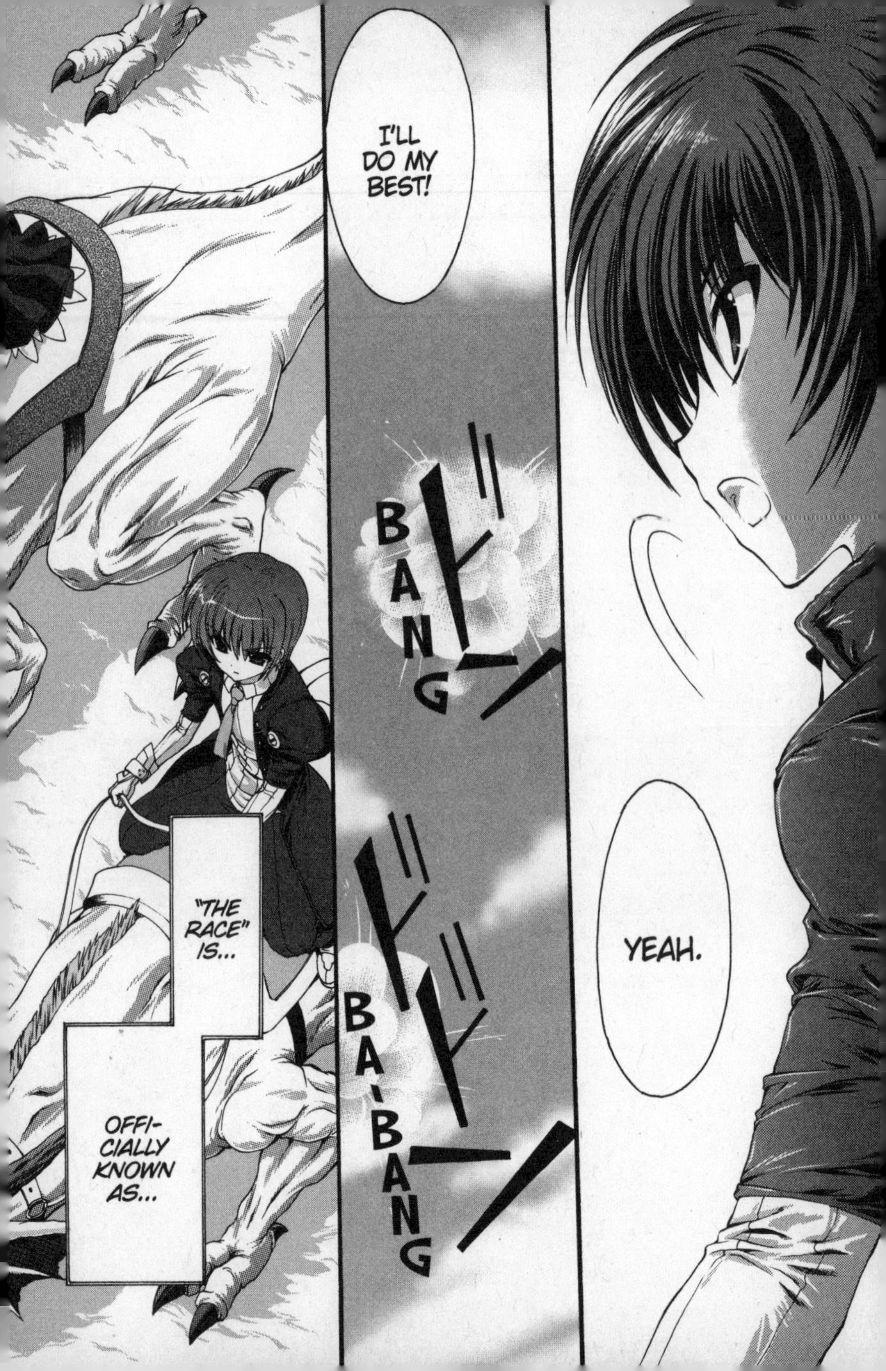
YEAH.
I'LL DO MY BEST!
BANG
BA-BANG
"THE RACE" IS...
OFFI-CIALLY KNOWN AS...

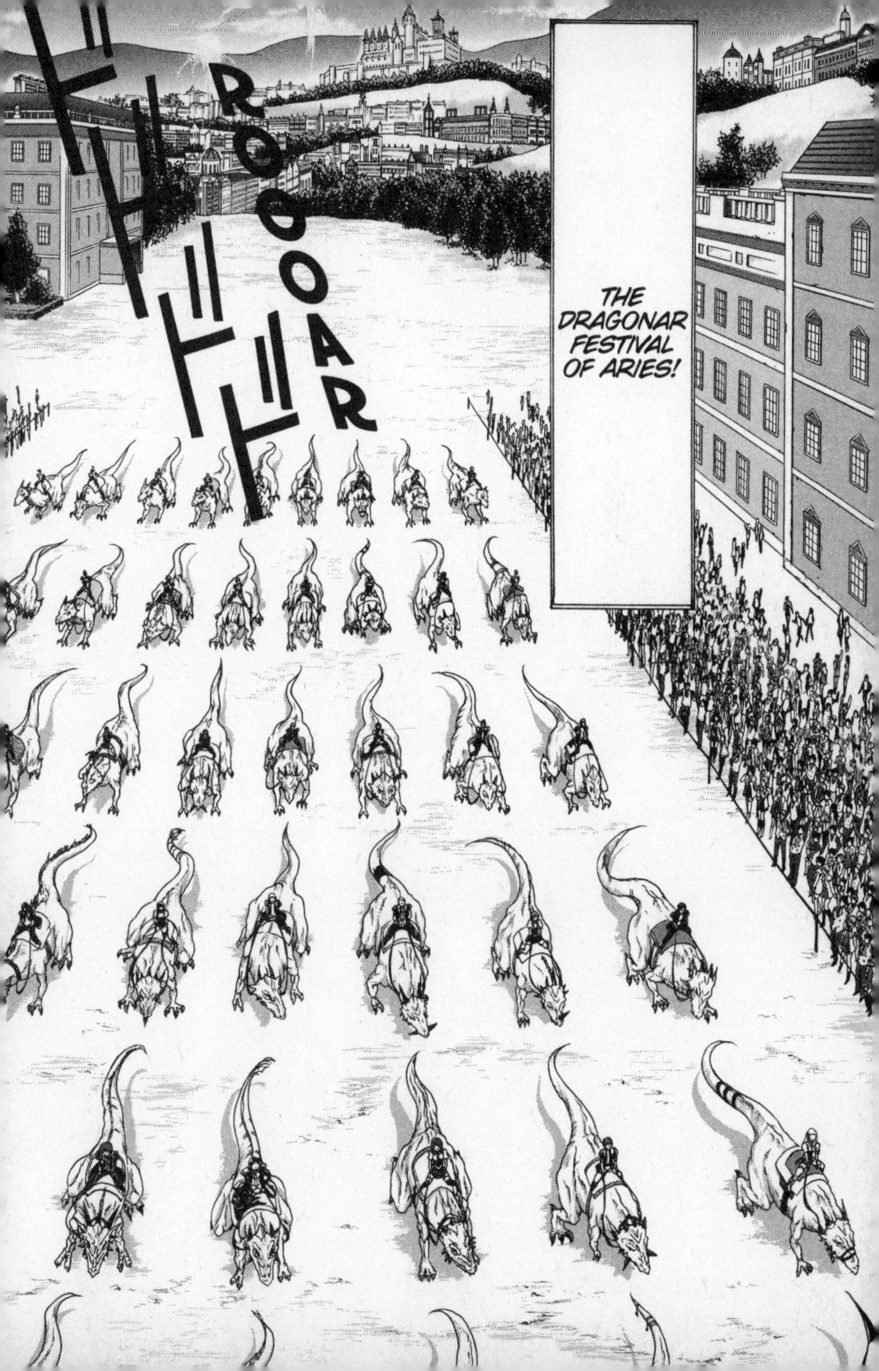

THE DRAGONAR FESTIVAL OF ARIES!
ROOOOAR

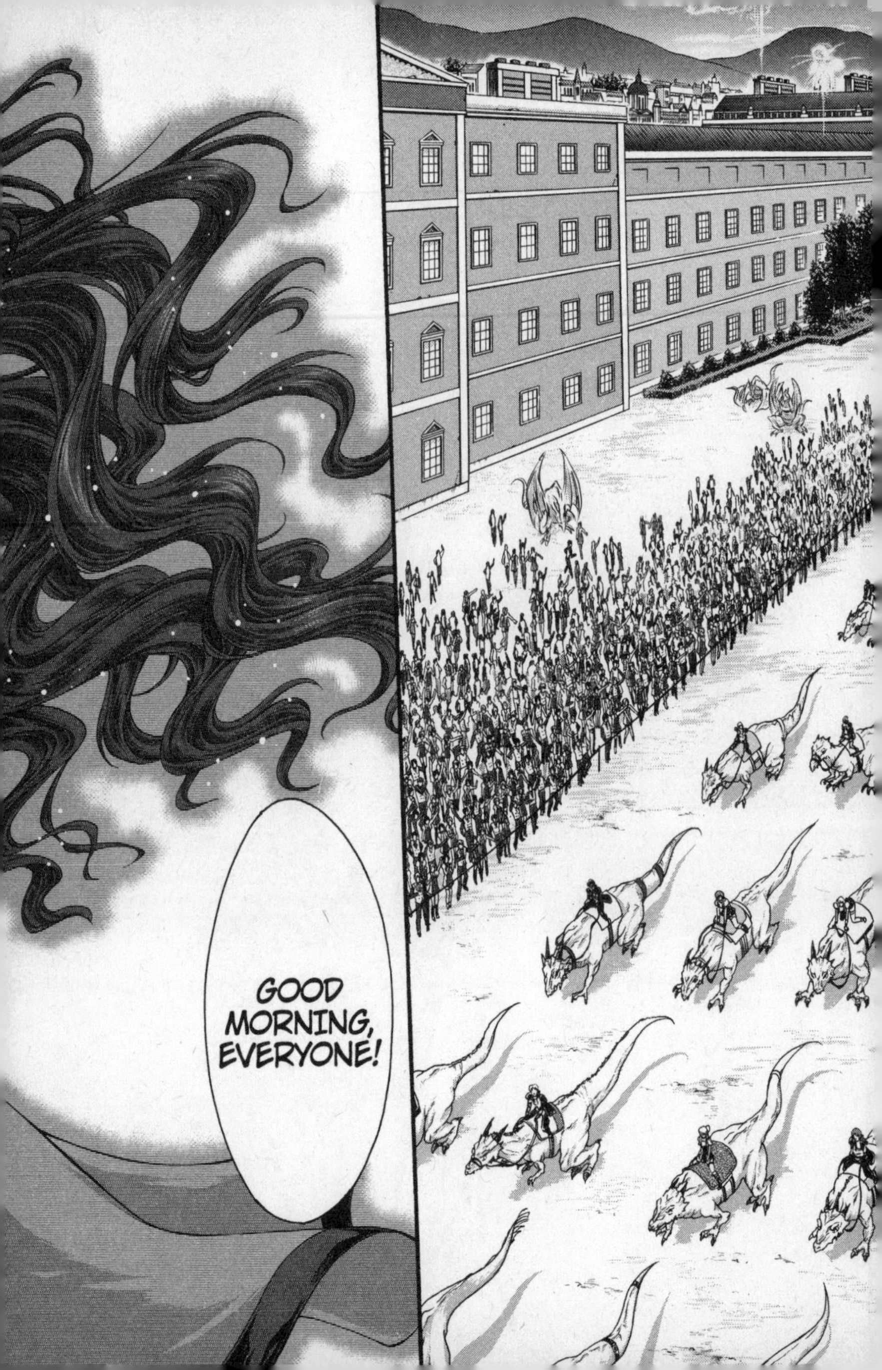
GOOD MORNING, EVERYONE!

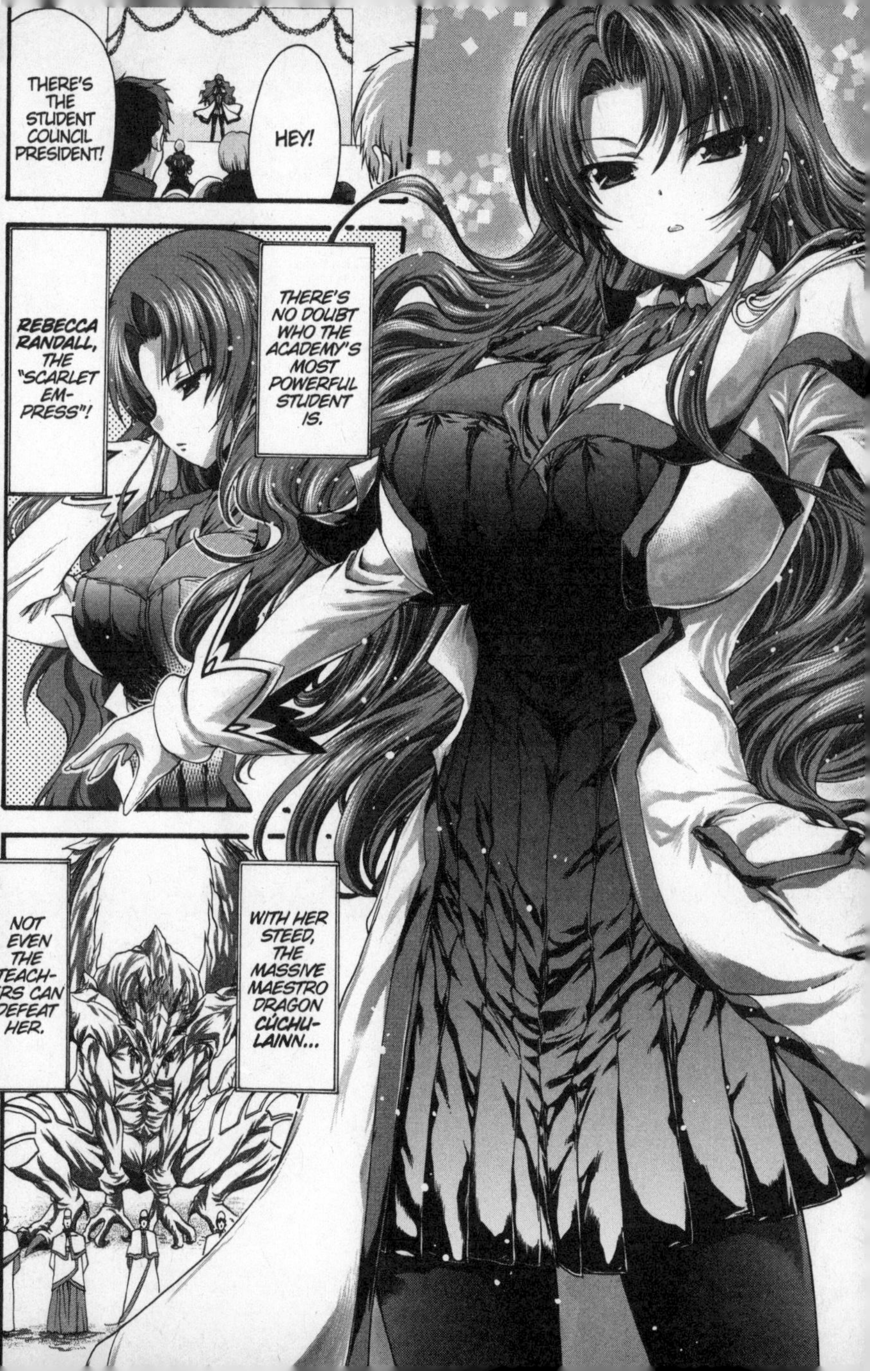
HEY!
THERE'S THE STUDENT COUNCIL PRESIDENT!
THERE'S NO DOUBT WHO THE ACADEMY'S MOST POWERFUL STUDENT IS.
REBECCA RANDALL, THE "SCARLET EM-PRESS"!
WITH HER STEED, THE MASSIVE MAESTRO DRAGON CÚCHU-LAINN...
NOT EVEN THE TEACH-ERS CAN DEFEAT HER.

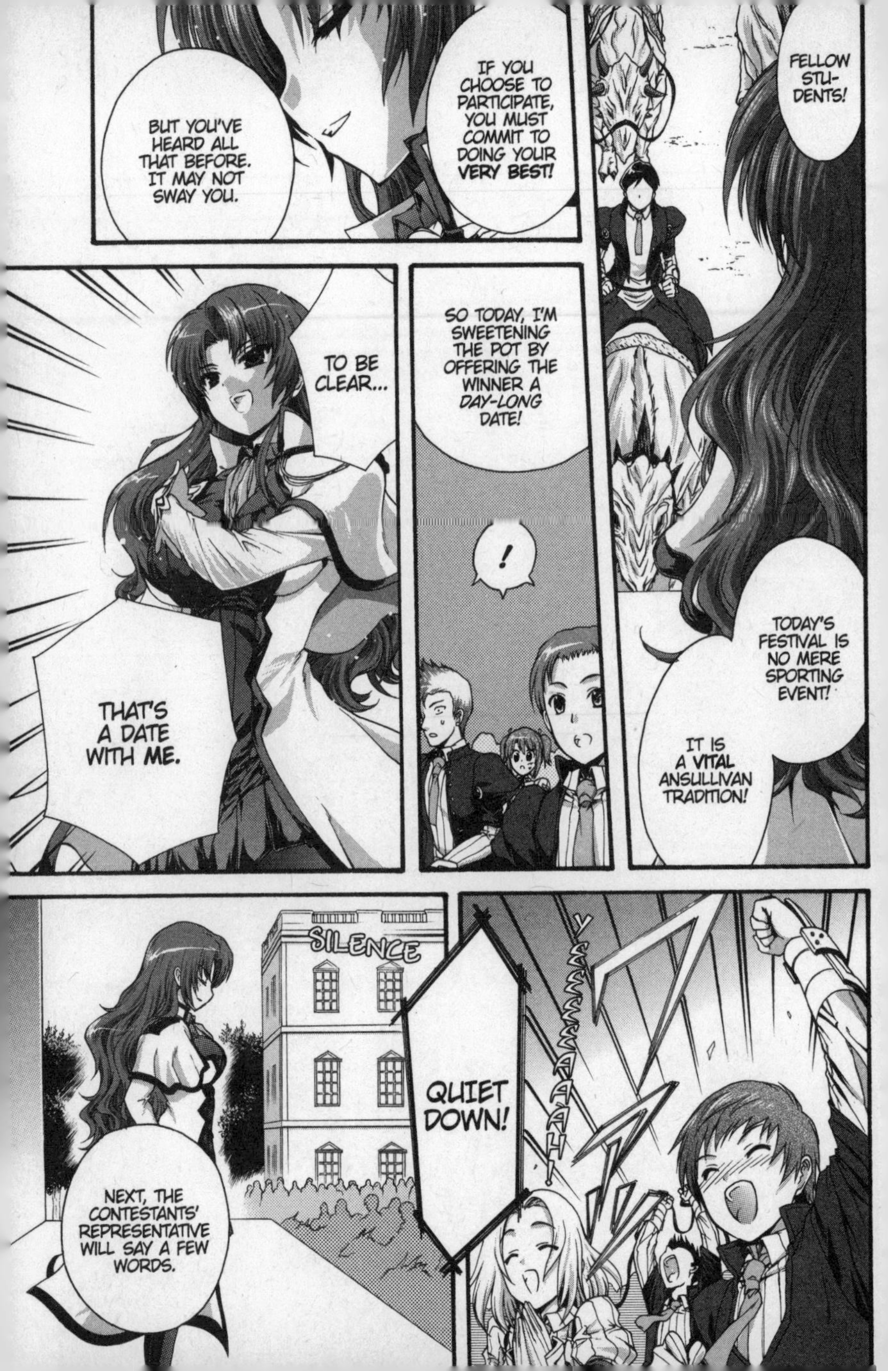
FELLOW STU-DENTS!
TODAY'S FESTIVAL IS NO MERE SPORTING EVENT!
IT IS A VITAL ANSULLIVAN TRADITION!
IF YOU CHOOSE TO PARTICIPATE, YOU MUST COMMIT TO DOING YOUR VERY BEST!
BUT YOU'VE HEARD ALL THAT BEFORE. IT MAY NOT SWAY YOU.
SO TODAY, I'M SWEETENING THE POT BY OFFERING THE WINNER A DAY-LONG DATE!
!
TO BE CLEAR...
THAT'S A DATE WITH ME.
YEEEEEAAAAAH!
QUIET DOWN!
SILENCE
NEXT, THE CONTESTANTS' REPRESENTATIVE WILL SAY A FEW WORDS.

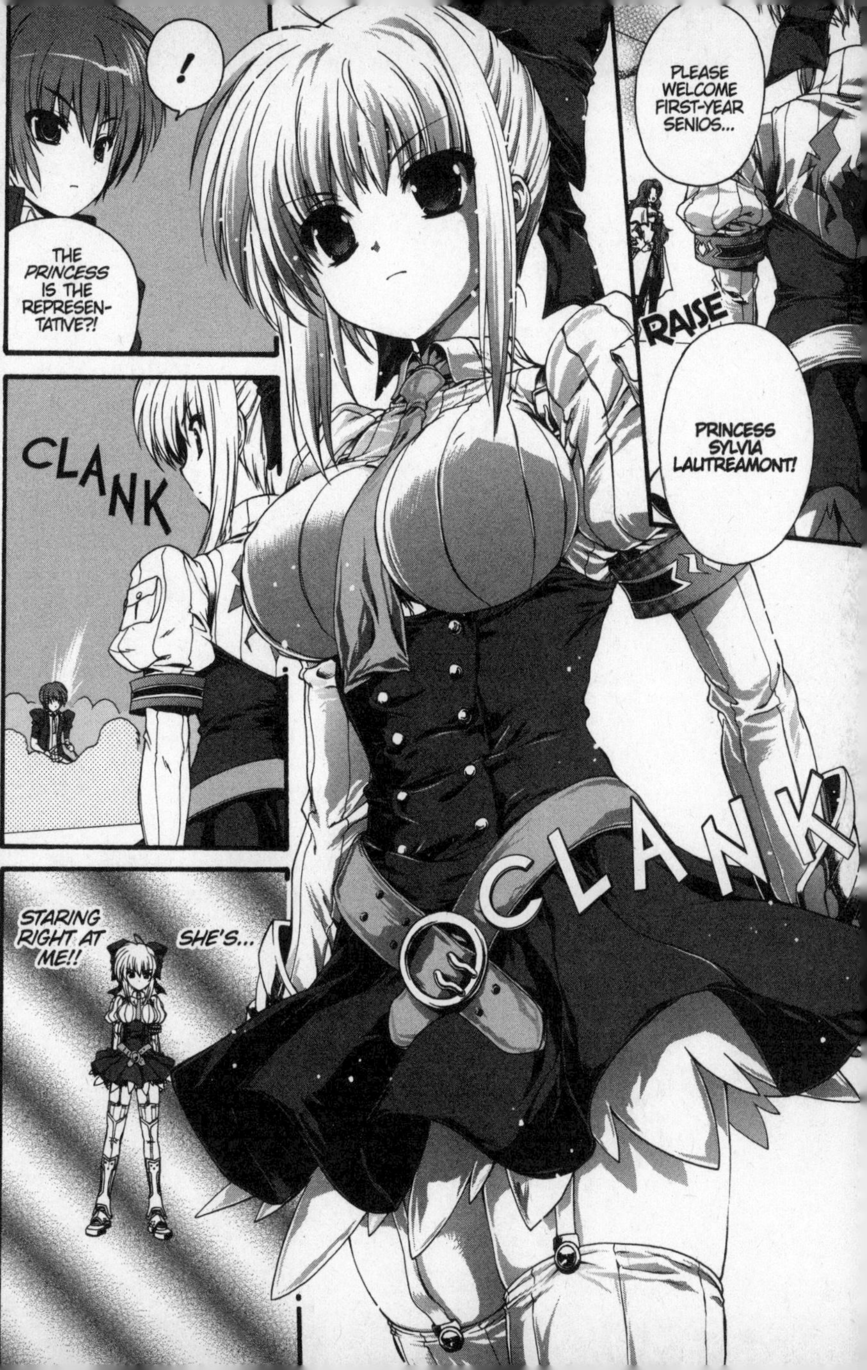
PLEASE WELCOME FIRST-YEAR SENIOS...
RAISE
PRINCESS SYLVIA LAUTREAMONT!
CLANK
!
THE PRINCESS IS THE REPRESEN-TATIVE?!
CLANK
SHE'S...
STARING RIGHT AT ME!!

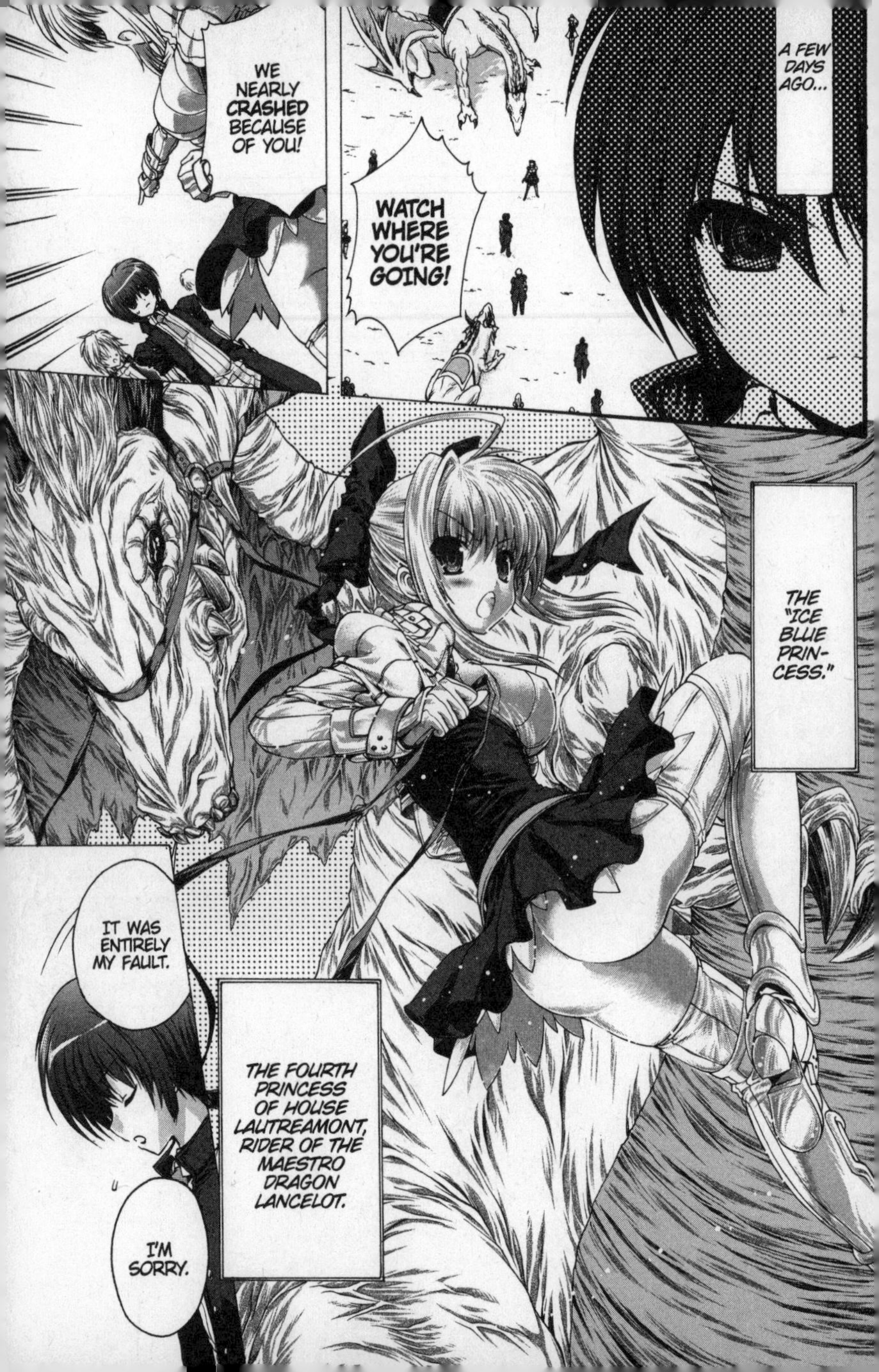
A FEW DAYS AGO...
WATCH WHERE YOU'RE GOING!
WE NEARLY CRASHED BECAUSE OF YOU!
THE "ICE BLUE PRIN-CESS."
THE FOURTH PRINCESS OF HOUSE LAUTREAMONT, RIDER OF THE MAESTRO DRAGON LANCELOT.
IT WAS ENTIRELY MY FAULT.
I'M SORRY.

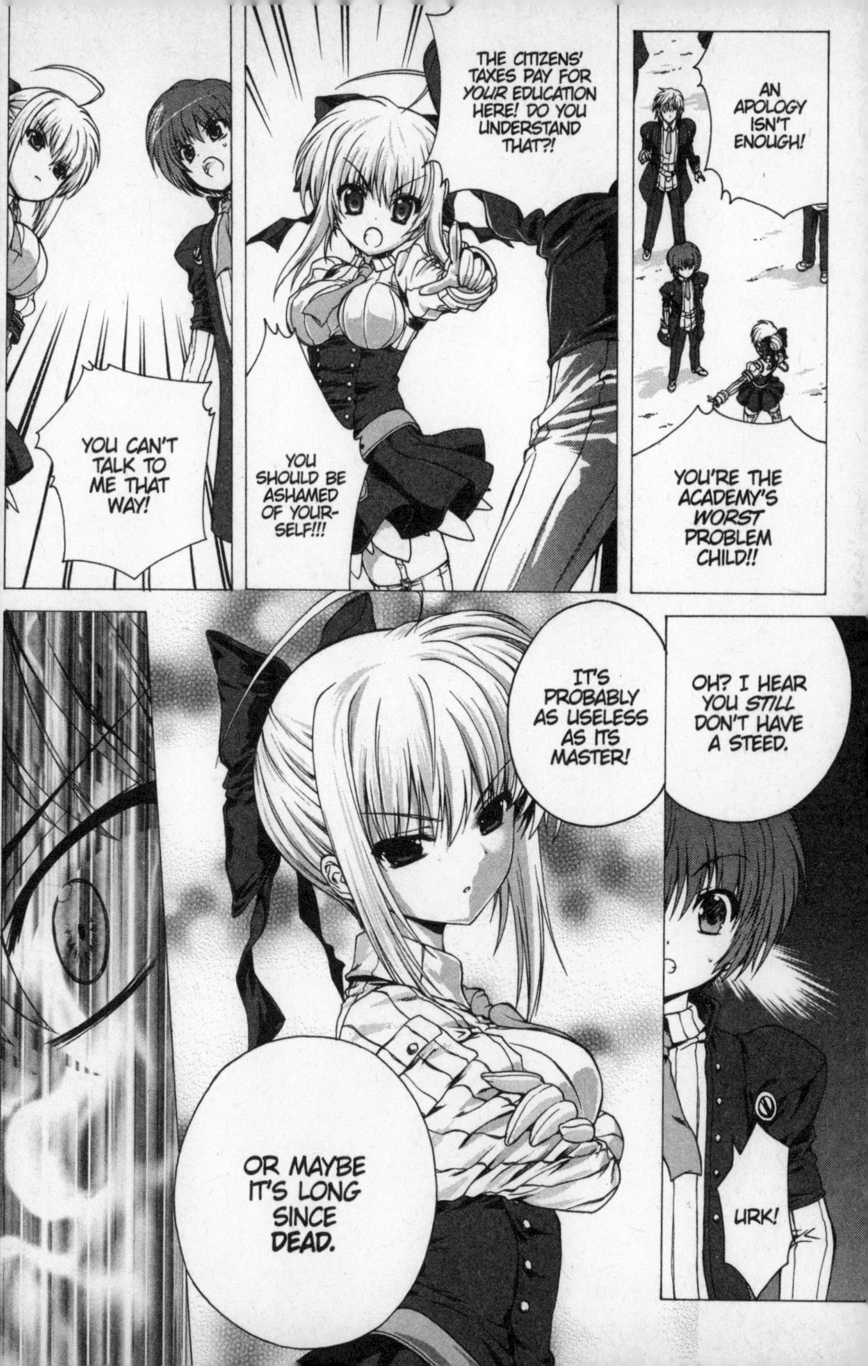
AN APOLOGY ISN'T ENOUGH!
YOU'RE THE ACADEMY'S *WORST* PROBLEM CHILD!!
THE CITIZENS' TAXES PAY FOR *YOUR* EDUCATION HERE! DO YOU UNDERSTAND THAT?!
YOU SHOULD BE ASHAMED OF YOUR-SELF!!!
YOU CAN'T TALK TO ME THAT WAY!
OH? I HEAR YOU *STILL* DON'T HAVE A STEED.
URK!
IT'S PROBABLY AS USELESS AS ITS MASTER!
OR MAYBE IT'S LONG SINCE DEAD.

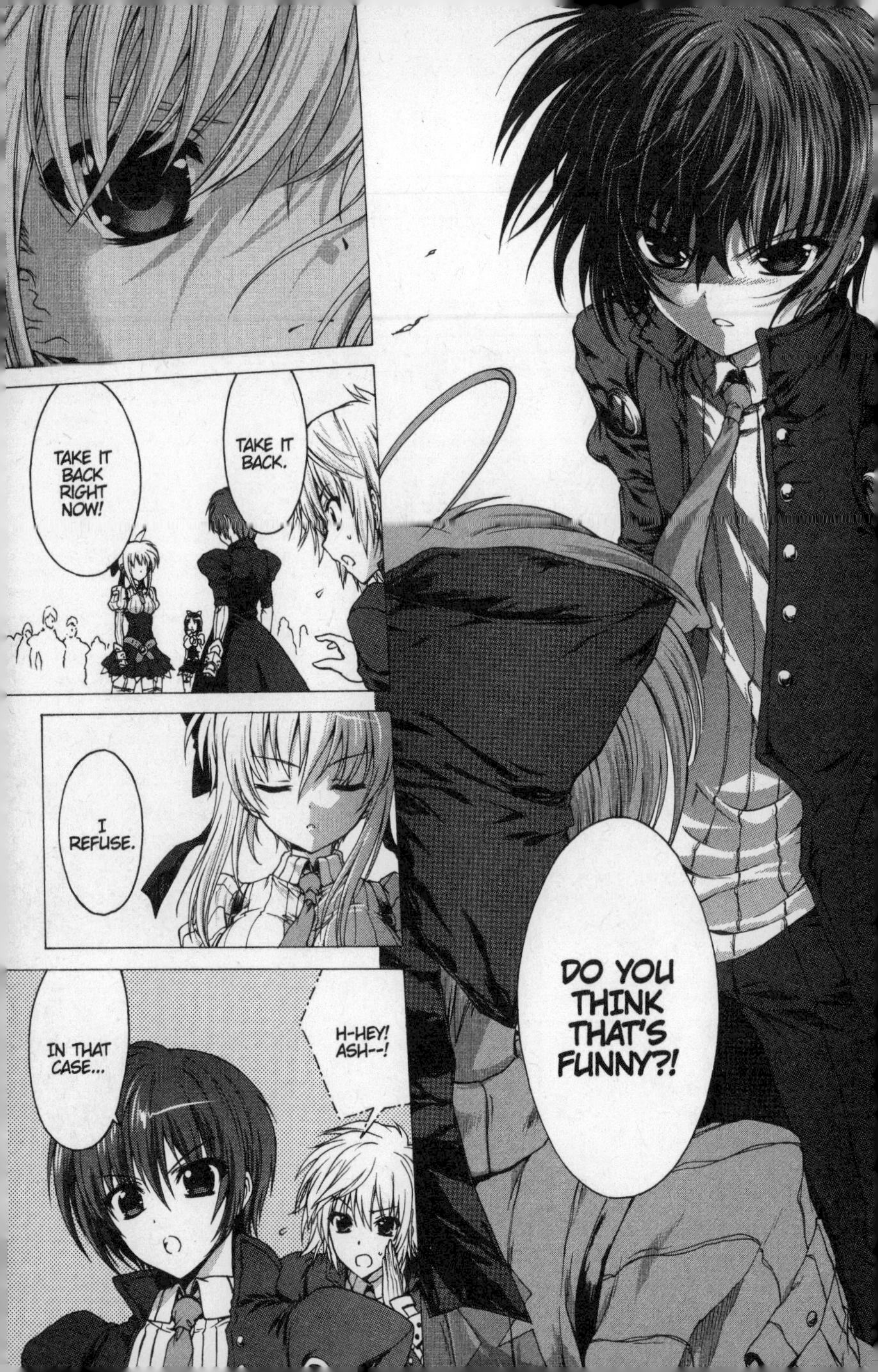
DO YOU THINK THAT'S FUNNY?!
TAKE IT BACK.
TAKE IT BACK RIGHT NOW!
I REFUSE.
H-HEY! ASH--!
IN THAT CASE...

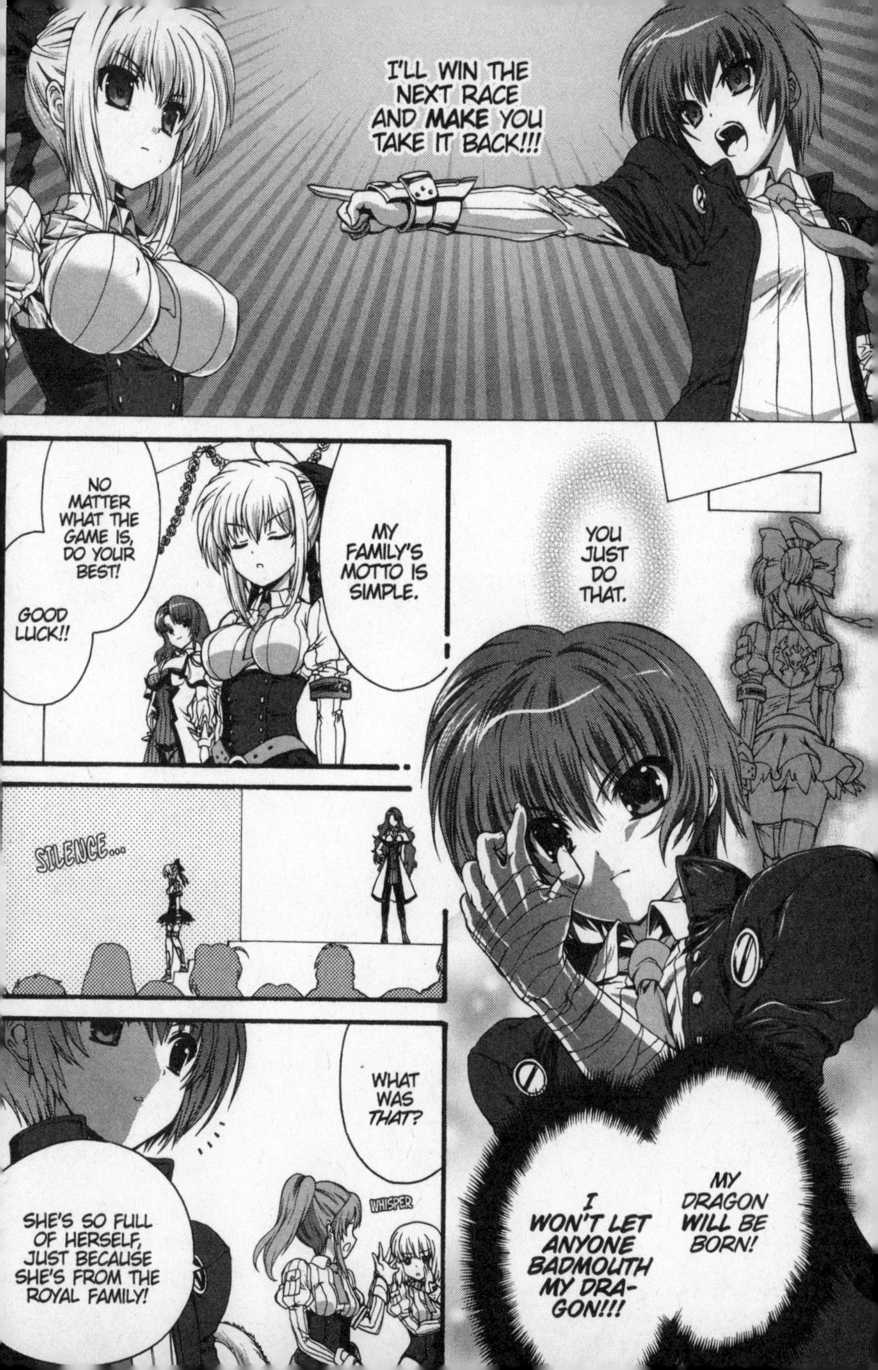
I'LL WIN THE NEXT RACE AND MAKE YOU TAKE IT BACK!!!
YOU JUST DO THAT.
MY DRAGON WILL BE BORN!
I WON'T LET ANYONE BADMOUTH MY DRA-GON!!!
MY FAMILY'S MOTTO IS SIMPLE.
NO MATTER WHAT THE GAME IS, DO YOUR BEST!
GOOD LUCK!!
SILENCE...
WHAT WAS THAT?
...
WHISPER
SHE'S SO FULL OF HERSELF, JUST BECAUSE SHE'S FROM THE ROYAL FAMILY!

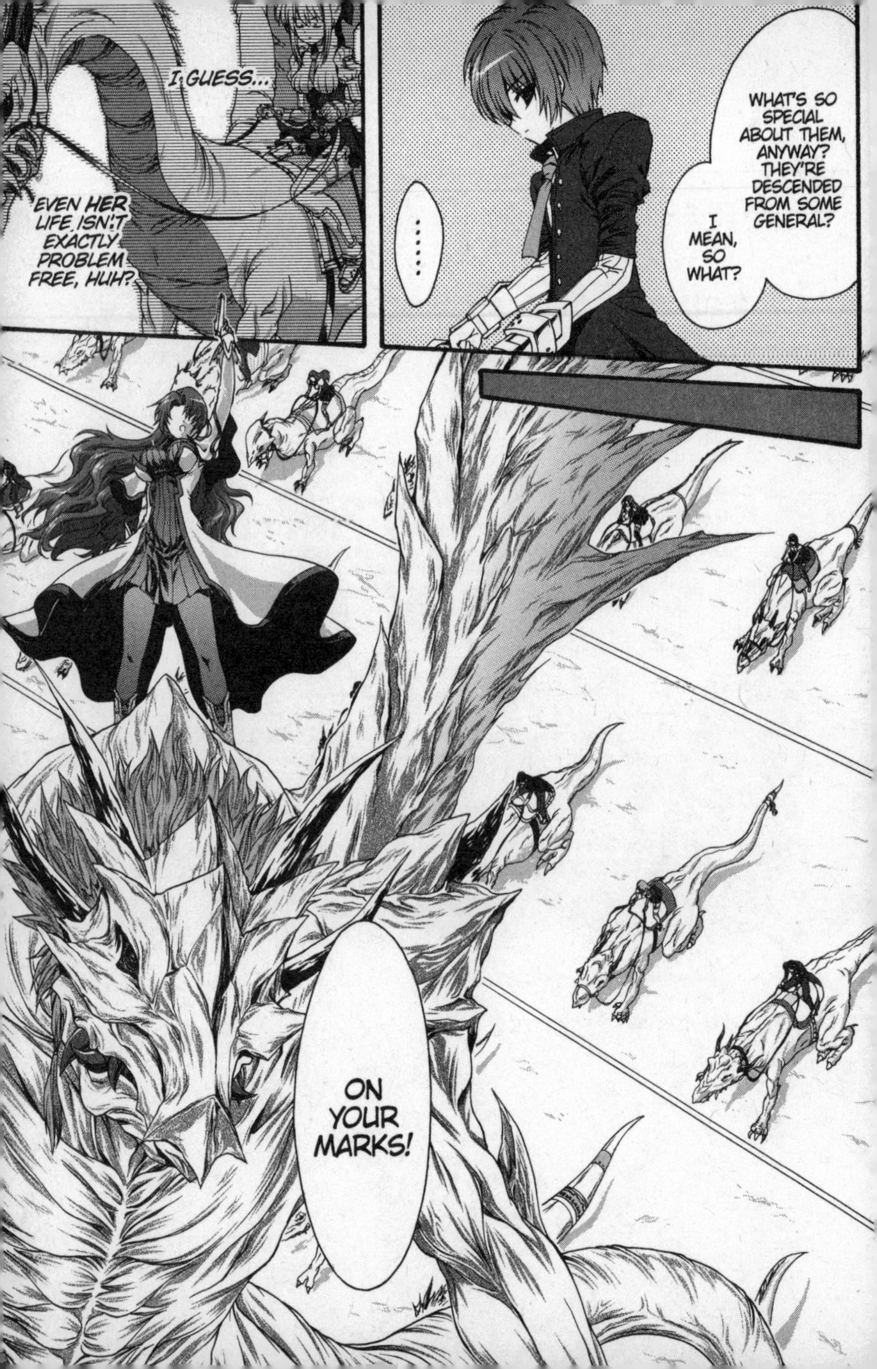
WHAT'S SO SPECIAL ABOUT THEM, ANYWAY? THEY'RE DESCENDED FROM SOME GENERAL?
I MEAN, SO WHAT?
......
I GUESS...
EVEN HER LIFE ISN'T EXACTLY PROBLEM FREE, HUH?
ON YOUR MARKS!

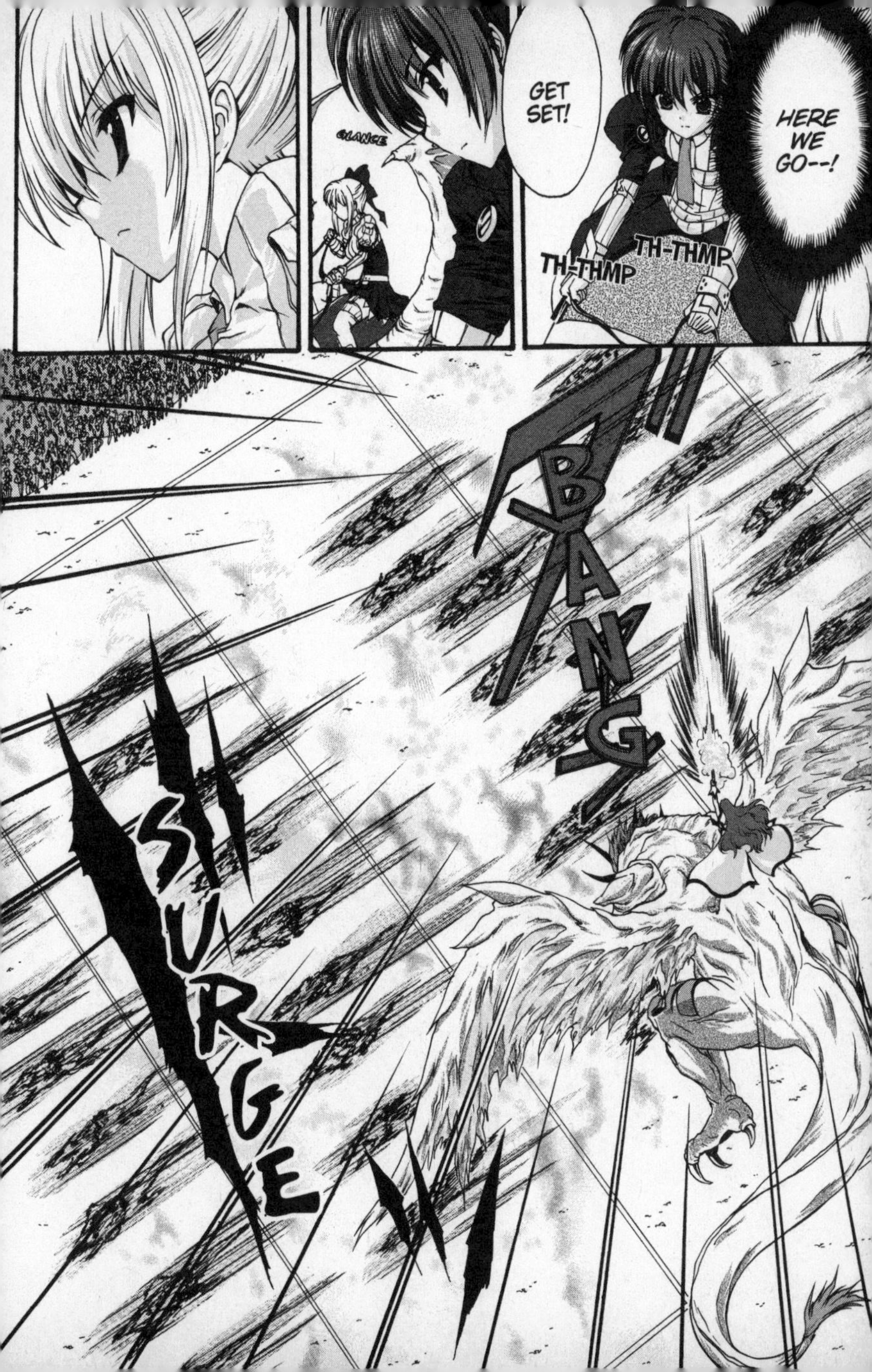
GET SET!
HERE WE GO--!
TH-THMP
TH-THMP
GLANCE
BANG
SURGE

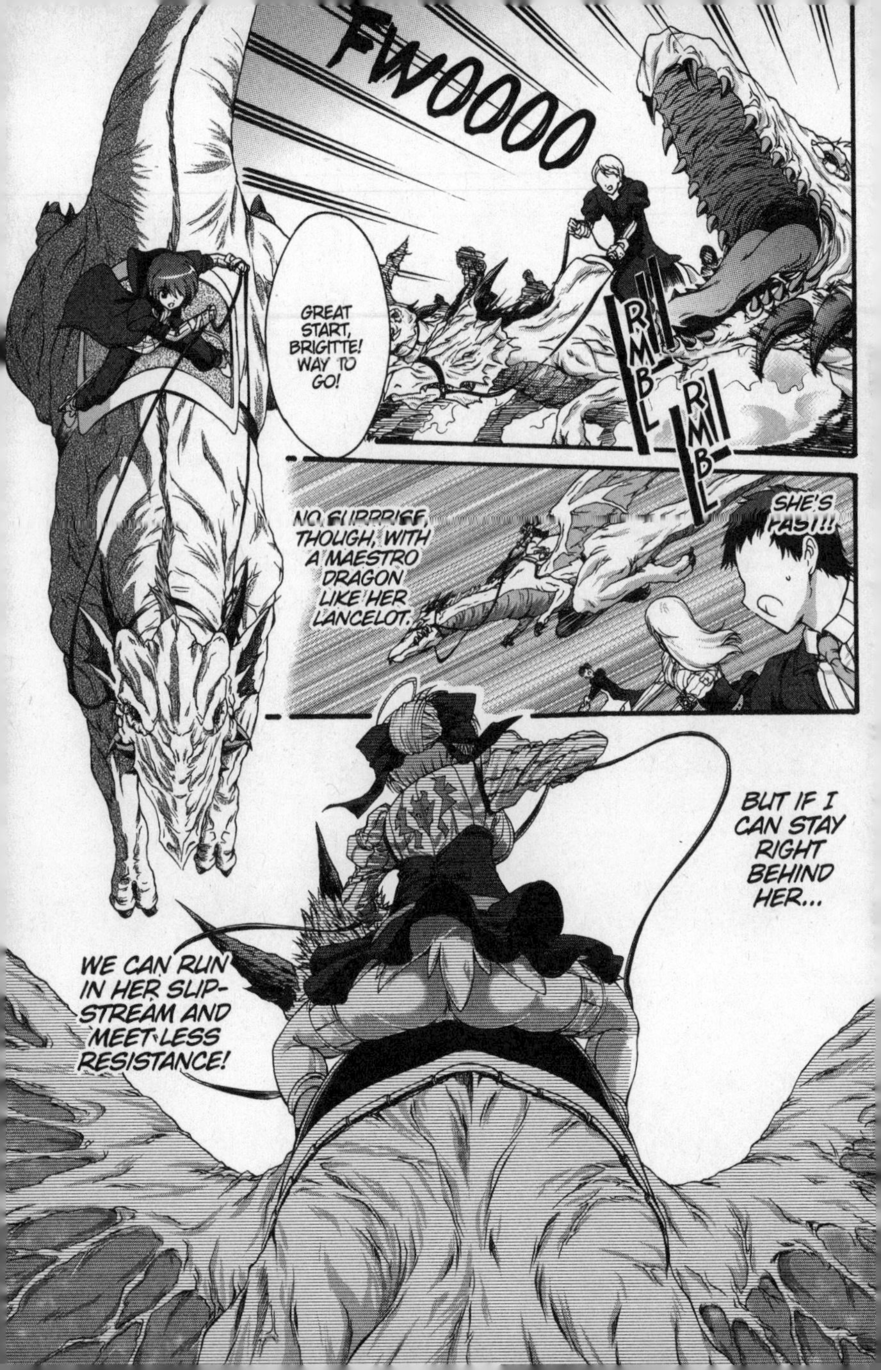
FWOOOO
RMBL
RMBL
GREAT START, BRIGITTE! WAY TO GO!
SHE'S FAST!!
NO SURPRISE, THOUGH, WITH A MAESTRO DRAGON LIKE HER LANCELOT.
BUT IF I CAN STAY RIGHT BEHIND HER...
WE CAN RUN IN HER SLIP-STREAM AND MEET LESS RESISTANCE!

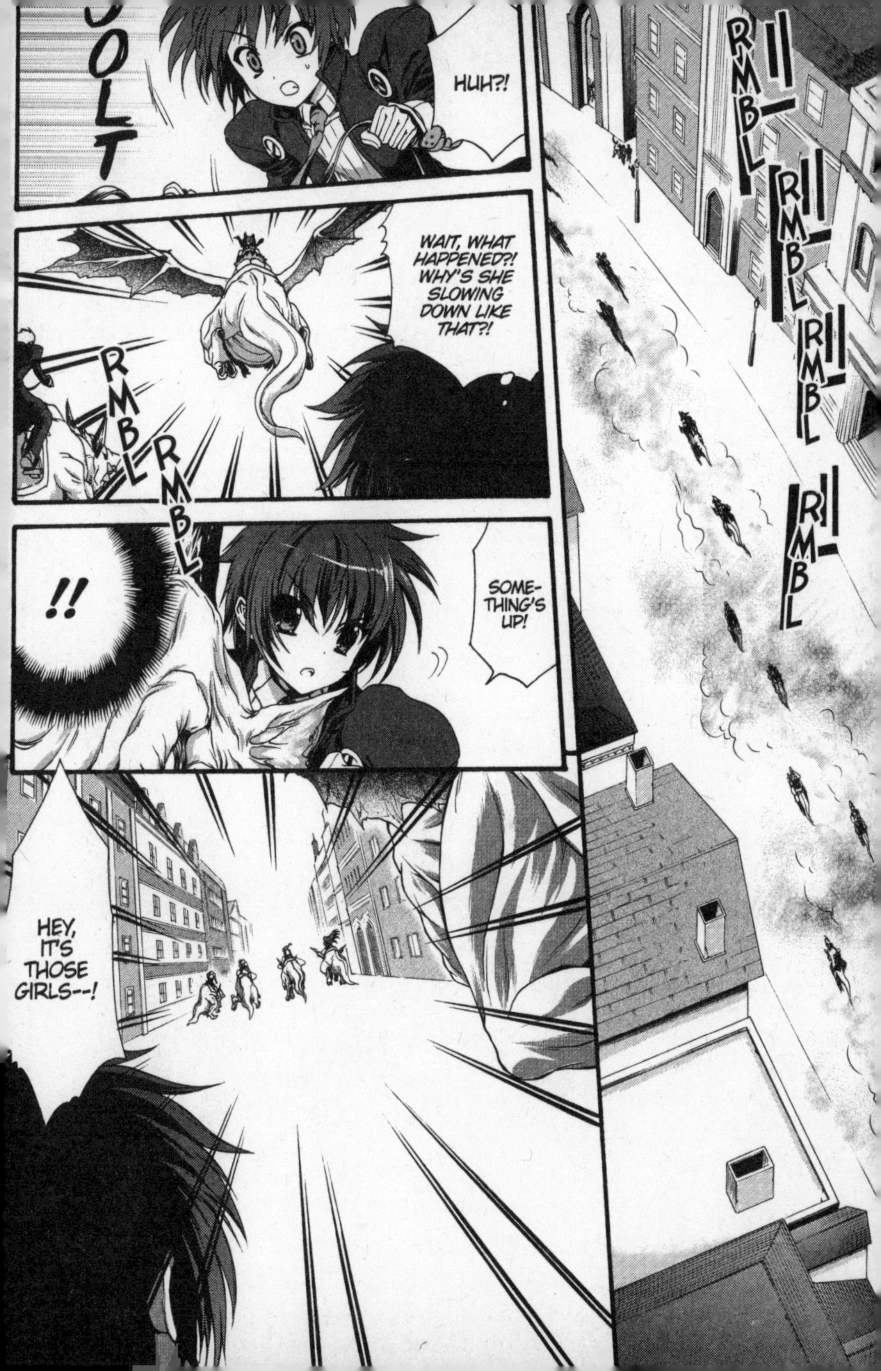
RMBL
RMBL
RMBL
RMBL
HUH?!
JOLT
WAIT, WHAT HAPPENED?! WHY'S SHE SLOWING DOWN LIKE THAT?!
RMBL
RMBL
SOME-THING'S UP!
!!
HEY, IT'S THOSE GIRLS--!

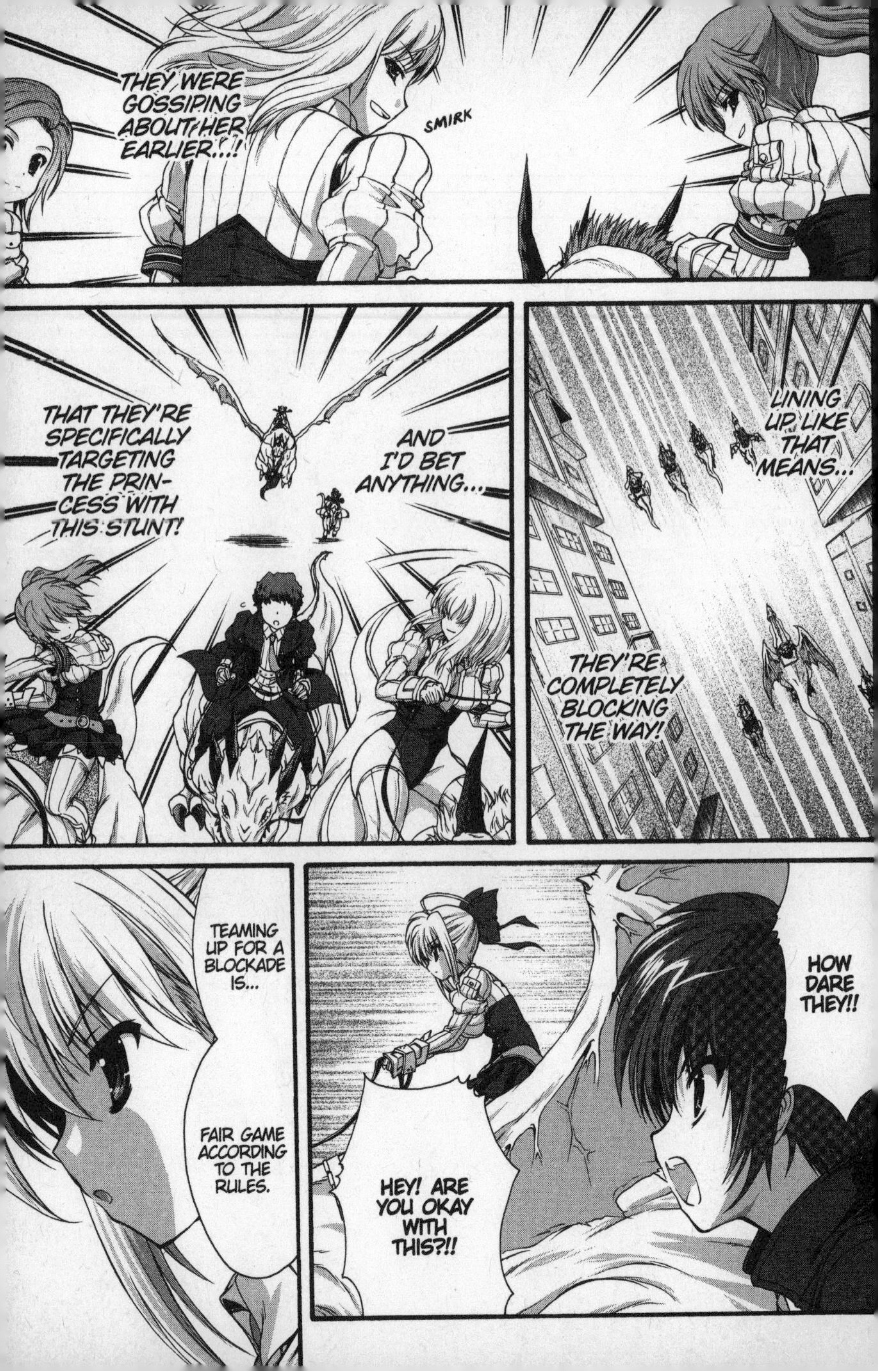
SMIRK
THEY WERE GOSSIPING ABOUT HER EARLIER...!
LINING UP LIKE THAT MEANS...
THEY'RE COMPLETELY BLOCKING THE WAY!
AND I'D BET ANYTHING...
THAT THEY'RE SPECIFICALLY TARGETING THE PRIN-CESS WITH THIS STUNT!
HOW DARE THEY!!
HEY! ARE YOU OKAY WITH THIS?!!
TEAMING UP FOR A BLOCKADE IS...
FAIR GAME ACCORDING TO THE RULES.

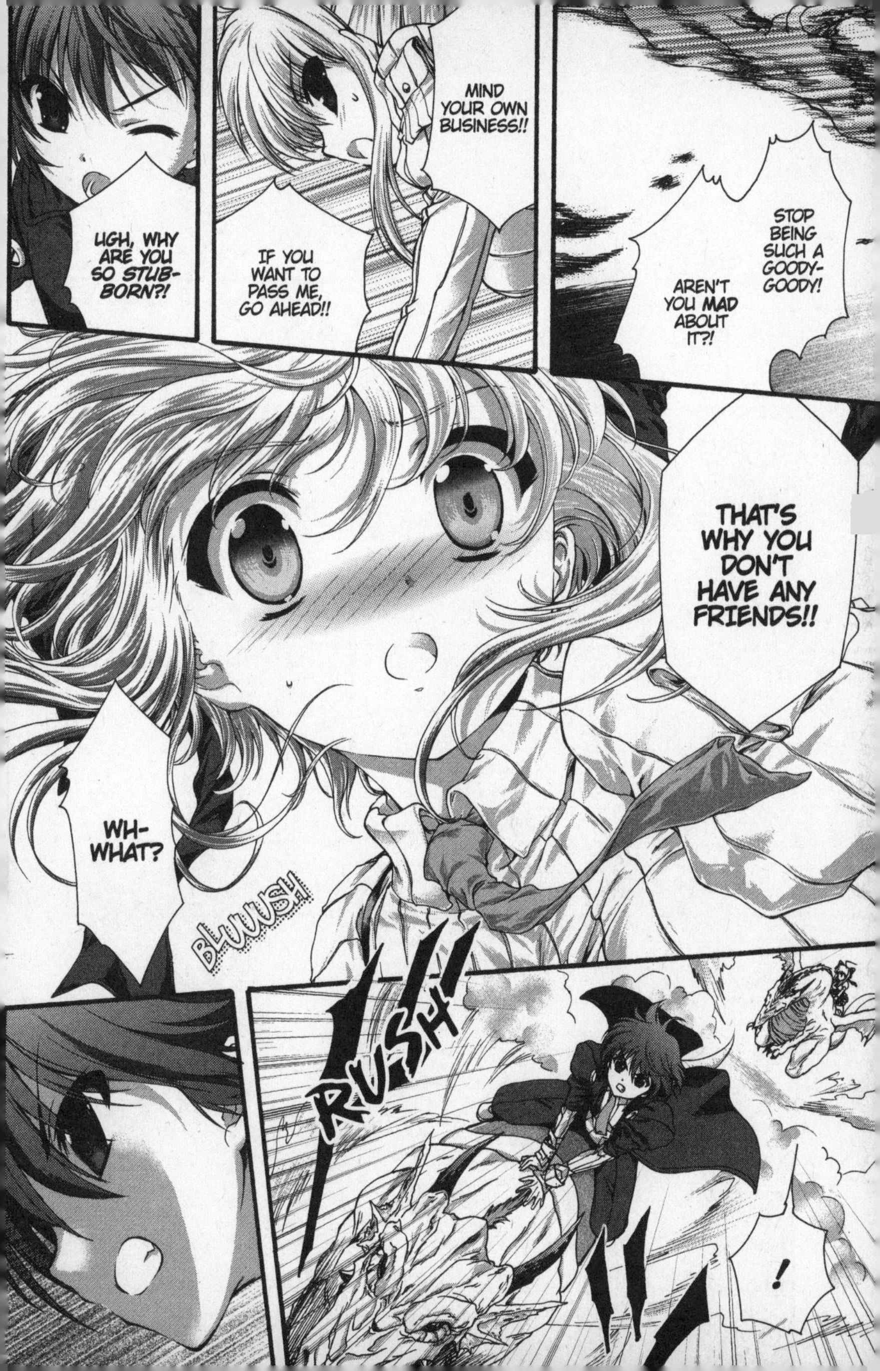
STOP BEING SUCH A GOODY-GOODY!
AREN'T YOU MAD ABOUT IT?!
MIND YOUR OWN BUSINESS!!
IF YOU WANT TO PASS ME, GO AHEAD!!
UGH, WHY ARE YOU SO STUB-BORN?!
THAT'S WHY YOU DON'T HAVE ANY FRIENDS!!
WH-WHAT?
BLUUUSH
RUSH
!

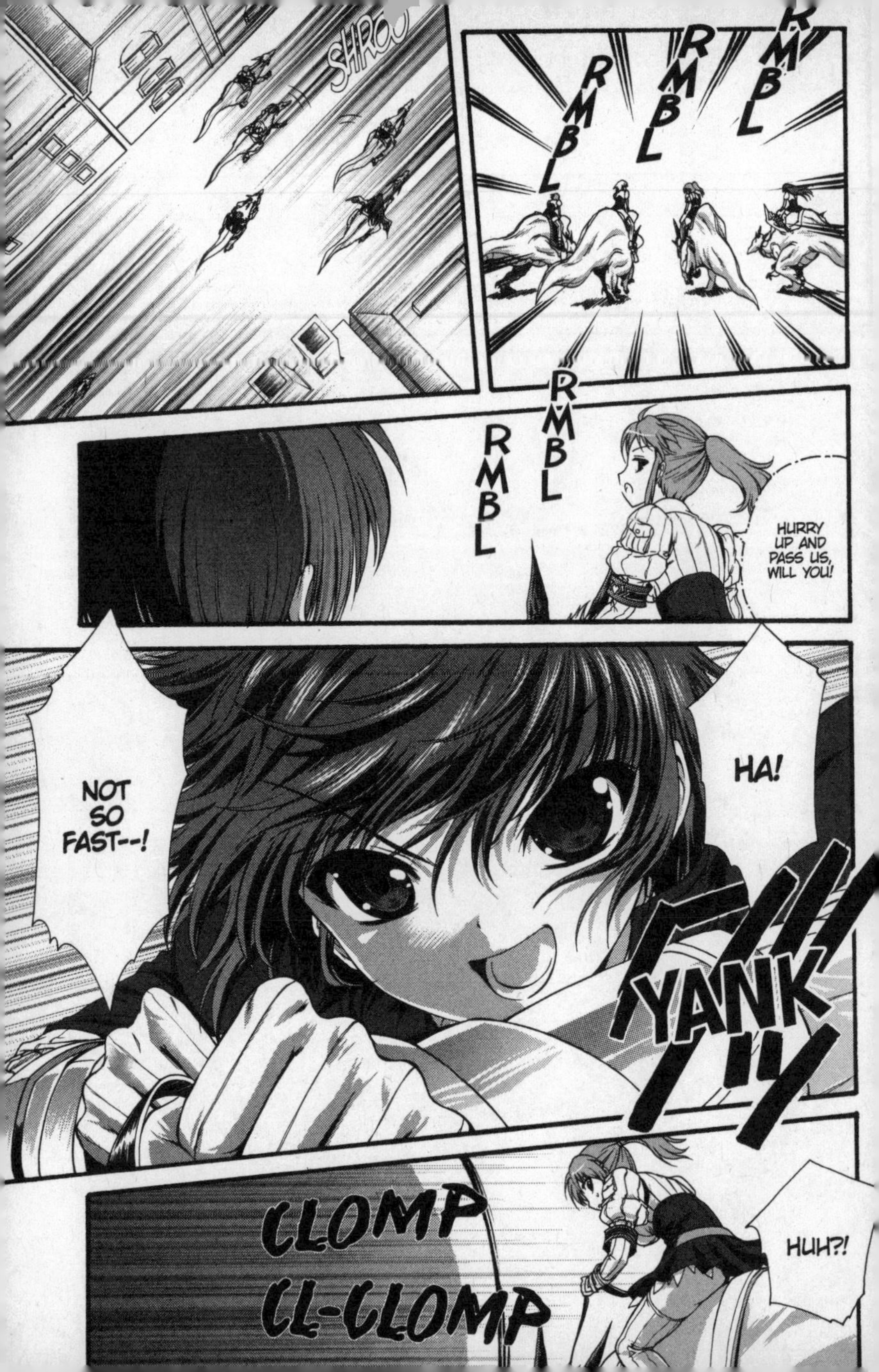
RMBL
RMBL
RMBL
RMBL
SHROO
RMBL
RMBL
HURRY UP AND PASS US, WILL YOU!
HA!
NOT SO FAST--!
YANK
HUH?!
CLOMP
CL-CLOMP

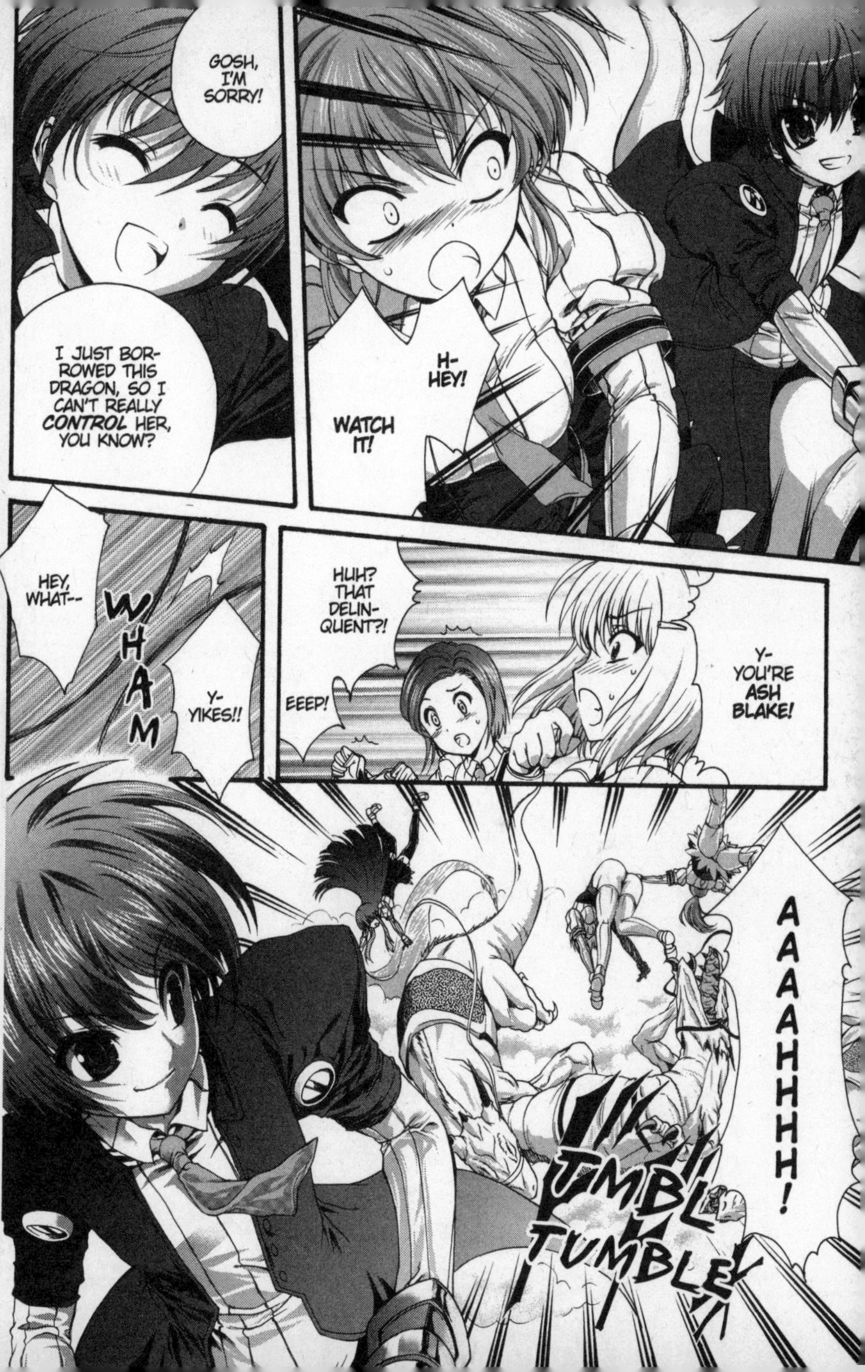
H- HEY!
WATCH IT!
GOSH, I'M SORRY!
I JUST BORROWED THIS DRAGON, SO I CAN'T REALLY **CONTROL** HER, YOU KNOW?
HUH? THAT DELINQUENT?!
Y- YOU'RE ASH BLAKE!
EEEP!
HEY, WHAT--
WHAM
Y- YIKES!!
AAAAHHHH!
TUMBLE

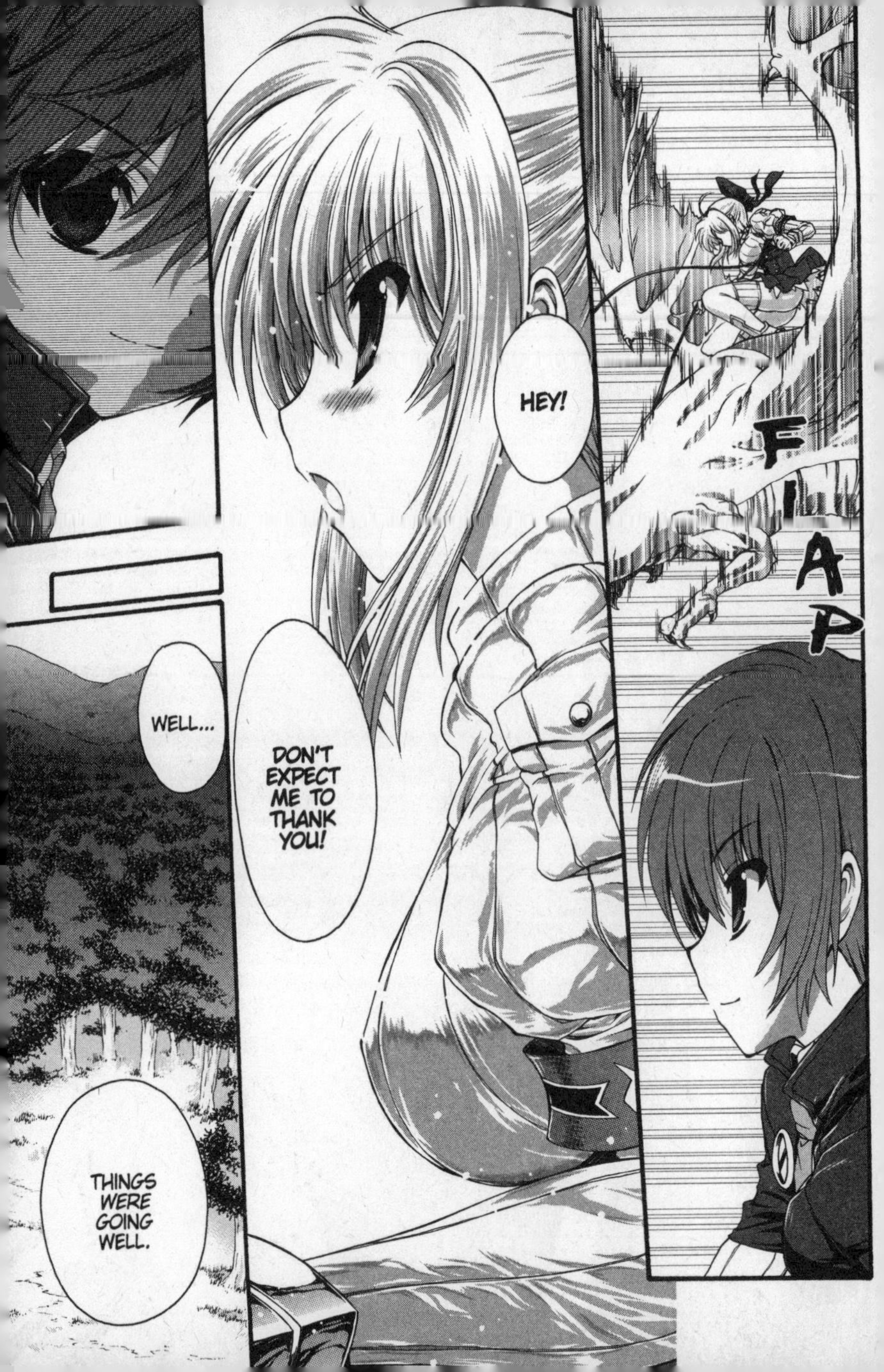
FLAP
HEY!
DON'T EXPECT ME TO THANK YOU!
WELL...
THINGS WERE GOING WELL.

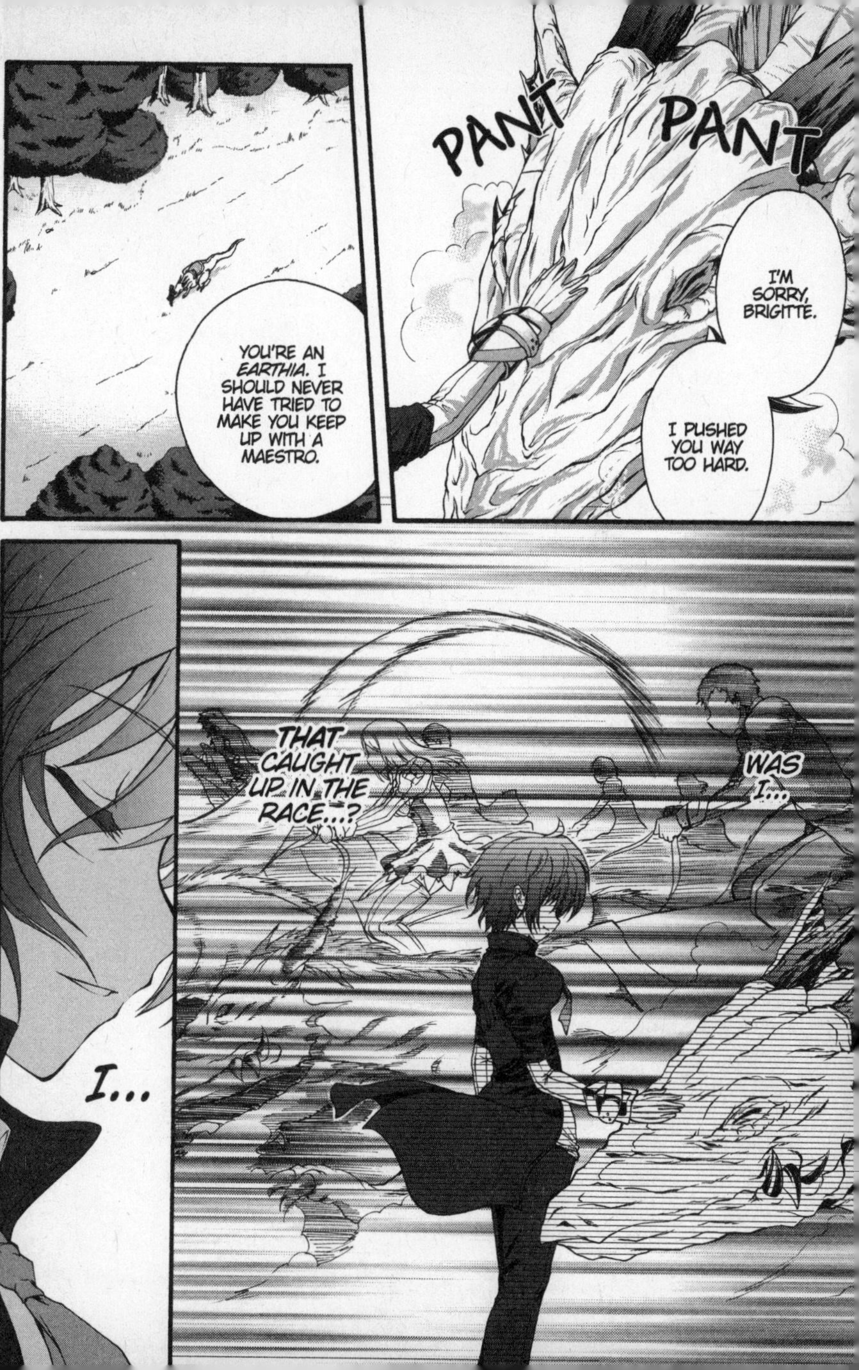
PANT PANT
I'M SORRY, BRIGITTE.
I PUSHED YOU WAY TOO HARD.
YOU'RE AN *EARTHIA*. I SHOULD NEVER HAVE TRIED TO MAKE YOU KEEP UP WITH A MAESTRO.
WAS I...
THAT CAUGHT UP IN THE RACE...?
I...

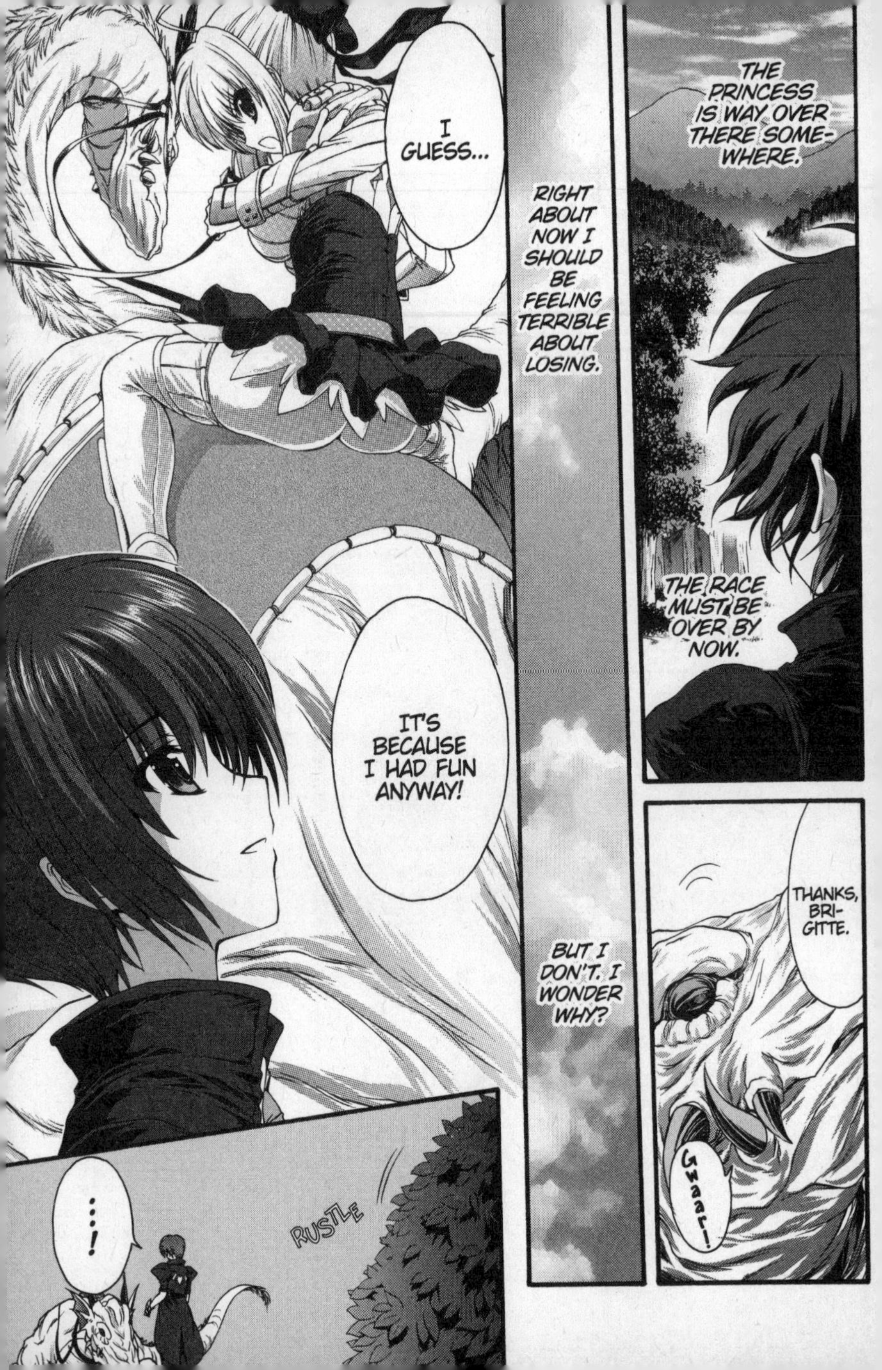
THE PRINCESS IS WAY OVER THERE SOME-WHERE.
THE RACE MUST BE OVER BY NOW.
THANKS, BRI-GITTE.
Gwaar!
RIGHT ABOUT NOW I SHOULD BE FEELING TERRIBLE ABOUT LOSING.
BUT I DON'T. I WONDER WHY?
I GUESS...
IT'S BECAUSE I HAD FUN ANYWAY!
RUSTLE
...!

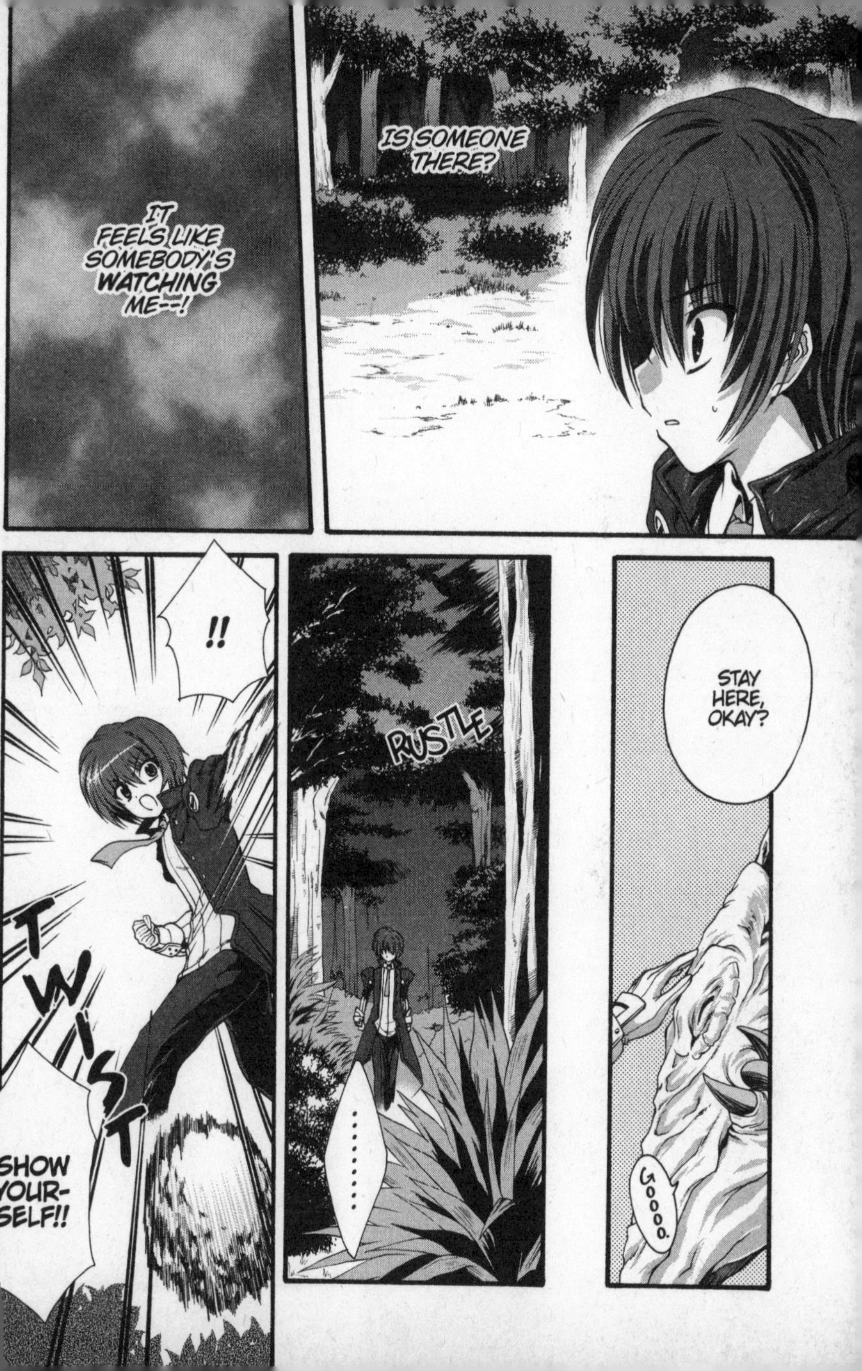
IS SOMEONE THERE?
IT FEELS LIKE SOMEBODY'S WATCHING ME--!
STAY HERE, OKAY?
GOOOO.
RUSTLE
......
!!
TWIST
SHOW YOUR-SELF!!

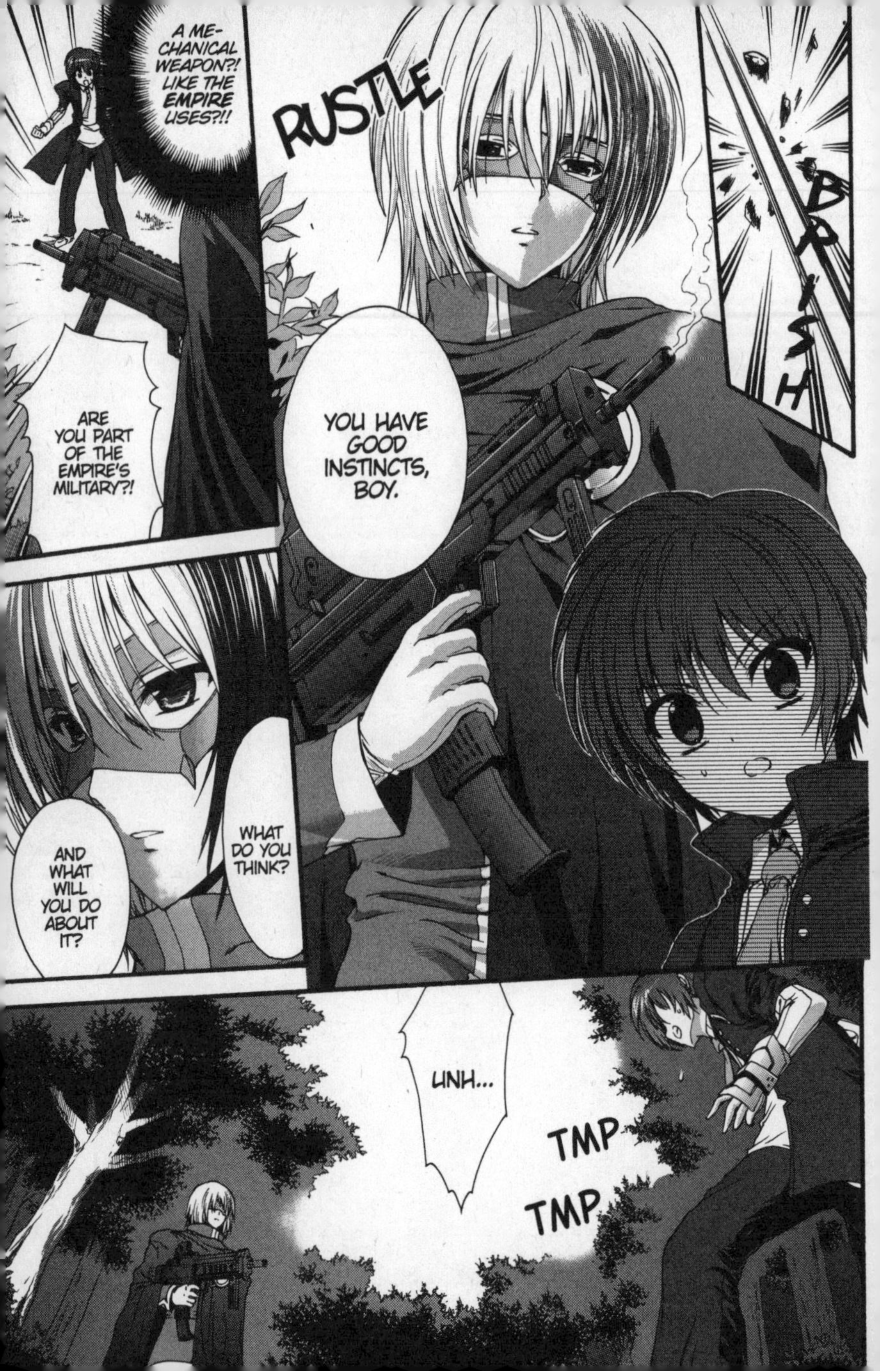
BRISH
A ME-CHANICAL WEAPON?! LIKE THE EMPIRE USES?!!
ARE YOU PART OF THE EMPIRE'S MILITARY?!
RUSTLE
YOU HAVE GOOD INSTINCTS, BOY.
WHAT DO YOU THINK?
AND WHAT WILL YOU DO ABOUT IT?
UNH...
TMP
TMP

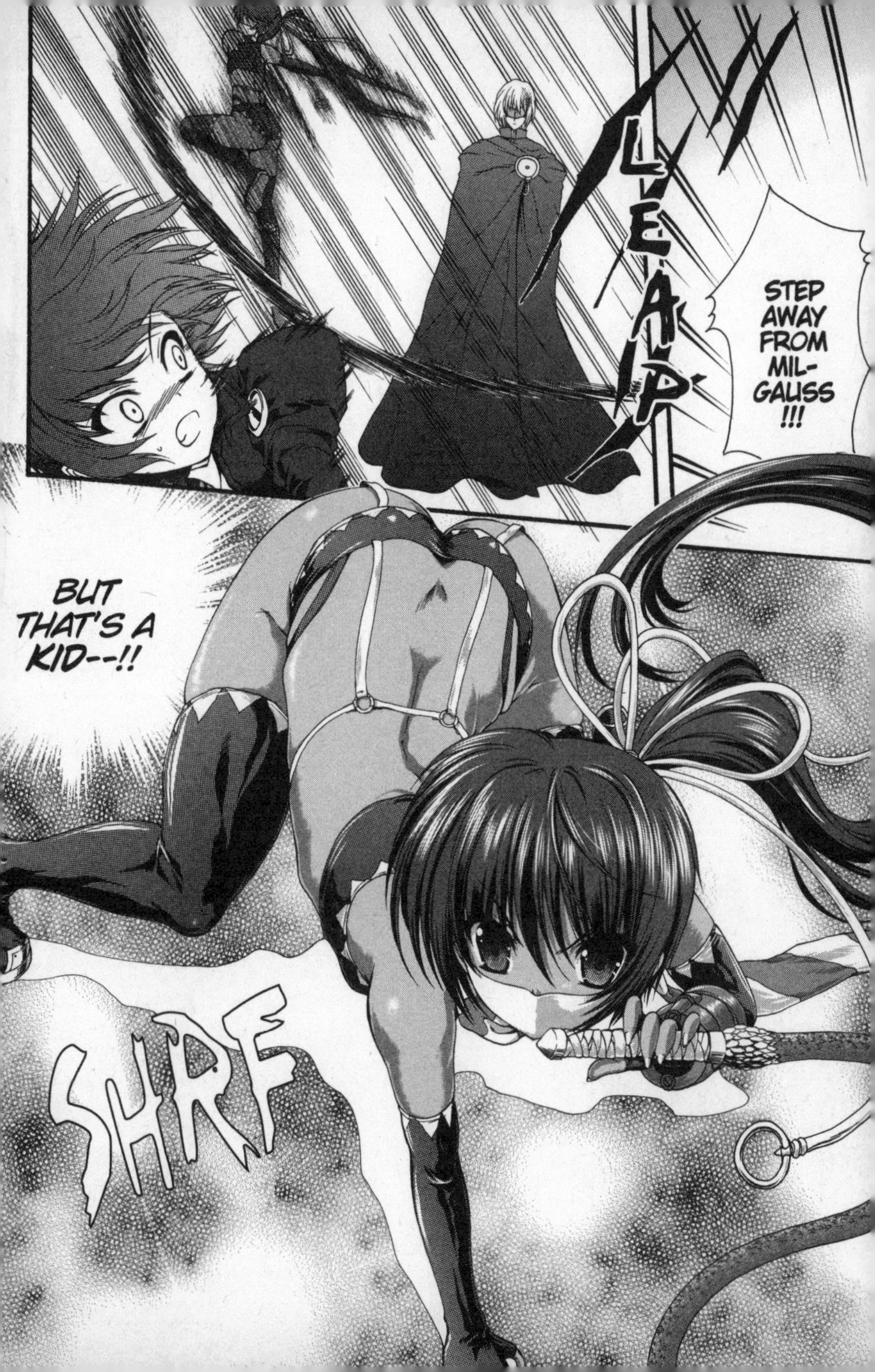
STEP AWAY FROM MIL-GAUSS !!!
LEAP
BUT THAT'S A KID--!!
SHRF

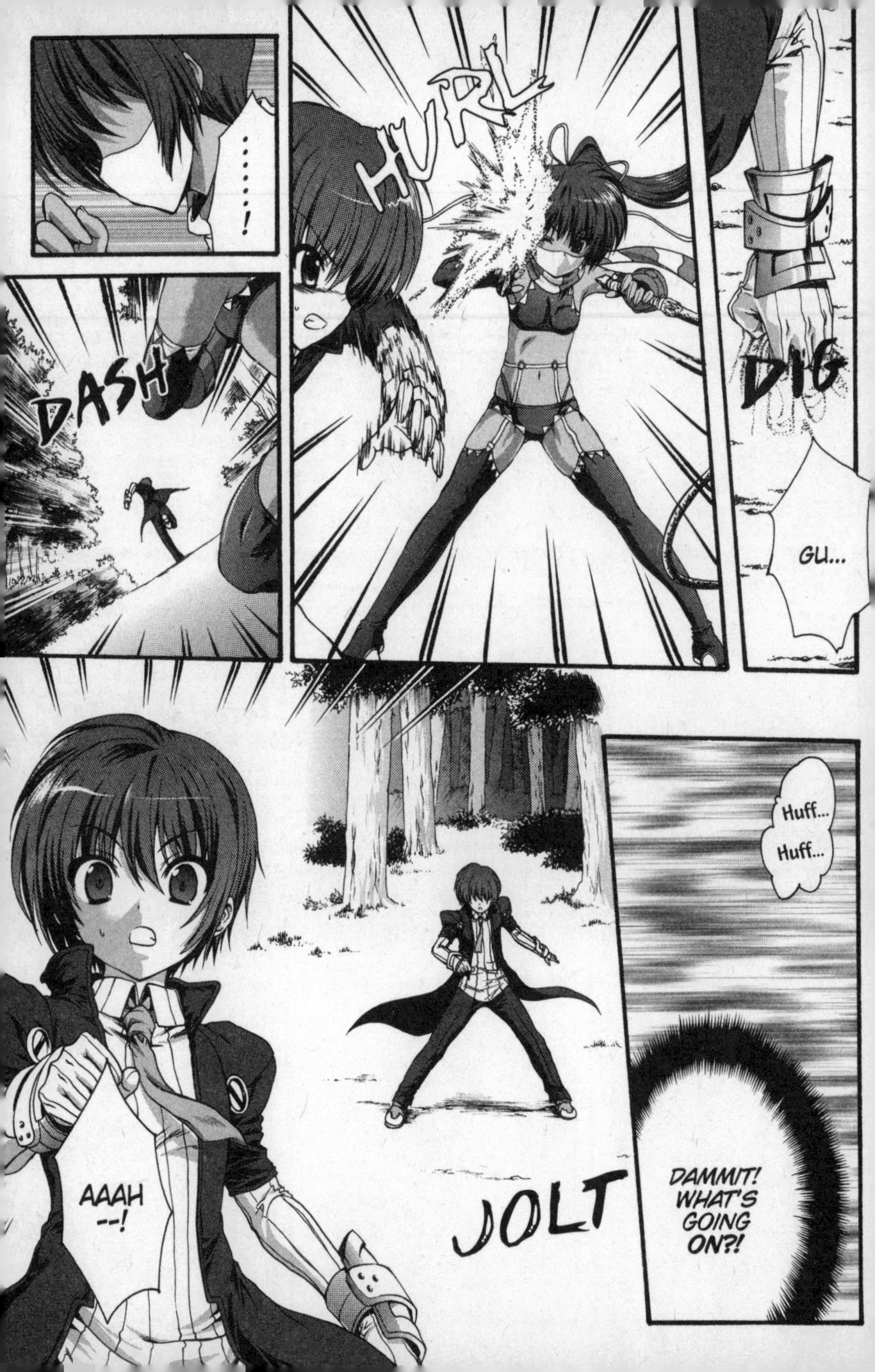
DIG
GU...
HURL
......!
DASH
Huff... Huff...
DAMMIT! WHAT'S GOING ON?!
JOLT
AAAH --!

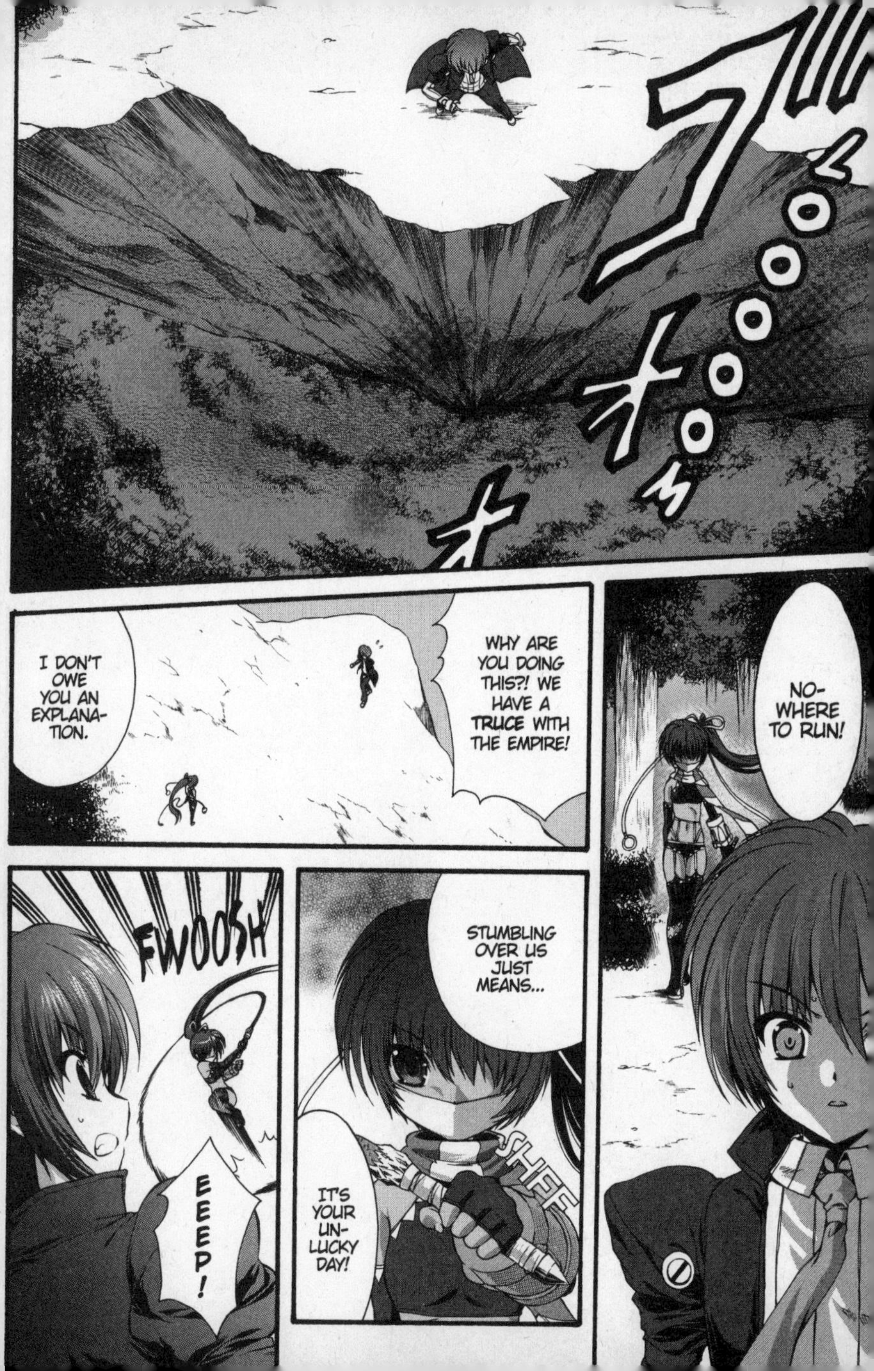
NO-WHERE TO RUN!
WHY ARE YOU DOING THIS?! WE HAVE A TRUCE WITH THE EMPIRE!
I DON'T OWE YOU AN EXPLANA-TION.
STUMBLING OVER US JUST MEANS...
SHFF
IT'S YOUR UN-LUCKY DAY!
FWOOSH
EEEP!

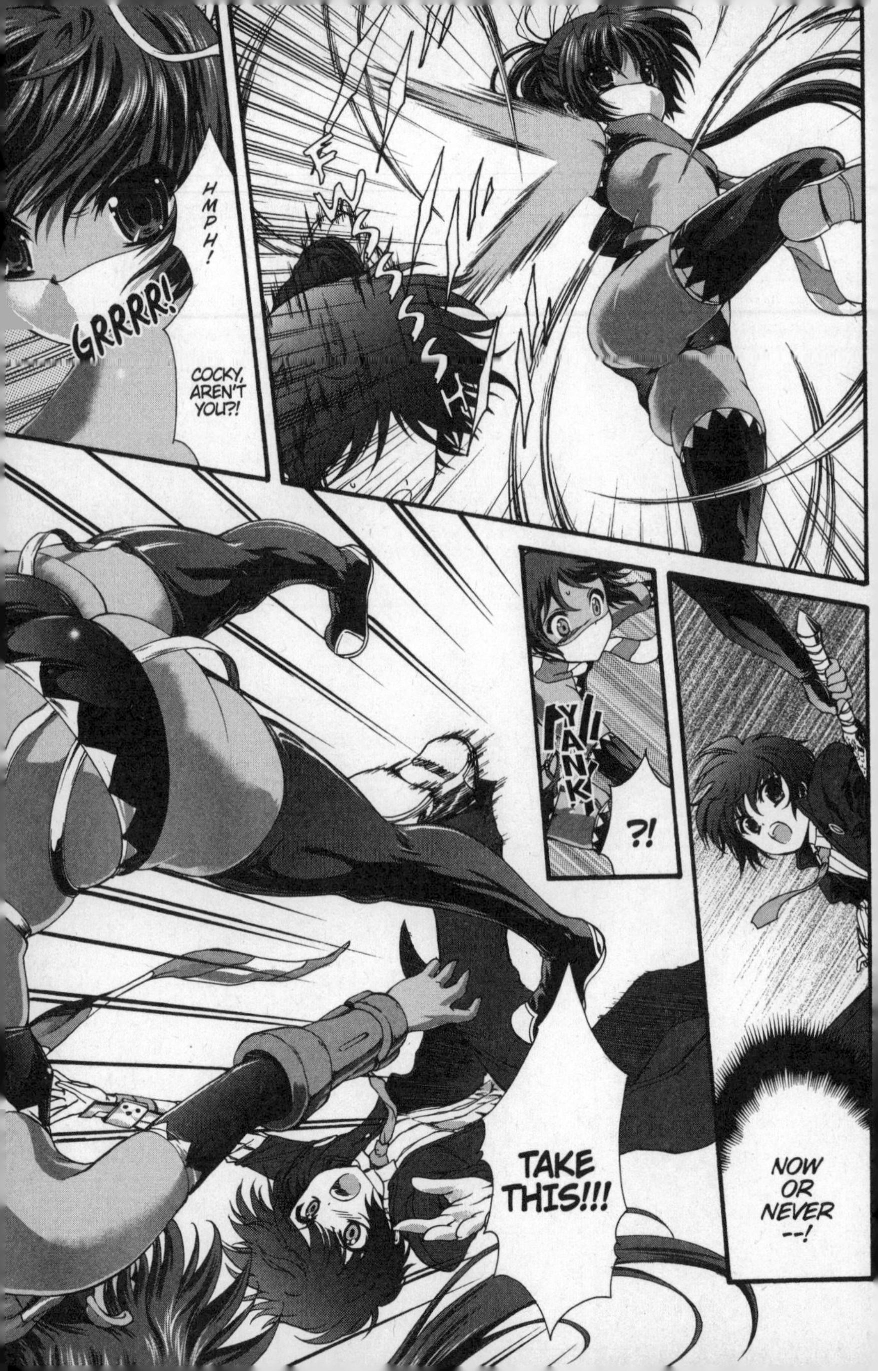
HMPH!
GRRRR!
COCKY, AREN'T YOU?!
NOW OR NEVER --!
YANK!
?!
TAKE THIS!!!

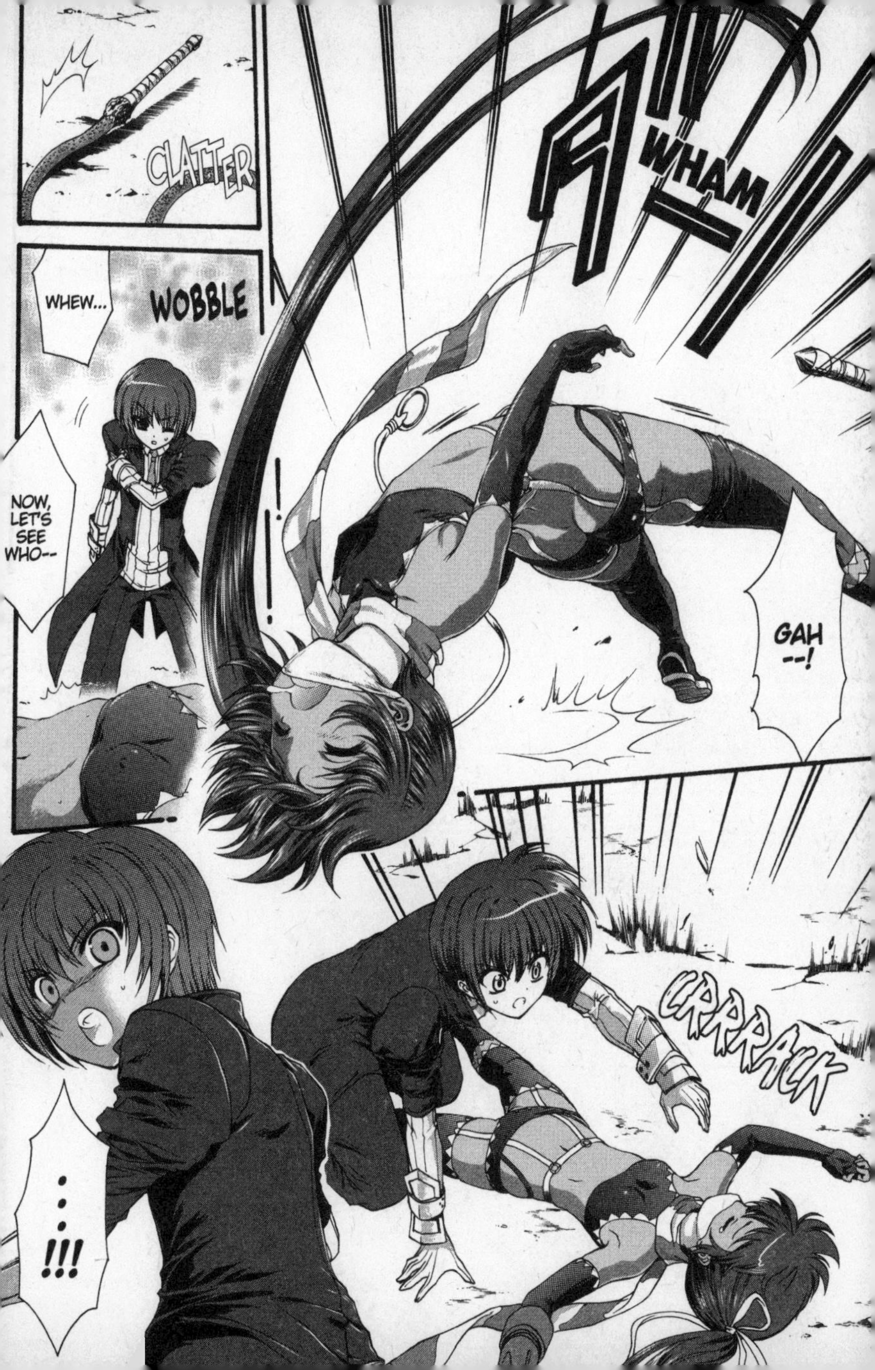
WHAM
!
GAH --!
CLATTER
WHEW...
WOBBLE
NOW, LET'S SEE WHO--
CRRRACK
...!!!

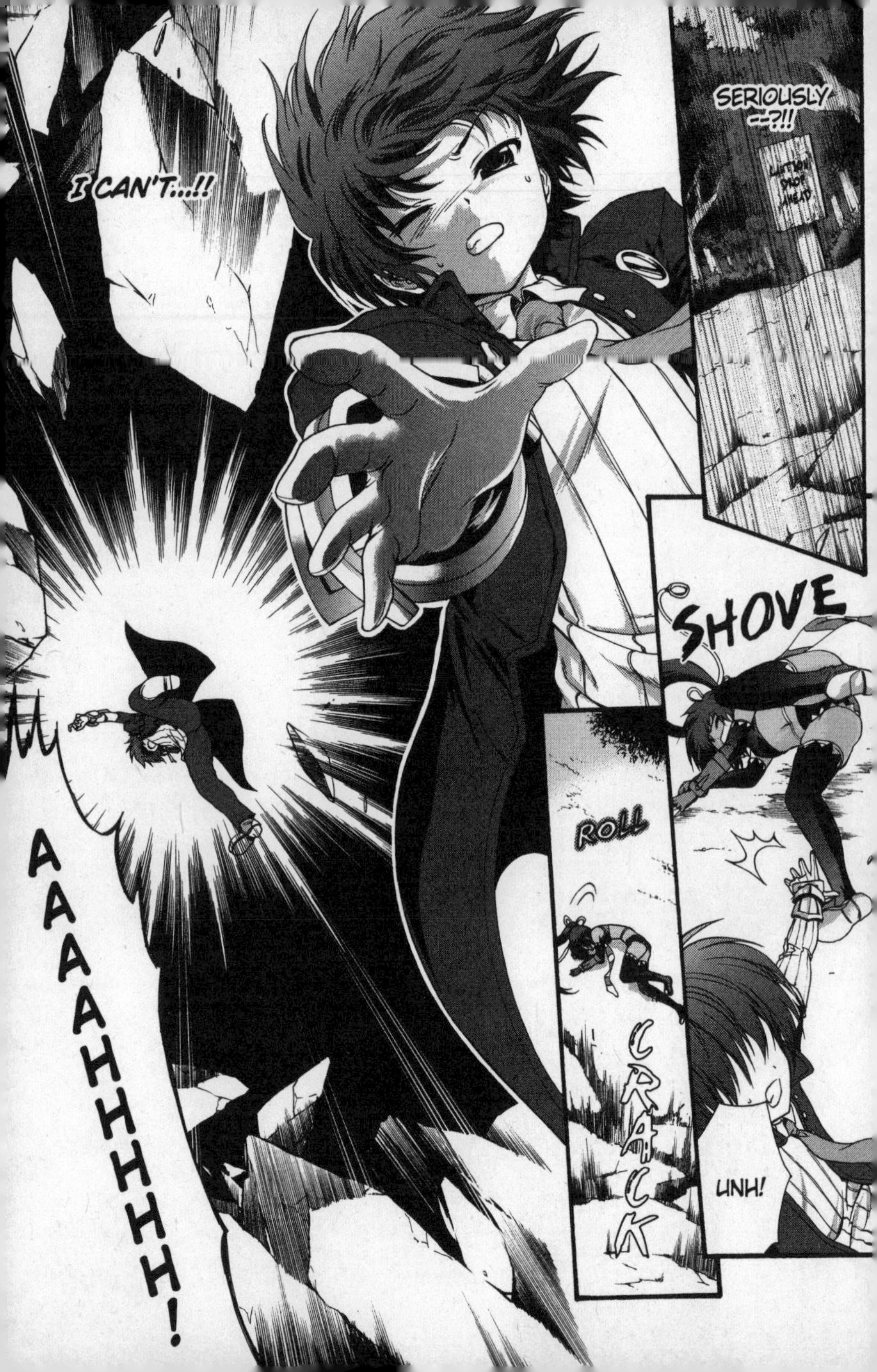
SERIOUSLY
--?!!
SHOVE
ROLL
CRACK
UNH!
I CAN'T...!!
AAAAHHHHHH!

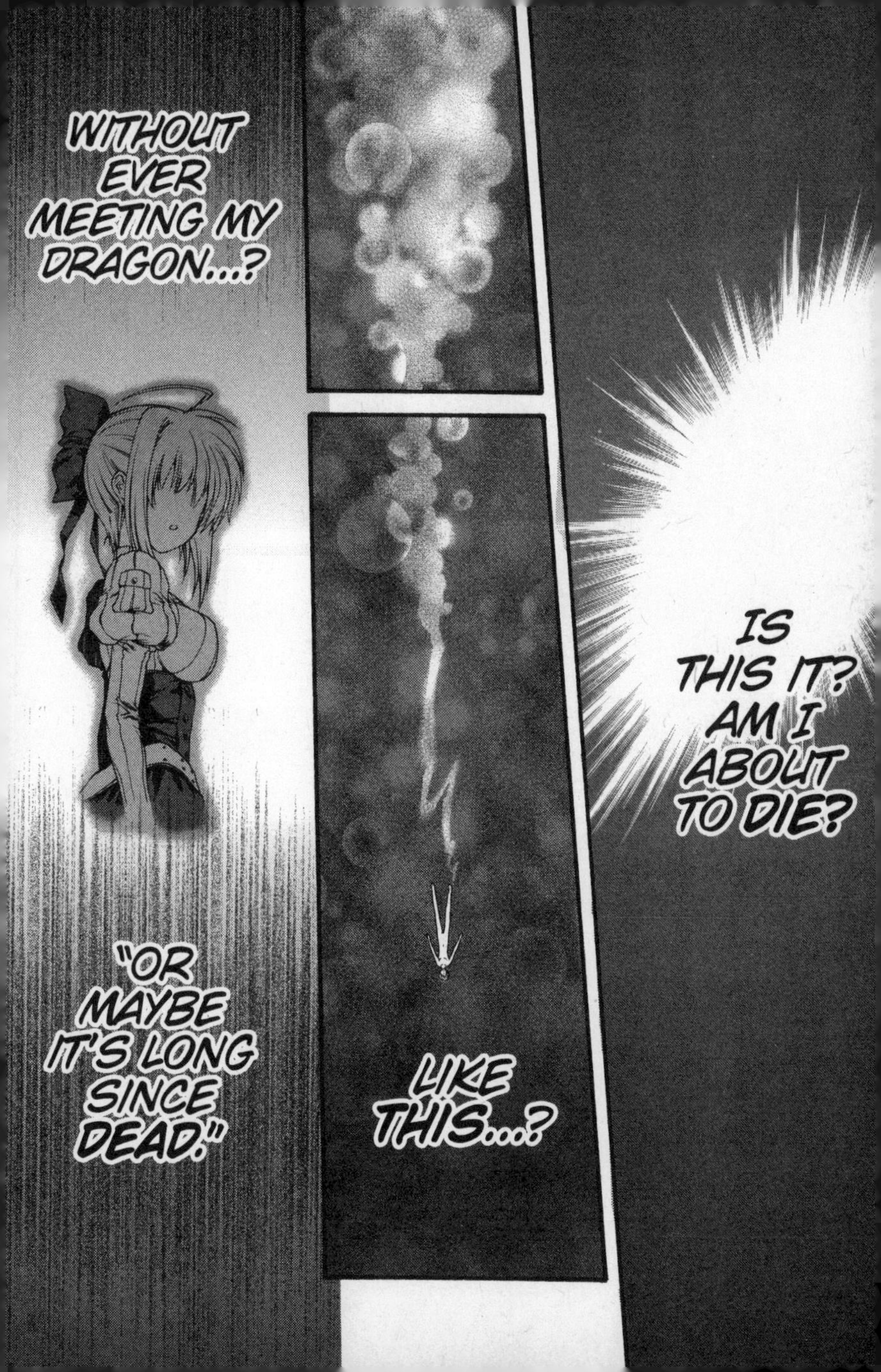
IS THIS IT? AM I ABOUT TO DIE?
LIKE THIS...?
WITHOUT EVER MEETING MY DRAGON...?
"OR MAYBE IT'S LONG SINCE DEAD."

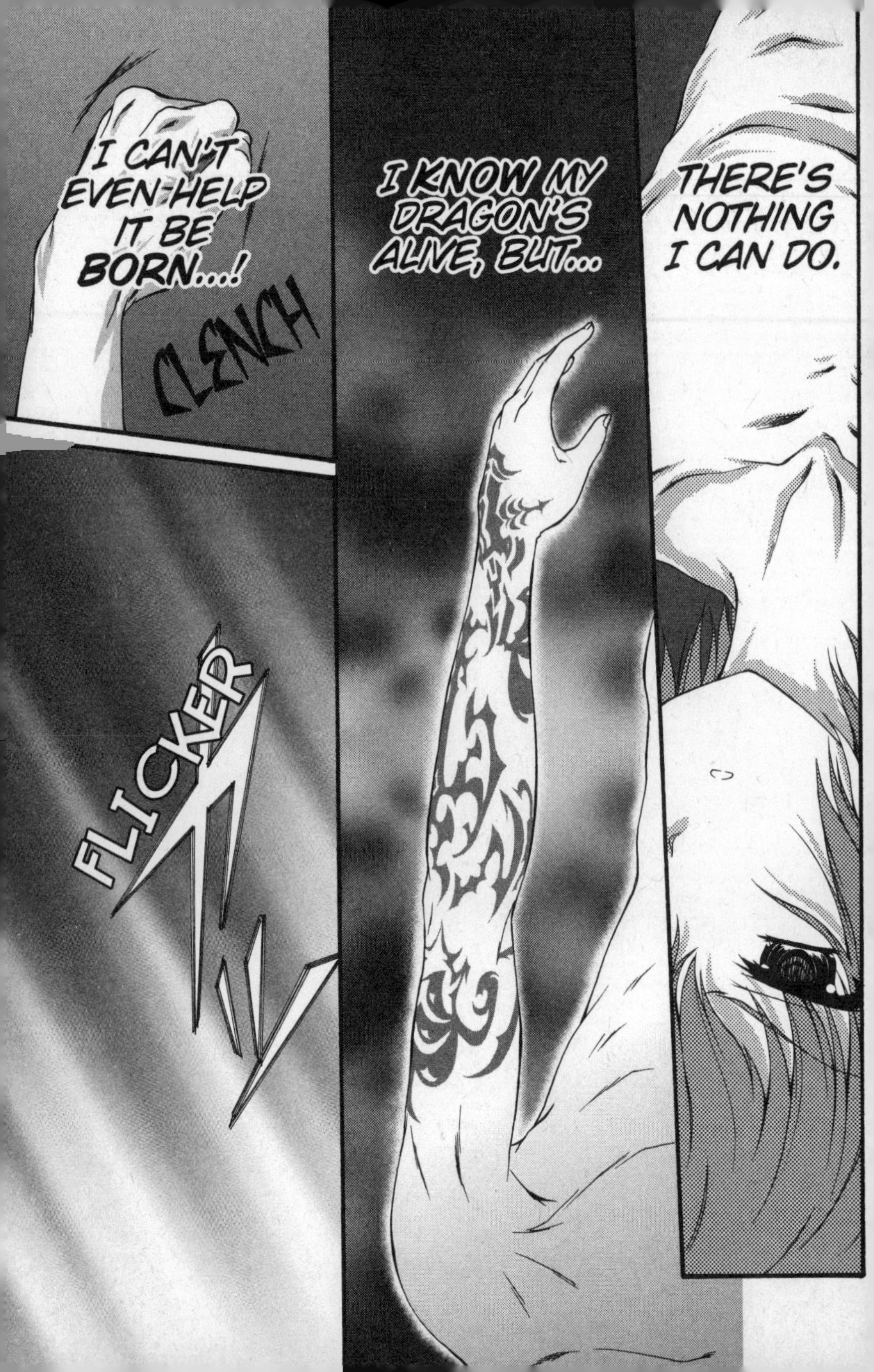
THERE'S NOTHING I CAN DO.
I KNOW MY DRAGON'S ALIVE, BUT...
I CAN'T EVEN HELP IT BE BORN...!
CLENCH
FLICKER

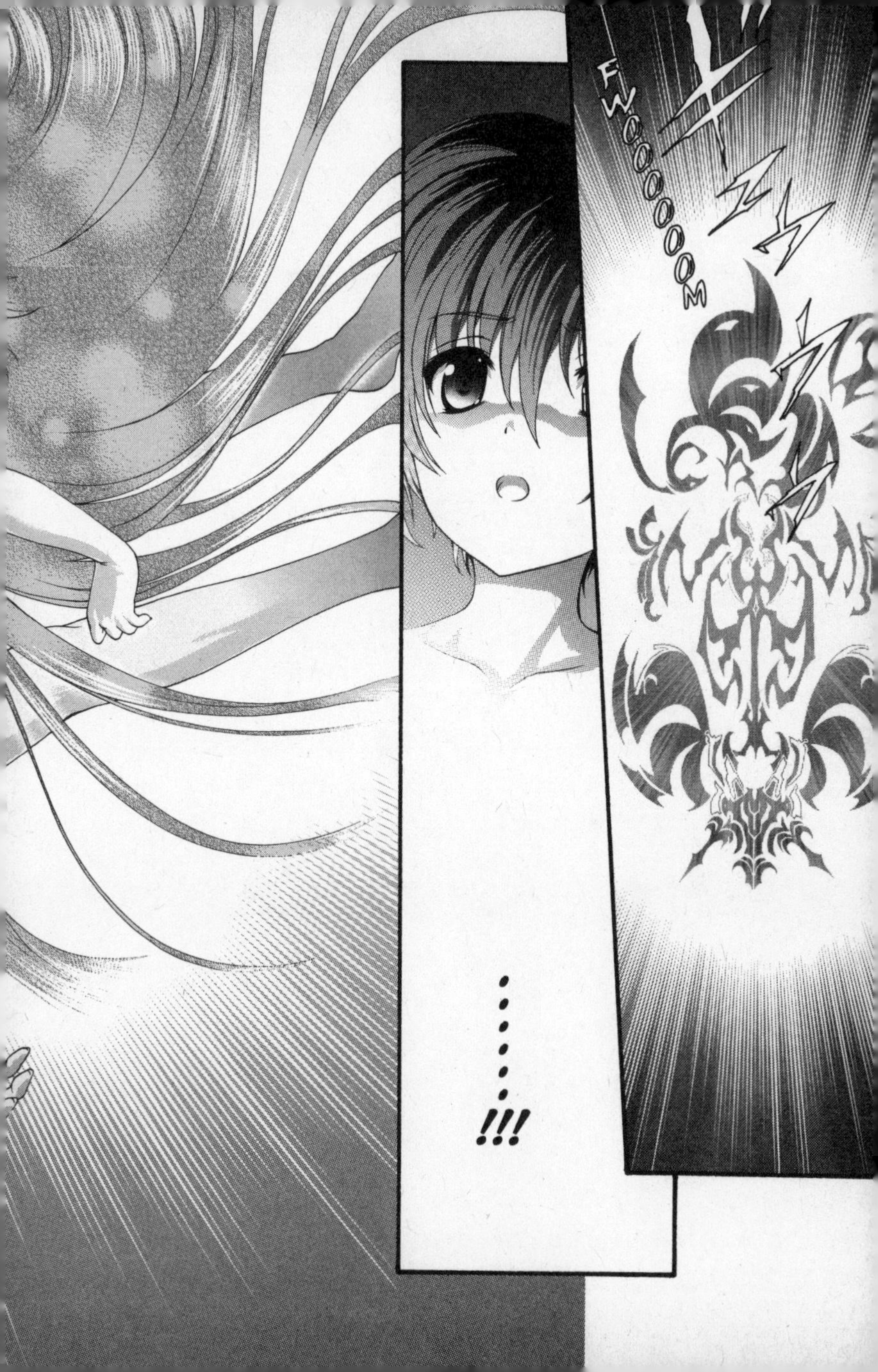
FWOOOOOOOM
......!!!

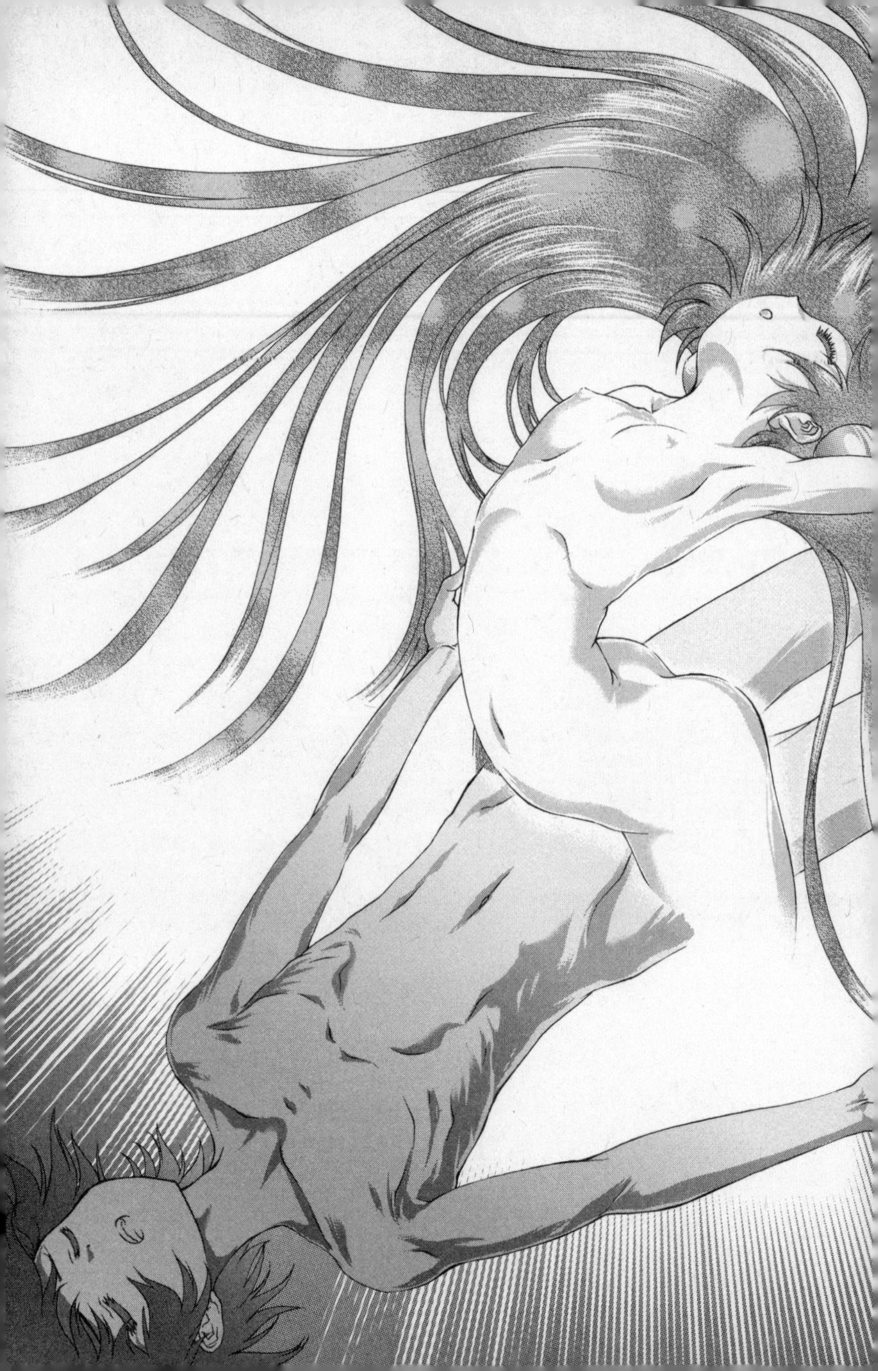

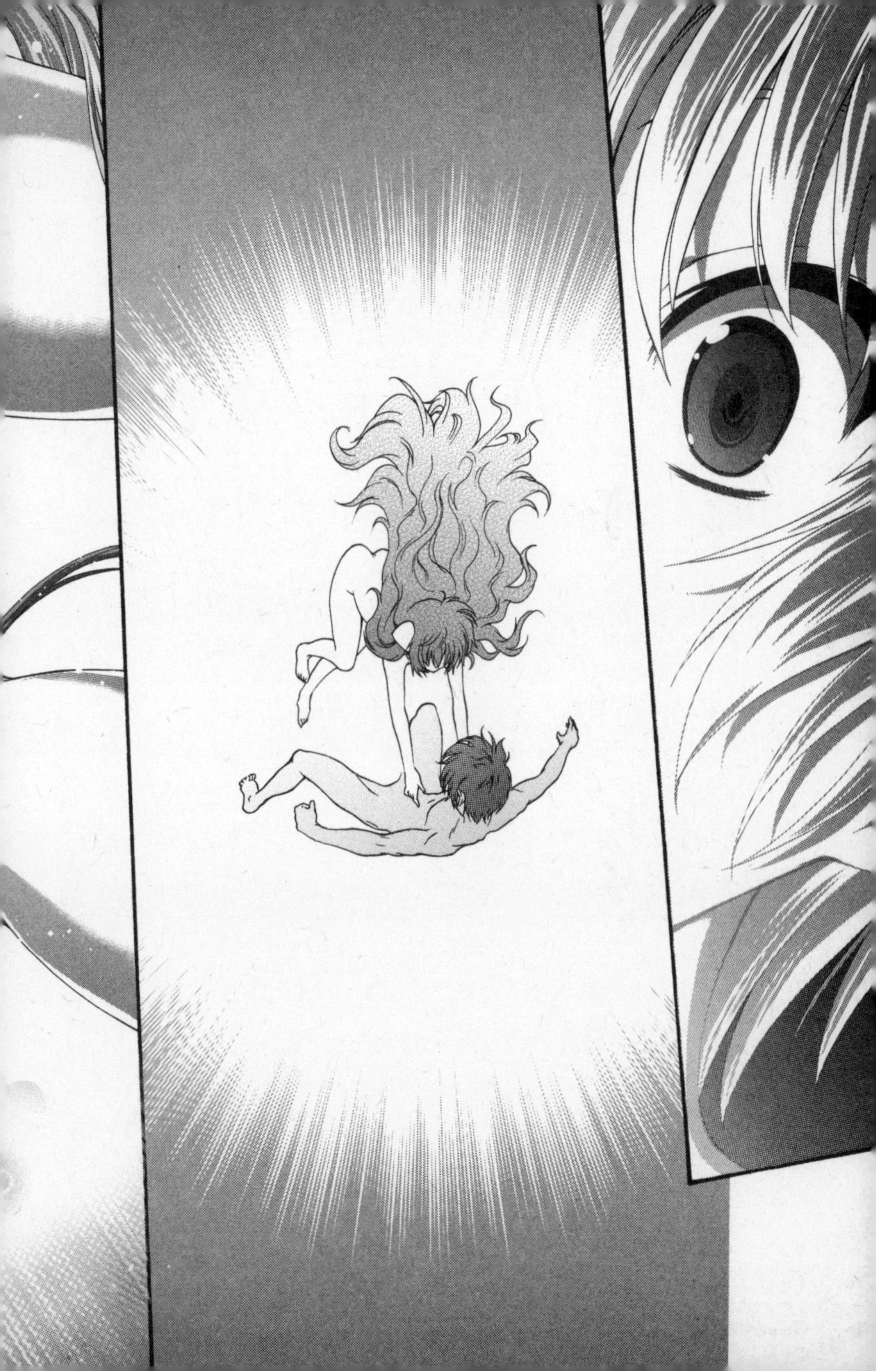

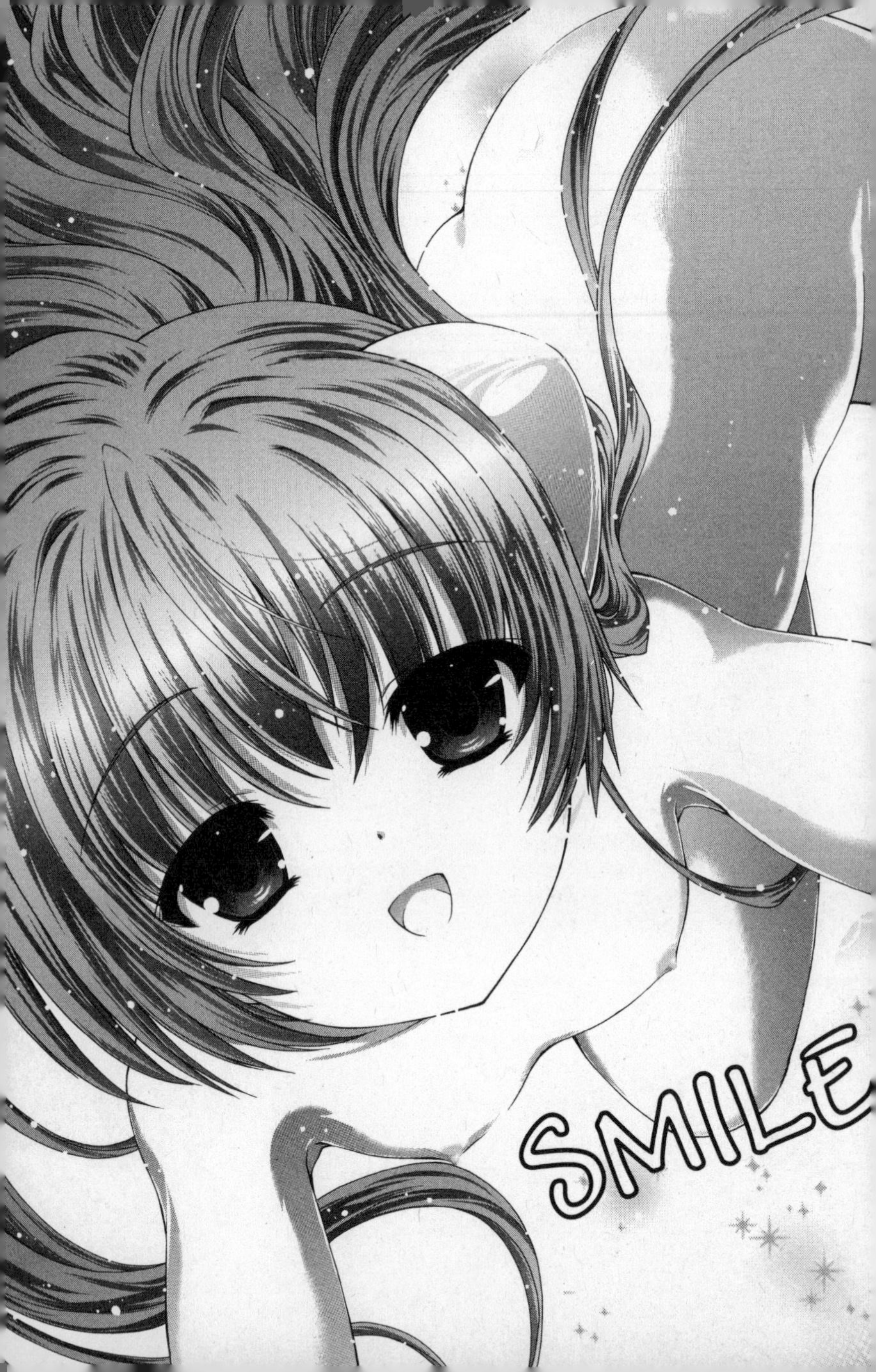
SMILE

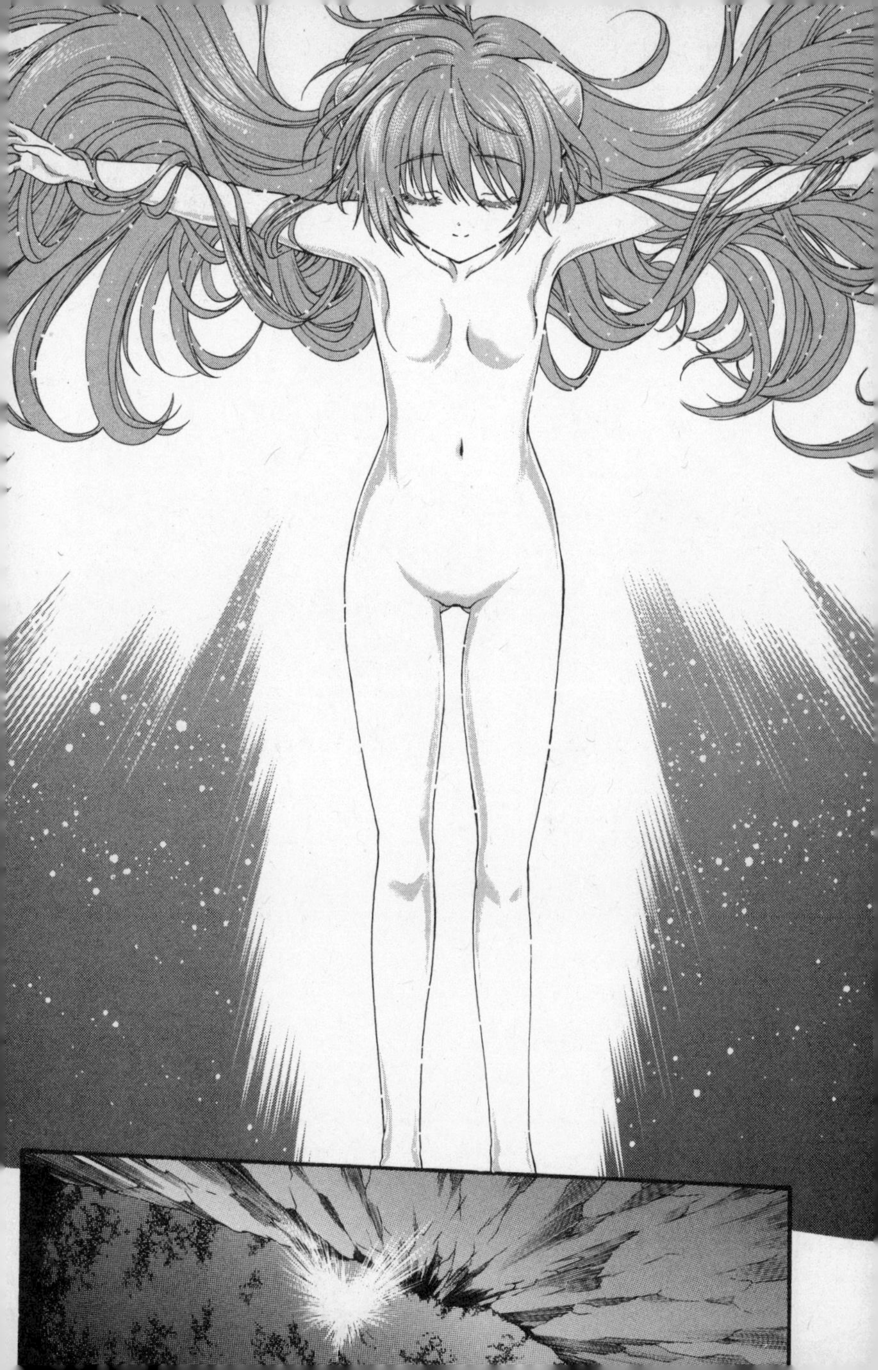

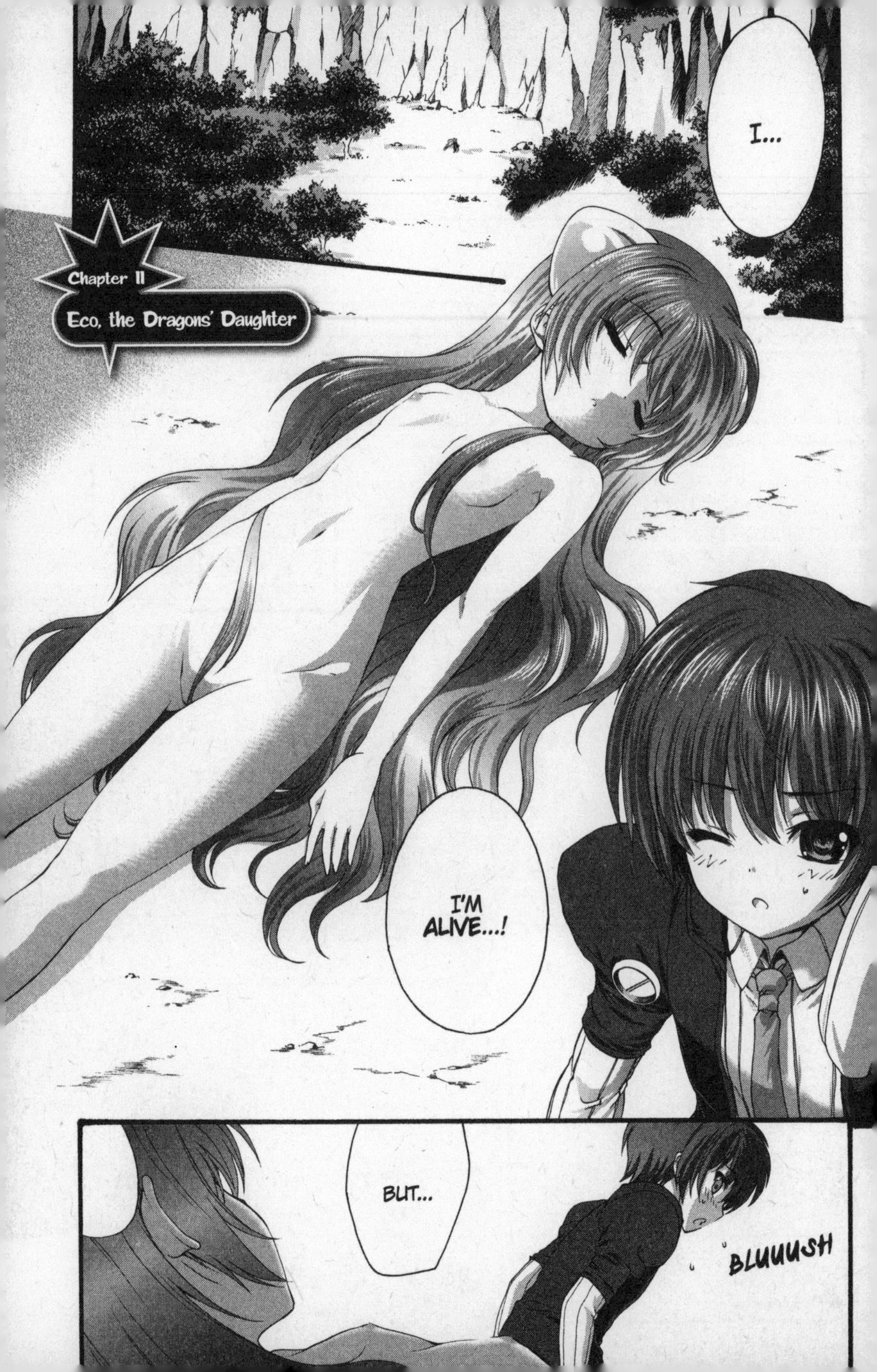
I...
Chapter 11
Eco, the Dragons' Daughter
I'M ALIVE...!
BUT...
BLUUUSH

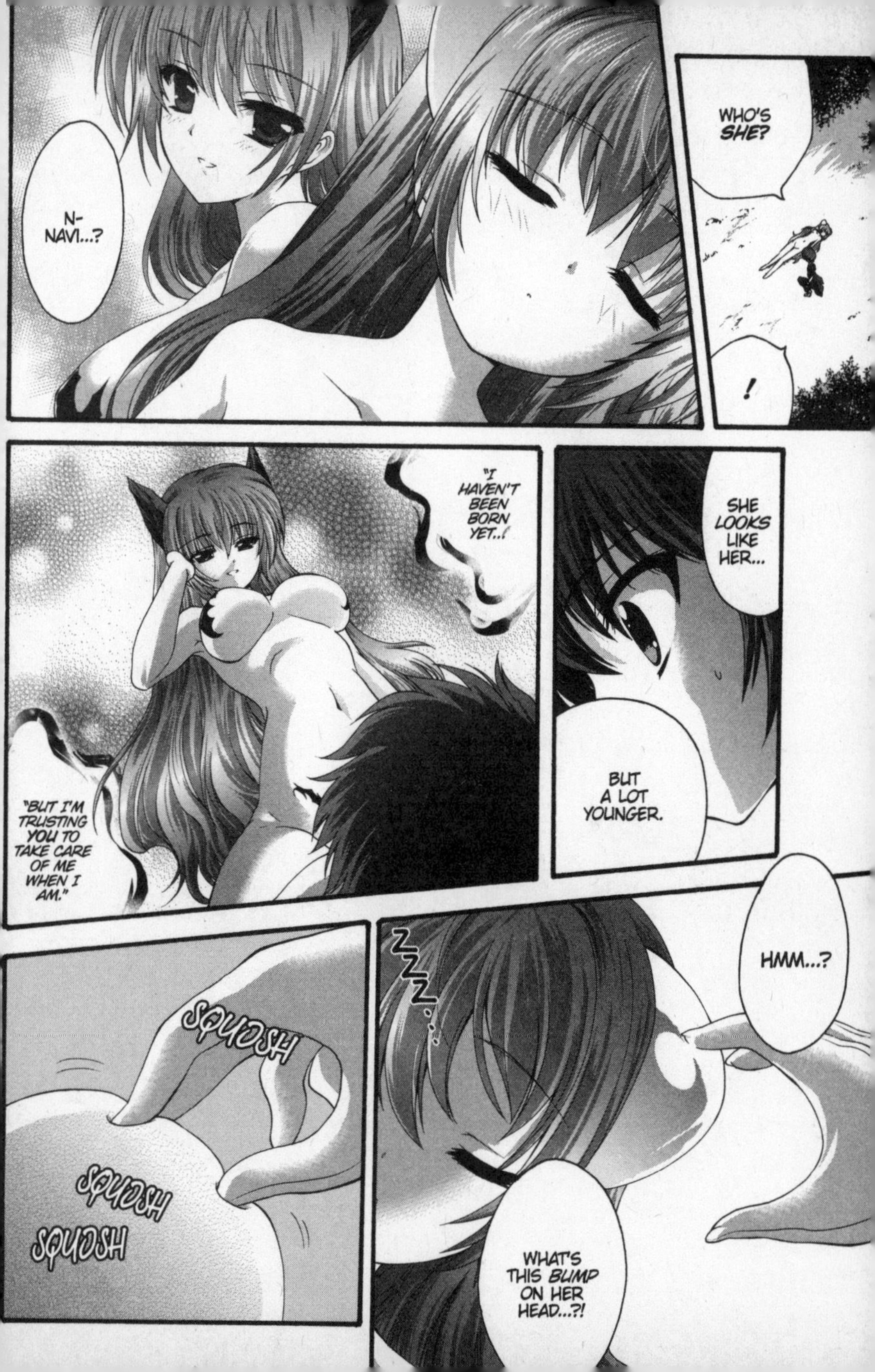
WHO'S SHE?
!
N-NAVI...?
SHE LOOKS LIKE HER...
BUT A LOT YOUNGER.
"I HAVEN'T BEEN BORN YET..."
"BUT I'M TRUSTING YOU TO TAKE CARE OF ME WHEN I AM."
ZZZ...
HMM...?
WHAT'S THIS BUMP ON HER HEAD...?!
SQUOSH
SQUOSH
SQUOSH

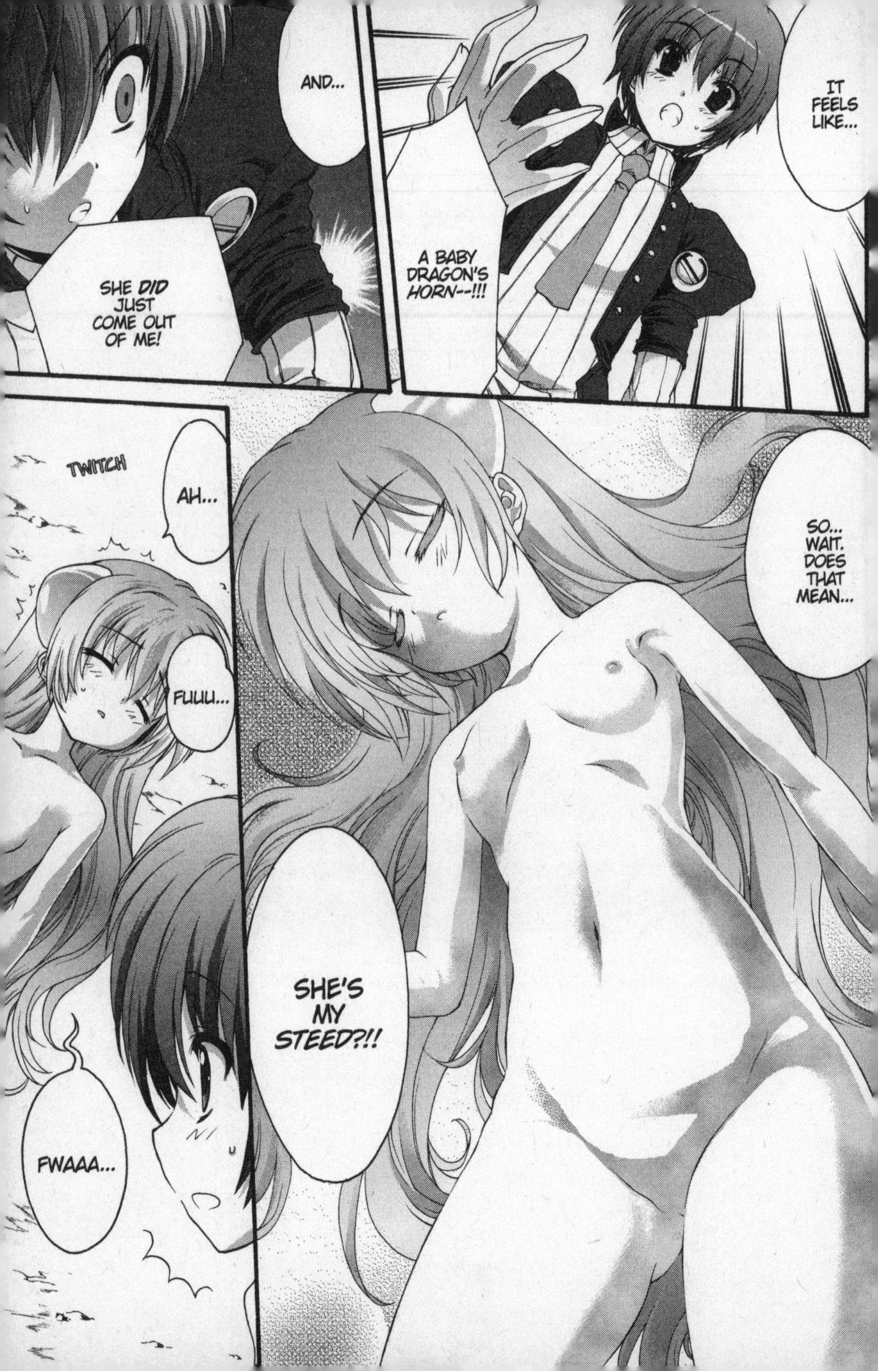
IT FEELS LIKE...
A BABY DRAGON'S HORN--!!!
AND...
SHE DID JUST COME OUT OF ME!
SO... WAIT. DOES THAT MEAN...
SHE'S MY STEED?!!
TWITCH
AH...
FUUU...
FWAAA...

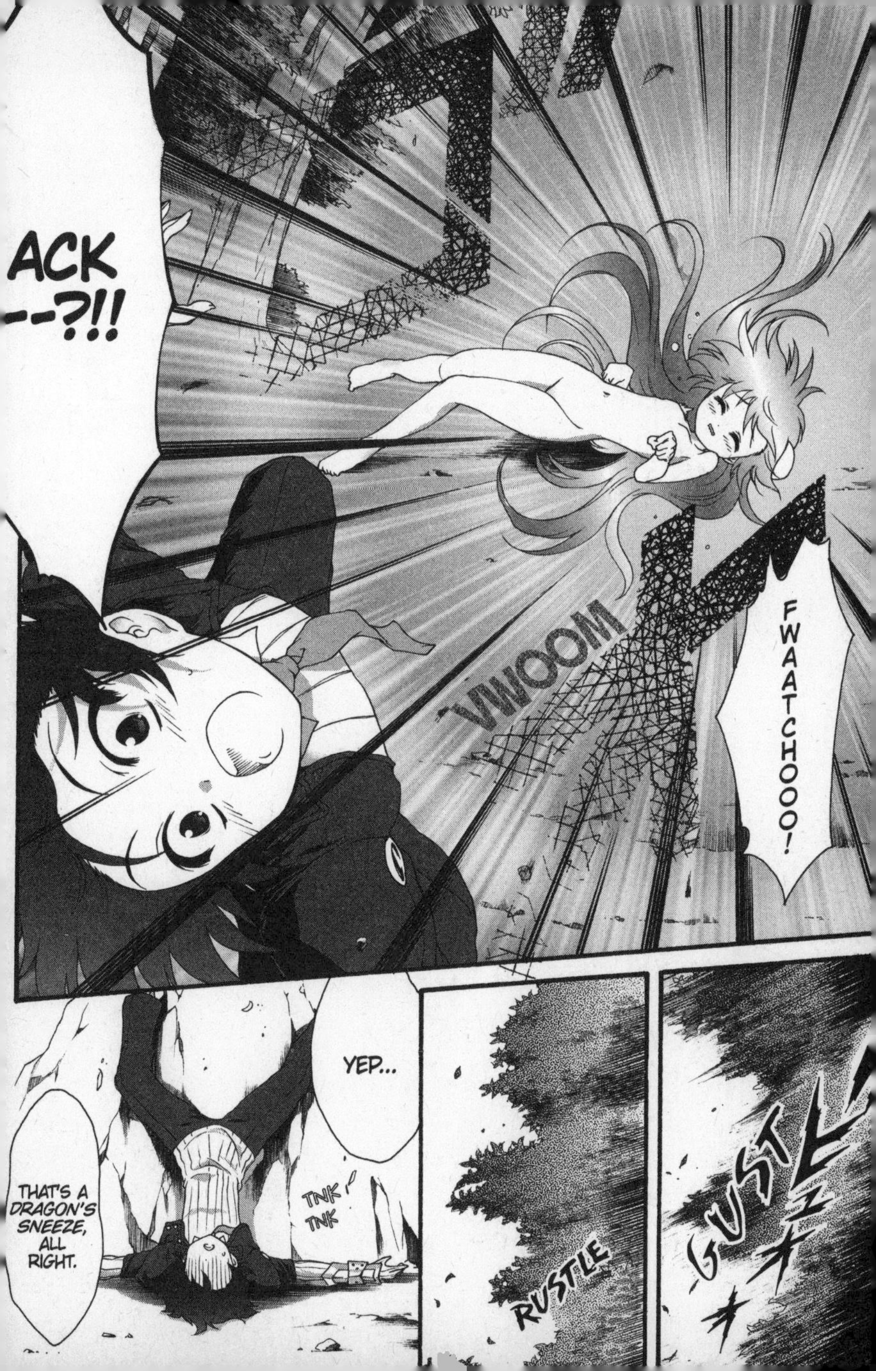
FWAATCHOOO!
VWOOM
ACK --?!!
GUST
RUSTLE
YEP...
TNK TNK
THAT'S A DRAGON'S SNEEZE, ALL RIGHT.

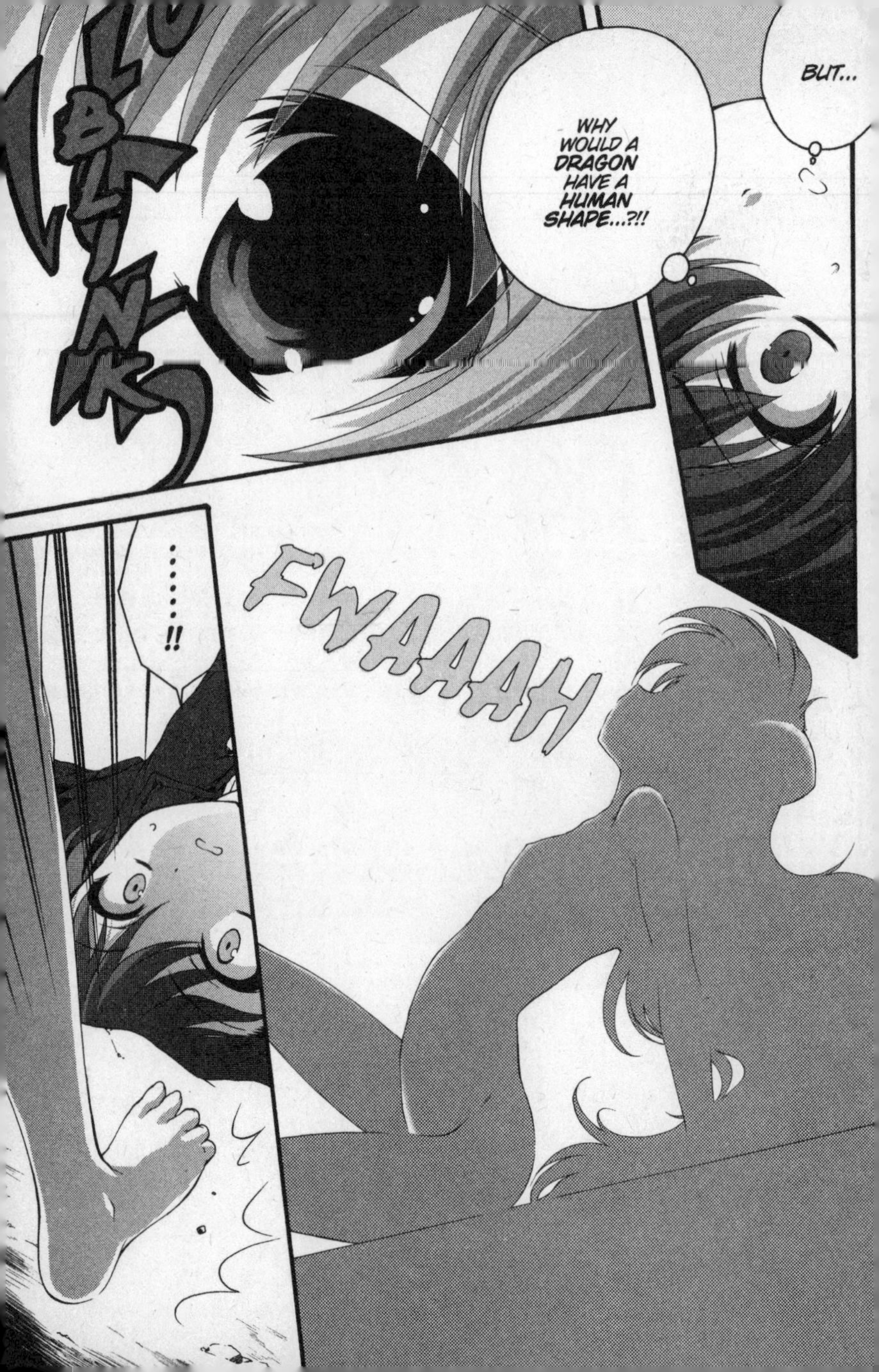
BUT...
WHY WOULD A DRAGON HAVE A HUMAN SHAPE...?!!
BLINK
FWAAAH
......!!

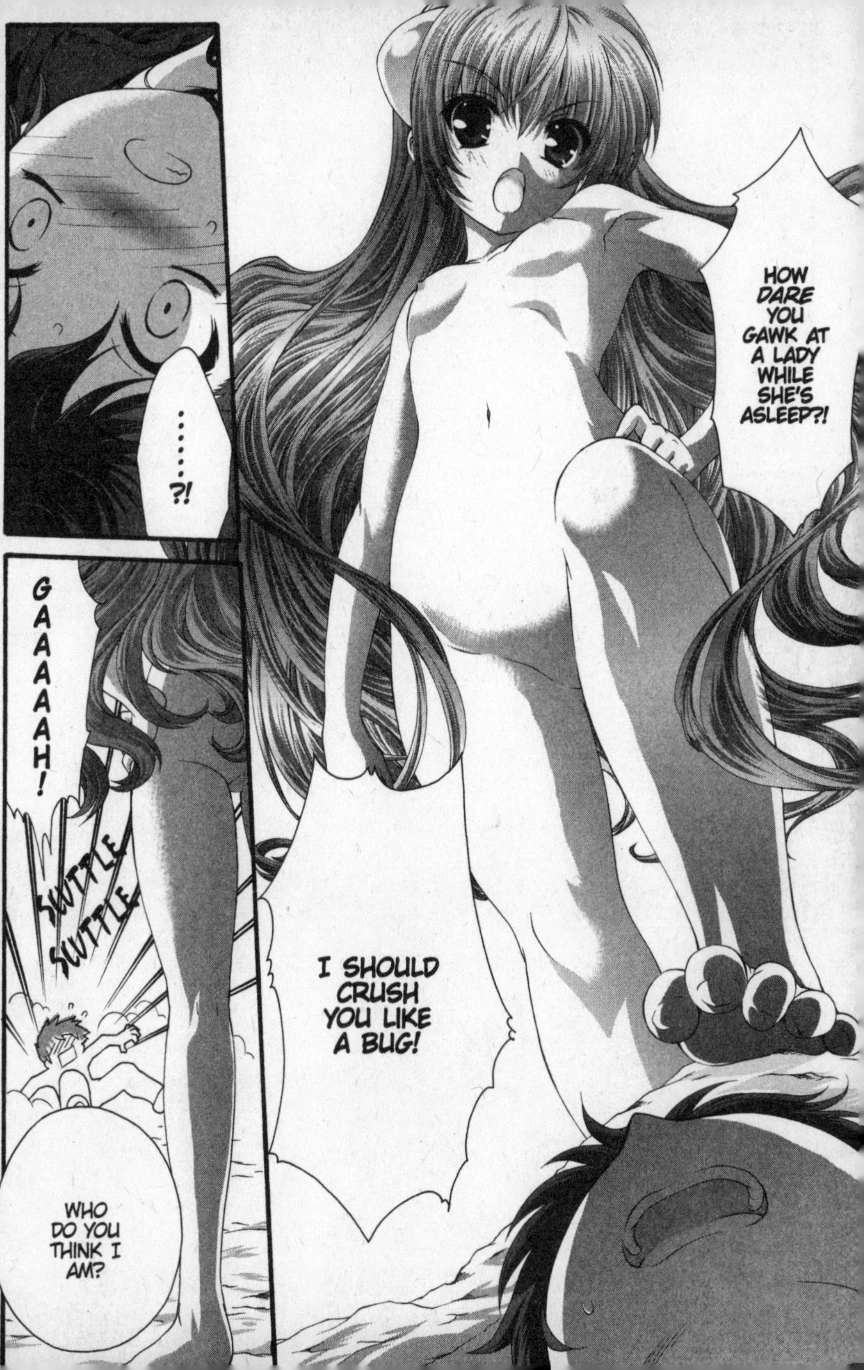
HOW DARE YOU GAWK AT A LADY WHILE SHE'S ASLEEP?!
I SHOULD CRUSH YOU LIKE A BUG!
......?!
GAAAAAAH!
SCUTTLE SCUTTLE
WHO DO YOU THINK I AM?

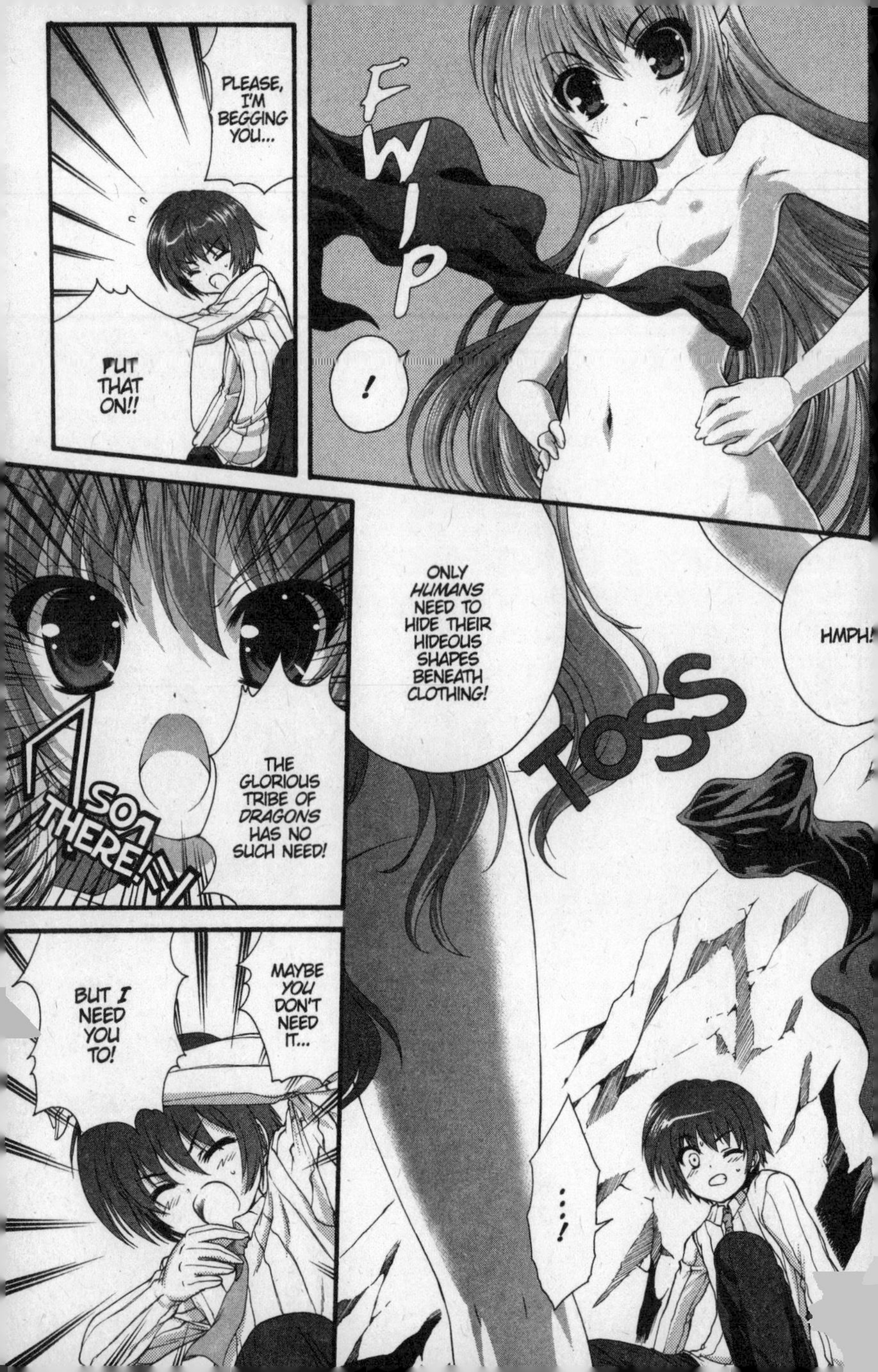
FWIP
!
PLEASE, I'M BEGGING YOU...
PUT THAT ON!!
HMPH!
ONLY HUMANS NEED TO HIDE THEIR HIDEOUS SHAPES BENEATH CLOTHING!
TOSS
...!
THE GLORIOUS TRIBE OF DRAGONS HAS NO SUCH NEED!
SO THERE!
MAYBE YOU DON'T NEED IT...
BUT I NEED YOU TO!

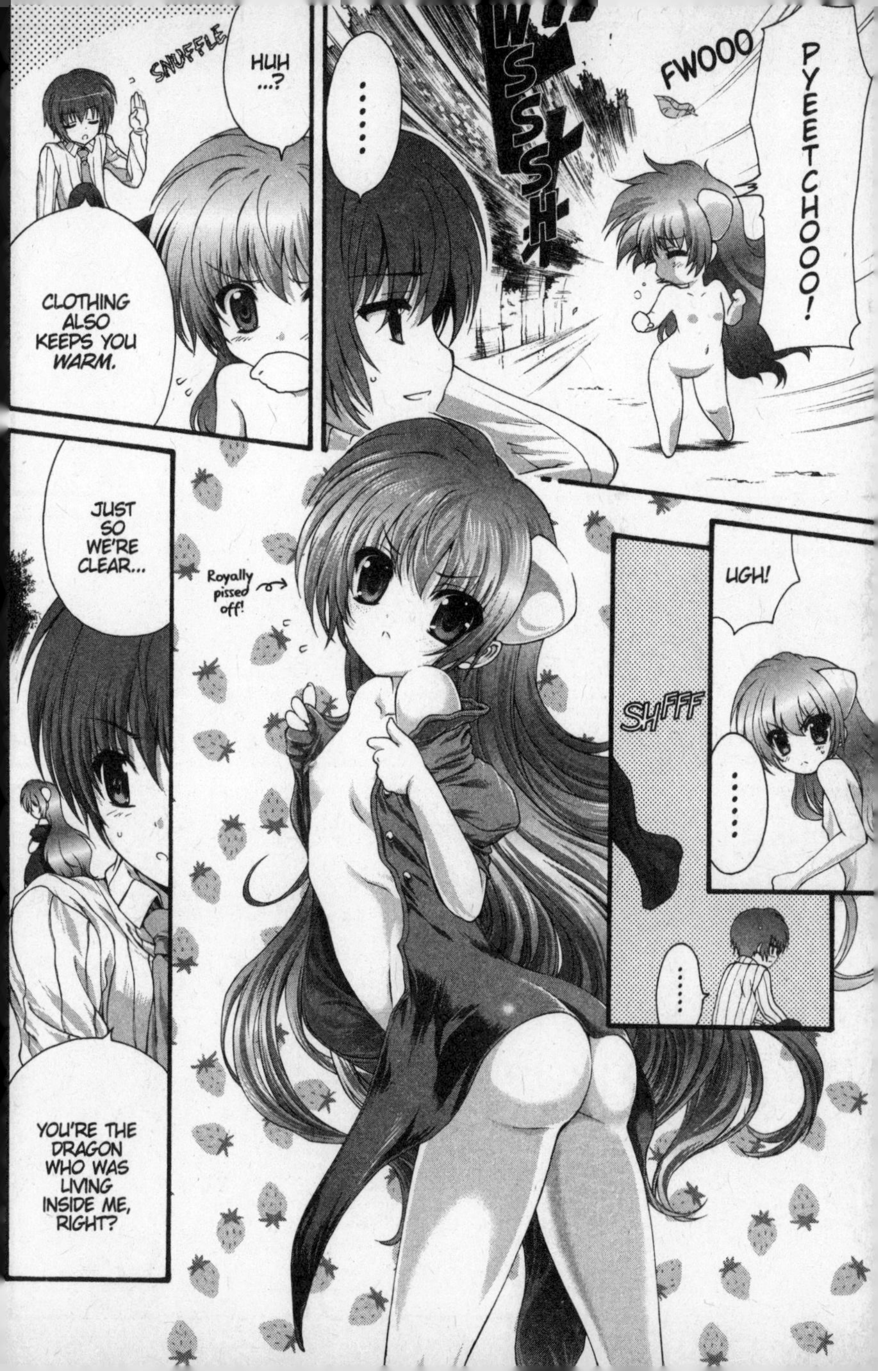
PYEETCHOOO!
FWOOO
WSSSH
......
HUH ...?
SNUFFLE
CLOTHING ALSO KEEPS YOU WARM.
UGH!
......
SHFFF
......
Royally pissed off!
JUST SO WE'RE CLEAR...
YOU'RE THE DRAGON WHO WAS LIVING INSIDE ME, RIGHT?

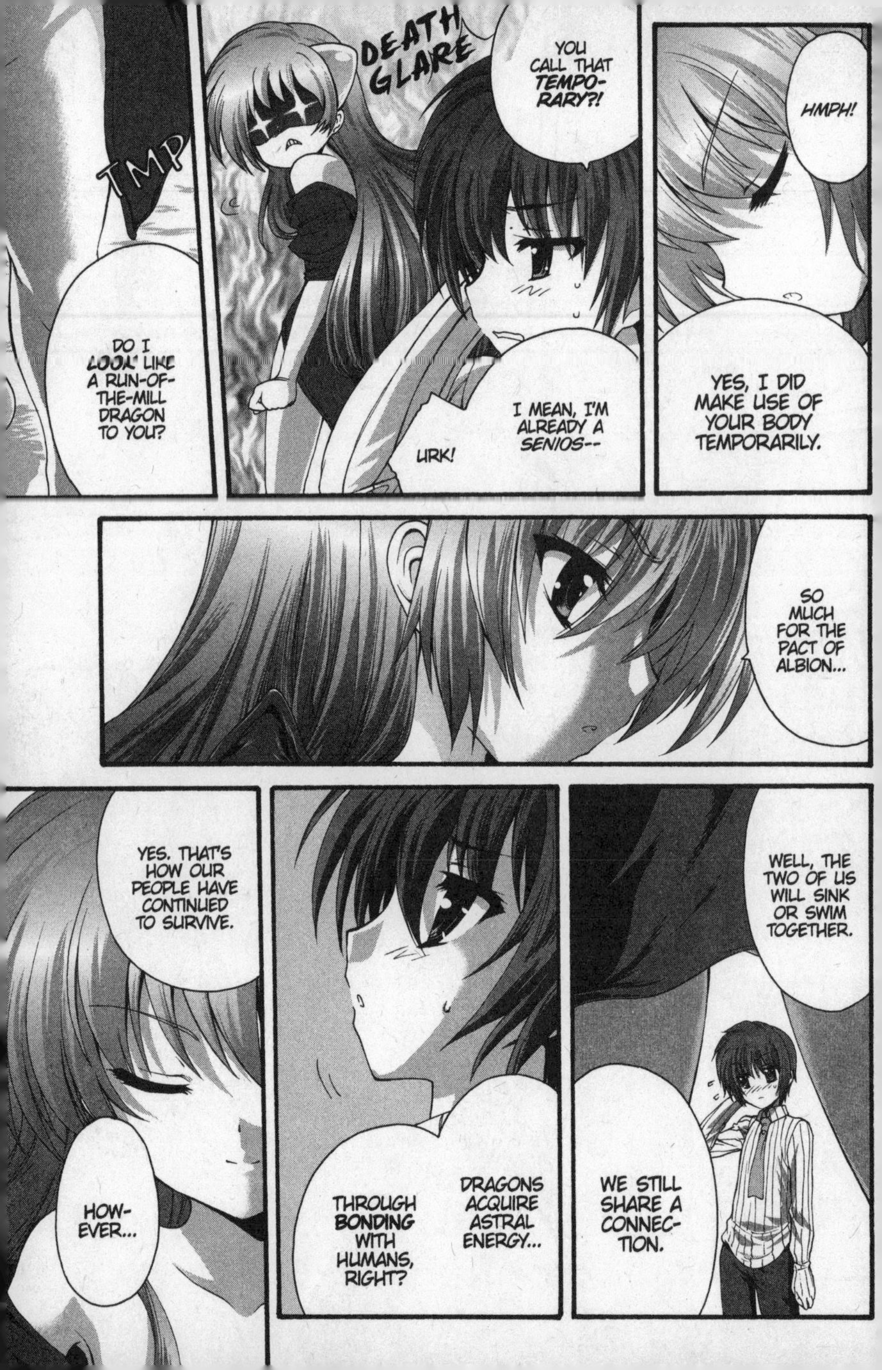
HMPH!
YES, I DID MAKE USE OF YOUR BODY TEMPORARILY.
YOU CALL THAT TEMPORARY?!
DEATH GLARE
I MEAN, I'M ALREADY A SENIOS--
URK!
TMP
DO I LOOK LIKE A RUN-OF-THE-MILL DRAGON TO YOU?
SO MUCH FOR THE PACT OF ALBION...
WELL, THE TWO OF US WILL SINK OR SWIM TOGETHER.
WE STILL SHARE A CONNECTION.
DRAGONS ACQUIRE ASTRAL ENERGY...
THROUGH BONDING WITH HUMANS, RIGHT?
YES. THAT'S HOW OUR PEOPLE HAVE CONTINUED TO SURVIVE.
HOW-EVER...

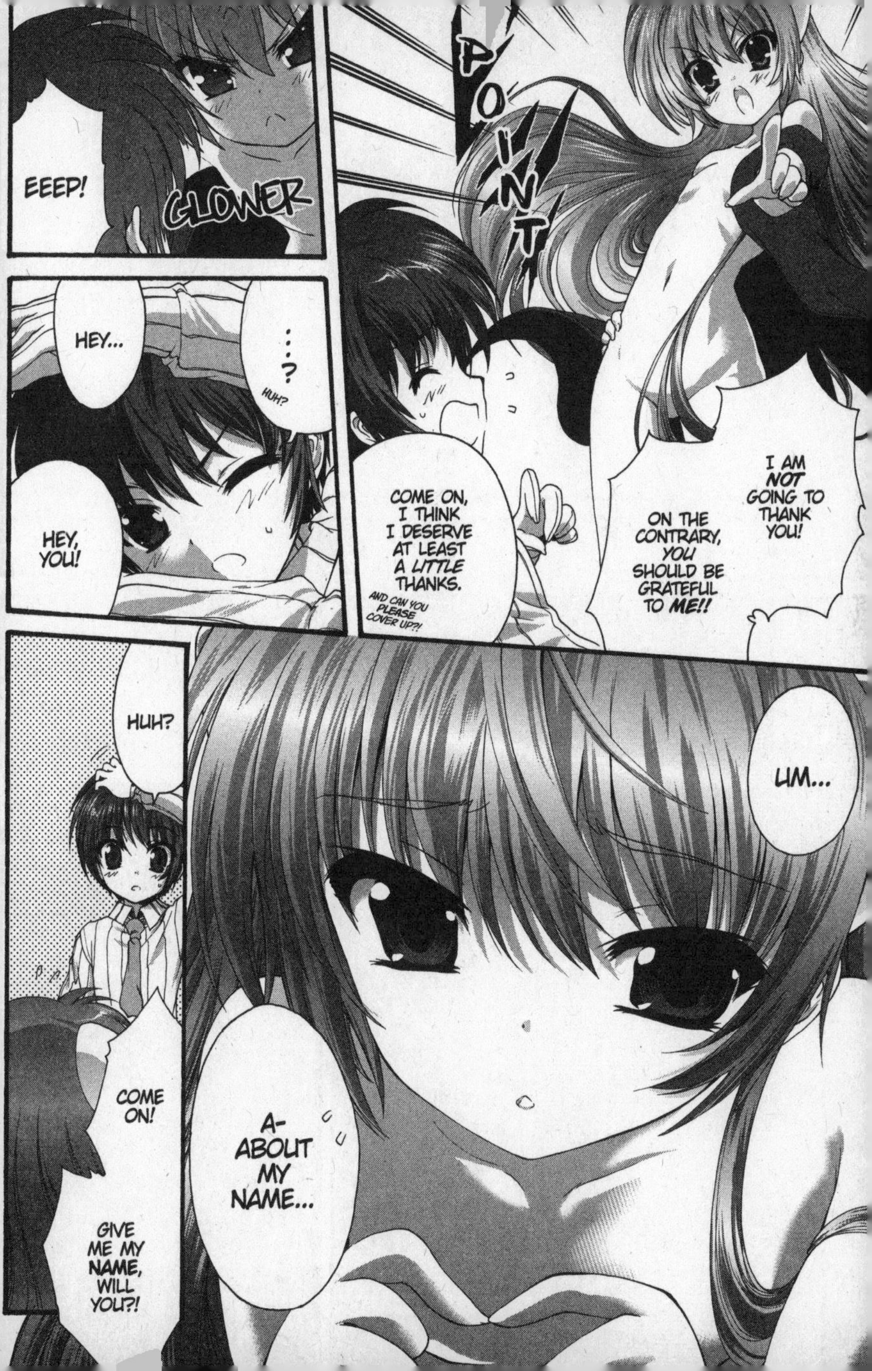
POINT
I AM NOT GOING TO THANK YOU!
ON THE CONTRARY, YOU SHOULD BE GRATEFUL TO ME!!
COME ON, I THINK I DESERVE AT LEAST A LITTLE THANKS.
AND CAN YOU PLEASE COVER UP?!
GLOWER
EEEP!
HEY...
...?
HUH?
HEY, YOU!
UM...
A-ABOUT MY NAME...
HUH?
COME ON!
GIVE ME MY NAME, WILL YOU?!

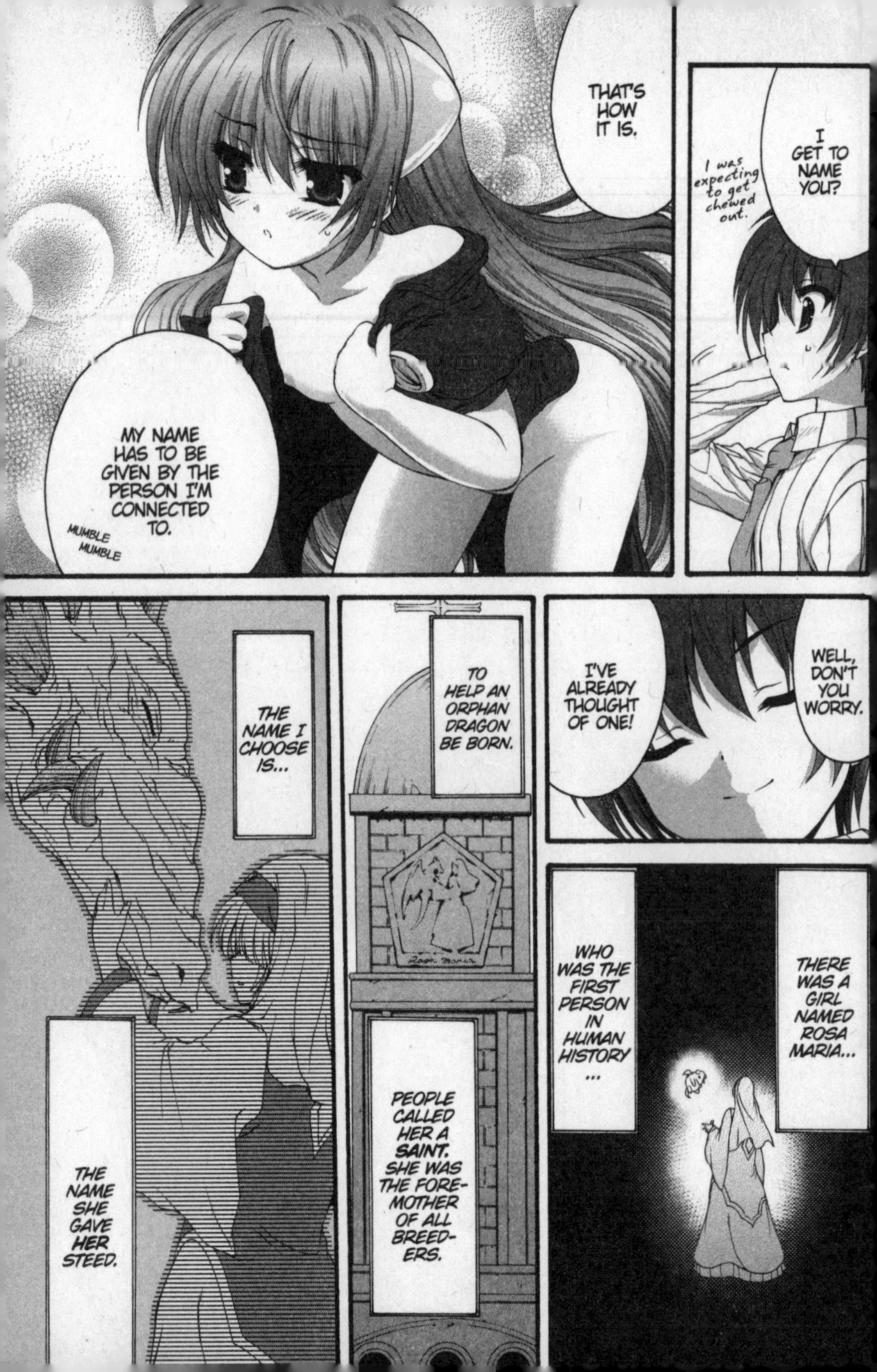
I GET TO NAME YOU?
I was expecting to get chewed out.
THAT'S HOW IT IS.
MY NAME HAS TO BE GIVEN BY THE PERSON I'M CONNECTED TO.
MUMBLE MUMBLE
WELL, DON'T YOU WORRY.
I'VE ALREADY THOUGHT OF ONE!
THERE WAS A GIRL NAMED ROSA MARIA...
WHO WAS THE FIRST PERSON IN HUMAN HISTORY...
TO HELP AN ORPHAN DRAGON BE BORN.
PEOPLE CALLED HER A SAINT. SHE WAS THE FORE-MOTHER OF ALL BREED-ERS.
THE NAME I CHOOSE IS...
THE NAME SHE GAVE HER STEED.

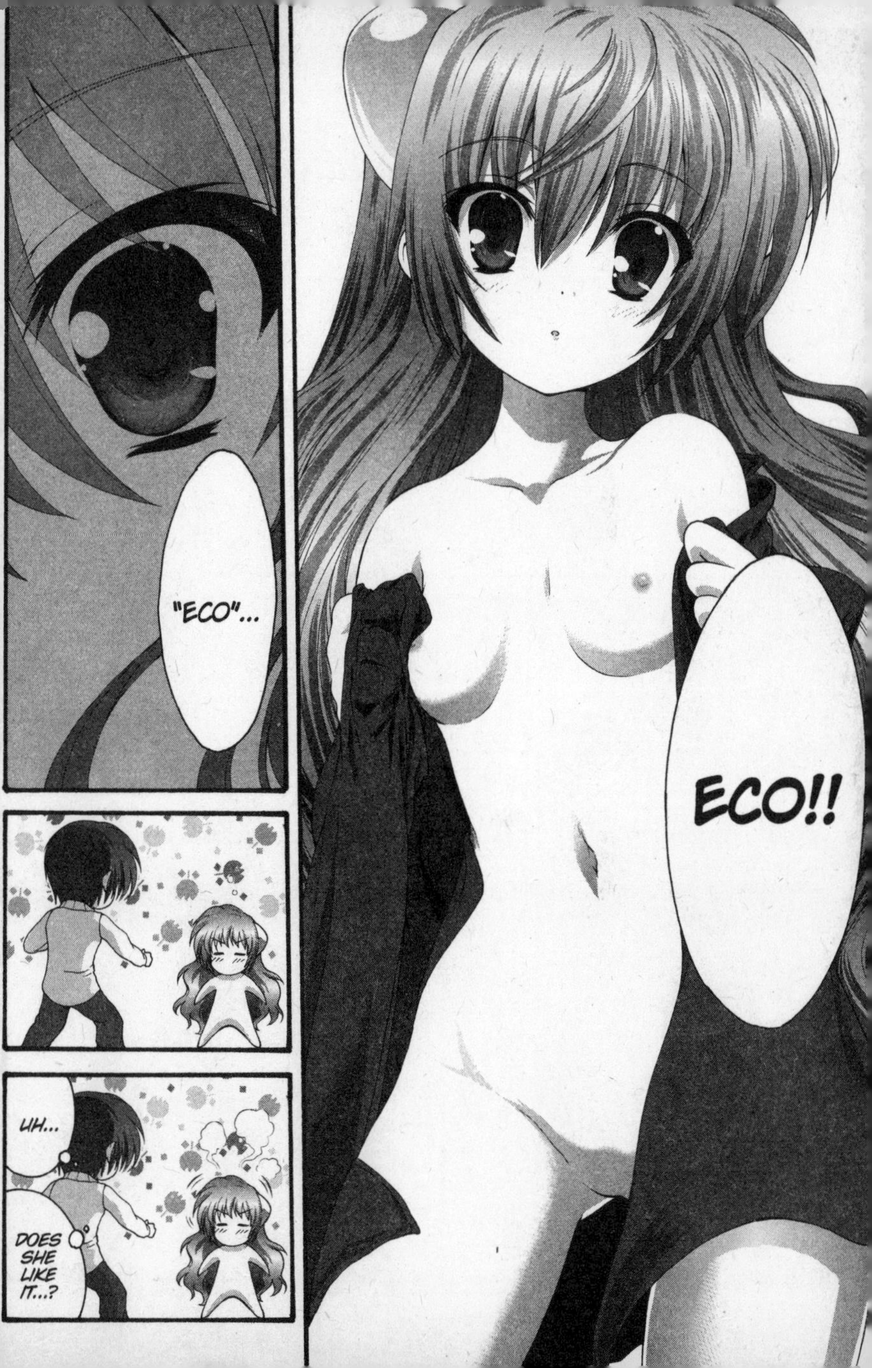
ECO!!
"ECO"...
UH...
DOES SHE LIKE IT...?

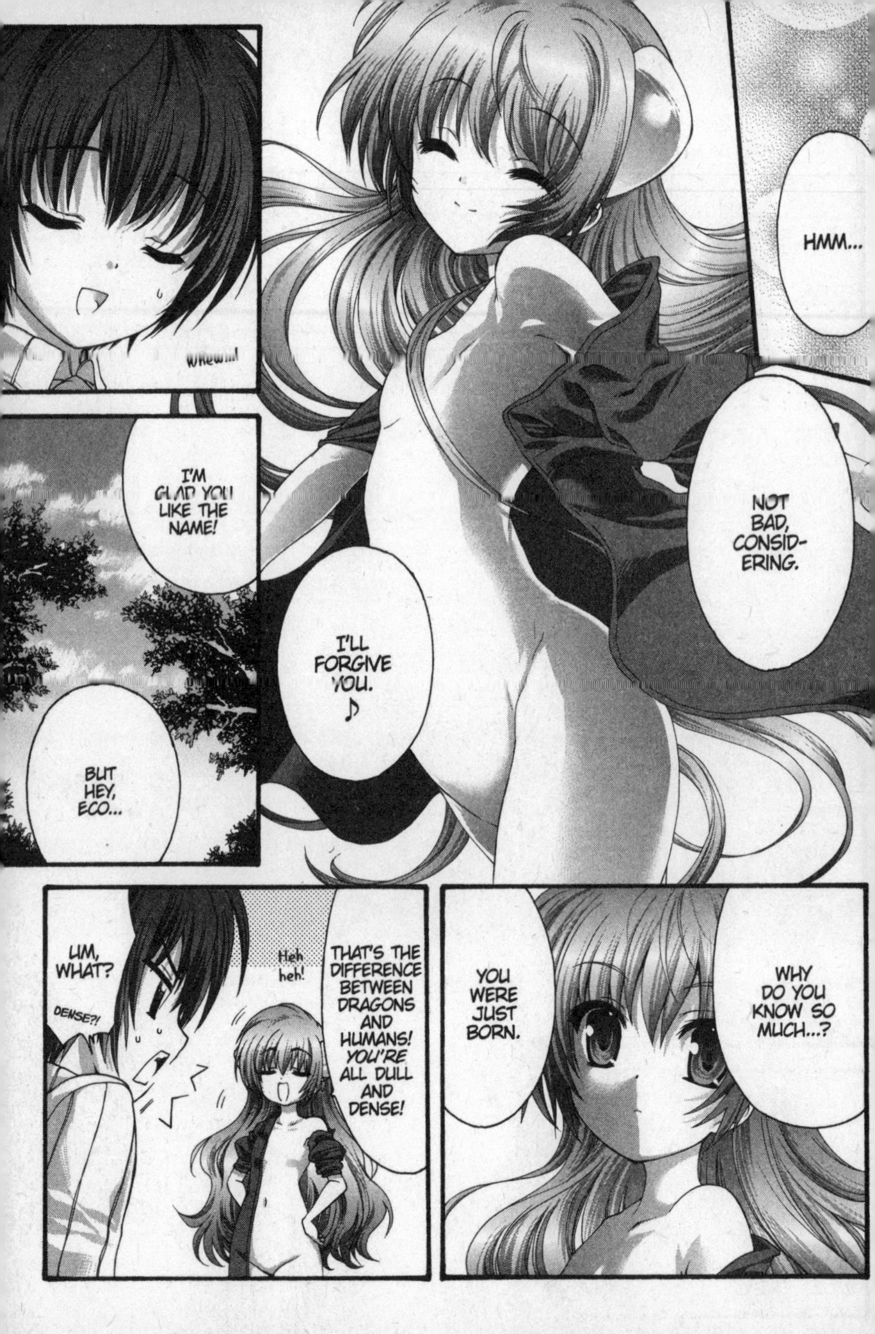
HMM...
NOT BAD, CONSID-ERING.
I'LL FORGIVE YOU. ♪
Whew!!
I'M GLAD YOU LIKE THE NAME!
BUT HEY, ECO...
WHY DO YOU KNOW SO MUCH...?
YOU WERE JUST BORN.
THAT'S THE DIFFERENCE BETWEEN DRAGONS AND HUMANS! *YOU'RE* ALL DULL AND DENSE!
Heh heh!
UM, WHAT?
DENSE?!

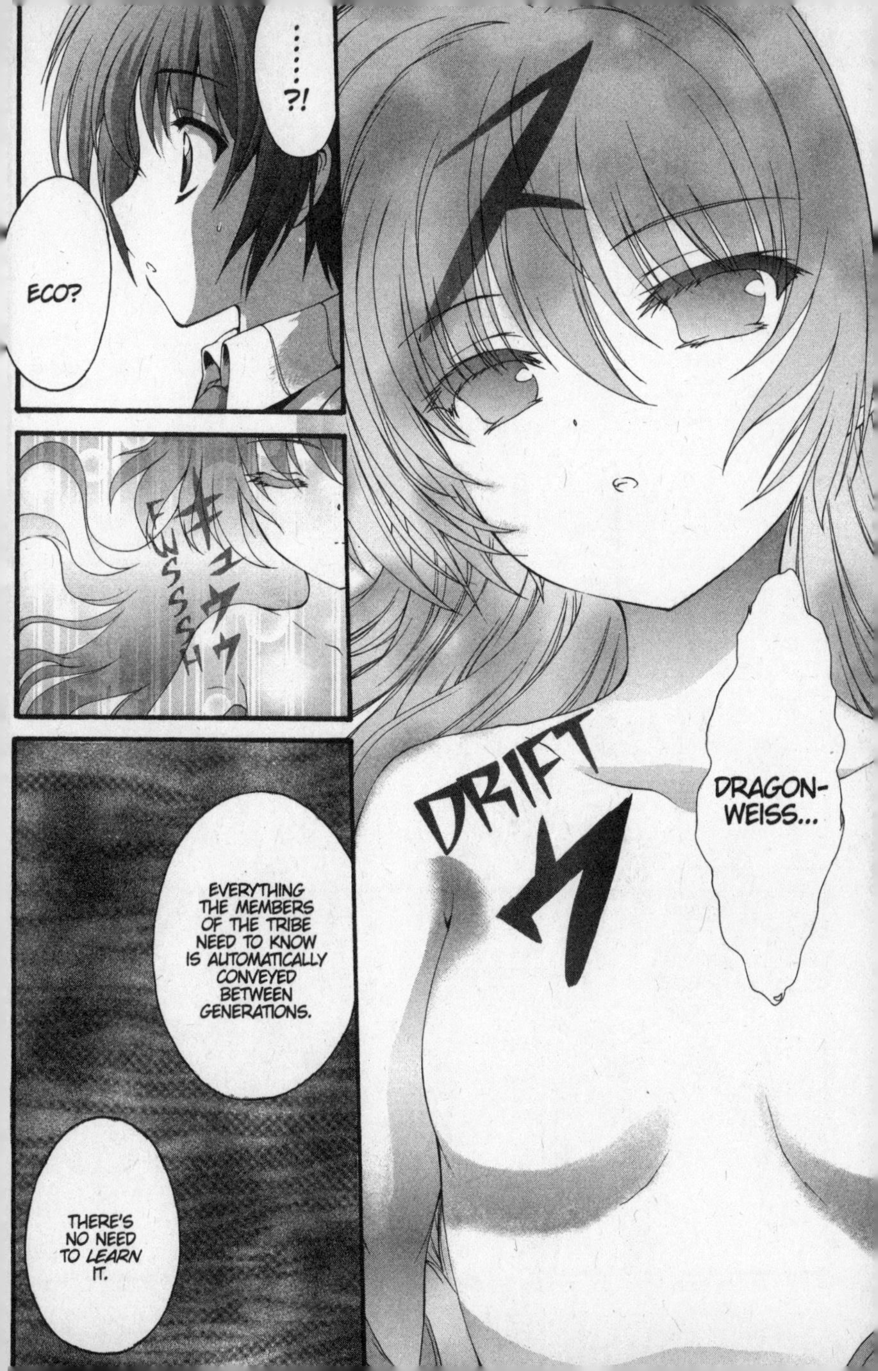
DRIFT
DRAGON-WEISS...
......?!
ECO?
FWSSSH
EVERYTHING THE MEMBERS OF THE TRIBE NEED TO KNOW IS AUTOMATICALLY CONVEYED BETWEEN GENERATIONS.
THERE'S NO NEED TO *LEARN* IT.

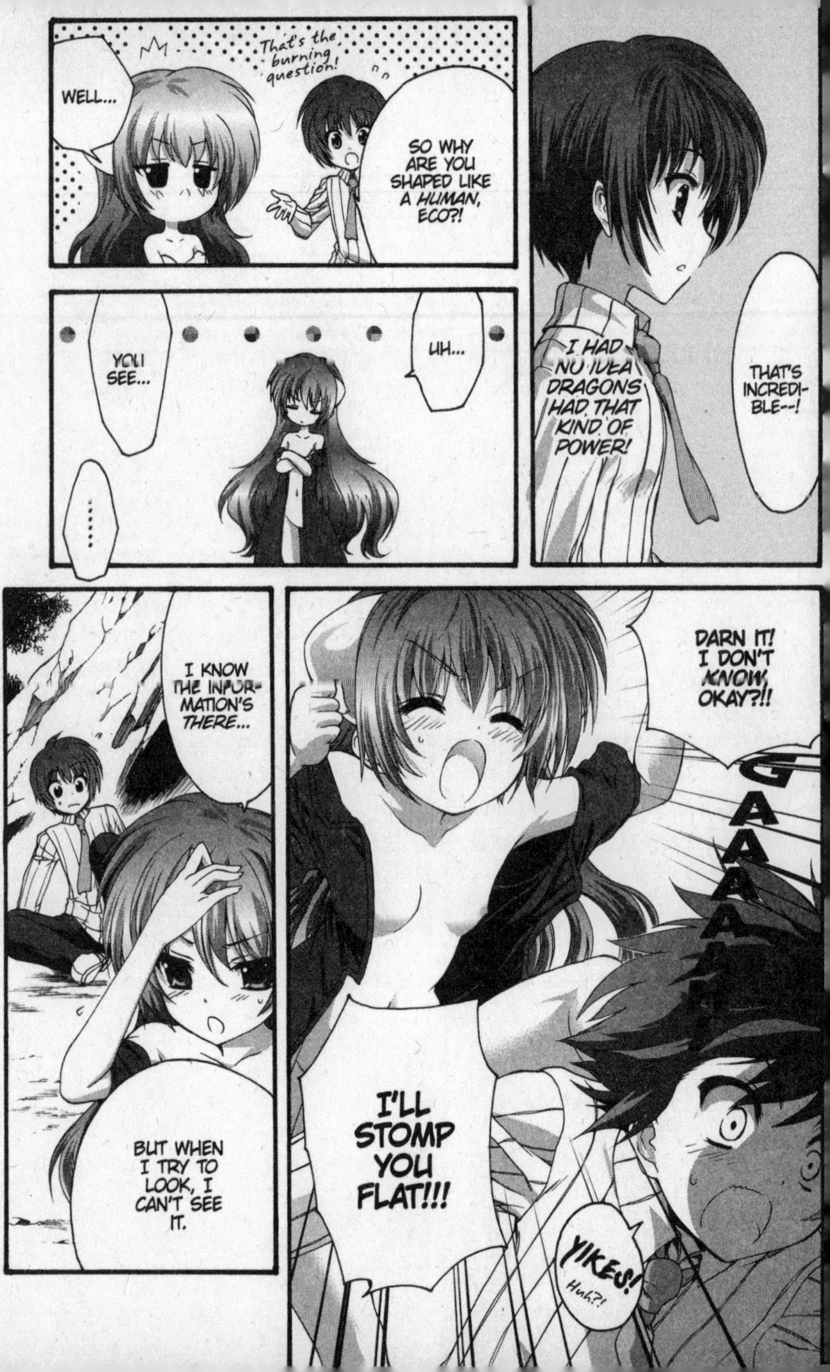
THAT'S INCREDIBLE--!
I HAD NO IDEA DRAGONS HAD THAT KIND OF POWER!
That's the burning question!
SO WHY ARE YOU SHAPED LIKE A *HUMAN*, ECO?!
WELL...
UH...
YOU SEE...
......
DARN IT! I DON'T *KNOW*, OKAY?!!
GAAAAA
I'LL STOMP YOU FLAT!!!
YIKES!
Huh?!
I KNOW THE INFORMATION'S *THERE*...
BUT WHEN I TRY TO LOOK, I CAN'T SEE IT.

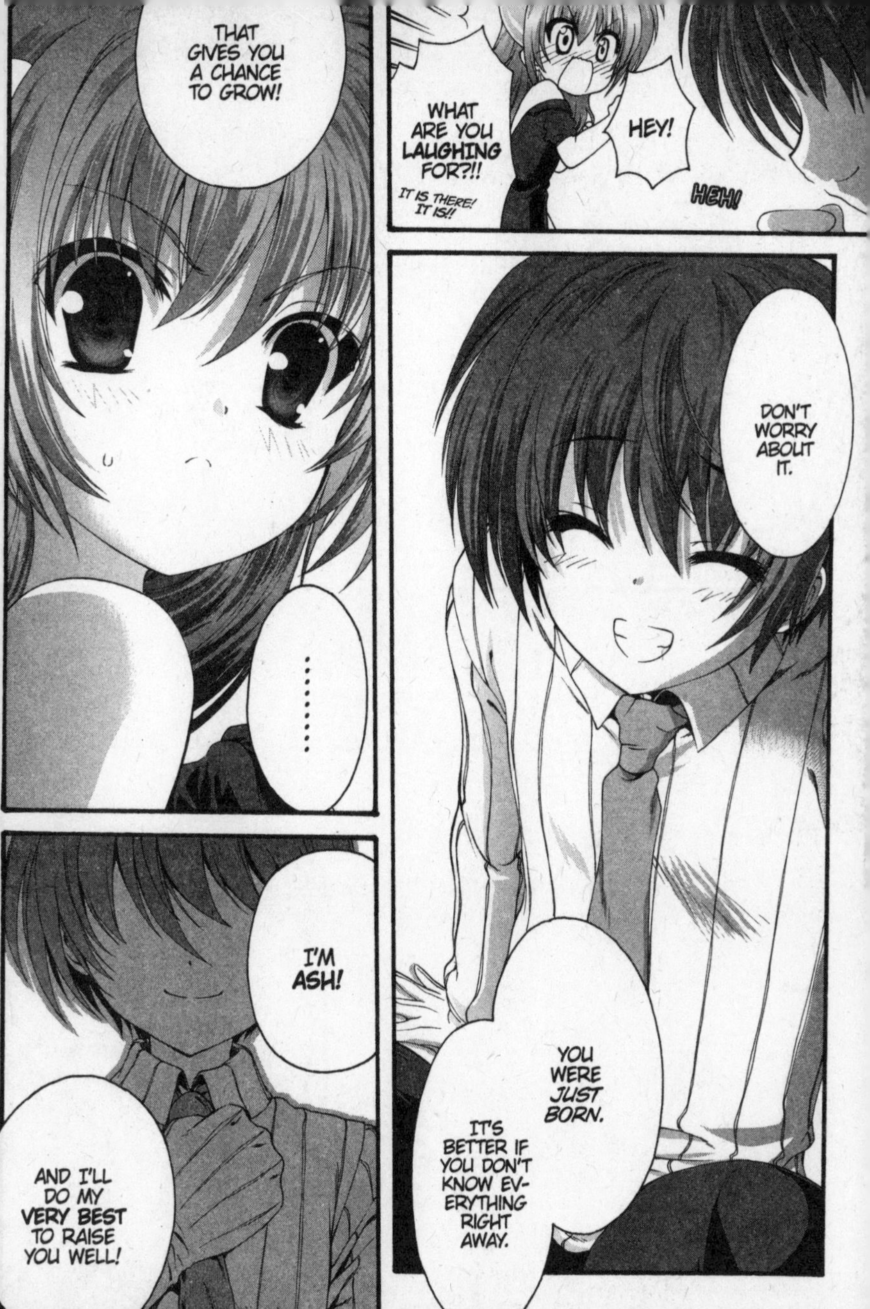
HEY!
HEH!
WHAT ARE YOU LAUGHING FOR?!!
IT IS THERE! IT IS!!
DON'T WORRY ABOUT IT.
YOU WERE JUST BORN.
IT'S BETTER IF YOU DON'T KNOW EV-ERYTHING RIGHT AWAY.
THAT GIVES YOU A CHANCE TO GROW!
......
I'M ASH!
AND I'LL DO MY VERY BEST TO RAISE YOU WELL!

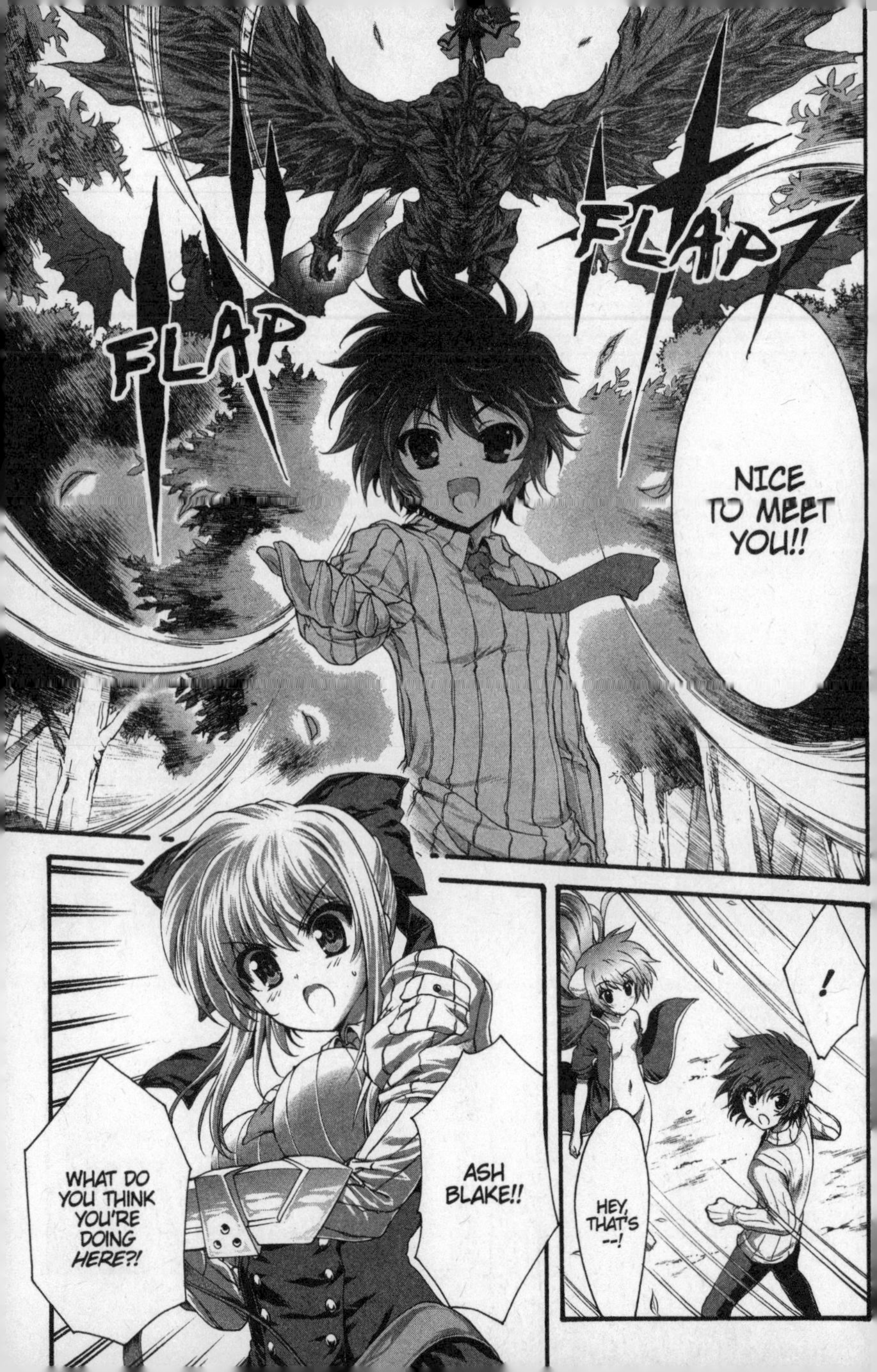
FLAP
NICE TO MEET YOU!!
FLAP
!
HEY, THAT'S --!
ASH BLAKE!!
WHAT DO YOU THINK YOU'RE DOING HERE?!

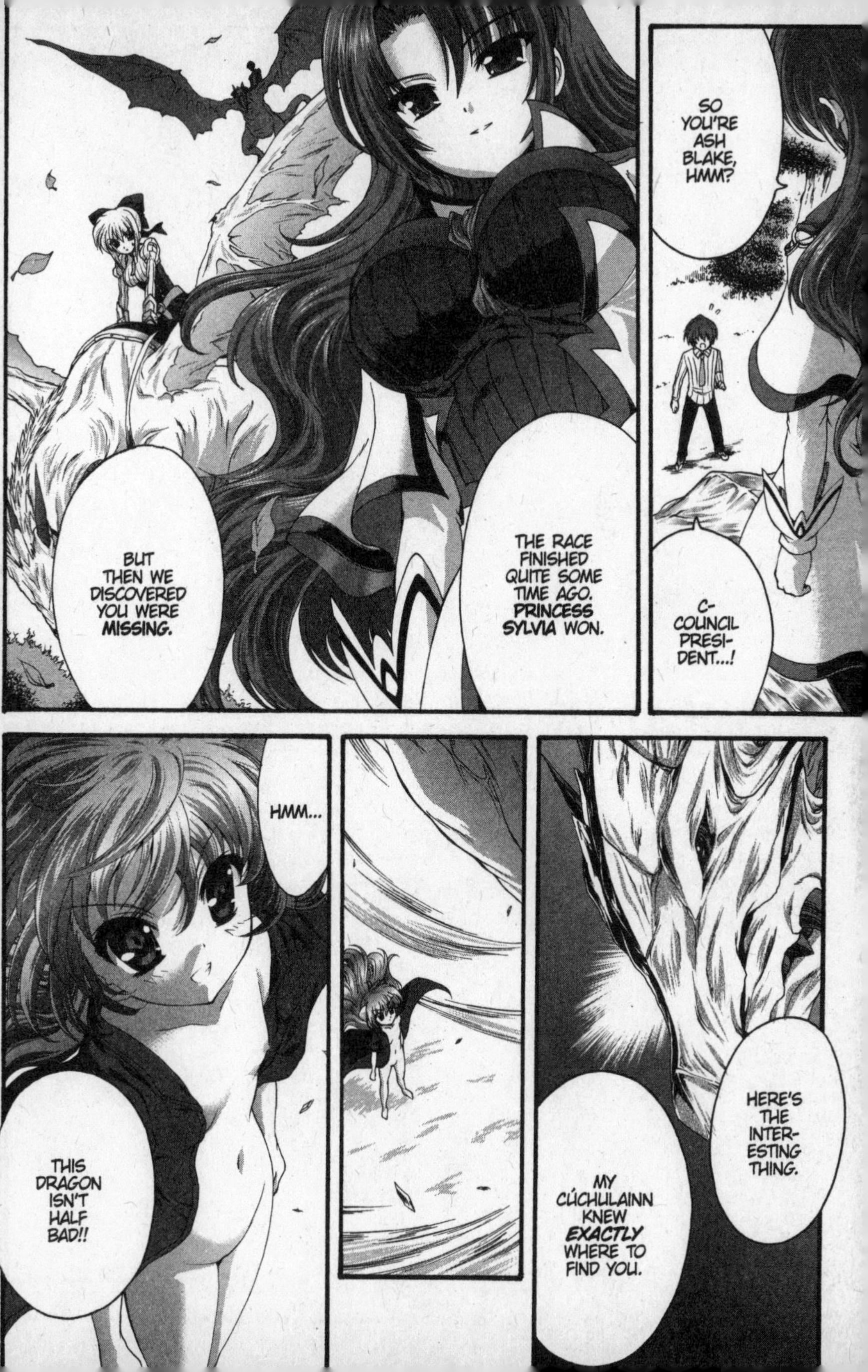
SO YOU'RE ASH BLAKE, HMM?
C-COUNCIL PRESI-DENT...!
THE RACE FINISHED QUITE SOME TIME AGO. **PRINCESS SYLVIA WON.**
BUT THEN WE DISCOVERED YOU WERE **MISSING.**
HERE'S THE INTER-ESTING THING.
MY CÚCHULAINN KNEW ***EXACTLY*** WHERE TO FIND YOU.
HMM...
THIS DRAGON ISN'T HALF BAD!!

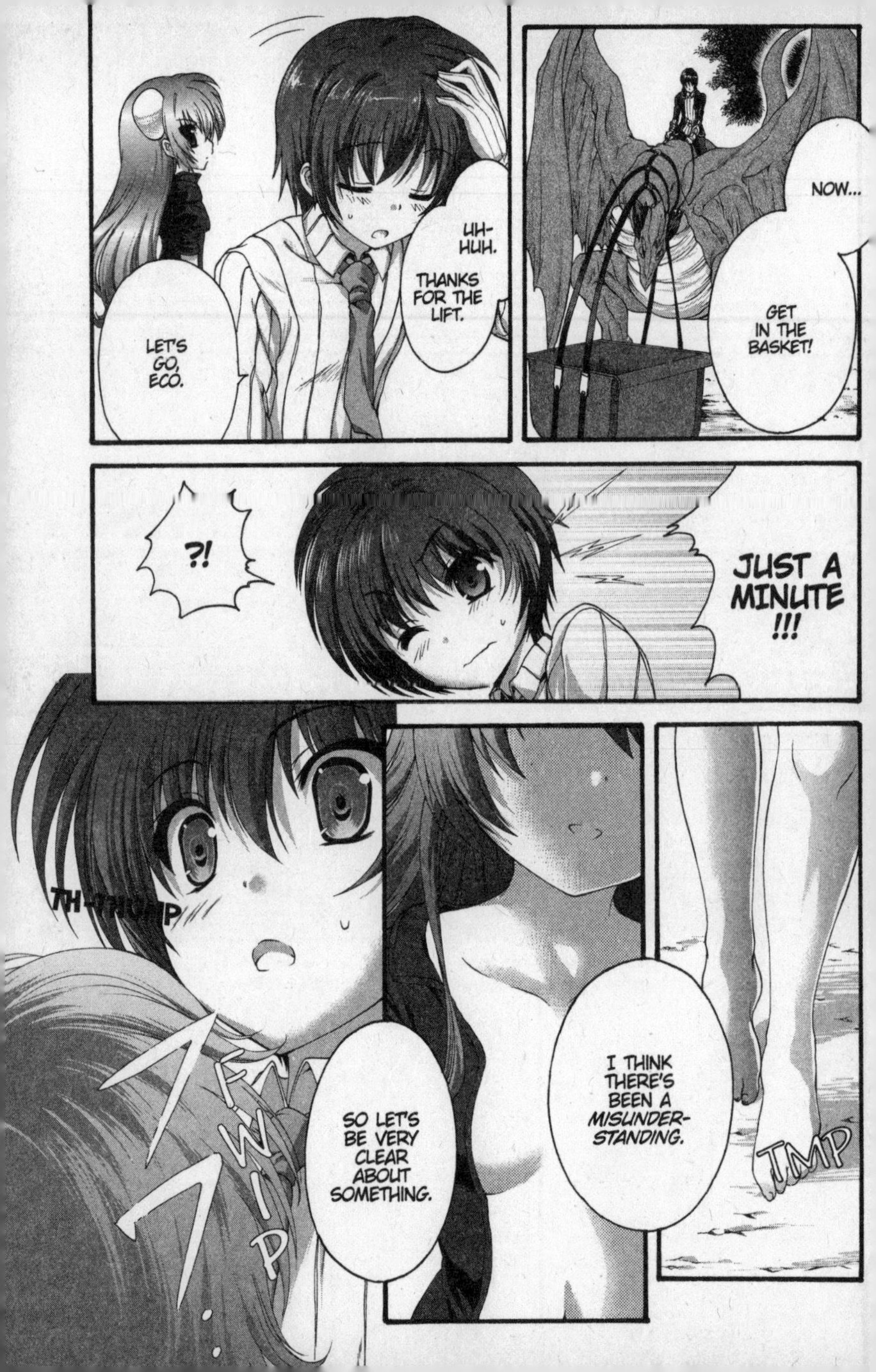
NOW...
GET IN THE BASKET!
UH-HUH.
THANKS FOR THE LIFT.
LET'S GO, ECO.
JUST A MINUTE !!!
?!
TMP
I THINK THERE'S BEEN A *MISUNDER-STANDING.*
SO LET'S BE VERY CLEAR ABOUT SOMETHING.
TH-THUMP
FWIP

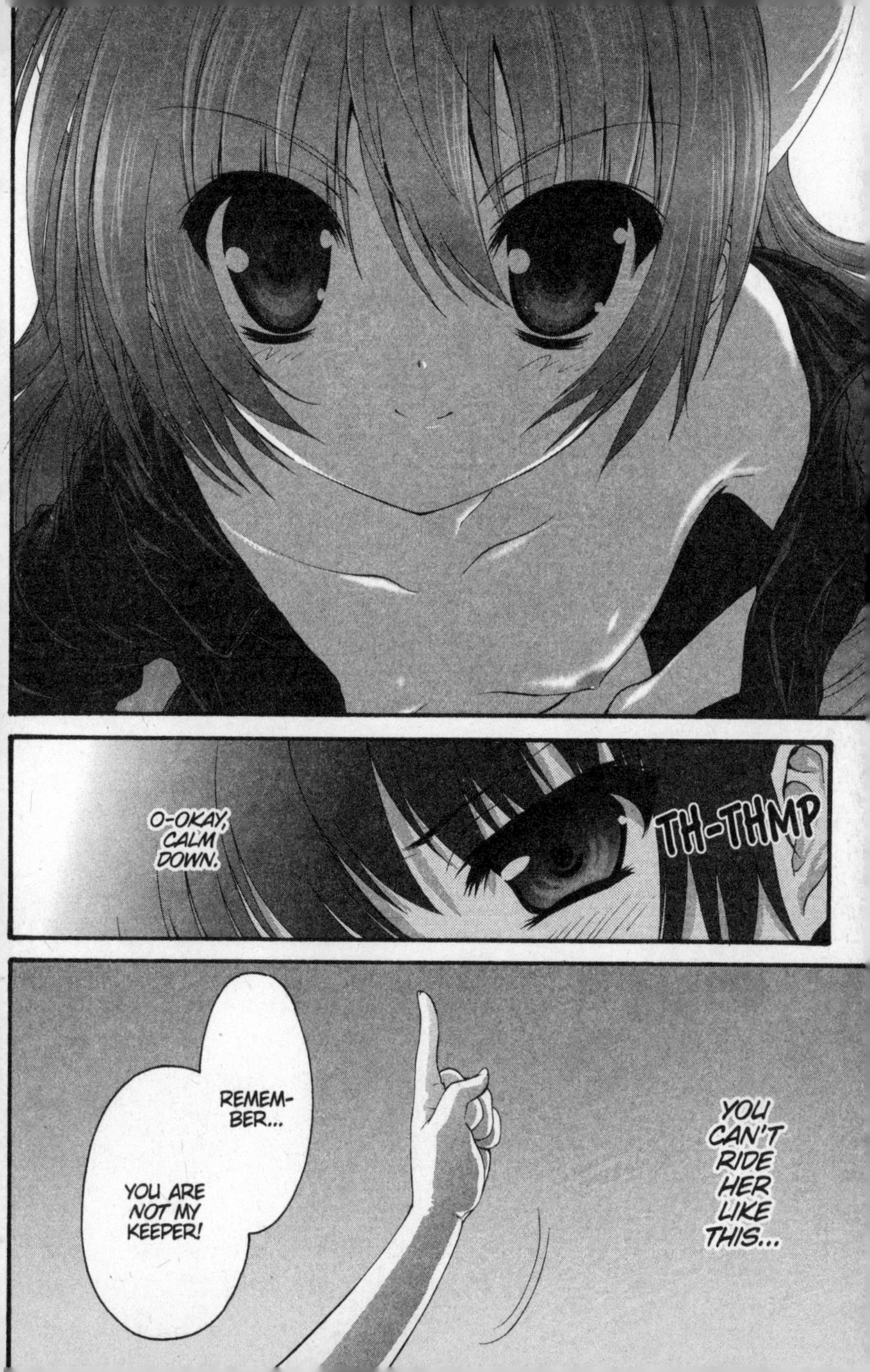
TH-THMP
O-OKAY, CALM DOWN.
YOU CAN'T RIDE HER LIKE THIS...
REMEMBER...
YOU ARE NOT MY KEEPER!

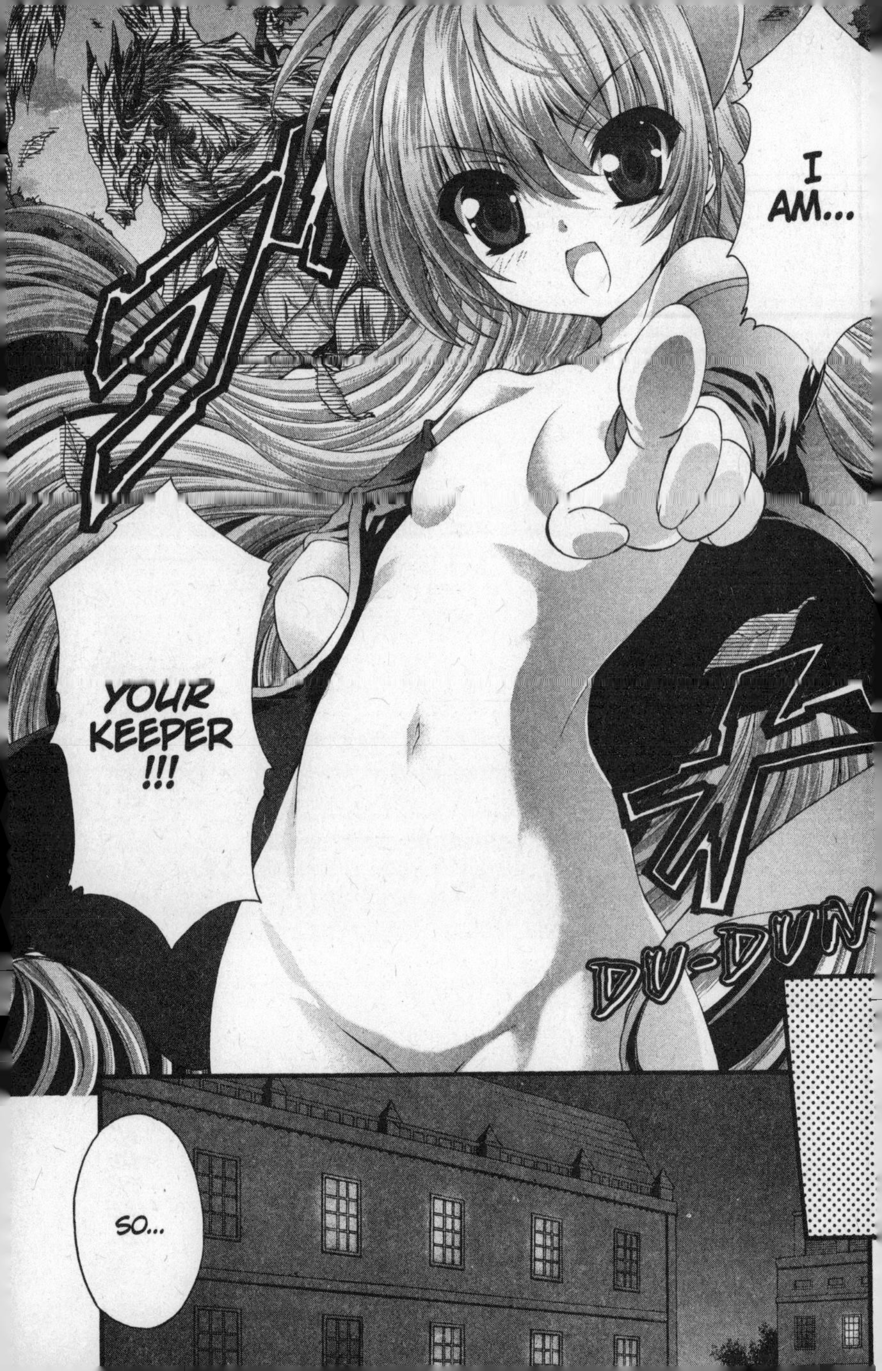
I AM...
YOUR KEEPER!!!
DU-DUN
SO...

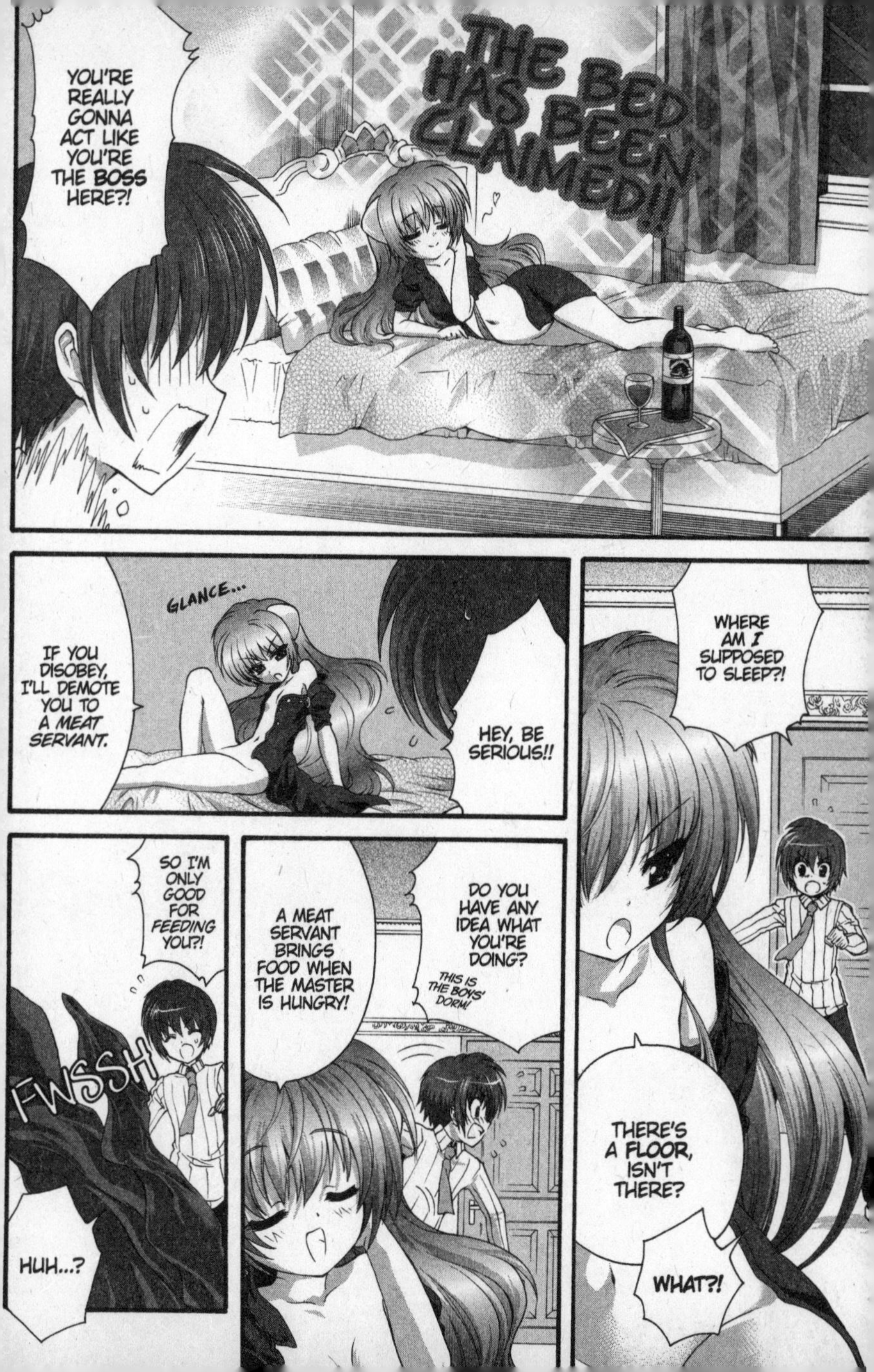
THE BED HAS BEEN CLAIMED!!
YOU'RE REALLY GONNA ACT LIKE YOU'RE THE BOSS HERE?!
WHERE AM I SUPPOSED TO SLEEP?!
THERE'S A FLOOR, ISN'T THERE?
WHAT?!
GLANCE...
HEY, BE SERIOUS!!
IF YOU DISOBEY, I'LL DEMOTE YOU TO A MEAT SERVANT.
DO YOU HAVE ANY IDEA WHAT YOU'RE DOING?
THIS IS THE BOYS' DORM!
A MEAT SERVANT BRINGS FOOD WHEN THE MASTER IS HUNGRY!
SO I'M ONLY GOOD FOR FEEDING YOU?!
FWSSH
HUH...?

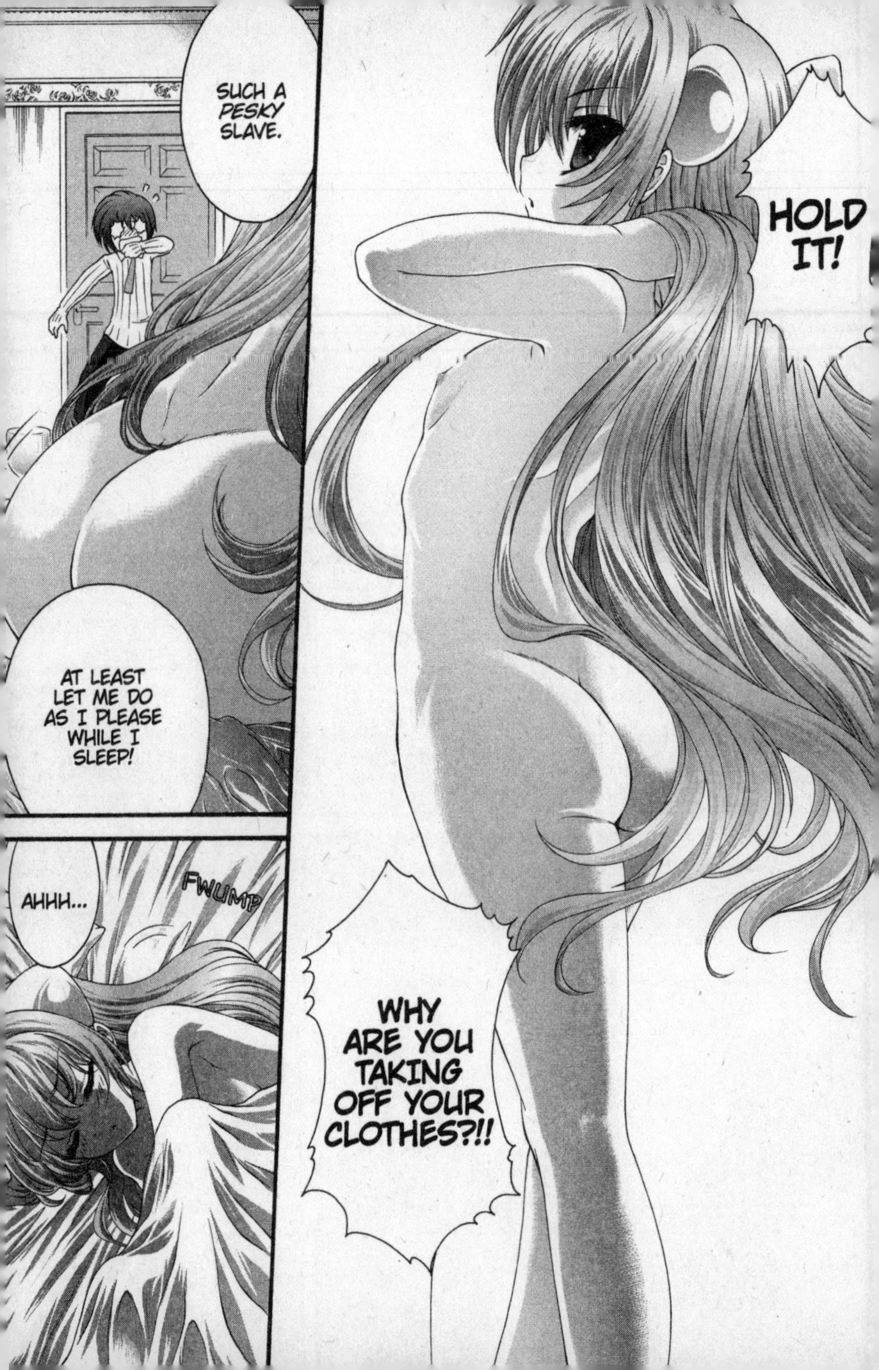
HOLD IT!
WHY ARE YOU TAKING OFF YOUR CLOTHES?!!
SUCH A PESKY SLAVE.
AT LEAST LET ME DO AS I PLEASE WHILE I SLEEP!
FWUMP
AHHH...

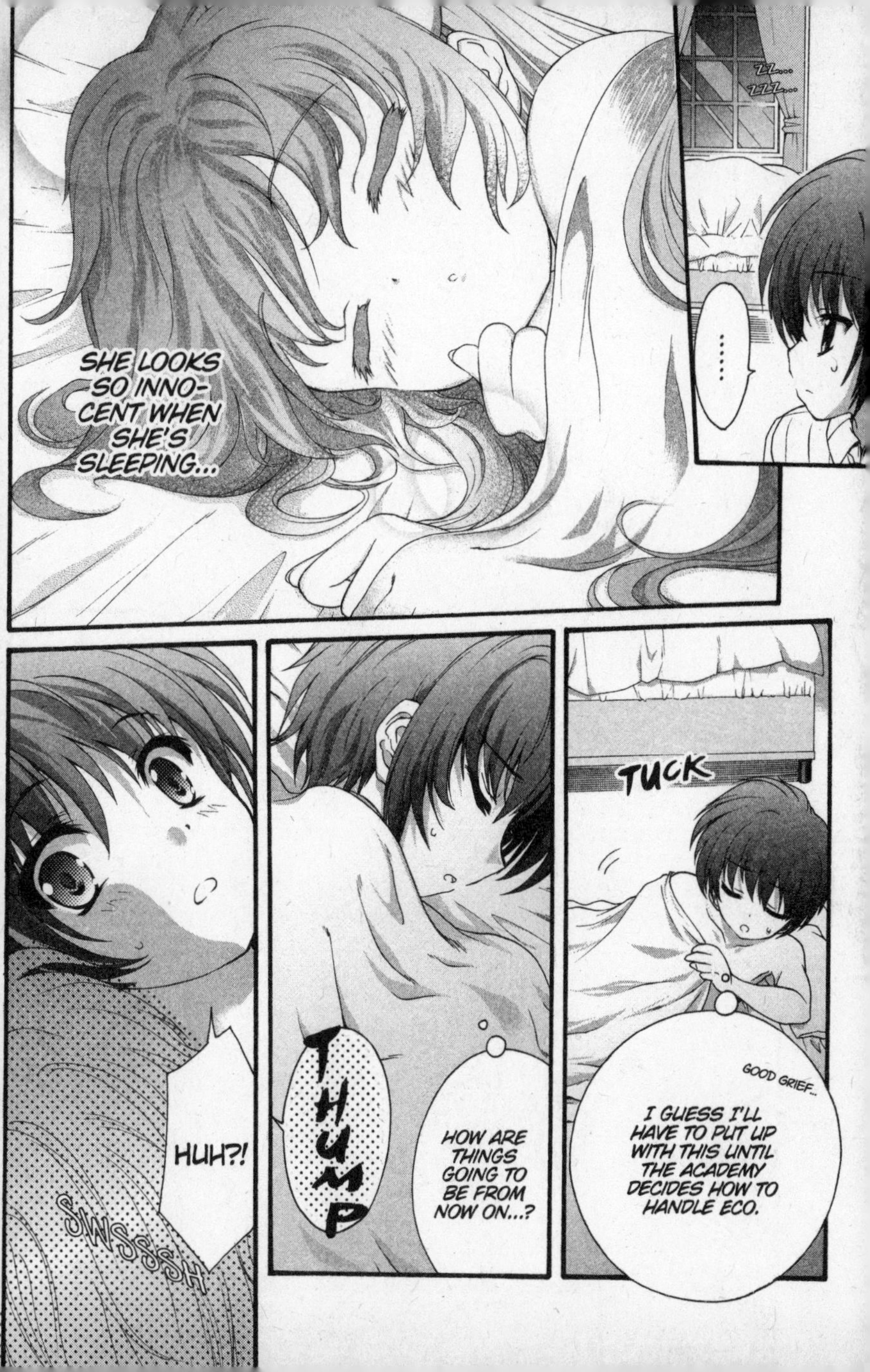
ZZZ...
ZZZ...
......
SHE LOOKS SO INNOCENT WHEN SHE'S SLEEPING...
TUCK
GOOD GRIEF...
I GUESS I'LL HAVE TO PUT UP WITH THIS UNTIL THE ACADEMY DECIDES HOW TO HANDLE ECO.
THUMP
HOW ARE THINGS GOING TO BE FROM NOW ON...?
HUH?!
SWSSSH

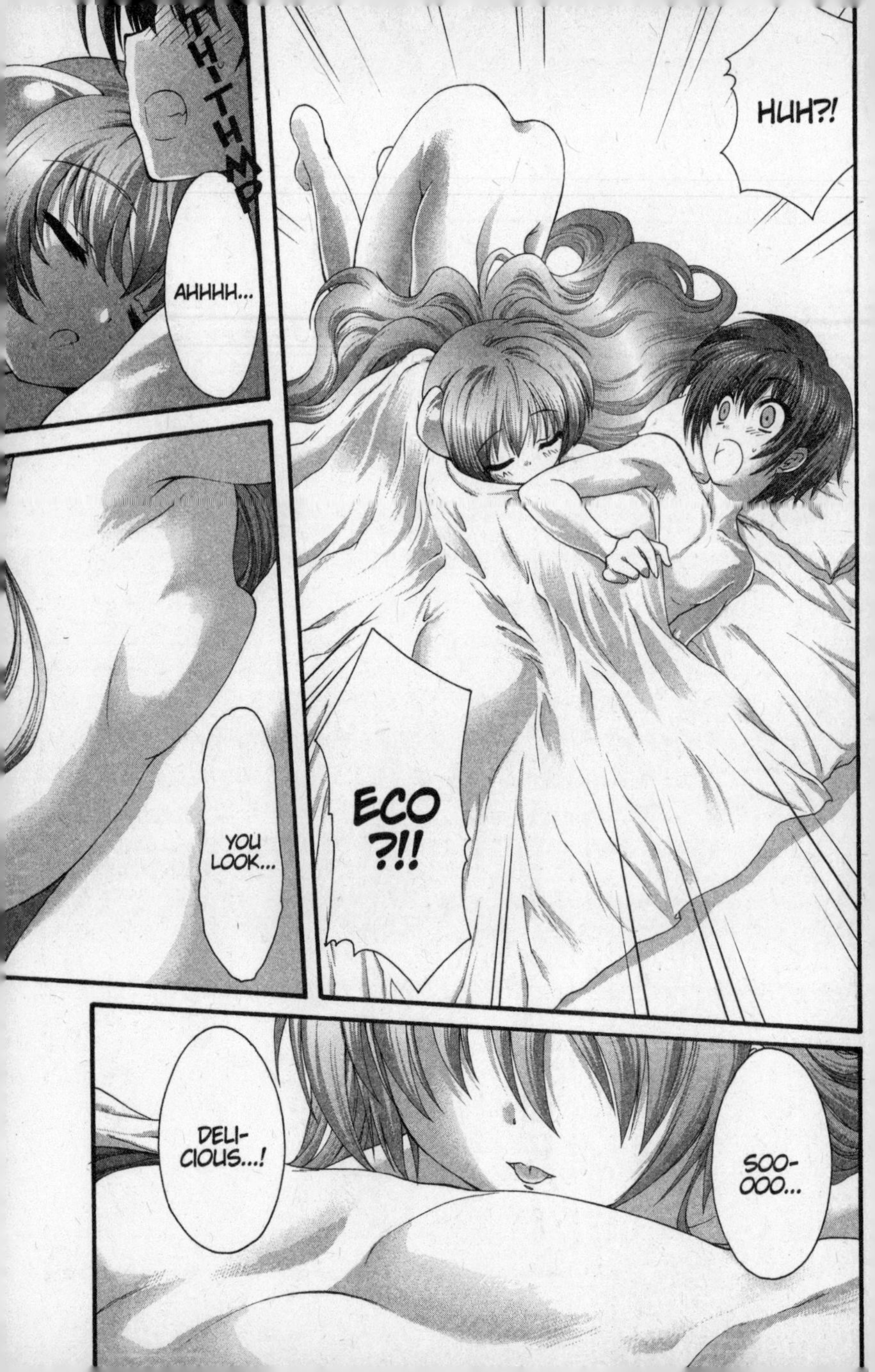
HUH?!
ECO ?!!
THMP
AHHHH...
YOU LOOK...
SOO-OOO...
DELI-CIOUS...!

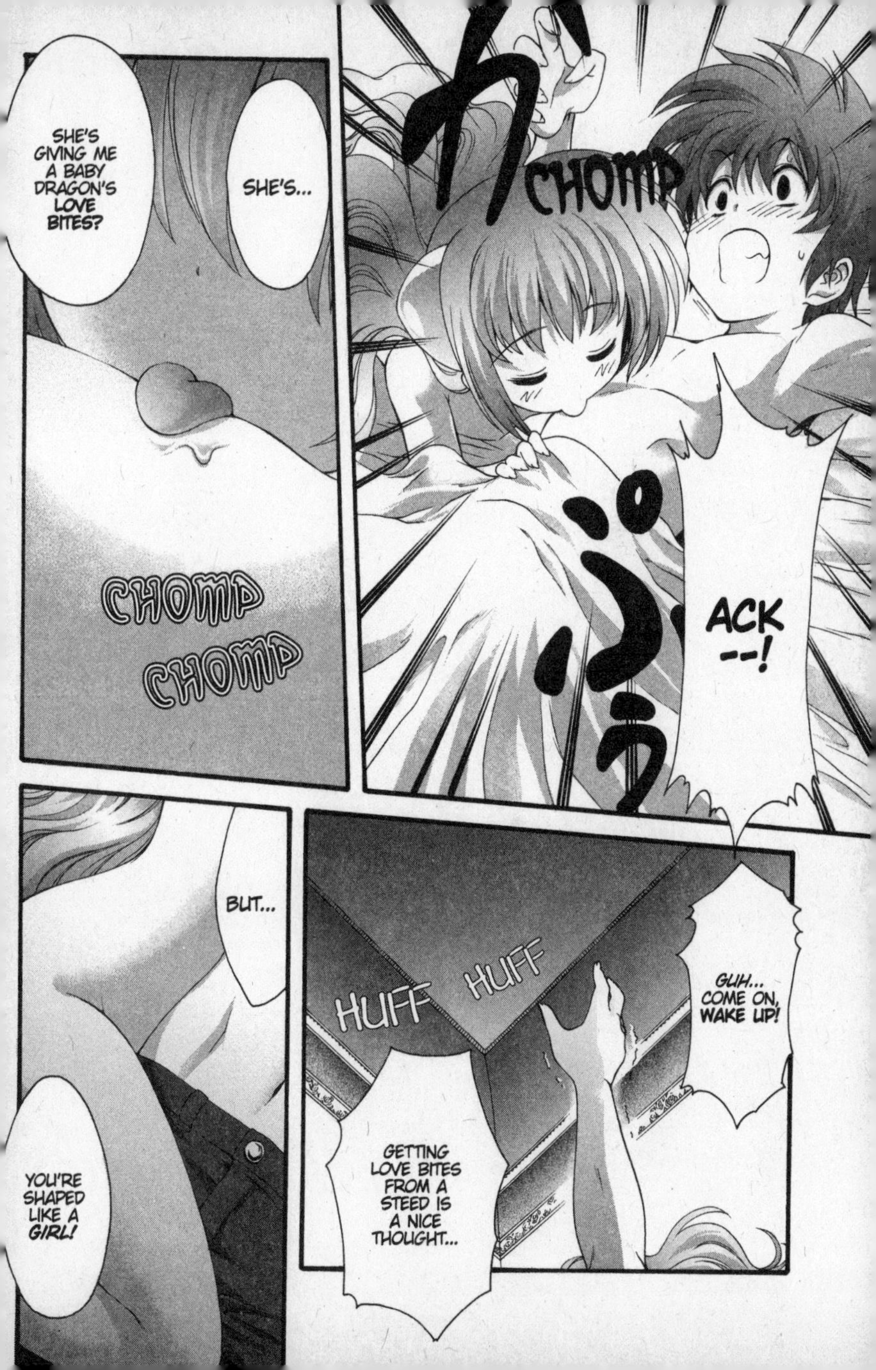
CHOMP
ACK --!
SHE'S...
SHE'S GIVING ME A BABY DRAGON'S LOVE BITES?
CHOMP
CHOMP
GUH... COME ON, WAKE UP!
HUFF HUFF
GETTING LOVE BITES FROM A STEED IS A NICE THOUGHT...
BUT...
YOU'RE SHAPED LIKE A *GIRL!*

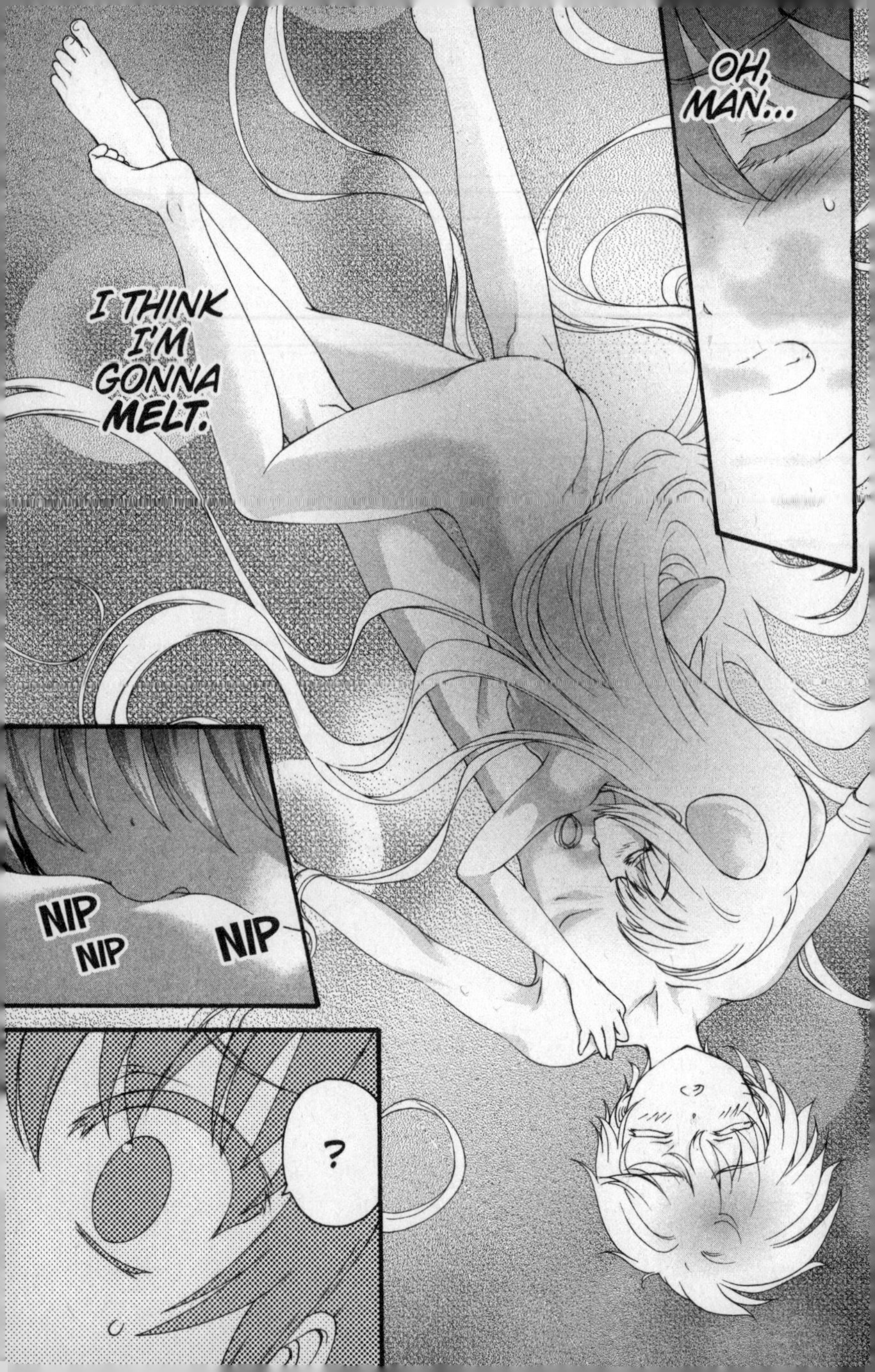
OH, MAN...
I THINK I'M GONNA MELT.
NIP NIP NIP
?

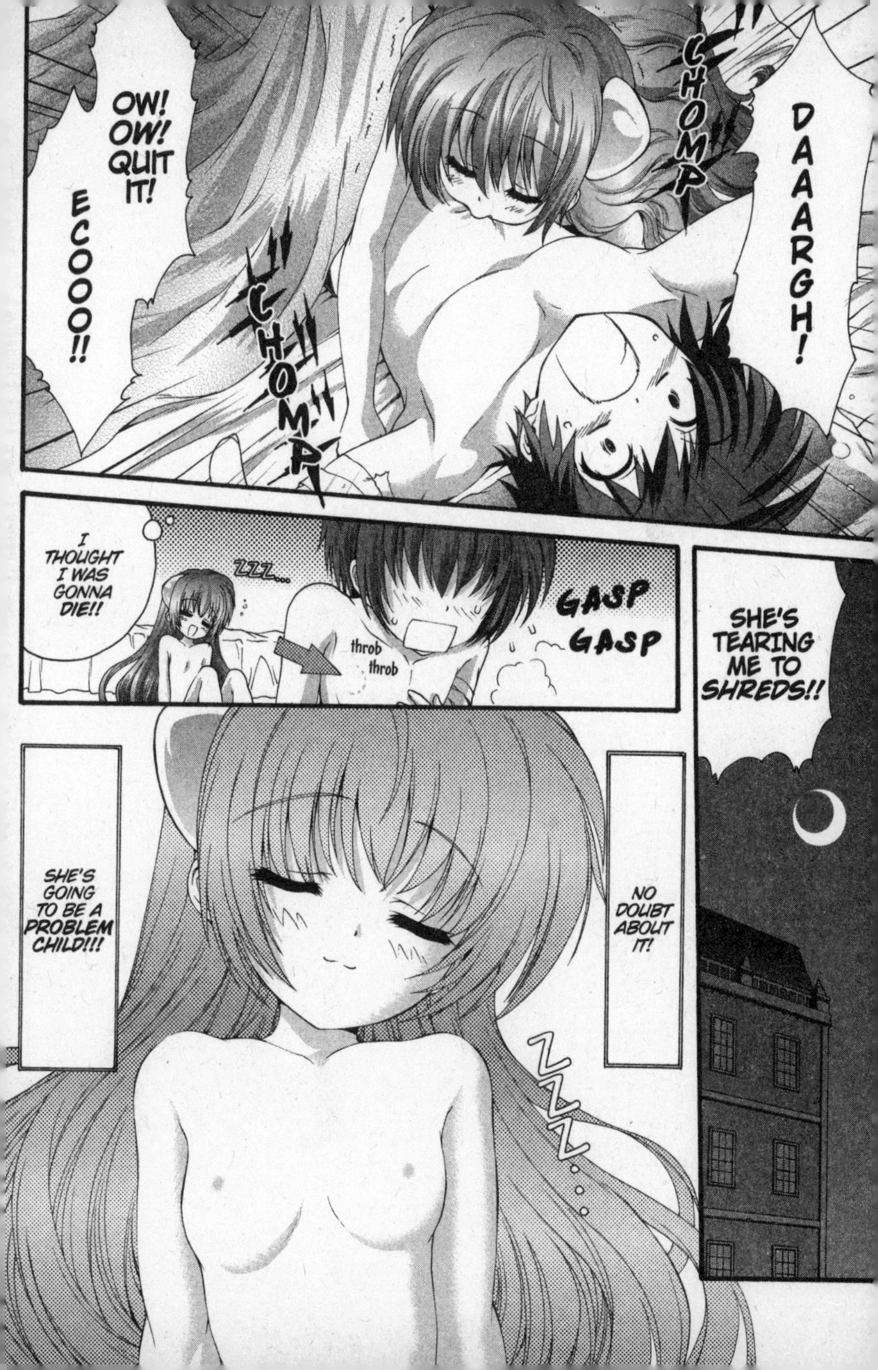
DAAAARGH!
CHOMP
OW! OW! QUIT IT!
CHOMP
ECOOOO!!
SHE'S TEARING ME TO SHREDS!!
GASP GASP
throb throb
ZZZ...
I THOUGHT I WAS GONNA DIE!!
NO DOUBT ABOUT IT!
SHE'S GOING TO BE A PROBLEM CHILD!!!
ZZZ...

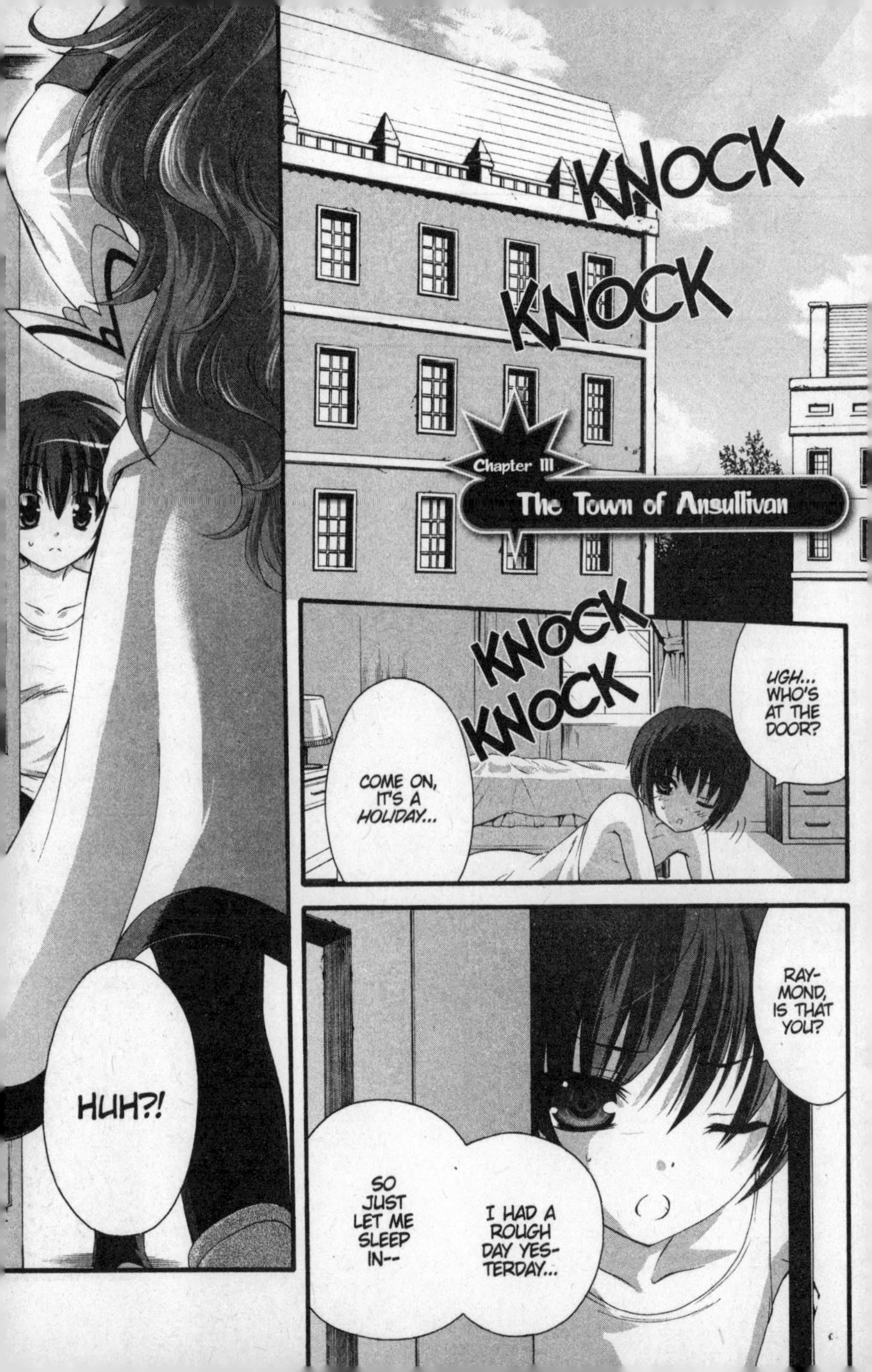
KNOCK KNOCK
Chapter III
The Town of Ansullivan
KNOCK KNOCK
UGH... WHO'S AT THE DOOR?
COME ON, IT'S A HOLIDAY...
RAY-MOND, IS THAT YOU?
I HAD A ROUGH DAY YES-TERDAY...
SO JUST LET ME SLEEP IN--
HUH?!

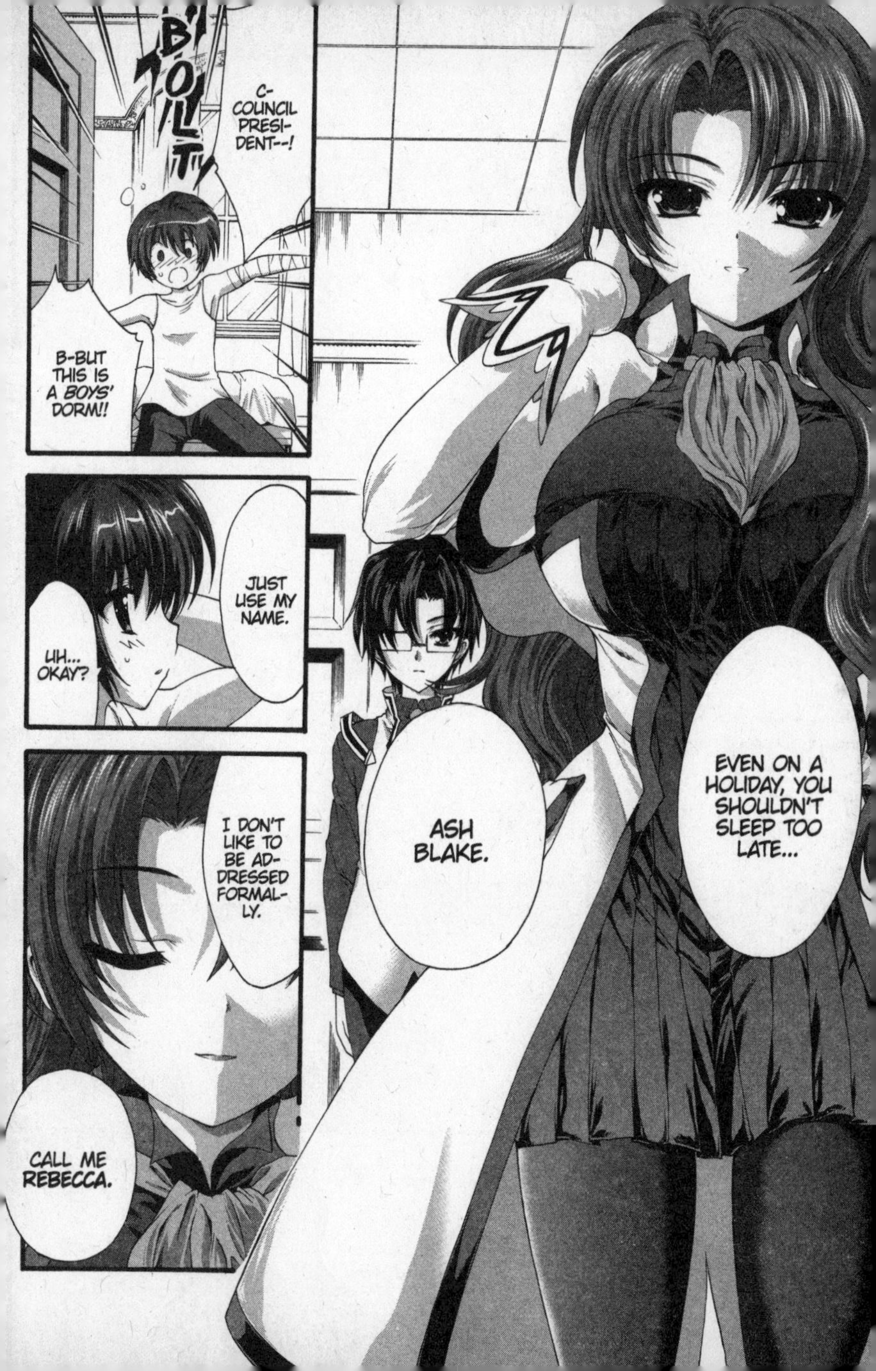
EVEN ON A HOLIDAY, YOU SHOULDN'T SLEEP TOO LATE...
ASH BLAKE.
BOLT
C-COUNCIL PRESI-DENT--!
B-BUT THIS IS A *BOYS'* DORM!!
JUST USE MY NAME.
UH... OKAY?
I DON'T LIKE TO BE AD-DRESSED FORMAL-LY.
CALL ME REBECCA.

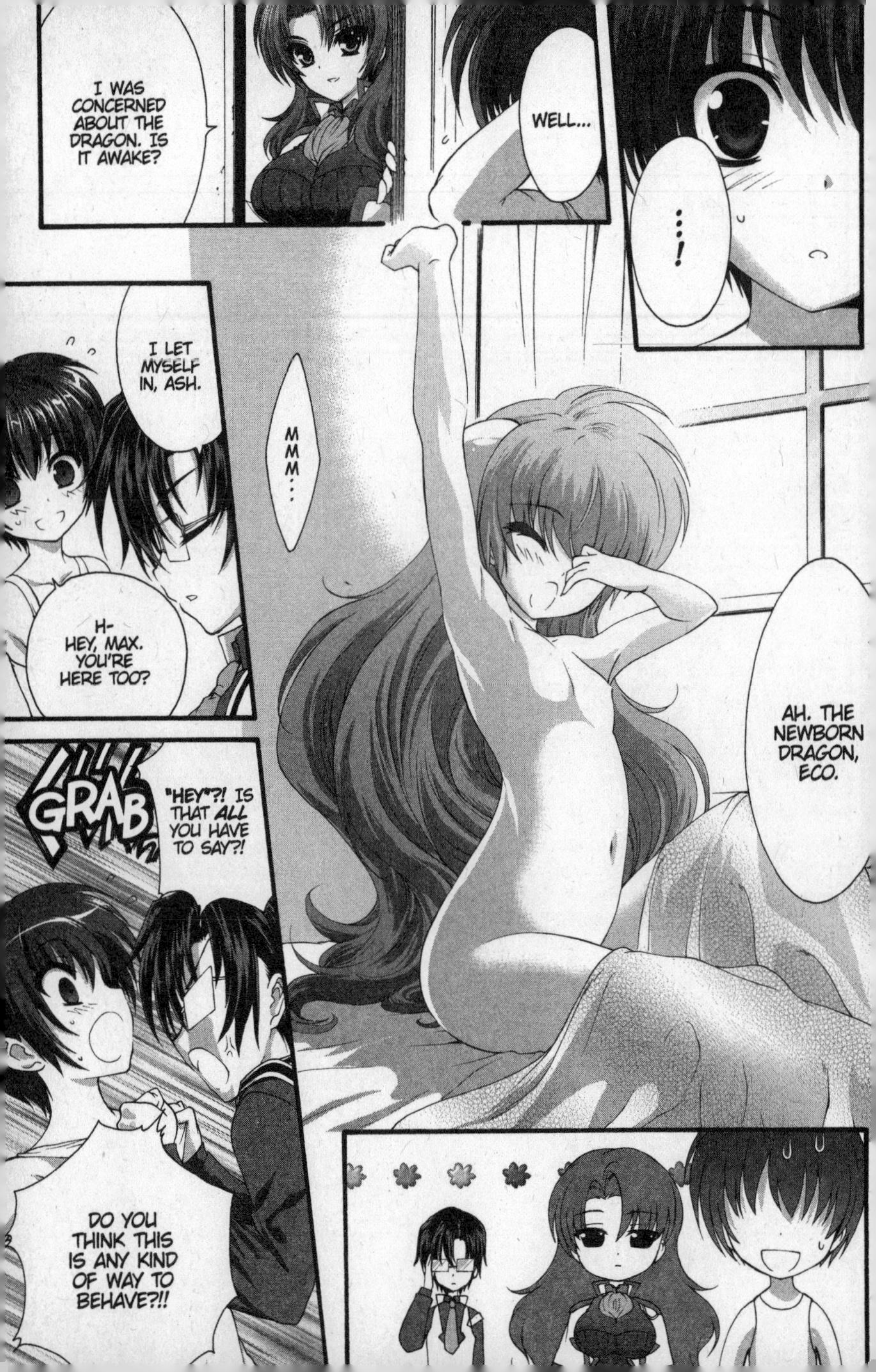
WELL...
...!
I WAS CONCERNED ABOUT THE DRAGON. IS IT AWAKE?
MMM...
AH. THE NEWBORN DRAGON, ECO.
I LET MYSELF IN, ASH.
H- HEY, MAX. YOU'RE HERE TOO?
GRAB
"HEY"?! IS THAT ALL YOU HAVE TO SAY?!
DO YOU THINK THIS IS ANY KIND OF WAY TO BEHAVE?!!

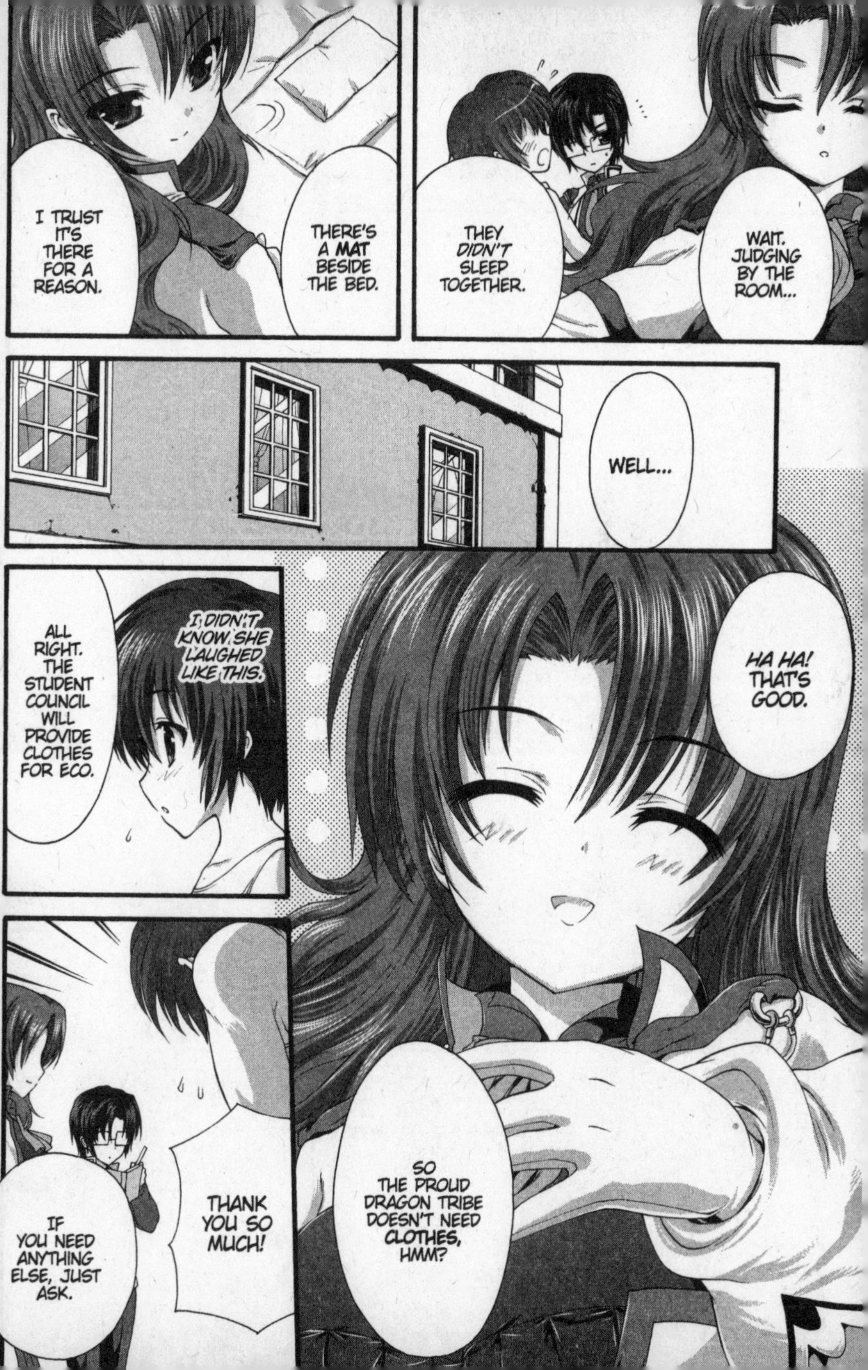
WAIT. JUDGING BY THE ROOM...
THEY *DIDN'T* SLEEP TOGETHER.
THERE'S A **MAT** BESIDE THE BED.
I TRUST IT'S THERE FOR A REASON.
WELL...
HA HA! THAT'S GOOD.
SO THE PROUD DRAGON TRIBE DOESN'T NEED CLOTHES, HMM?
ALL RIGHT. THE STUDENT COUNCIL WILL PROVIDE CLOTHES FOR ECO.
I DIDN'T KNOW SHE LAUGHED LIKE THIS.
THANK YOU SO MUCH!
IF YOU NEED ANYTHING ELSE, JUST ASK.

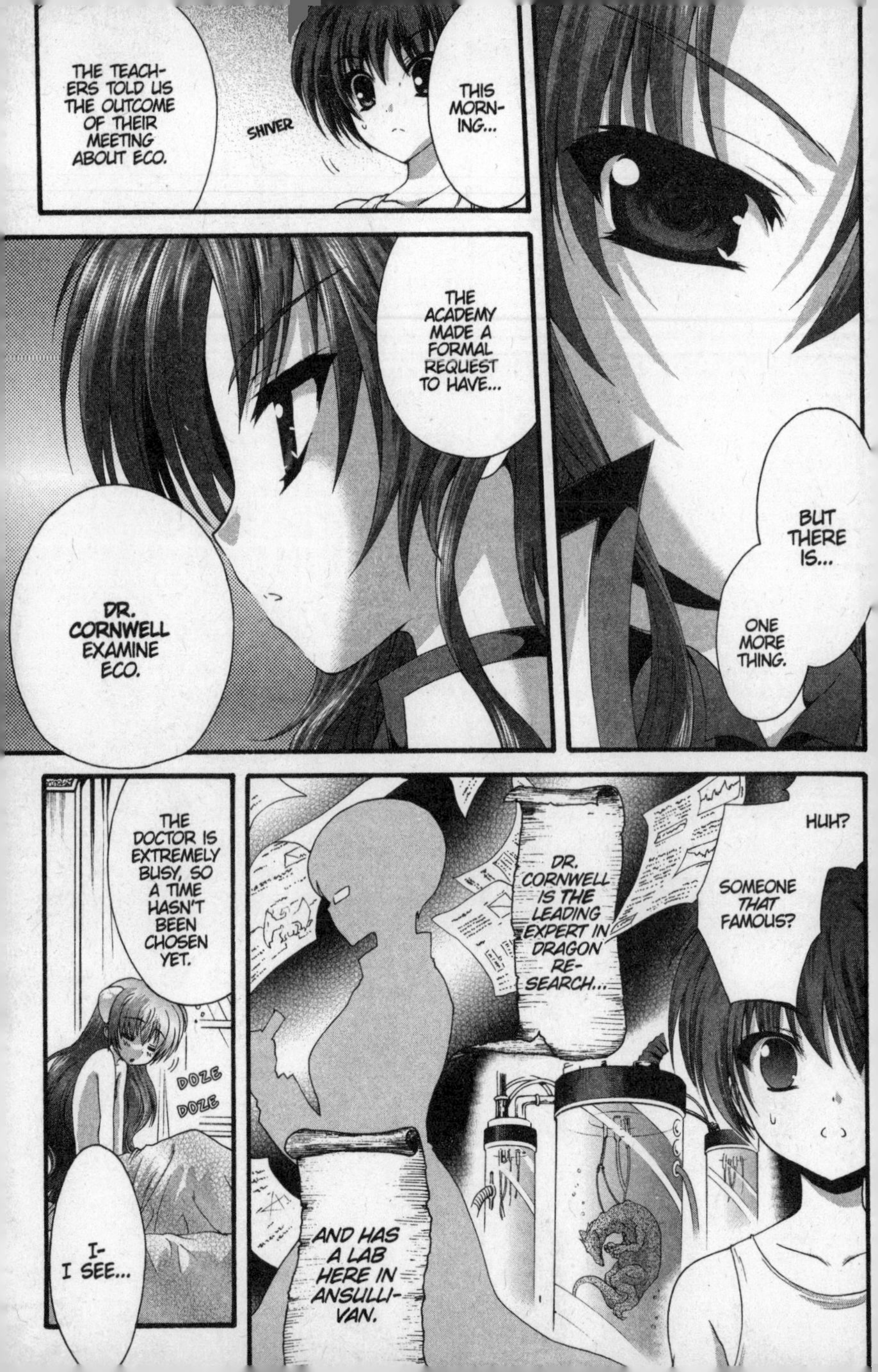
THIS MORNING...
THE TEACHERS TOLD US THE OUTCOME OF THEIR MEETING ABOUT ECO.
SHIVER
THE ACADEMY MADE A FORMAL REQUEST TO HAVE...
DR. CORNWELL EXAMINE ECO.
BUT THERE IS...
ONE MORE THING.
HUH?
SOMEONE THAT FAMOUS?
DR. CORNWELL IS THE LEADING EXPERT IN DRAGON RE-SEARCH...
AND HAS A LAB HERE IN ANSULLI-VAN.
THE DOCTOR IS EXTREMELY BUSY, SO A TIME HASN'T BEEN CHOSEN YET.
DOZE DOZE
I- I SEE...

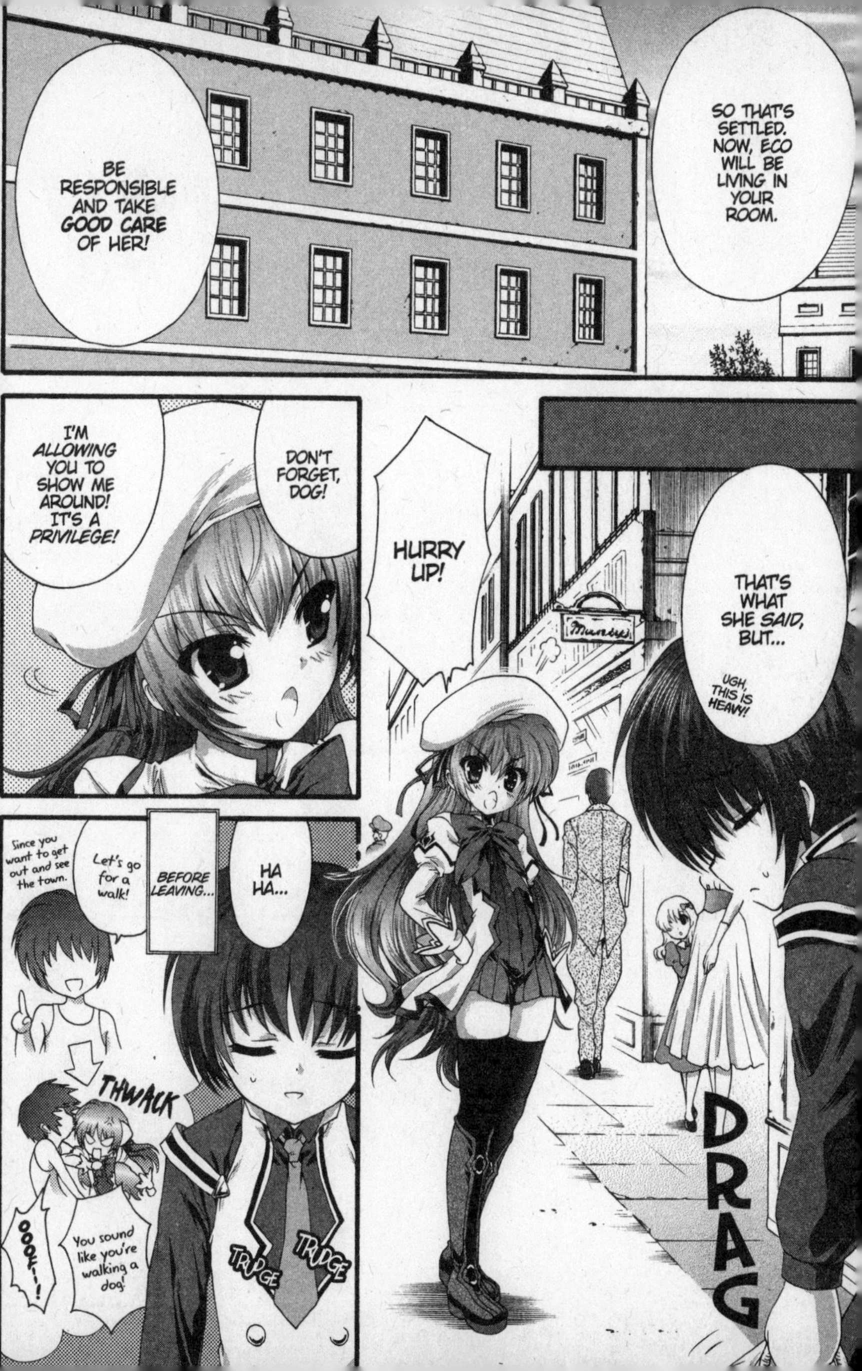
SO THAT'S SETTLED. NOW, ECO WILL BE LIVING IN YOUR ROOM.
BE RESPONSIBLE AND TAKE GOOD CARE OF HER!
HURRY UP!
THAT'S WHAT SHE SAID, BUT...
UGH, THIS IS HEAVY!
DRAG
DON'T FORGET, DOG!
I'M ALLOWING YOU TO SHOW ME AROUND! IT'S A PRIVILEGE!
HA HA...
BEFORE LEAVING...
Let's go for a walk!
Since you want to get out and see the town.
THWACK
TRUDGE
TRUDGE
You sound like you're walking a dog!
OOOF!!

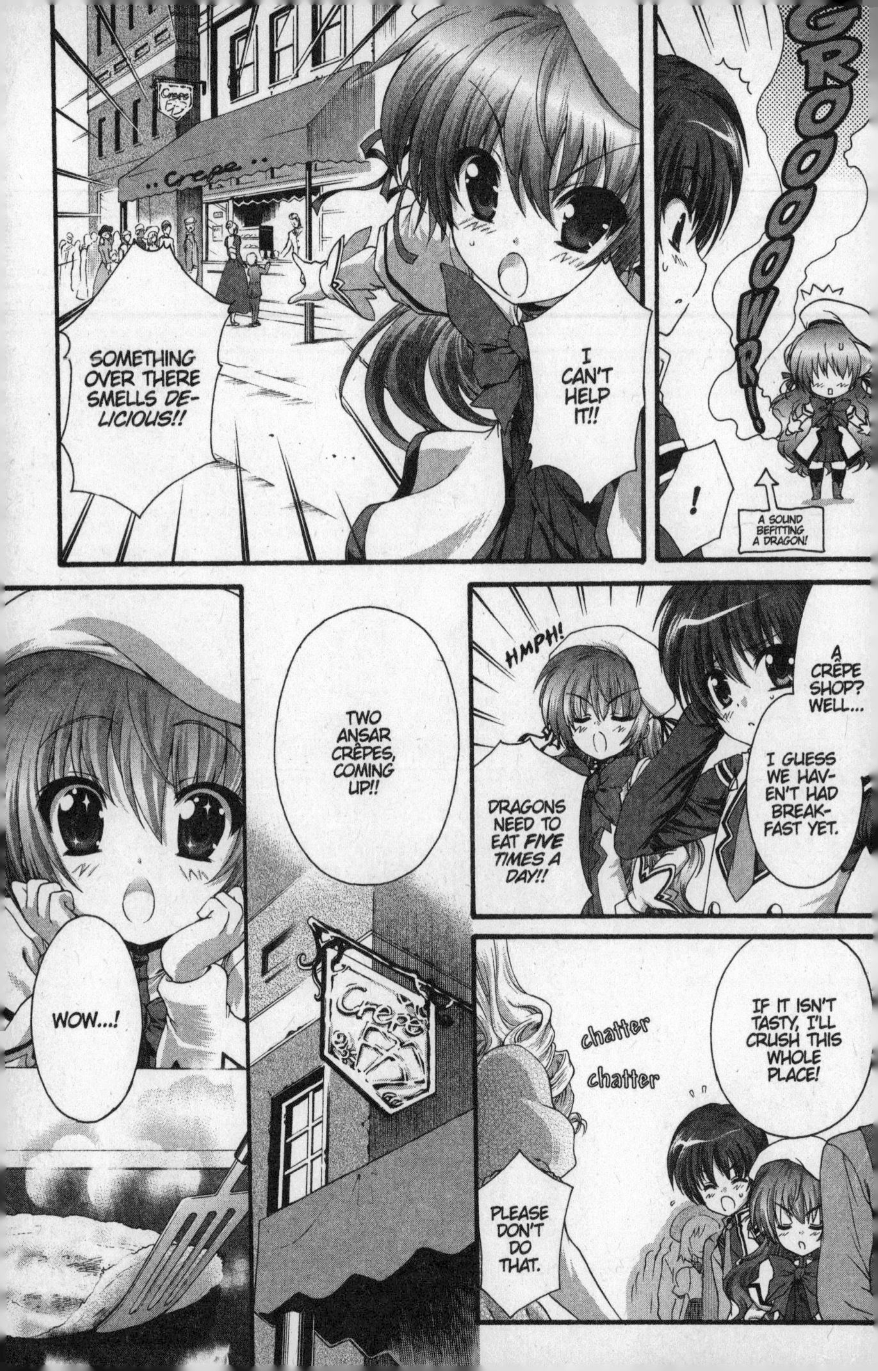
GROOOOWR
A SOUND BEFITTING A DRAGON!
!
I CAN'T HELP IT!!
SOMETHING OVER THERE SMELLS DE-LICIOUS!!
A CRÊPE SHOP? WELL...
I GUESS WE HAV-EN'T HAD BREAK-FAST YET.
HMPH!
DRAGONS NEED TO EAT *FIVE TIMES* A DAY!!
IF IT ISN'T TASTY, I'LL CRUSH THIS WHOLE PLACE!
chatter
chatter
PLEASE DON'T DO THAT.
TWO ANSAR CRÊPES, COMING UP!!
WOW...!

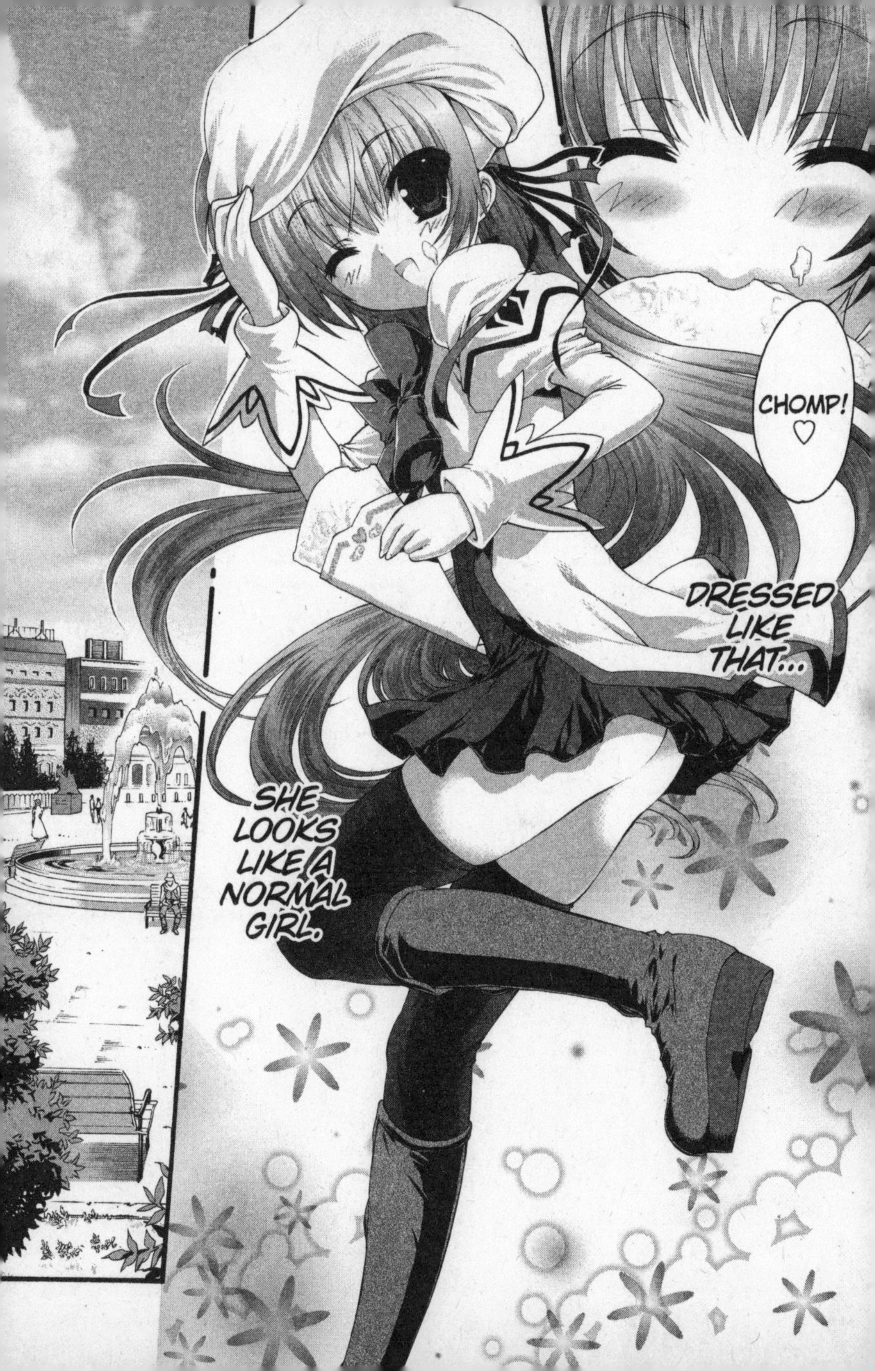
CHOMP! ♡
DRESSED LIKE THAT...
SHE LOOKS LIKE A NORMAL GIRL.

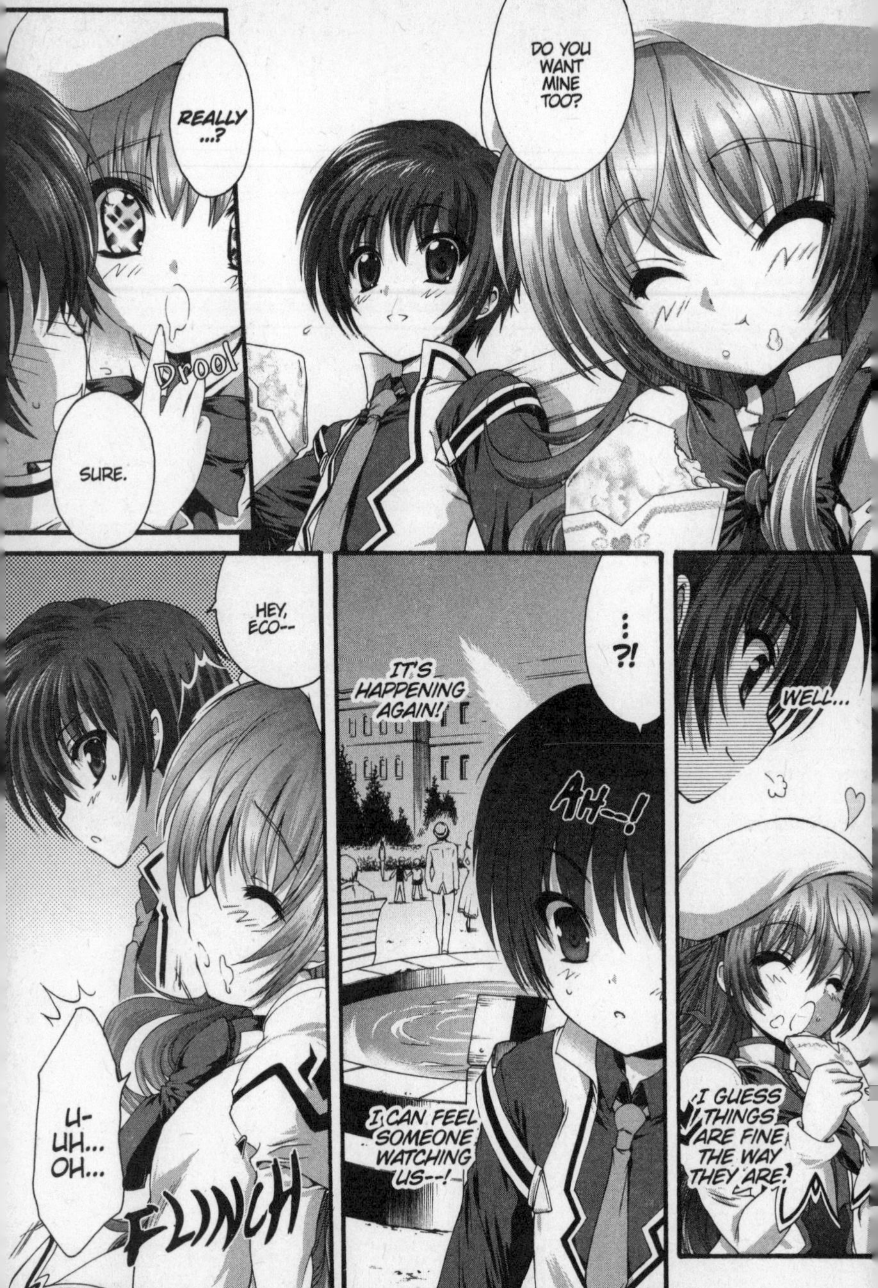
DO YOU WANT MINE TOO?
REALLY ...?
Drool
SURE.
WELL...
I GUESS THINGS ARE FINE THE WAY THEY ARE.
...?!
IT'S HAPPENING AGAIN!
AH--!
I CAN FEEL SOMEONE WATCHING US--!
HEY, ECO--
U-UH... OH...
FLINCH

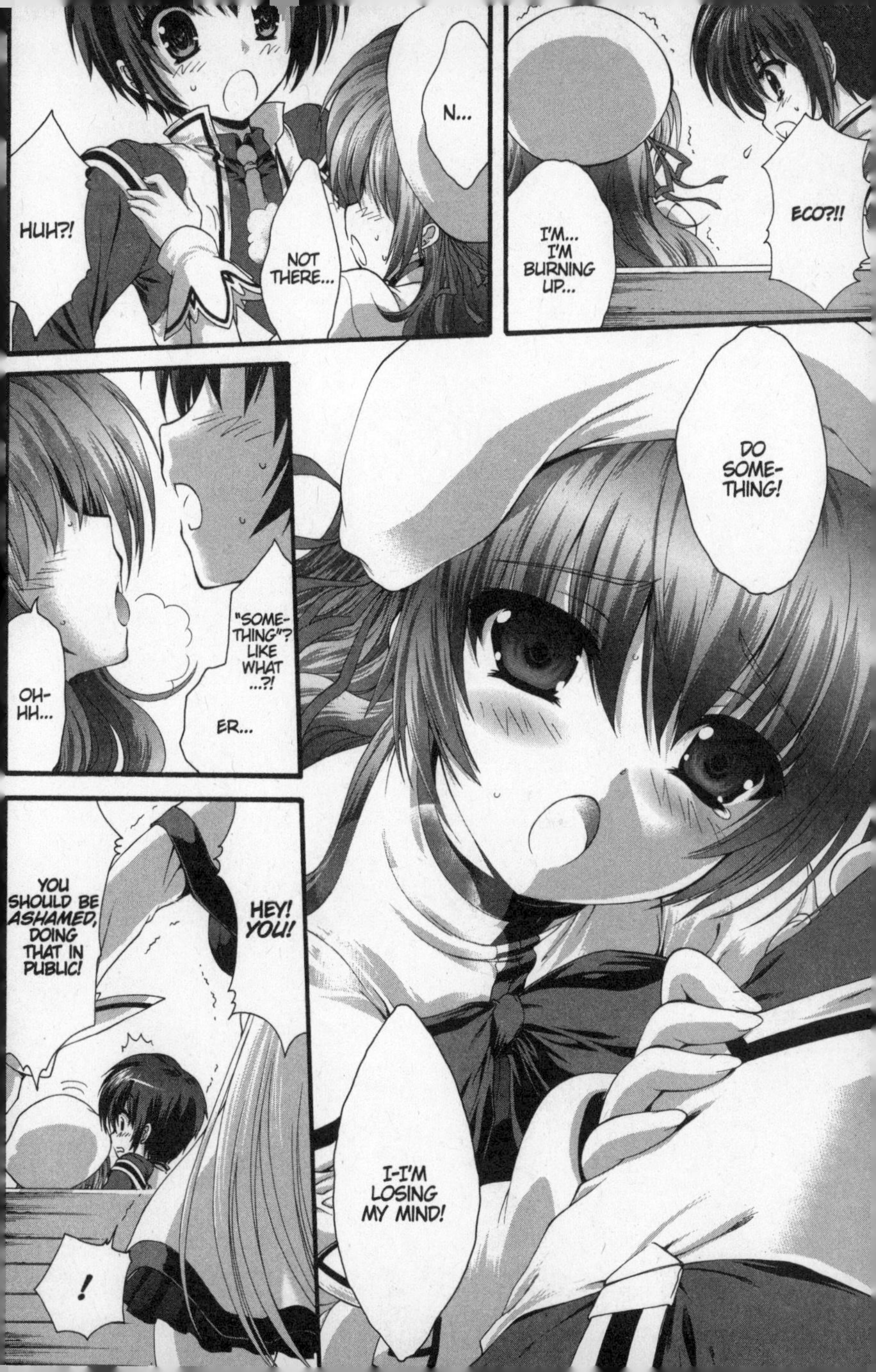
ECO?!!
I'M... I'M BURNING UP...
N...
NOT THERE...
HUH?!
DO SOME-THING!
I-I'M LOSING MY MIND!
"SOME-THING"? LIKE WHAT ...?!
ER...
OH-HH...
HEY! *YOU!*
YOU SHOULD BE *ASHAMED*, DOING THAT IN PUBLIC!
!

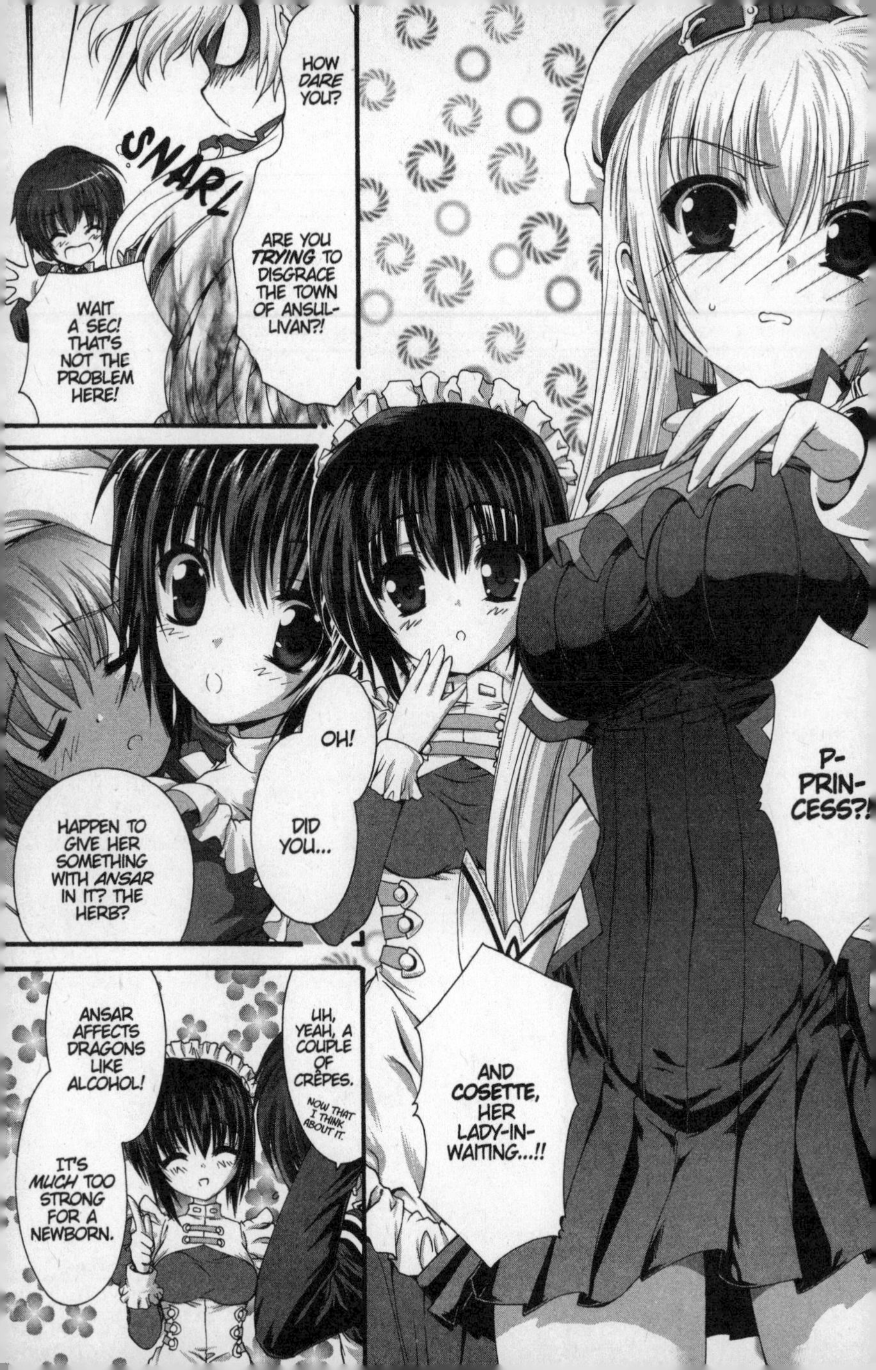
P-PRINCESS?!
AND COSETTE, HER LADY-IN-WAITING...!!
HOW *DARE* YOU?
ARE YOU *TRYING* TO DISGRACE THE TOWN OF ANSULLIVAN?!
SNARL
WAIT A SEC! THAT'S NOT THE PROBLEM HERE!
OH!
DID YOU...
HAPPEN TO GIVE HER SOMETHING WITH *ANSAR* IN IT? THE HERB?
UH, YEAH, A COUPLE OF CRÊPES.
NOW THAT I THINK ABOUT IT.
ANSAR AFFECTS DRAGONS LIKE ALCOHOL!
IT'S *MUCH* TOO STRONG FOR A NEWBORN.

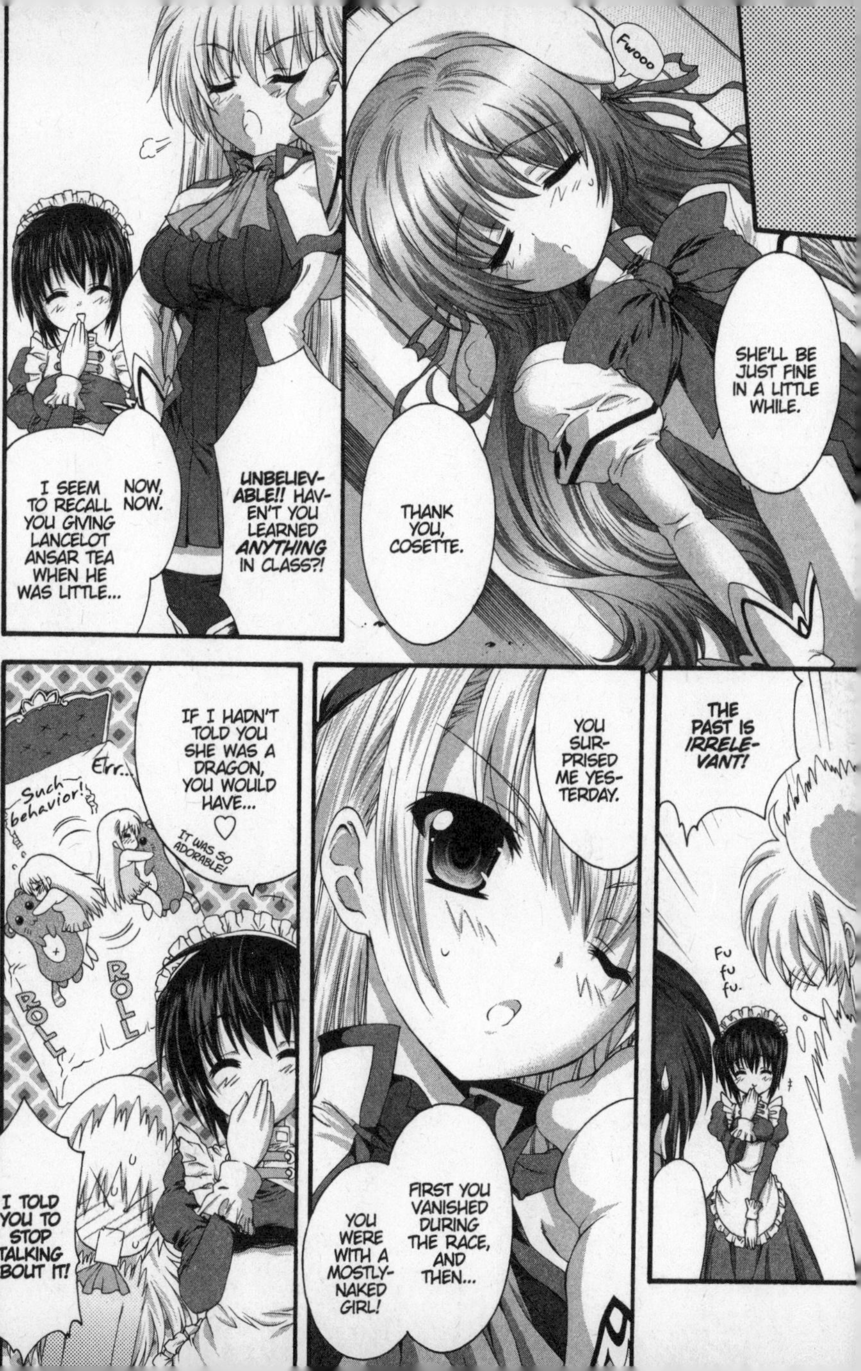
Fwooo
SHE'LL BE JUST FINE IN A LITTLE WHILE.
THANK YOU, COSETTE.
UNBELIEVABLE!! HAVEN'T YOU LEARNED ANYTHING IN CLASS?!
NOW, NOW.
I SEEM TO RECALL YOU GIVING LANCELOT ANSAR TEA WHEN HE WAS LITTLE...
THE PAST IS IRRELEVANT!
Fu fu fu.
YOU SURPRISED ME YESTERDAY.
FIRST YOU VANISHED DURING THE RACE, AND THEN...
YOU WERE WITH A MOSTLY-NAKED GIRL!
IF I HADN'T TOLD YOU SHE WAS A DRAGON, YOU WOULD HAVE... ♡
Err...
IT WAS SO ADORABLE!
Such behavior!
ROLL
ROLL
I TOLD YOU TO STOP TALKING ABOUT IT!

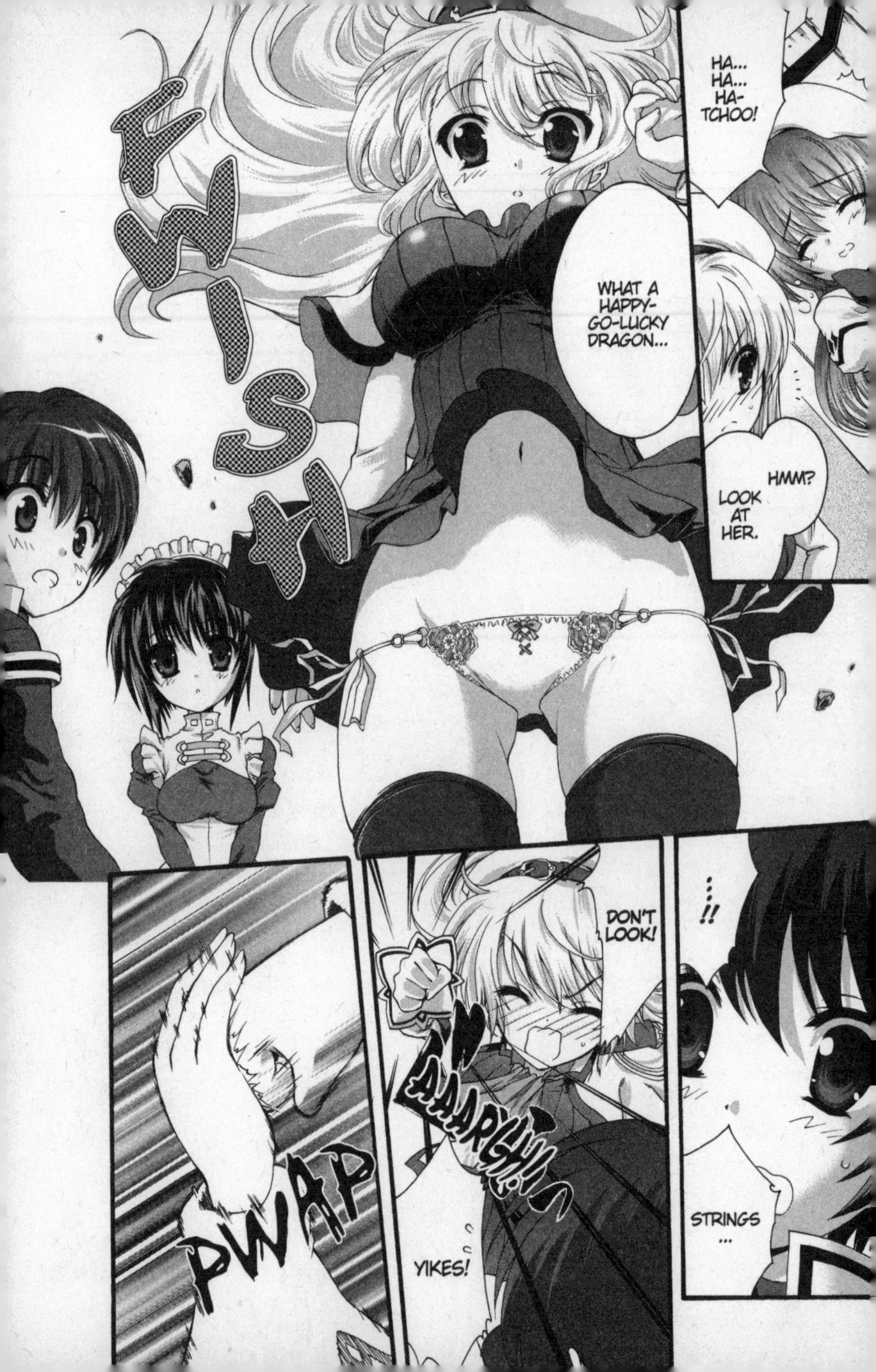
HA... HA... HA-TCHOO!
WHAT A HAPPY-GO-LUCKY DRAGON...
HMM?
LOOK AT HER.
FWISH
...!!
STRINGS ...
DON'T LOOK!
AAARGH!!
YIKES!
PWAP

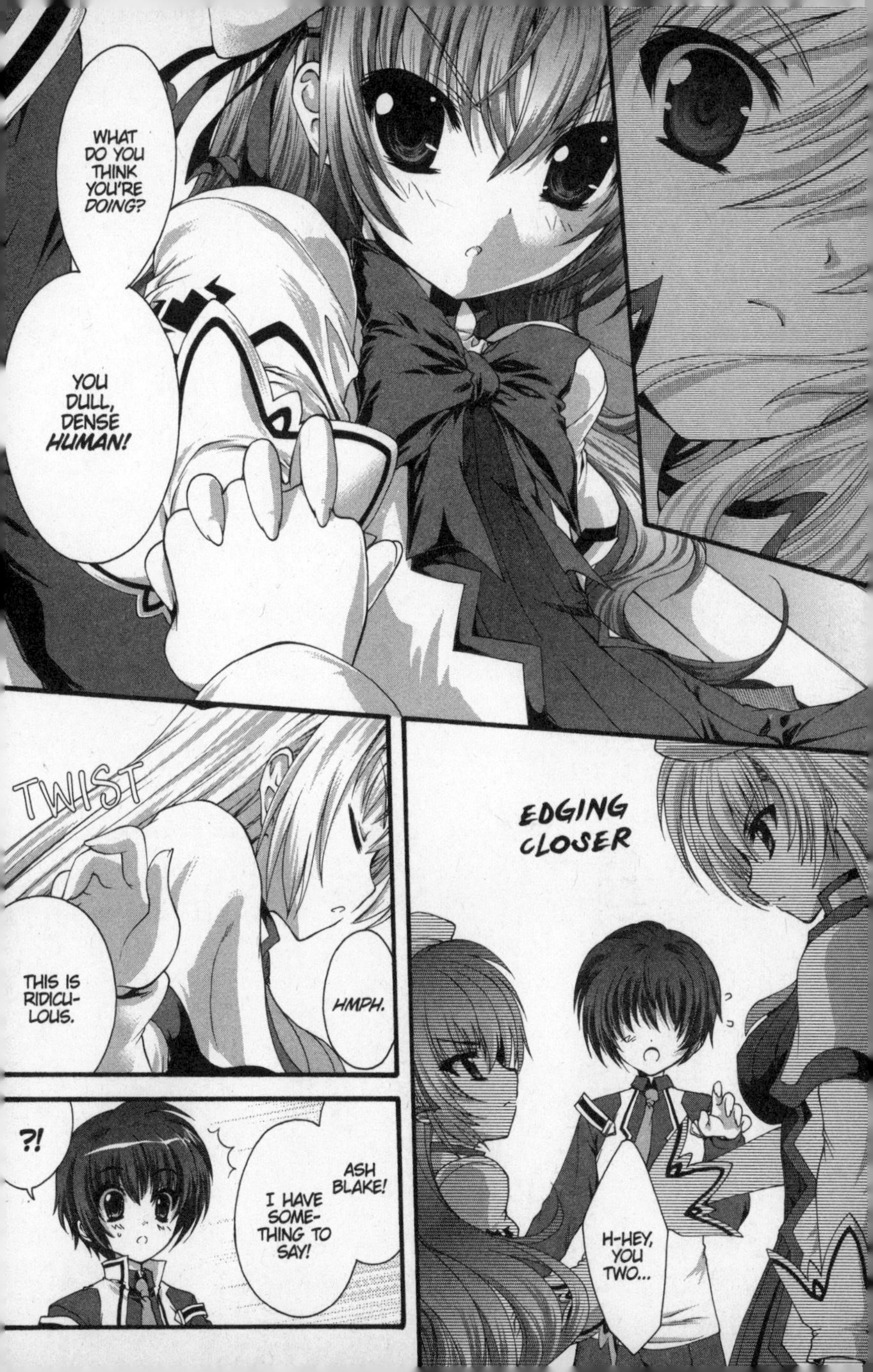
WHAT DO YOU THINK YOU'RE DOING?
YOU DULL, DENSE HUMAN!
EDGING CLOSER
H-HEY, YOU TWO...
TWIST
HMPH.
THIS IS RIDICU-LOUS.
ASH BLAKE! I HAVE SOME-THING TO SAY!
?!

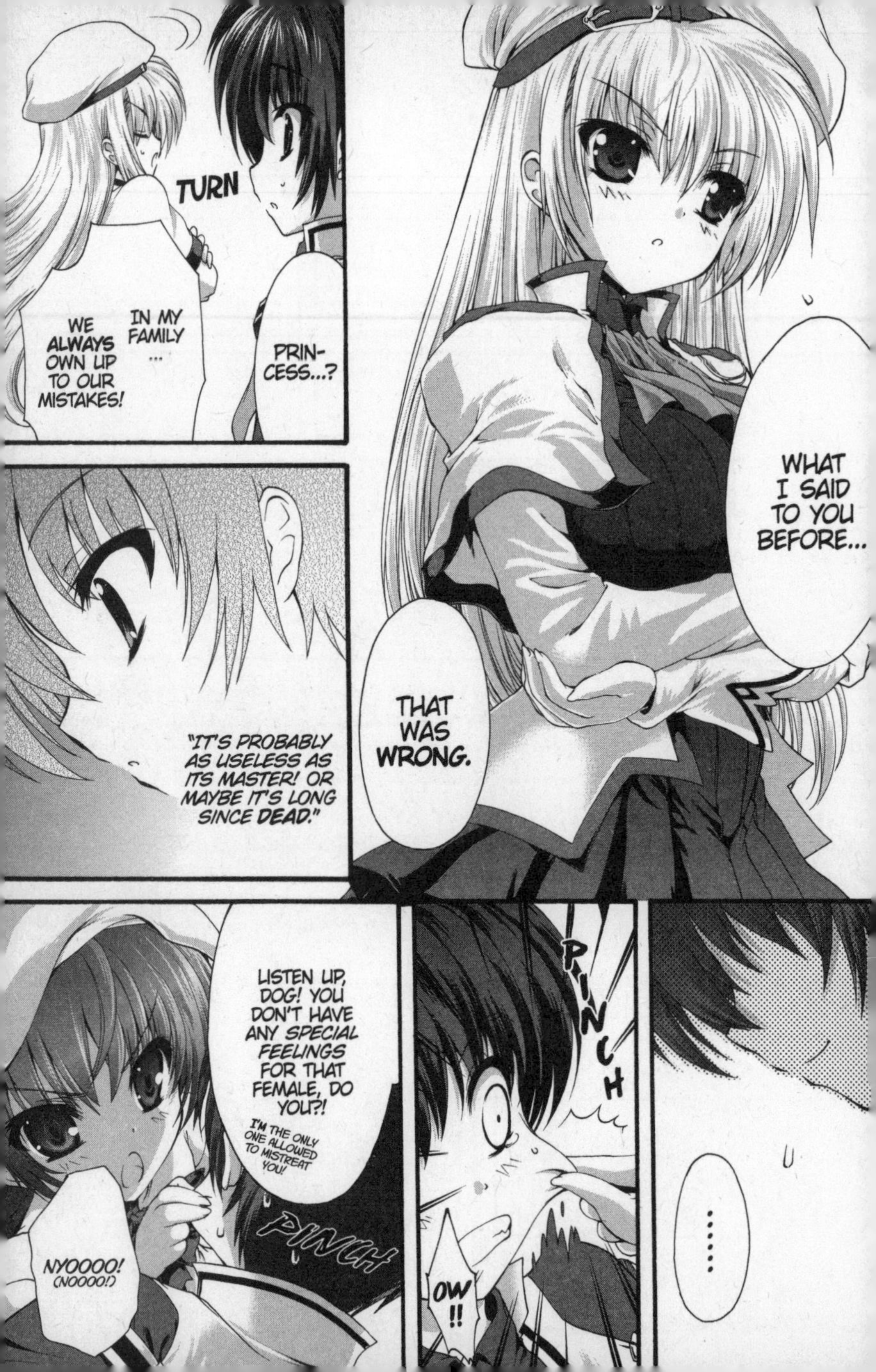
WHAT I SAID TO YOU BEFORE...
THAT WAS WRONG.
TURN
PRIN-CESS...?
IN MY FAMILY ...
WE ALWAYS OWN UP TO OUR MISTAKES!
"IT'S PROBABLY AS USELESS AS ITS MASTER! OR MAYBE IT'S LONG SINCE DEAD."
......
PINCH
OW!!
LISTEN UP, DOG! YOU DON'T HAVE ANY SPECIAL FEELINGS FOR THAT FEMALE, DO YOU?!
I'M THE ONLY ONE ALLOWED TO MISTREAT YOU!
PINCH
NYOOOO! (NOOOO!)

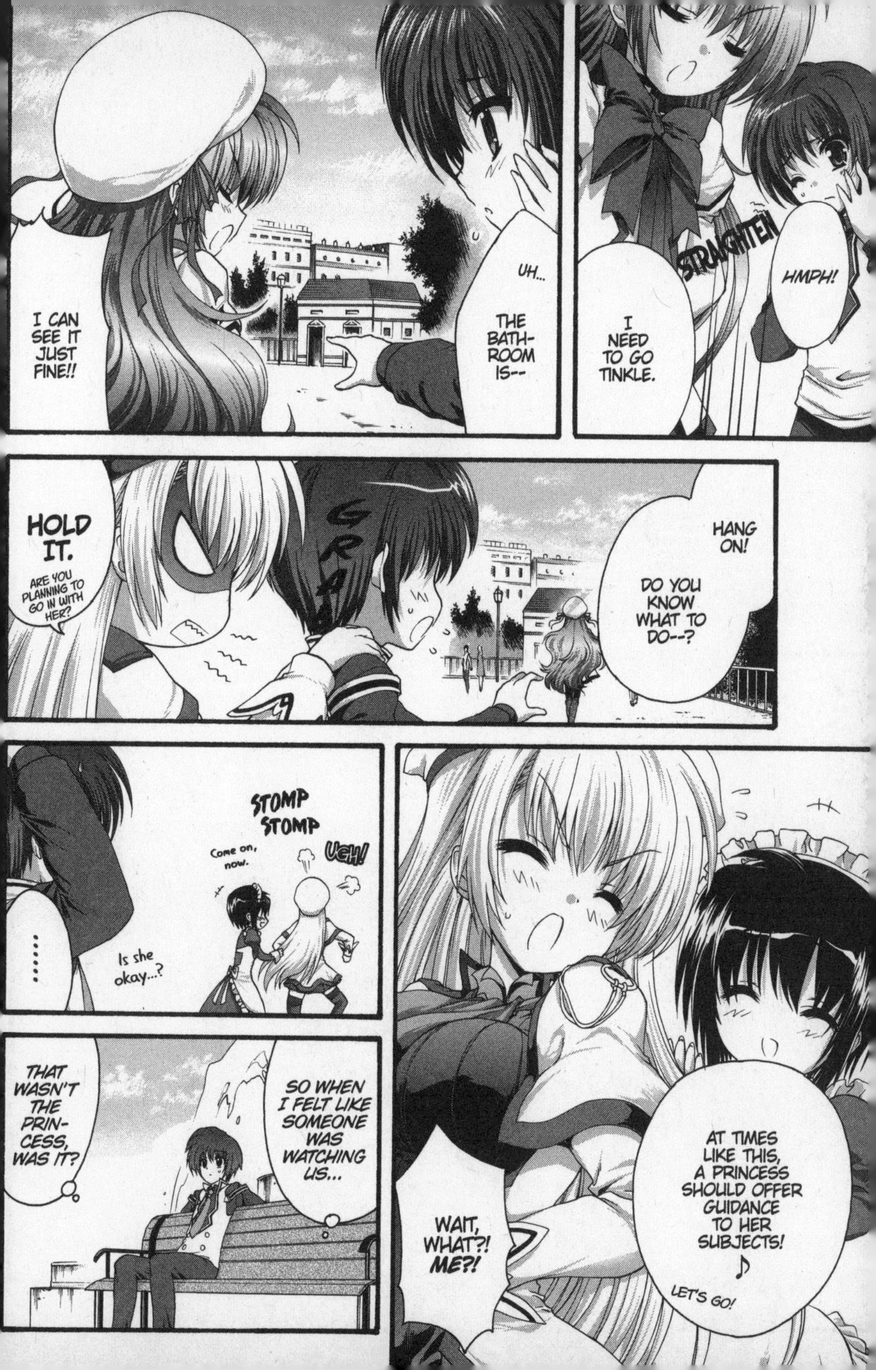
HMPH!
STRAIGHTEN
I NEED TO GO TINKLE.
UH...
THE BATH-ROOM IS--
I CAN SEE IT JUST FINE!!
HANG ON!
DO YOU KNOW WHAT TO DO--?
GRAB
HOLD IT.
ARE YOU PLANNING TO GO IN WITH HER?
AT TIMES LIKE THIS, A PRINCESS SHOULD OFFER GUIDANCE TO HER SUBJECTS! ♪
LET'S GO!
WAIT, WHAT?! ME?!
STOMP STOMP
UGH!
Come on, now.
Is she okay...?
......
SO WHEN I FELT LIKE SOMEONE WAS WATCHING US...
THAT WASN'T THE PRIN-CESS, WAS IT?

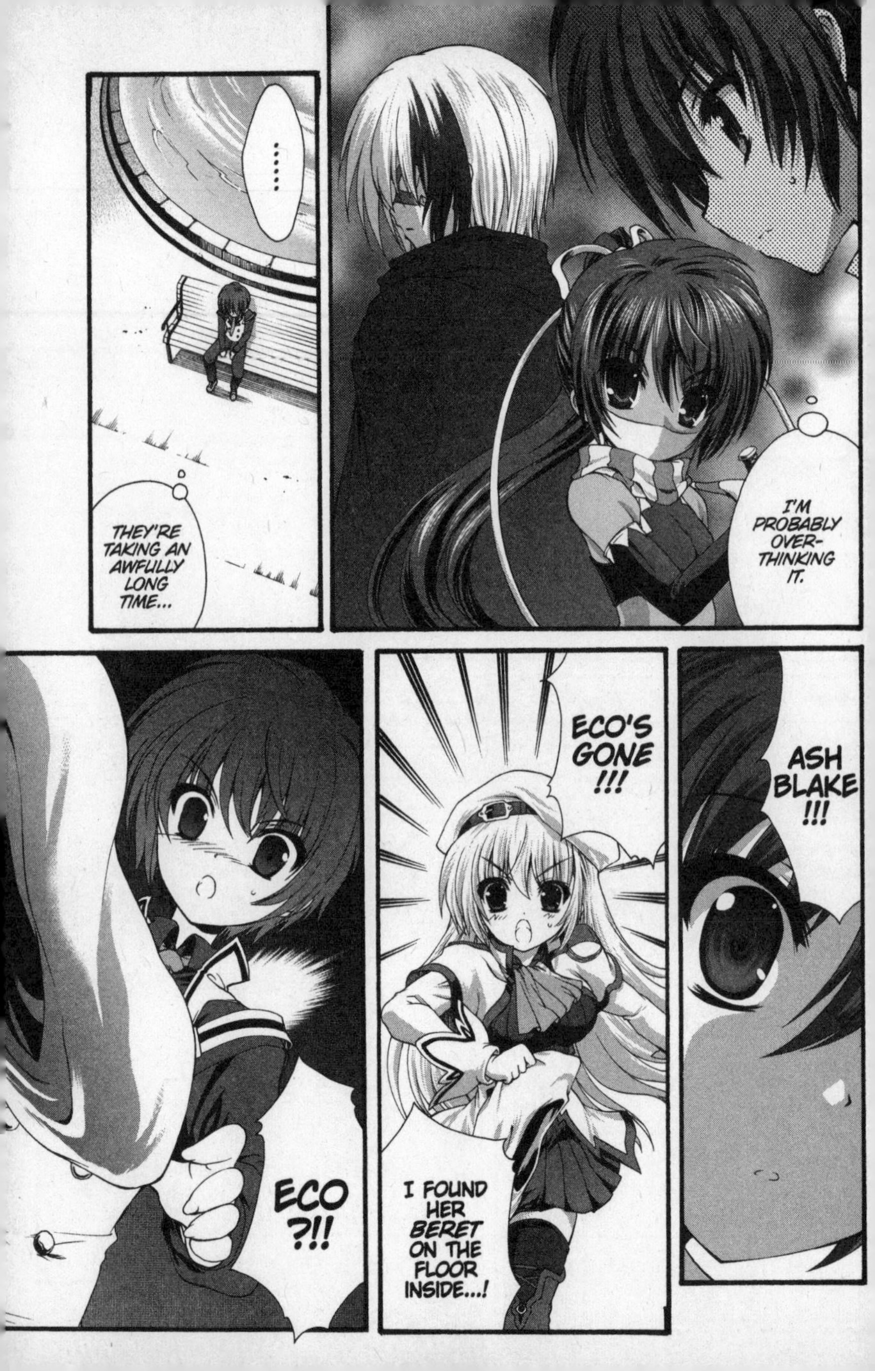

I'M PROBABLY OVER-THINKING IT.
......
THEY'RE TAKING AN AWFULLY LONG TIME...
ASH BLAKE!!!
ECO'S GONE!!!
I FOUND HER BERET ON THE FLOOR INSIDE...!
ECO?!!

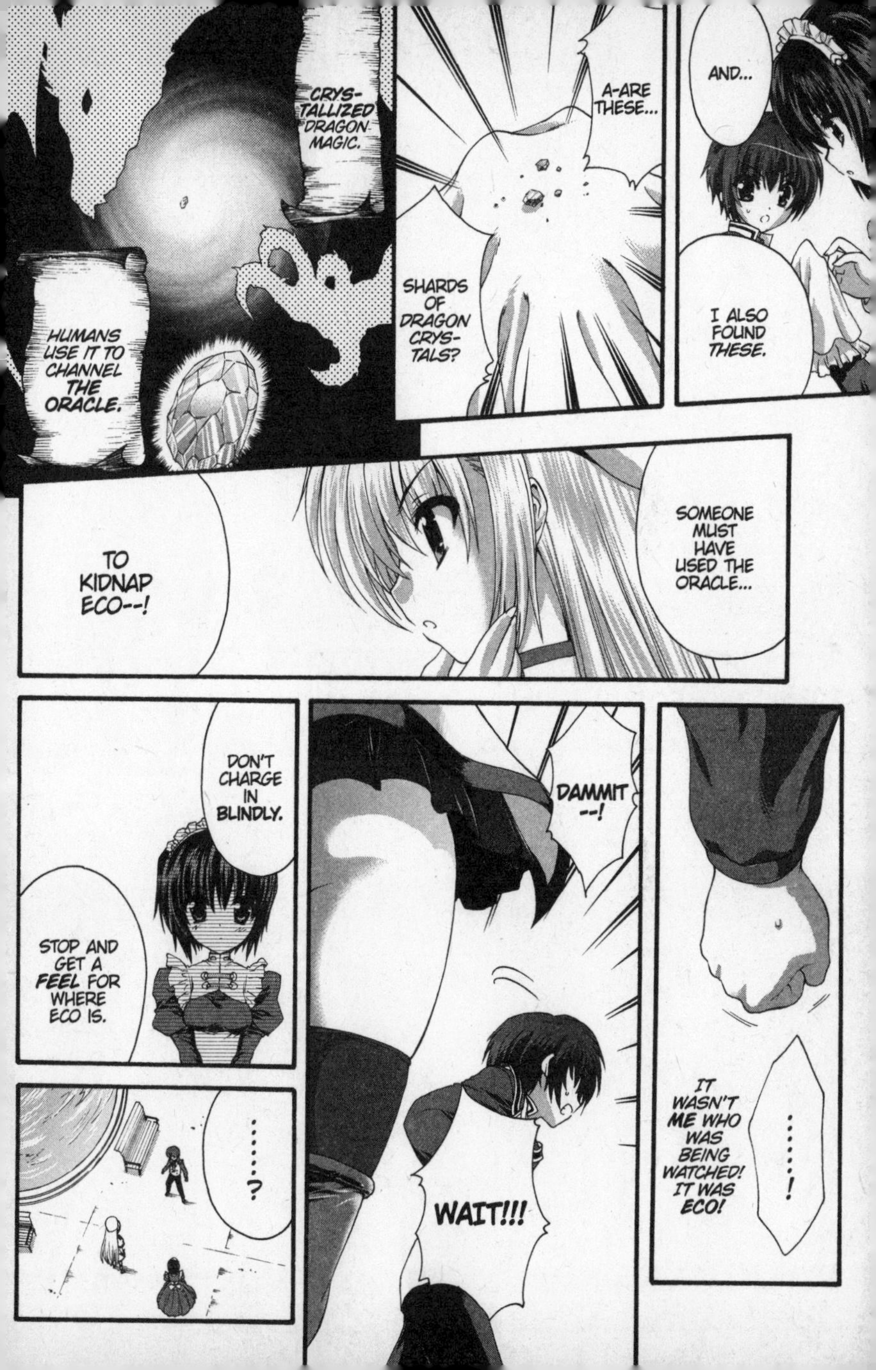
AND...
I ALSO FOUND THESE.
A-ARE THESE...
SHARDS OF DRAGON CRYSTALS?
CRYSTALLIZED DRAGON MAGIC.
HUMANS USE IT TO CHANNEL THE ORACLE.
SOMEONE MUST HAVE USED THE ORACLE...
TO KIDNAP ECO--!
......!
IT WASN'T ME WHO WAS BEING WATCHED! IT WAS ECO!
DAMMIT--!
WAIT!!!
DON'T CHARGE IN BLINDLY.
STOP AND GET A FEEL FOR WHERE ECO IS.
......?

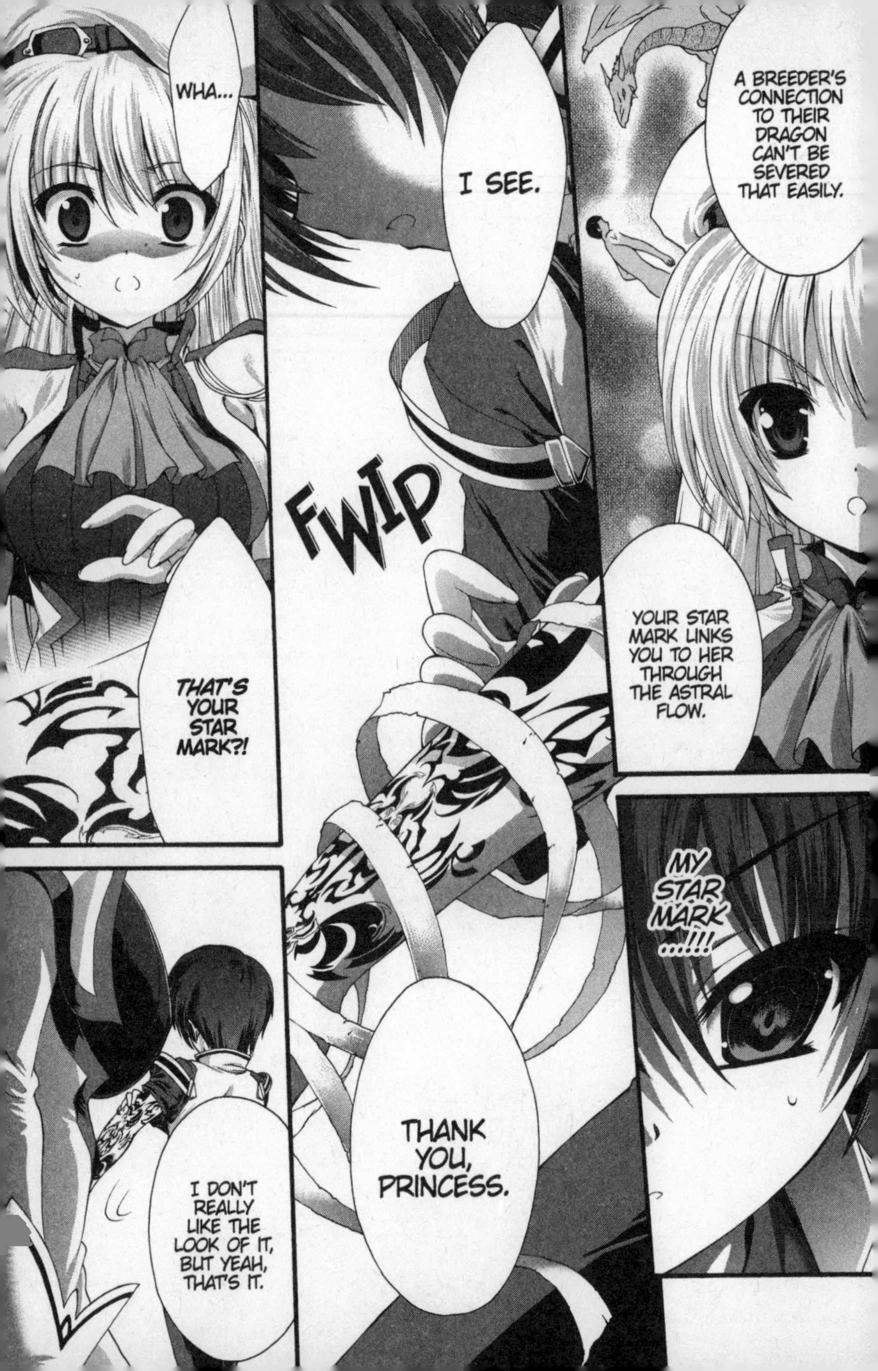
A BREEDER'S CONNECTION TO THEIR DRAGON CAN'T BE SEVERED THAT EASILY.
YOUR STAR MARK LINKS YOU TO HER THROUGH THE ASTRAL FLOW.
MY STAR MARK...!!!
I SEE.
FWIP
THANK YOU, PRINCESS.
WHA...
THAT'S YOUR STAR MARK?!
I DON'T REALLY LIKE THE LOOK OF IT, BUT YEAH, THAT'S IT.

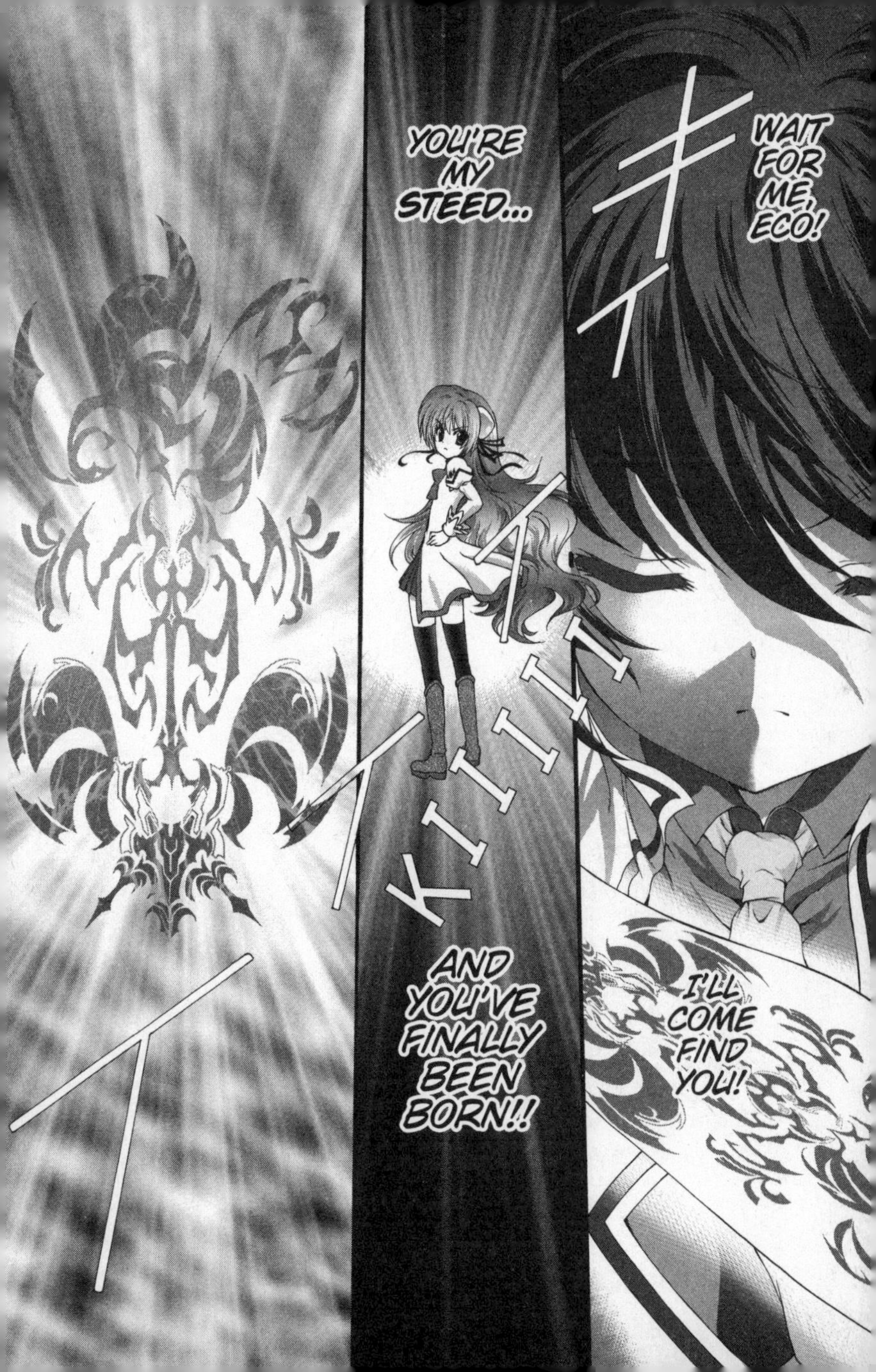
WAIT FOR ME, ECO!
I'LL COME FIND YOU!
YOU'RE MY STEED...
AND YOU'VE FINALLY BEEN BORN!!

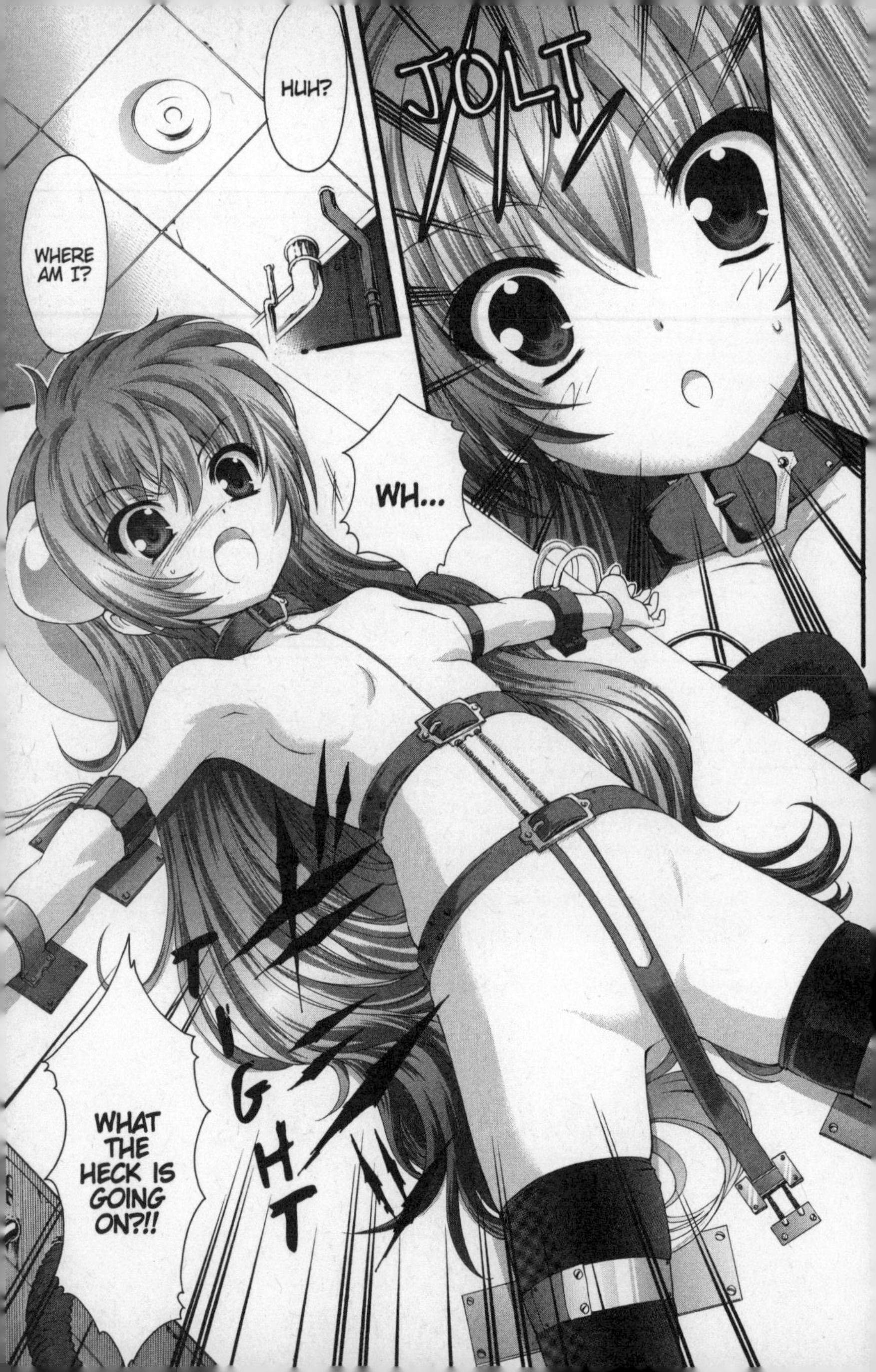
JOLT
HUH?
WHERE AM I?
WH...
TIGHT
WHAT THE HECK IS GOING ON?!!

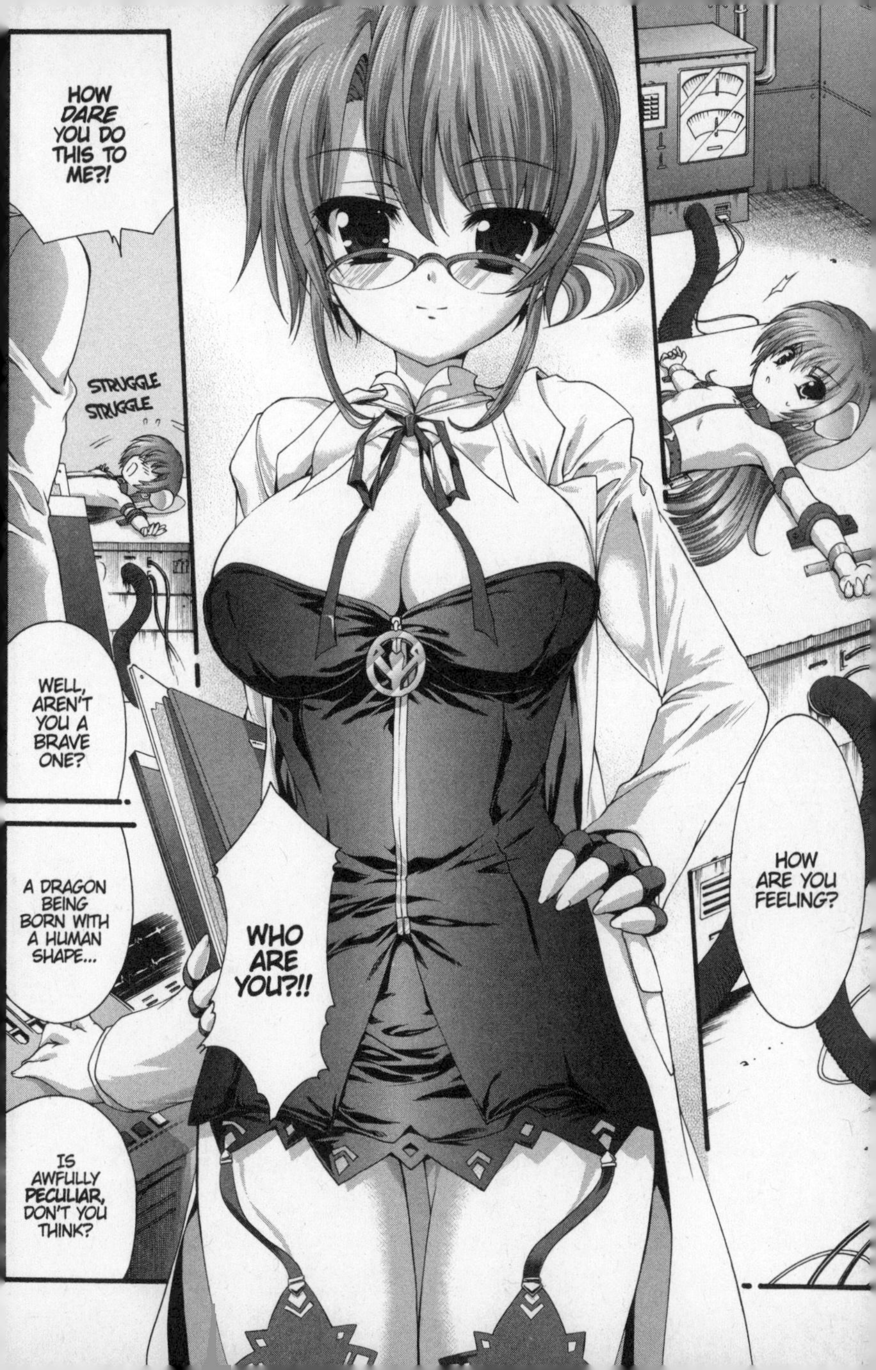
HOW ARE YOU FEELING?
HOW DARE YOU DO THIS TO ME?!
STRUGGLE STRUGGLE
WELL, AREN'T YOU A BRAVE ONE?
WHO ARE YOU?!!
A DRAGON BEING BORN WITH A HUMAN SHAPE...
IS AWFULLY PECULIAR, DON'T YOU THINK?

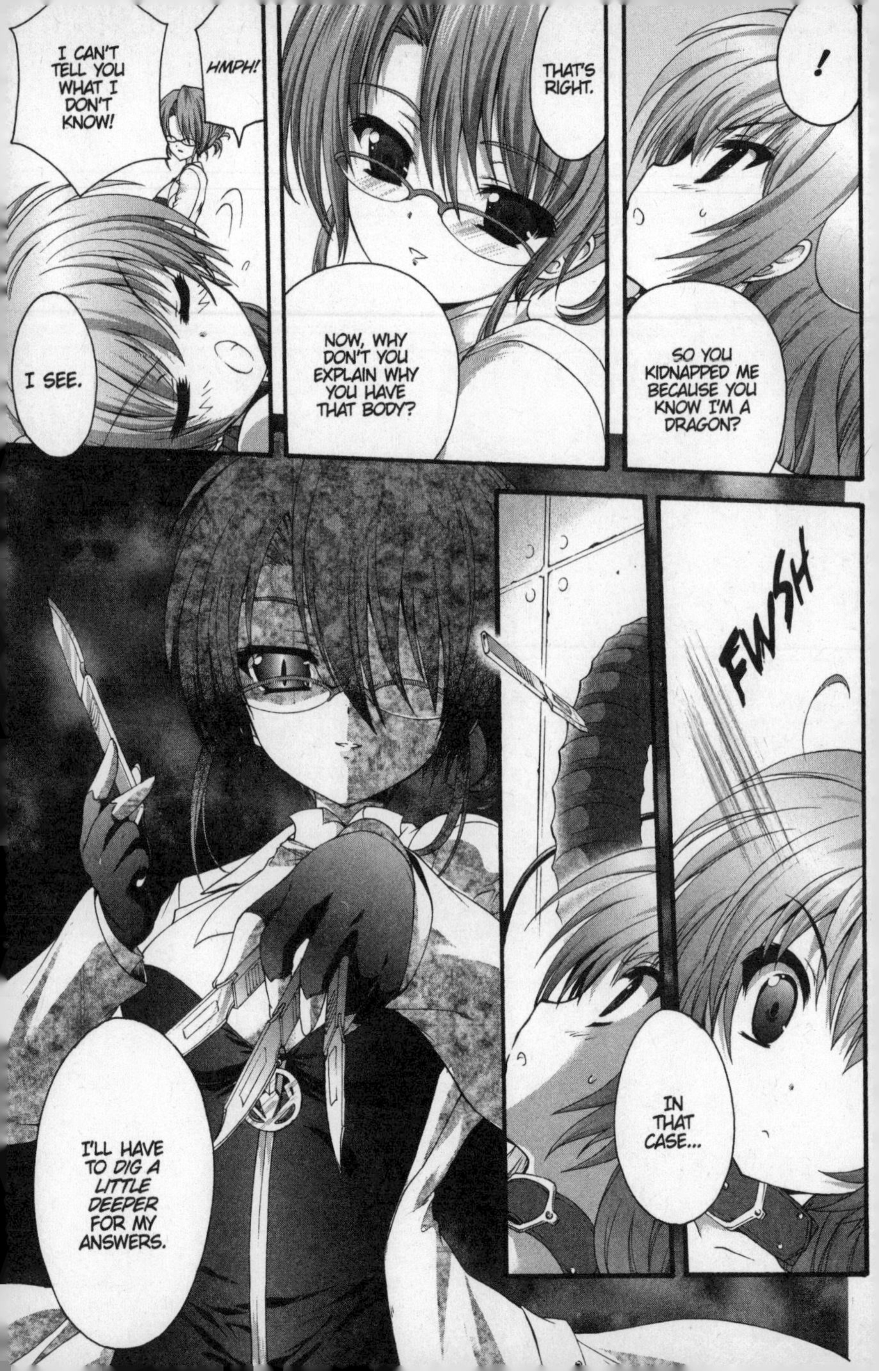
!
SO YOU KIDNAPPED ME BECAUSE YOU KNOW I'M A DRAGON?
THAT'S RIGHT.
NOW, WHY DON'T YOU EXPLAIN WHY YOU HAVE THAT BODY?
HMPH!
I CAN'T TELL YOU WHAT I DON'T KNOW!
I SEE.
FWSH
IN THAT CASE...
I'LL HAVE TO DIG A LITTLE DEEPER FOR MY ANSWERS.

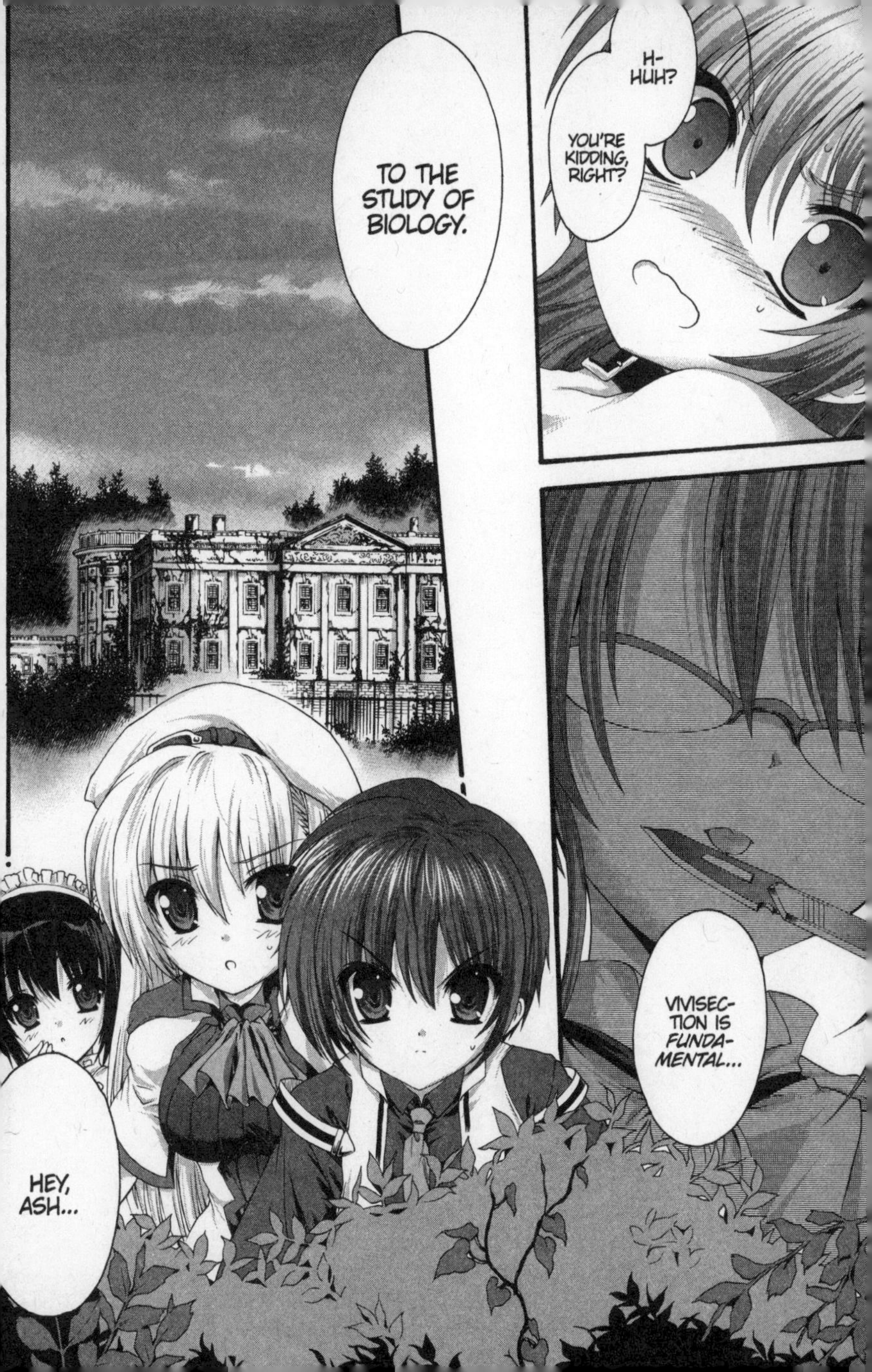
H-HUH?
YOU'RE KIDDING, RIGHT?
VIVISECTION IS FUNDAMENTAL...
TO THE STUDY OF BIOLOGY.
HEY, ASH...

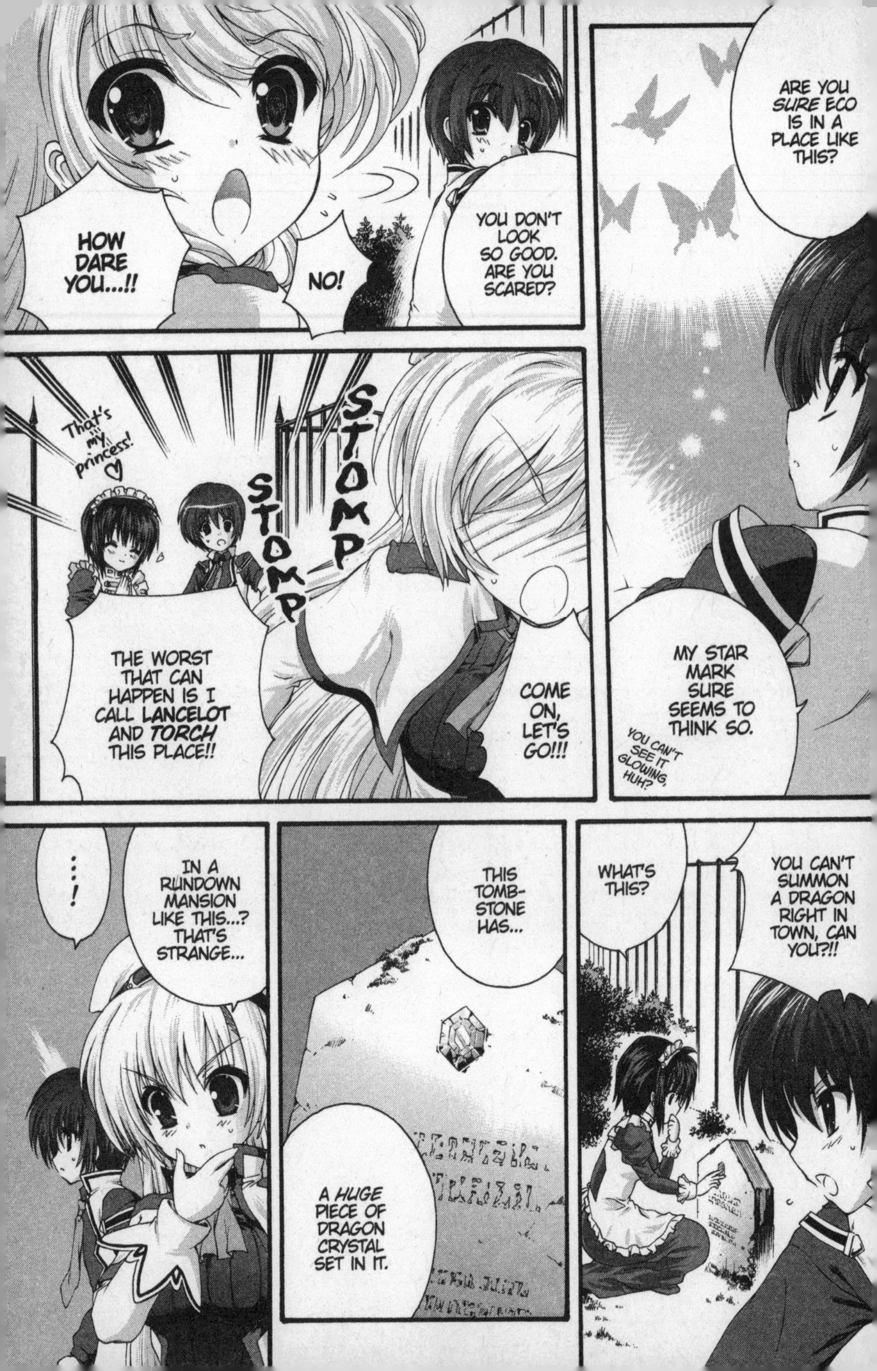
ARE YOU SURE ECO IS IN A PLACE LIKE THIS?
MY STAR MARK SURE SEEMS TO THINK SO.
YOU CAN'T SEE IT GLOWING, HUH?
YOU DON'T LOOK SO GOOD. ARE YOU SCARED?
NO!
HOW DARE YOU...!!
STOMP
STOMP
COME ON, LET'S GO!!!
That's my princess! ♡
THE WORST THAT CAN HAPPEN IS I CALL LANCELOT AND TORCH THIS PLACE!!
YOU CAN'T SUMMON A DRAGON RIGHT IN TOWN, CAN YOU?!!
WHAT'S THIS?
THIS TOMBSTONE HAS...
A HUGE PIECE OF DRAGON CRYSTAL SET IN IT.
IN A RUNDOWN MANSION LIKE THIS...? THAT'S STRANGE...
...!

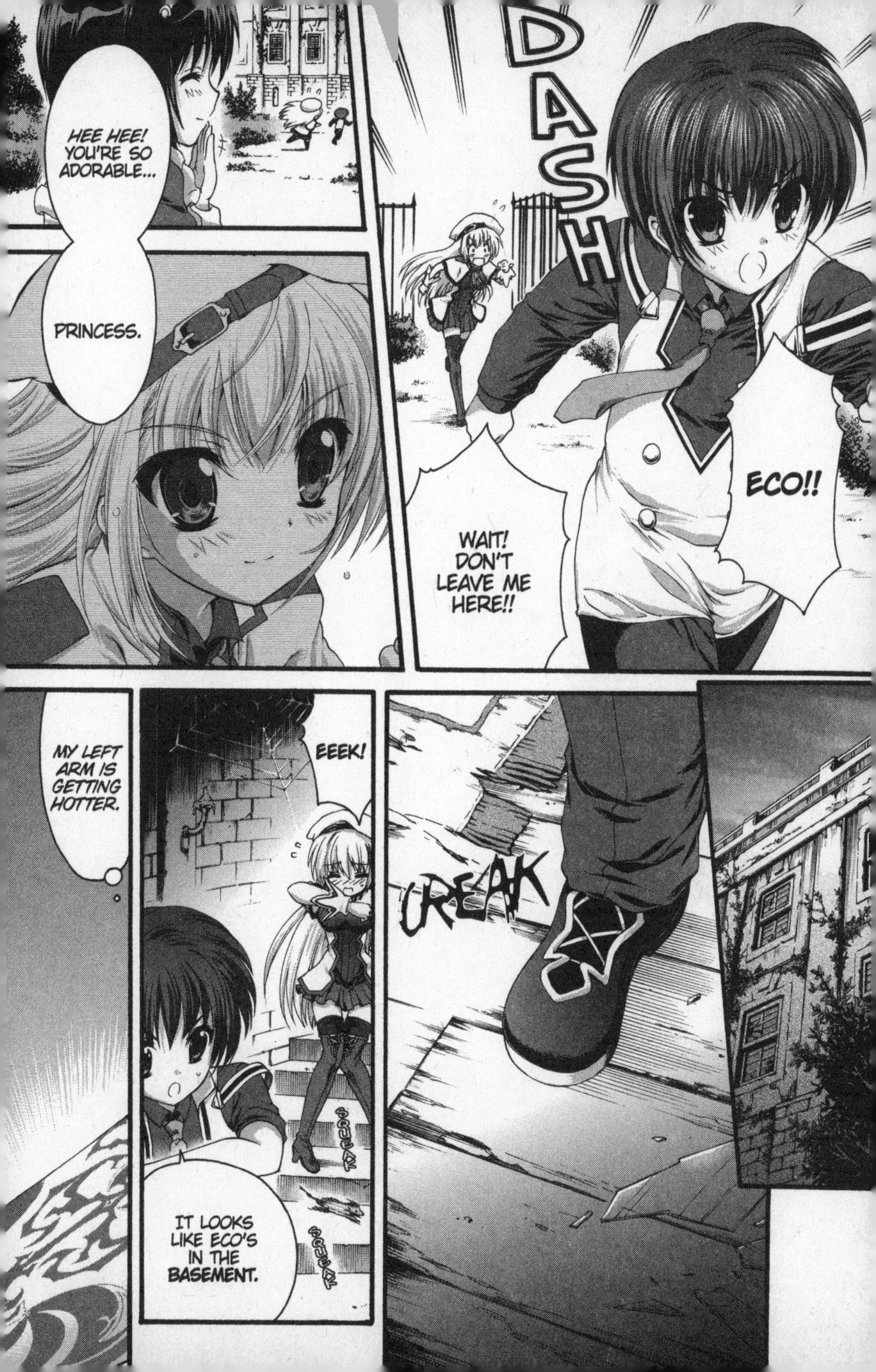
DASH
ECO!!
WAIT! DON'T LEAVE ME HERE!!
HEE HEE! YOU'RE SO ADORABLE...
PRINCESS.
CREAK
EEEK!
SQUEAK
SQUEAK
IT LOOKS LIKE ECO'S IN THE BASEMENT.
MY LEFT ARM IS GETTING HOTTER.

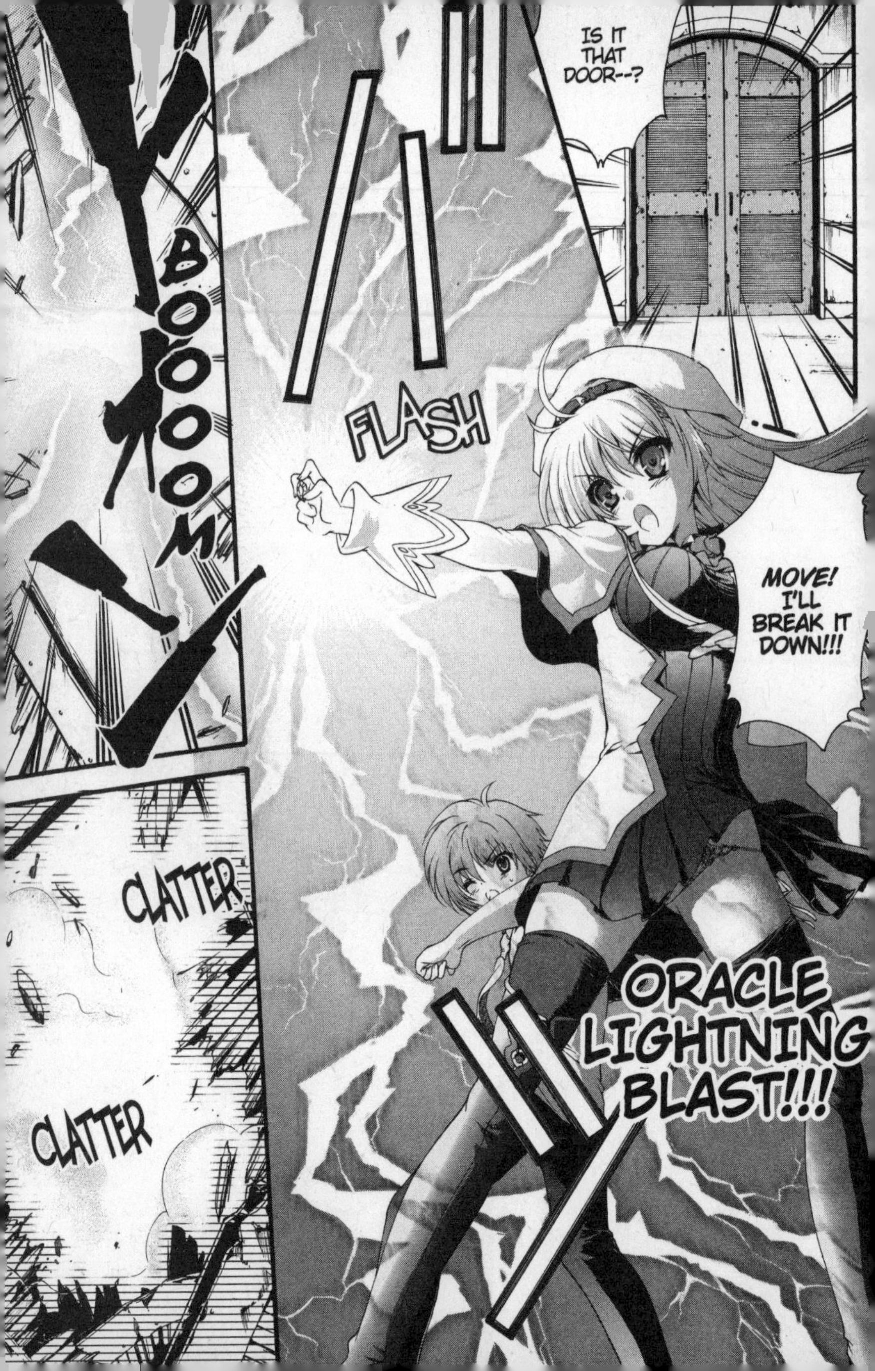
IS IT THAT DOOR--?
MOVE! I'LL BREAK IT DOWN!!!
FLASH
ORACLE LIGHTNING BLAST!!!
BOOOOM
CLATTER
CLATTER

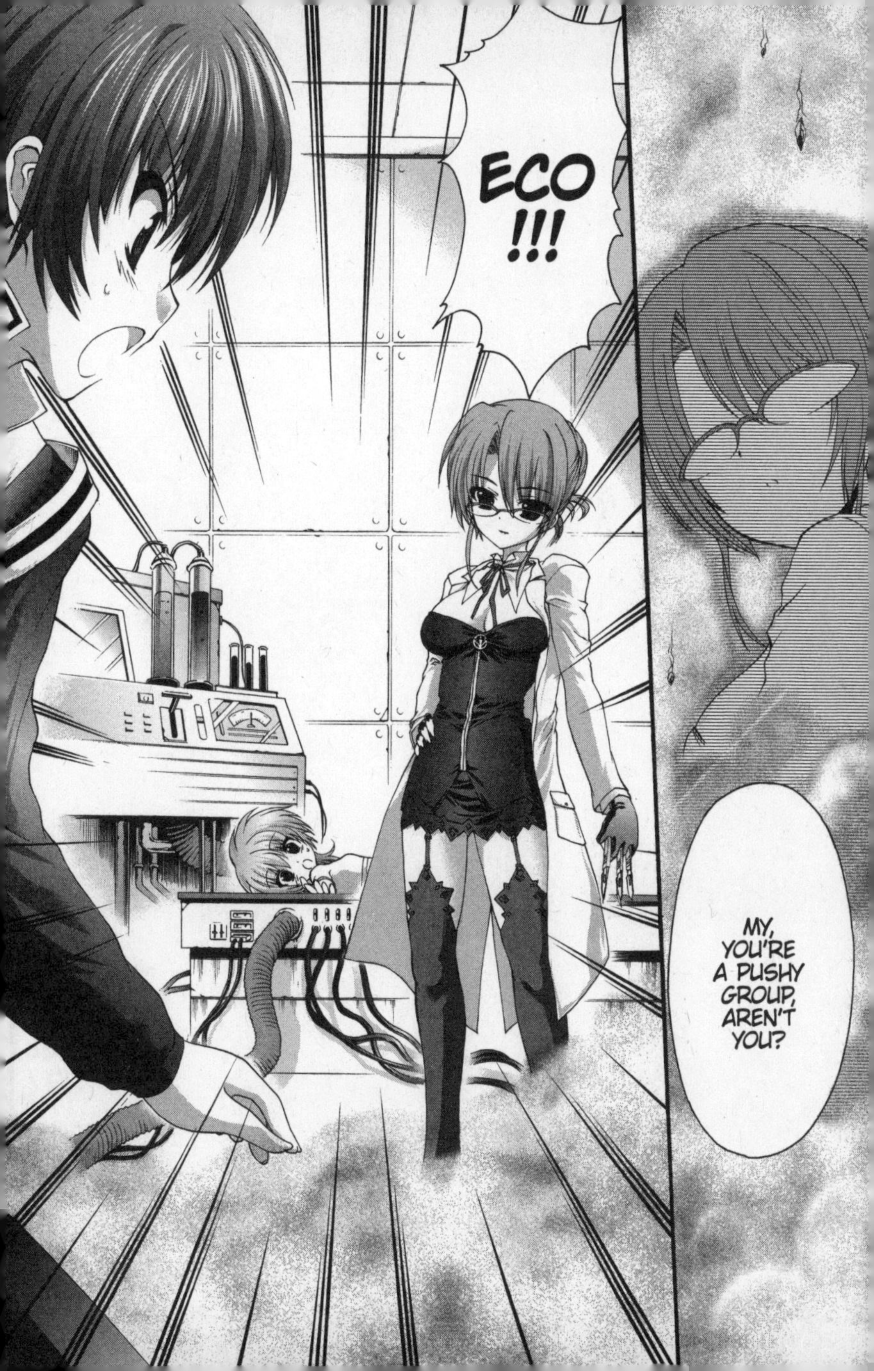
MY, YOU'RE A PUSHY GROUP, AREN'T YOU?
ECO !!!

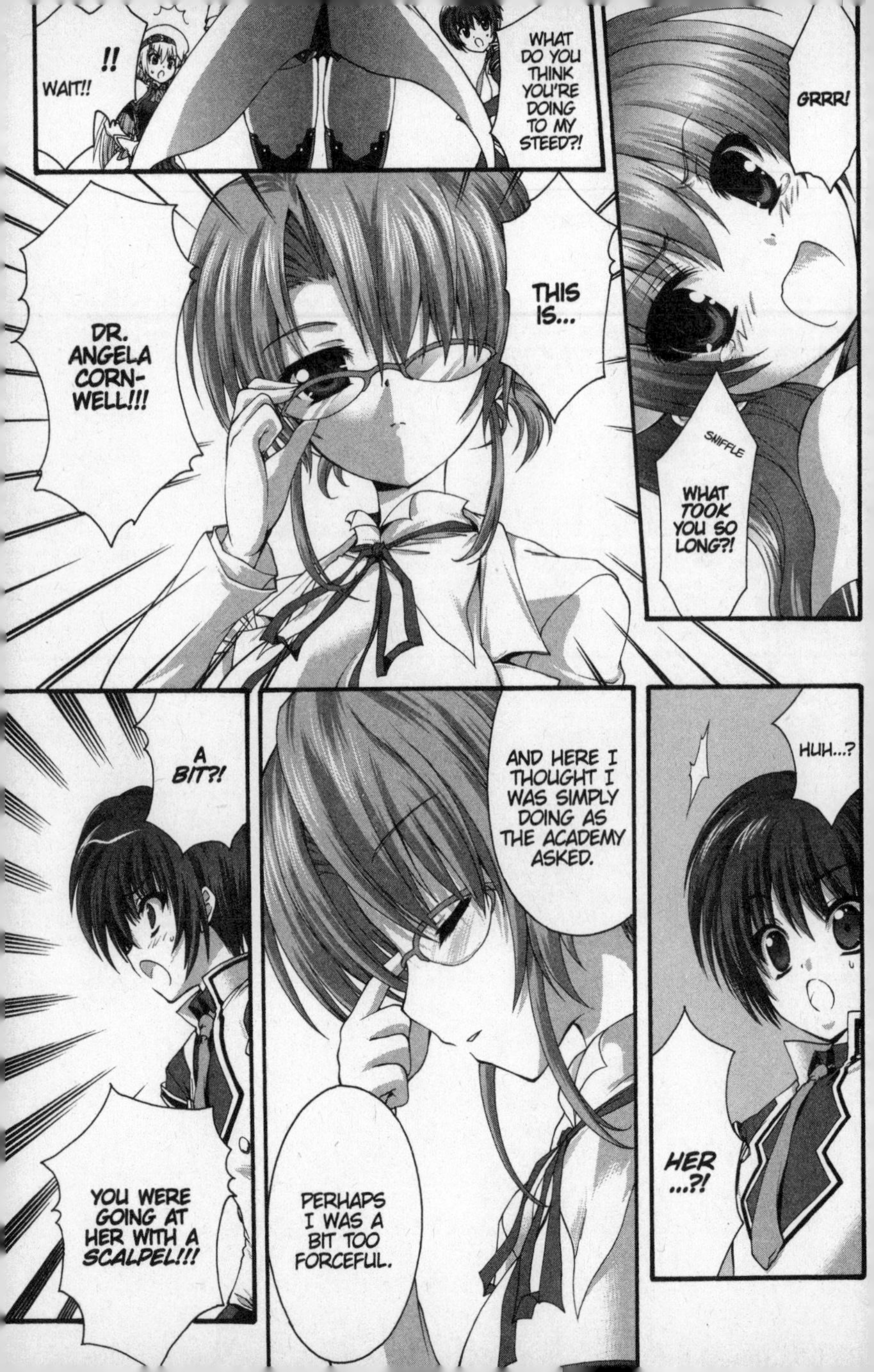

GRRR!
SNIFFLE
WHAT TOOK YOU SO LONG?!
WHAT DO YOU THINK YOU'RE DOING TO MY STEED?!
!!
WAIT!!
THIS IS...
DR. ANGELA CORN-WELL!!!
HUH...?
HER ...?!
AND HERE I THOUGHT I WAS SIMPLY DOING AS THE ACADEMY ASKED.
PERHAPS I WAS A BIT TOO FORCEFUL.
A BIT?!
YOU WERE GOING AT HER WITH A SCALPEL!!!

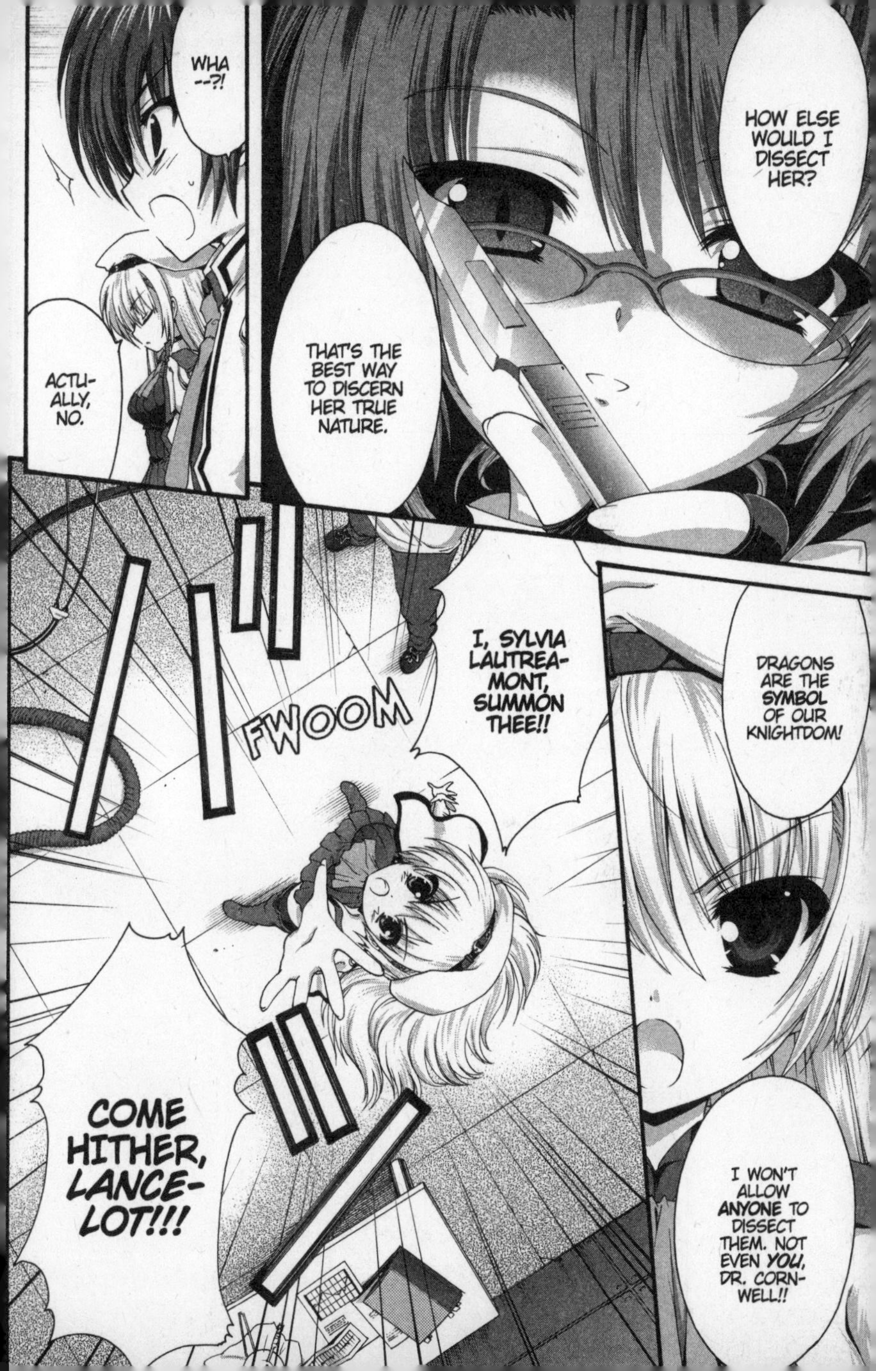
HOW ELSE WOULD I DISSECT HER?
THAT'S THE BEST WAY TO DISCERN HER TRUE NATURE.
WHA--?!
ACTU-ALLY, NO.
DRAGONS ARE THE SYMBOL OF OUR KNIGHTDOM!
I WON'T ALLOW ANYONE TO DISSECT THEM. NOT EVEN YOU, DR. CORN-WELL!!
I, SYLVIA LAUTREA-MONT, SUMMON THEE!!
FWOOM
COME HITHER, LANCE-LOT!!!

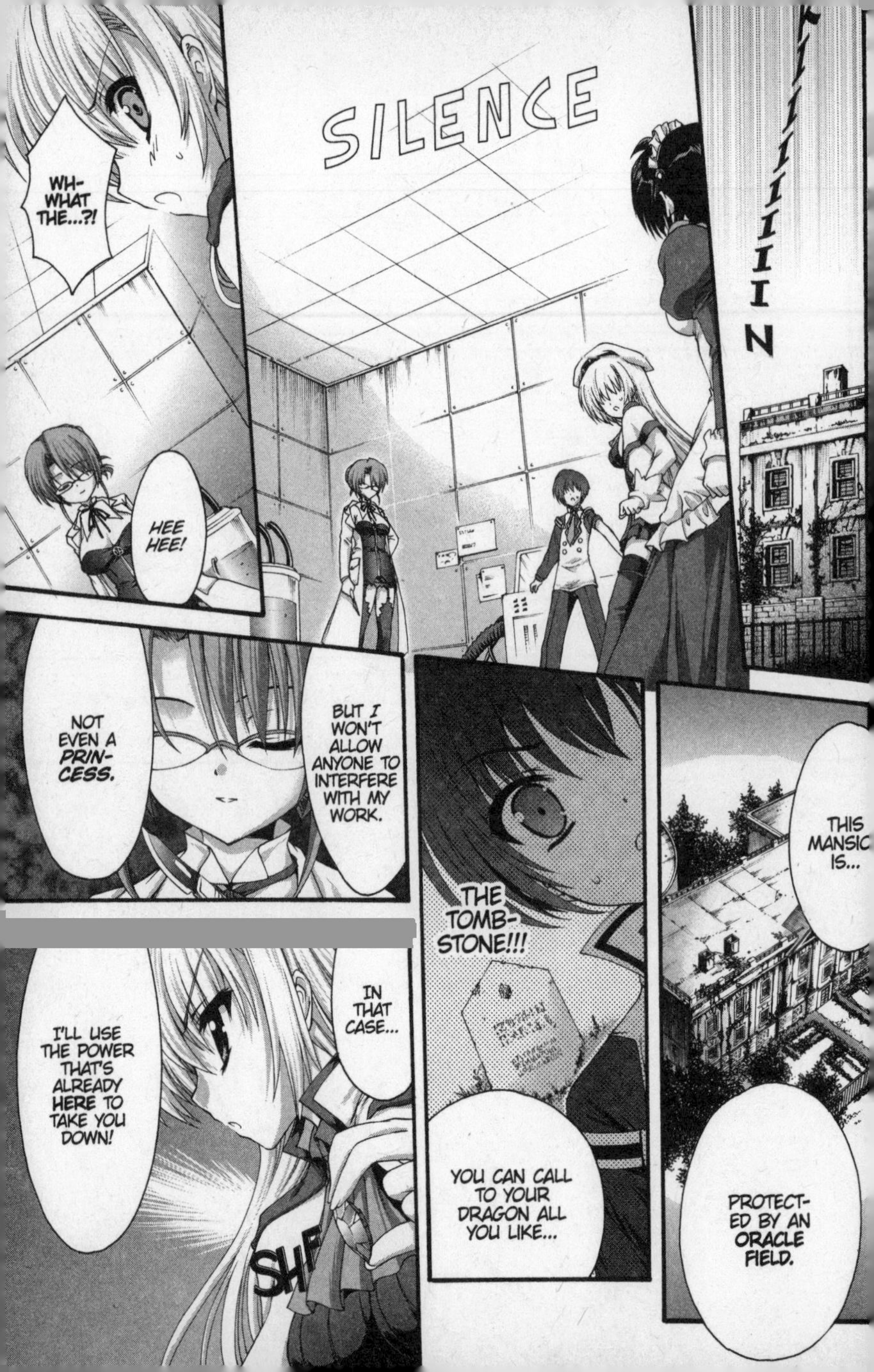
IIIIIIIN
SILENCE
WH-WHAT THE...?!
HEE HEE!
THIS MANSIC IS...
PROTECT-ED BY AN ORACLE FIELD.
THE TOMB-STONE!!!
YOU CAN CALL TO YOUR DRAGON ALL YOU LIKE...
BUT I WON'T ALLOW ANYONE TO INTERFERE WITH MY WORK.
NOT EVEN A *PRIN-CESS.*
IN THAT CASE...
I'LL USE THE POWER THAT'S ALREADY HERE TO TAKE YOU DOWN!
SHF

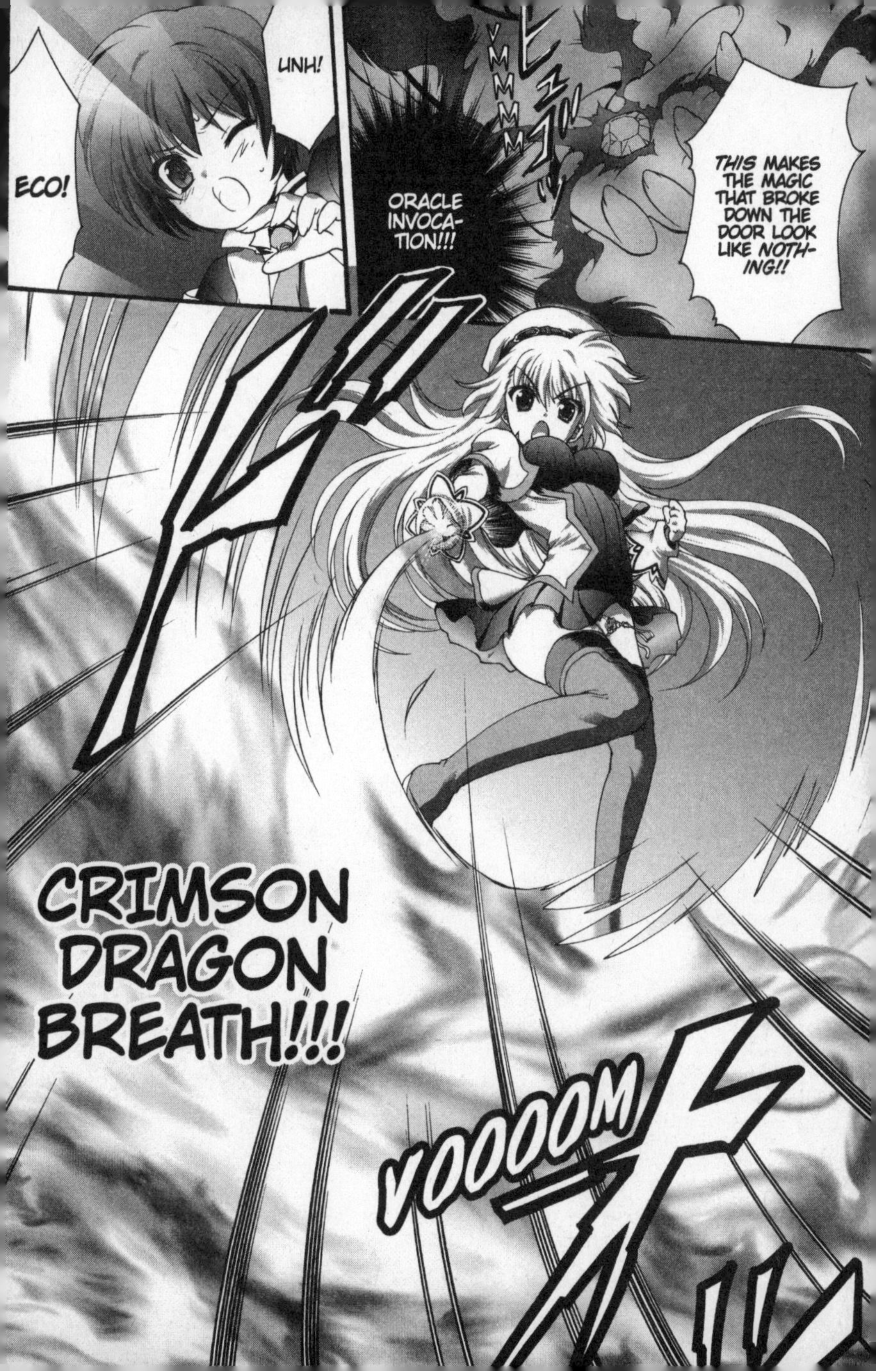
THIS MAKES THE MAGIC THAT BROKE DOWN THE DOOR LOOK LIKE NOTHING!!
VMMMM
ORACLE INVOCATION!!!
UNH!
ECO!
CRIMSON DRAGON BREATH!!!
VOOOOM

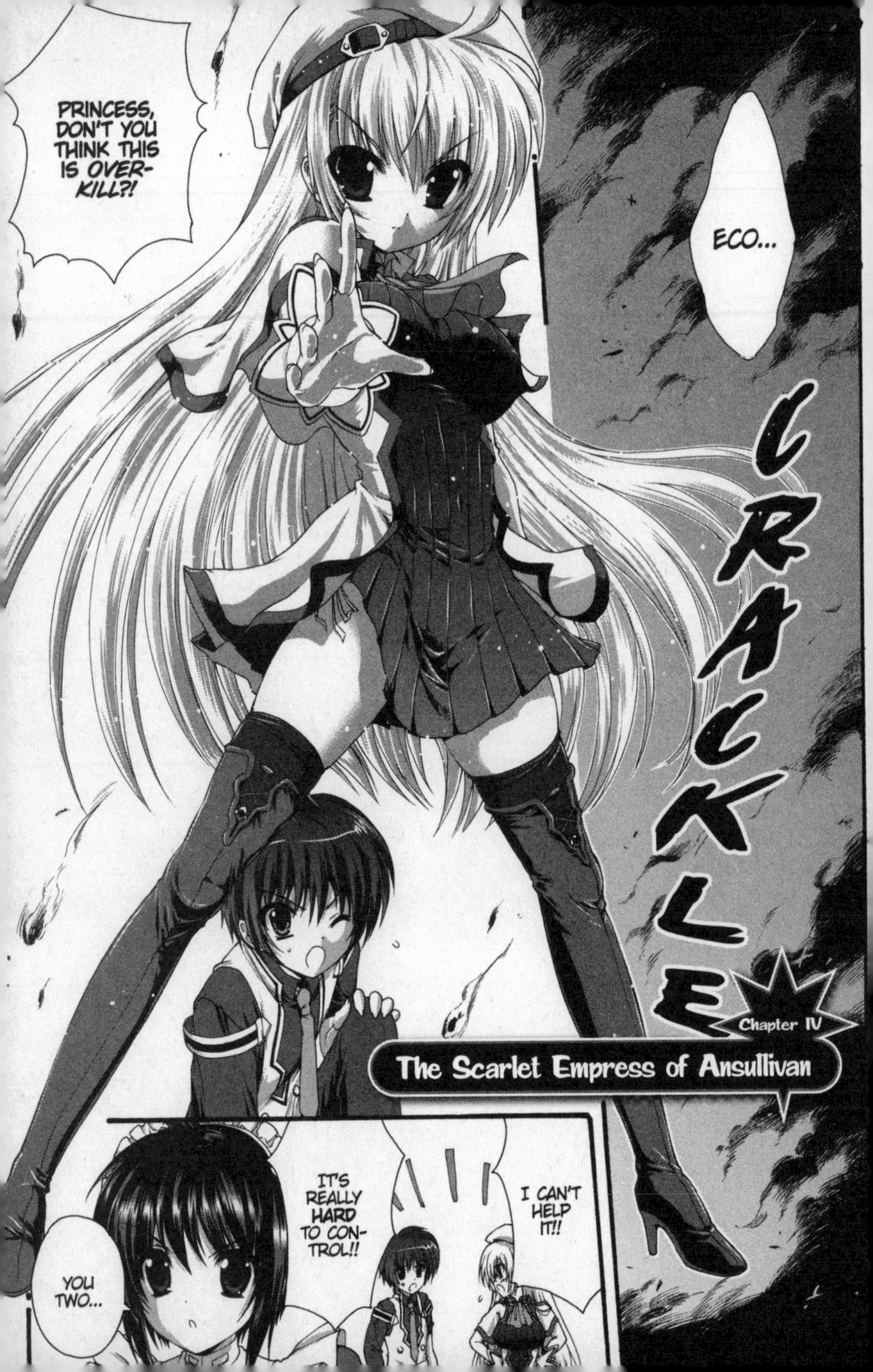
ECO...
PRINCESS, DON'T YOU THINK THIS IS OVER-KILL?!
CRACKLE
Chapter IV
The Scarlet Empress of Ansullivan
I CAN'T HELP IT!!
IT'S REALLY HARD TO CON-TROL!!
YOU TWO...

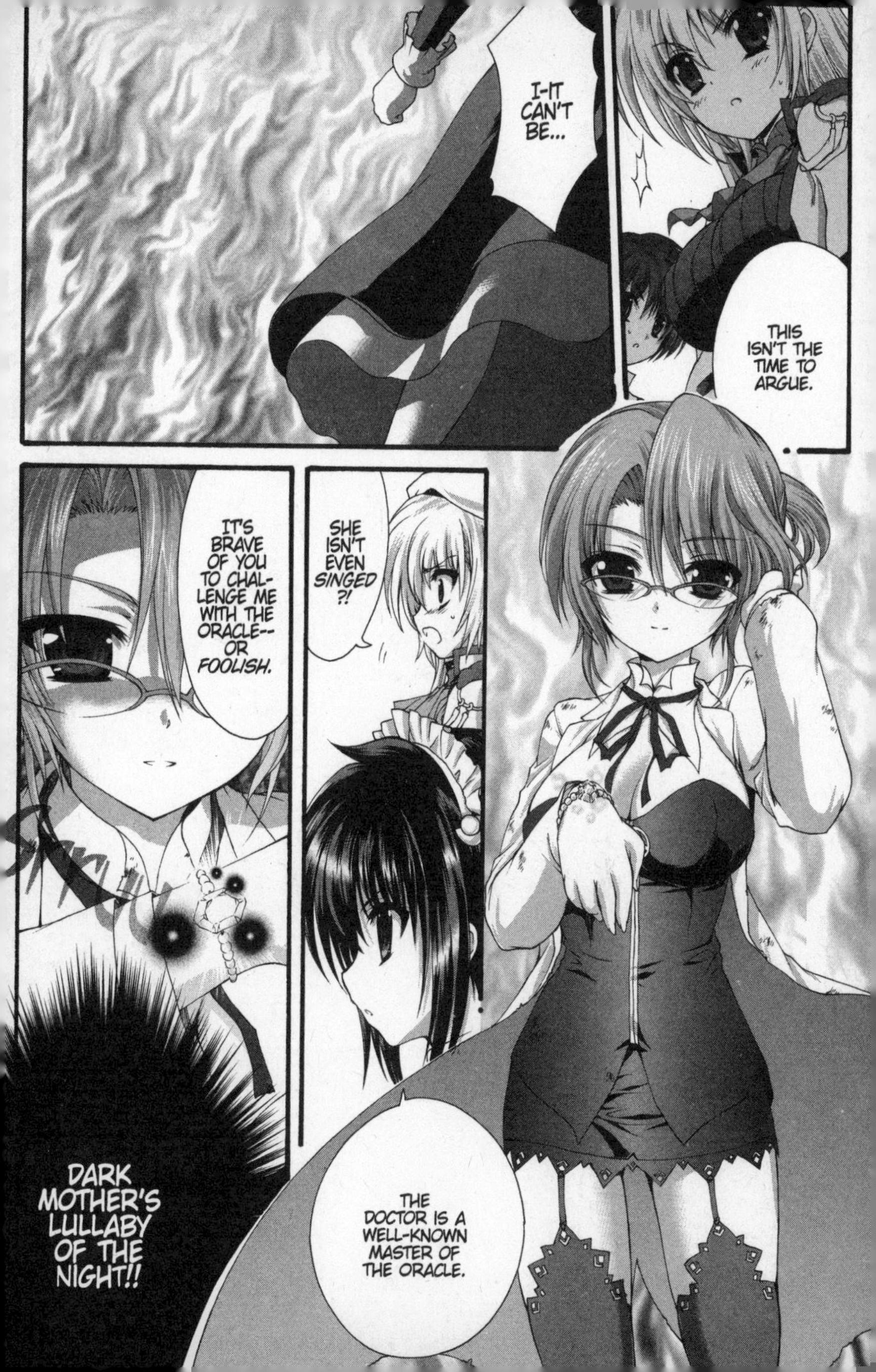
THIS ISN'T THE TIME TO ARGUE.
I-IT CAN'T BE...
SHE ISN'T EVEN SINGED?!
THE DOCTOR IS A WELL-KNOWN MASTER OF THE ORACLE.
IT'S BRAVE OF YOU TO CHAL-LENGE ME WITH THE ORACLE--OR FOOLISH.
DARK MOTHER'S LULLABY OF THE NIGHT!!

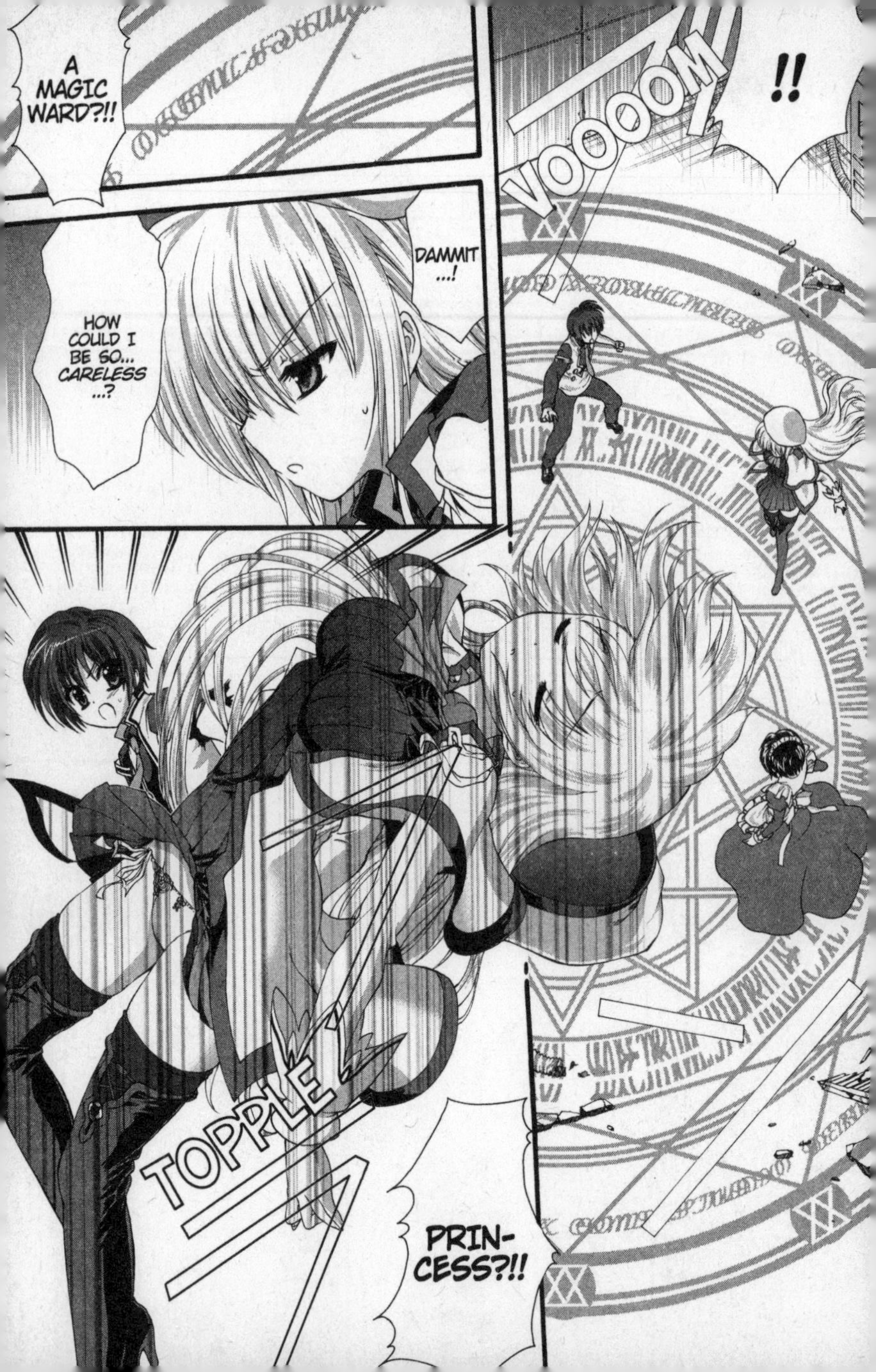
!!
VOOOOM
A MAGIC WARD?!!
DAMMIT ...!
HOW COULD I BE SO... CARELESS ...?
TOPPLE
PRIN-CESS?!!

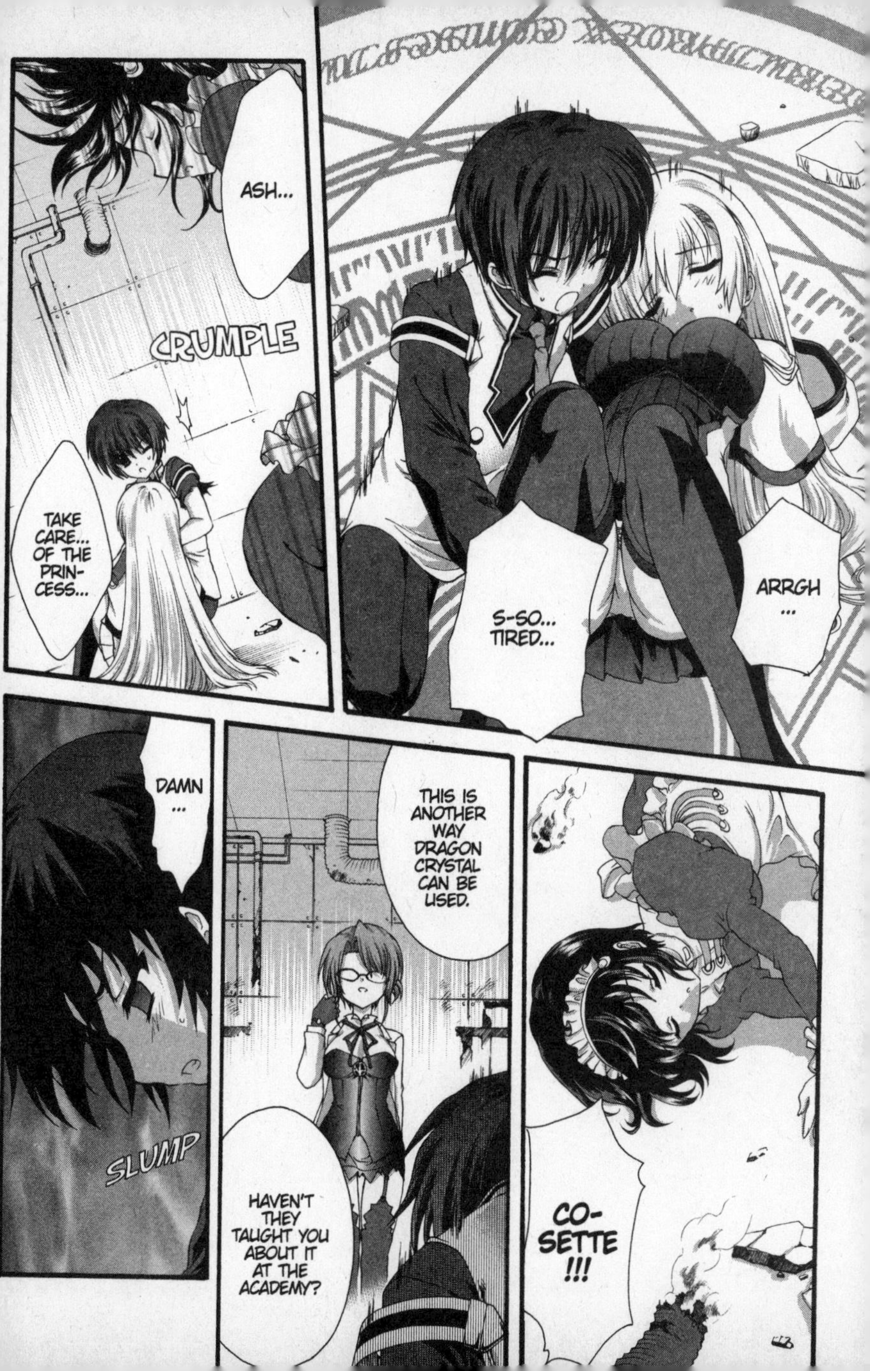
ARRGH ...
S-SO... TIRED...
ASH...
CRUMPLE
TAKE CARE... OF THE PRIN-CESS...
CO-SETTE !!!
THIS IS ANOTHER WAY DRAGON CRYSTAL CAN BE USED.
HAVEN'T THEY TAUGHT YOU ABOUT IT AT THE ACADEMY?
DAMN ...
SLUMP

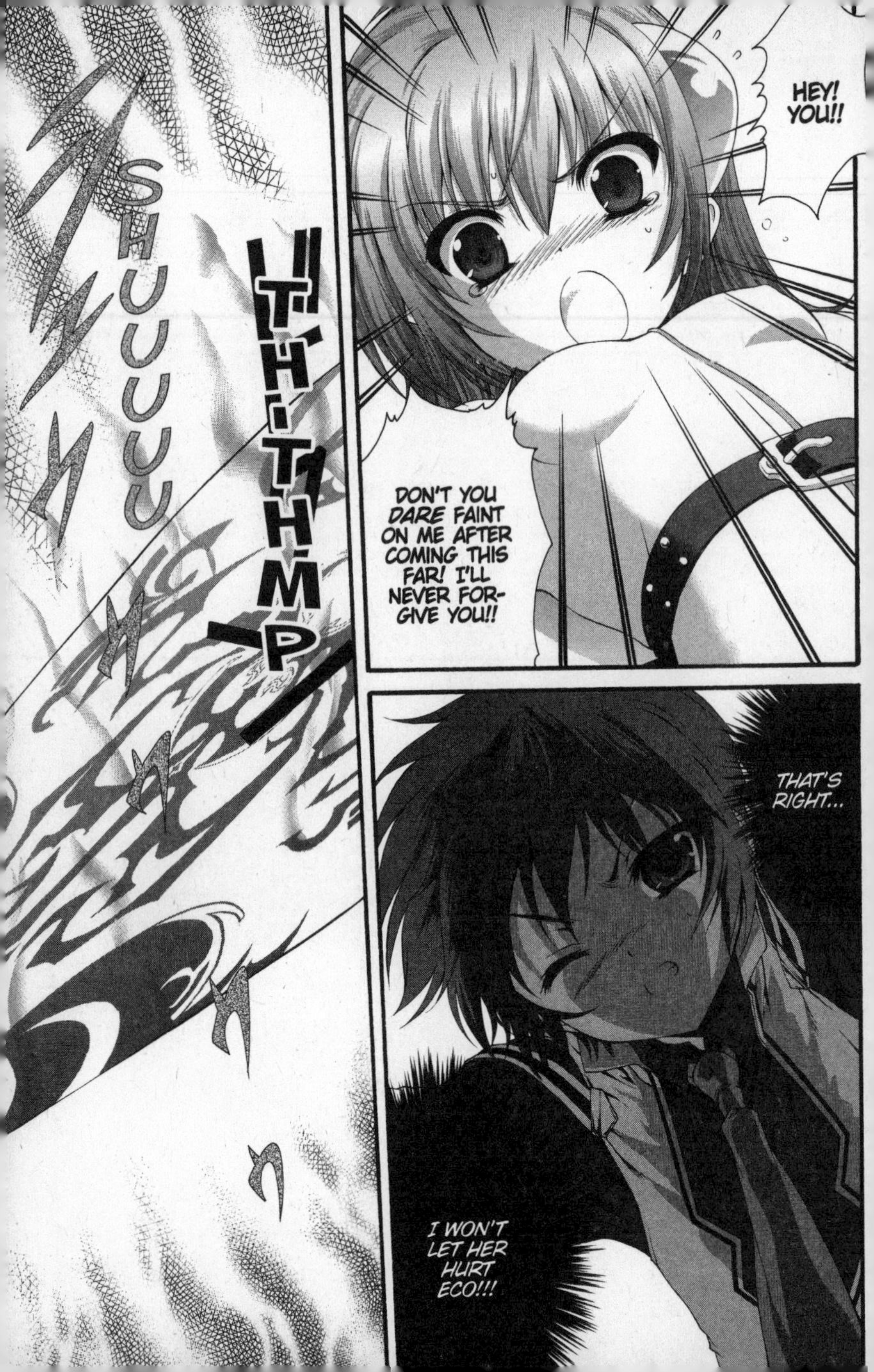
HEY! YOU!!
DON'T YOU *DARE* FAINT ON ME AFTER COMING THIS FAR! I'LL NEVER FOR-GIVE YOU!!
THAT'S RIGHT...
I WON'T LET HER HURT ECO!!!
TH-THMP
SHUUUUU

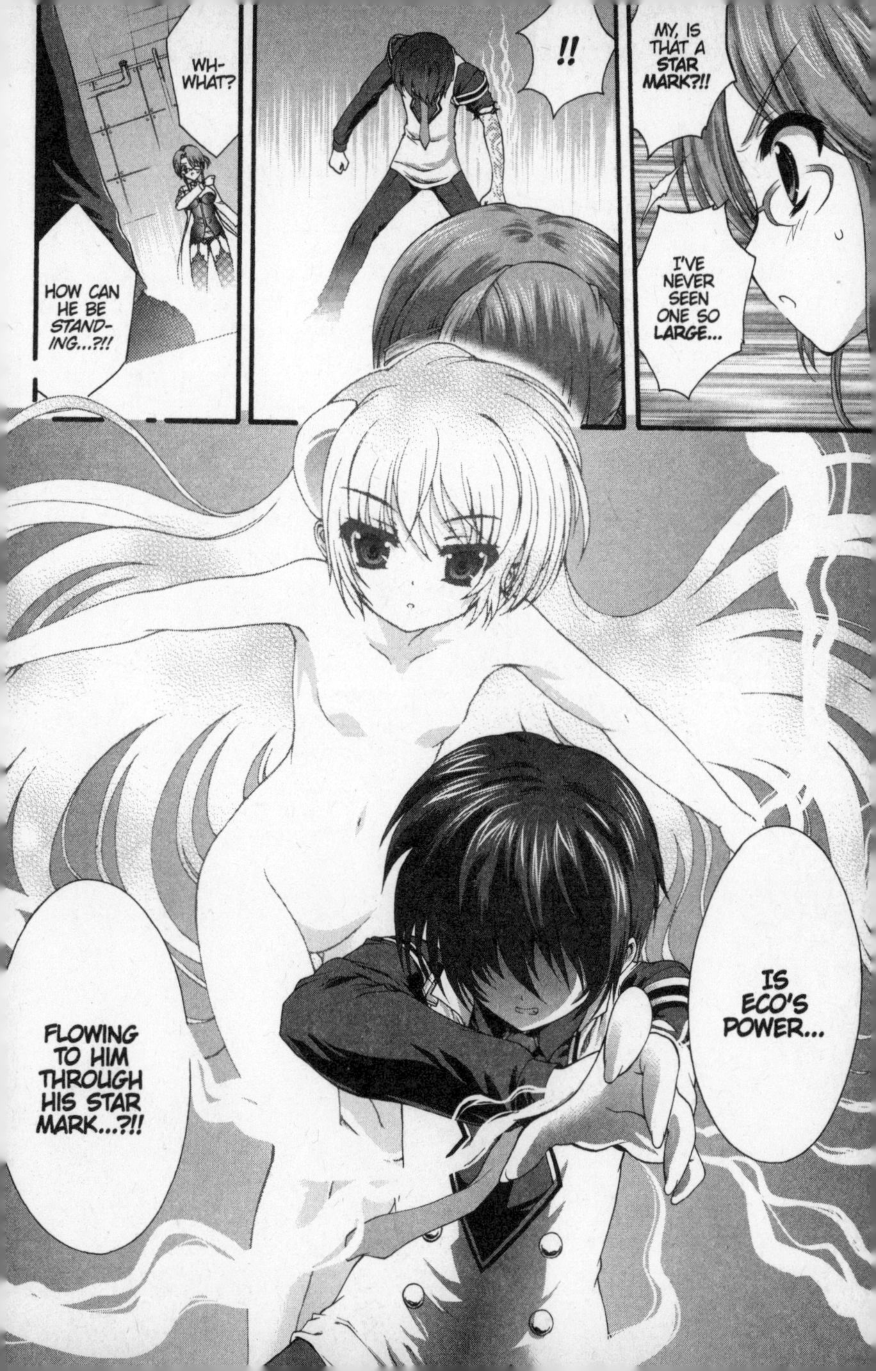
MY, IS THAT A STAR MARK?!!
I'VE NEVER SEEN ONE SO LARGE...
!!
WH-WHAT?
HOW CAN HE BE STAND-ING...?!!
IS ECO'S POWER...
FLOWING TO HIM THROUGH HIS STAR MARK...?!!

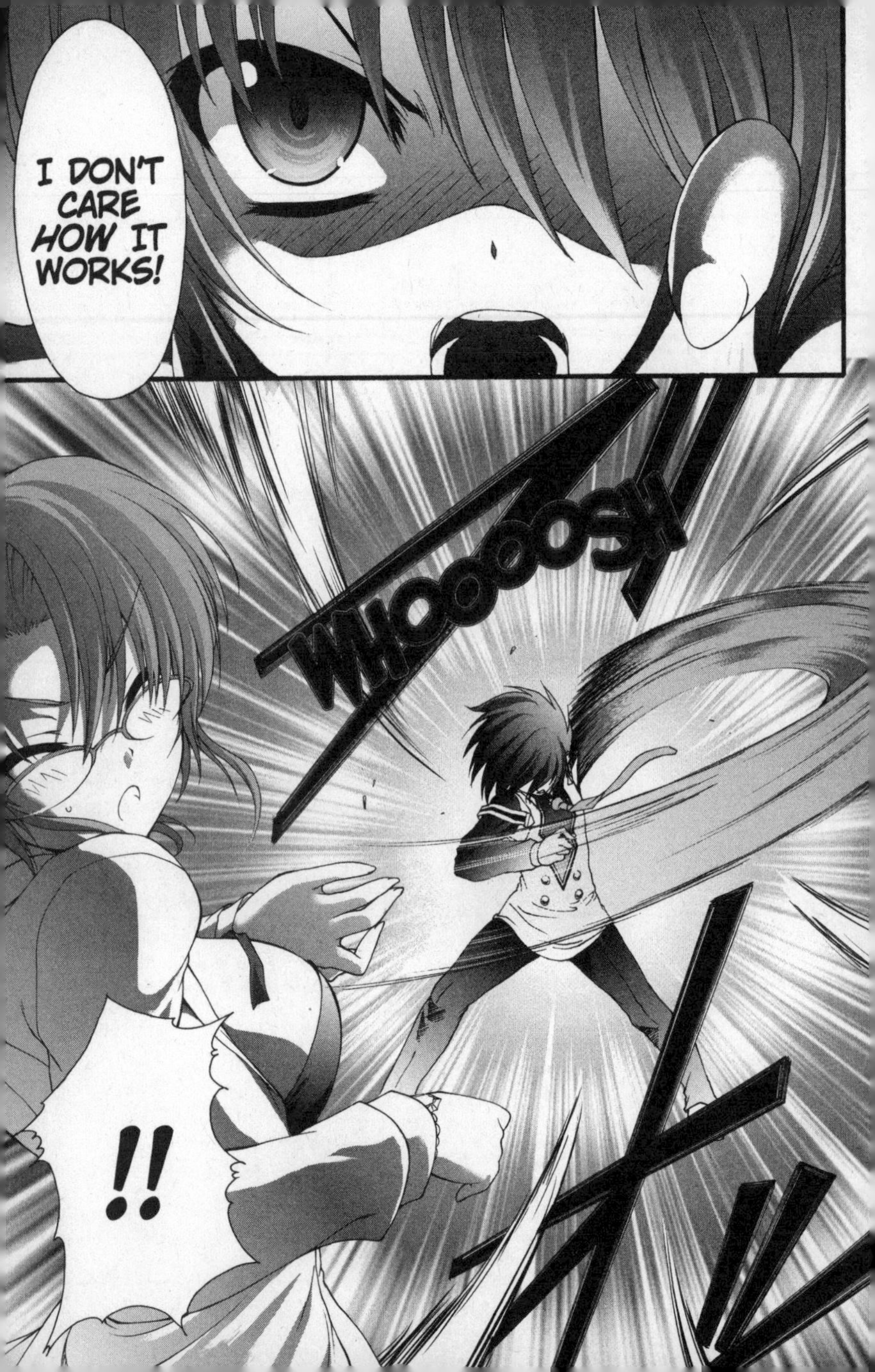
I DON'T CARE *HOW* IT WORKS!
WHOOOOOSH
!!

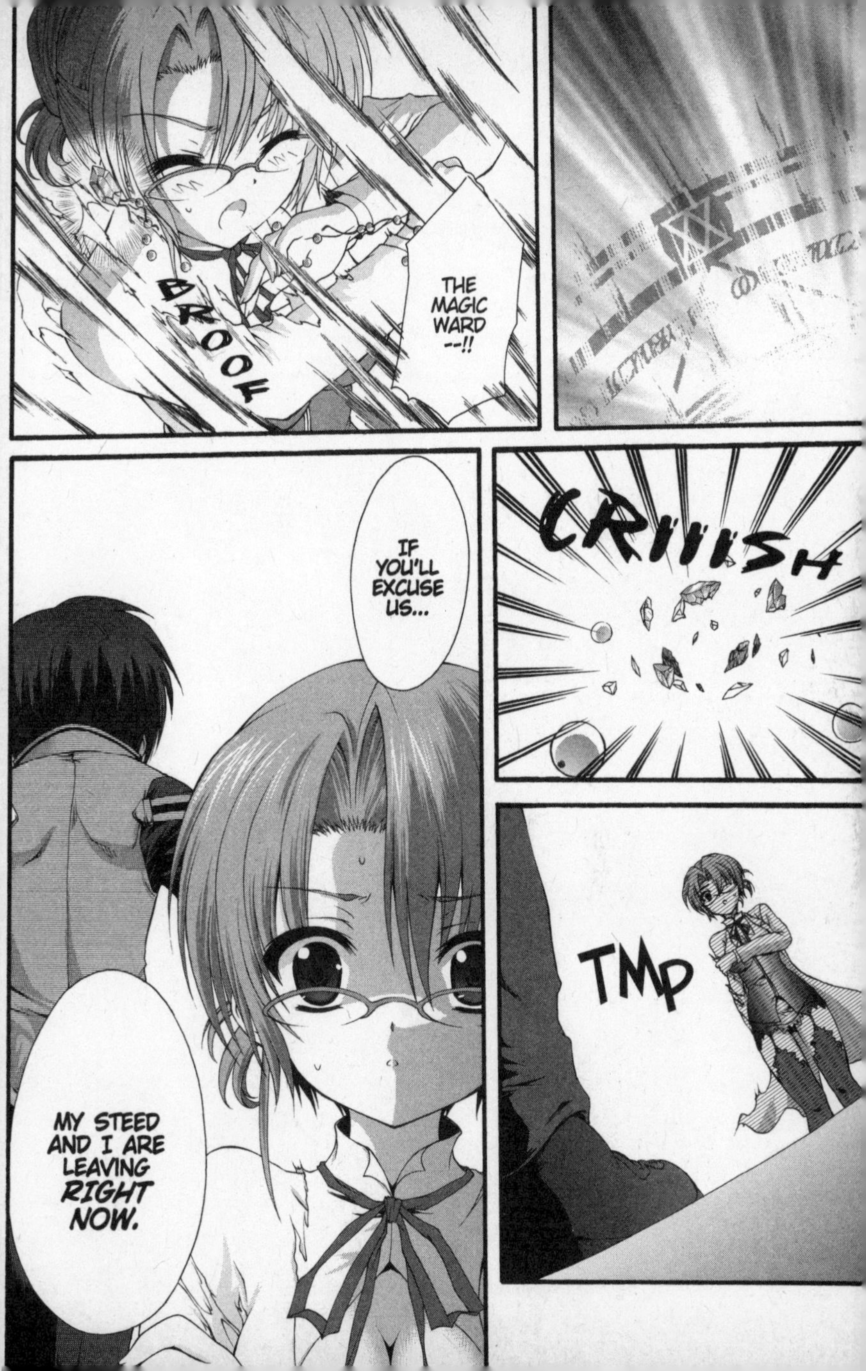
THE MAGIC WARD --!!
BROOOF
CRIIISH
TMP
IF YOU'LL EXCUSE US...
MY STEED AND I ARE LEAVING RIGHT NOW.

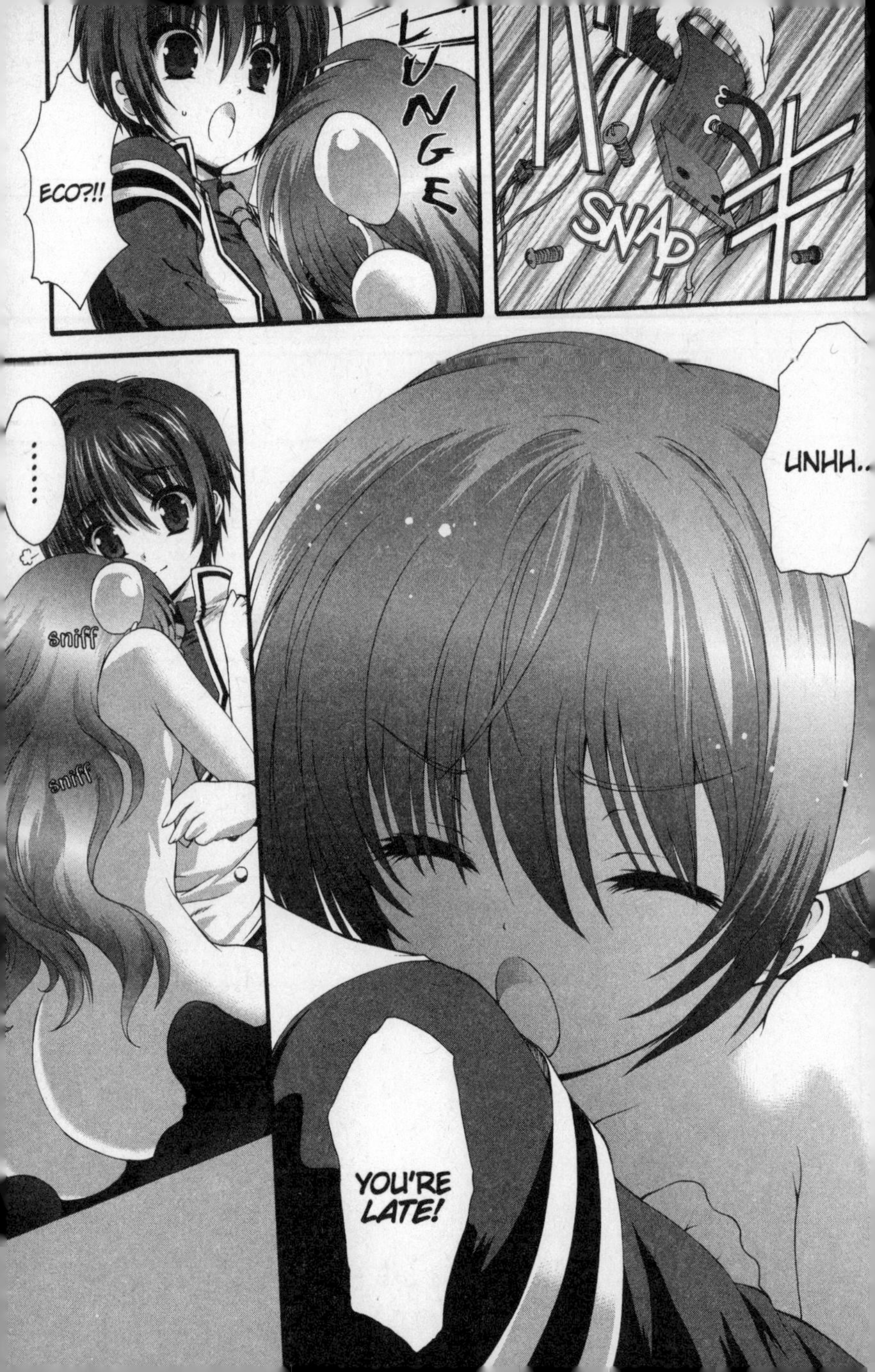

SNAP
LUNGE
ECO?!!
UNHH..
YOU'RE LATE!
......
sniff
sniff

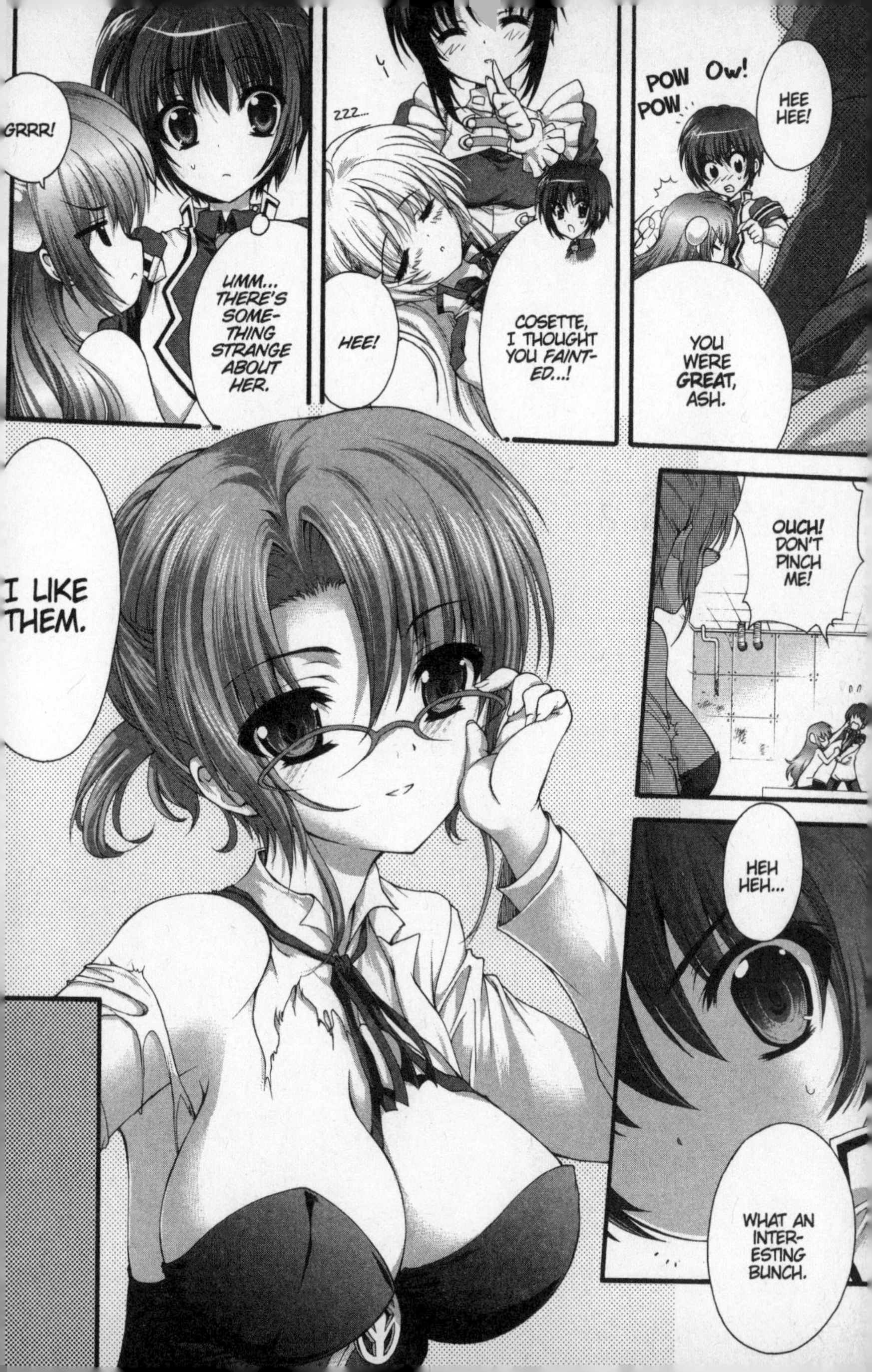
HEE HEE!
POW POW
Ow!
YOU WERE GREAT, ASH.
zzz...
COSETTE, I THOUGHT YOU FAINT-ED...!
HEE!
GRRR!
UMM... THERE'S SOME-THING STRANGE ABOUT HER.
OUCH! DON'T PINCH ME!
HEH HEH...
WHAT AN INTER-ESTING BUNCH.
I LIKE THEM.

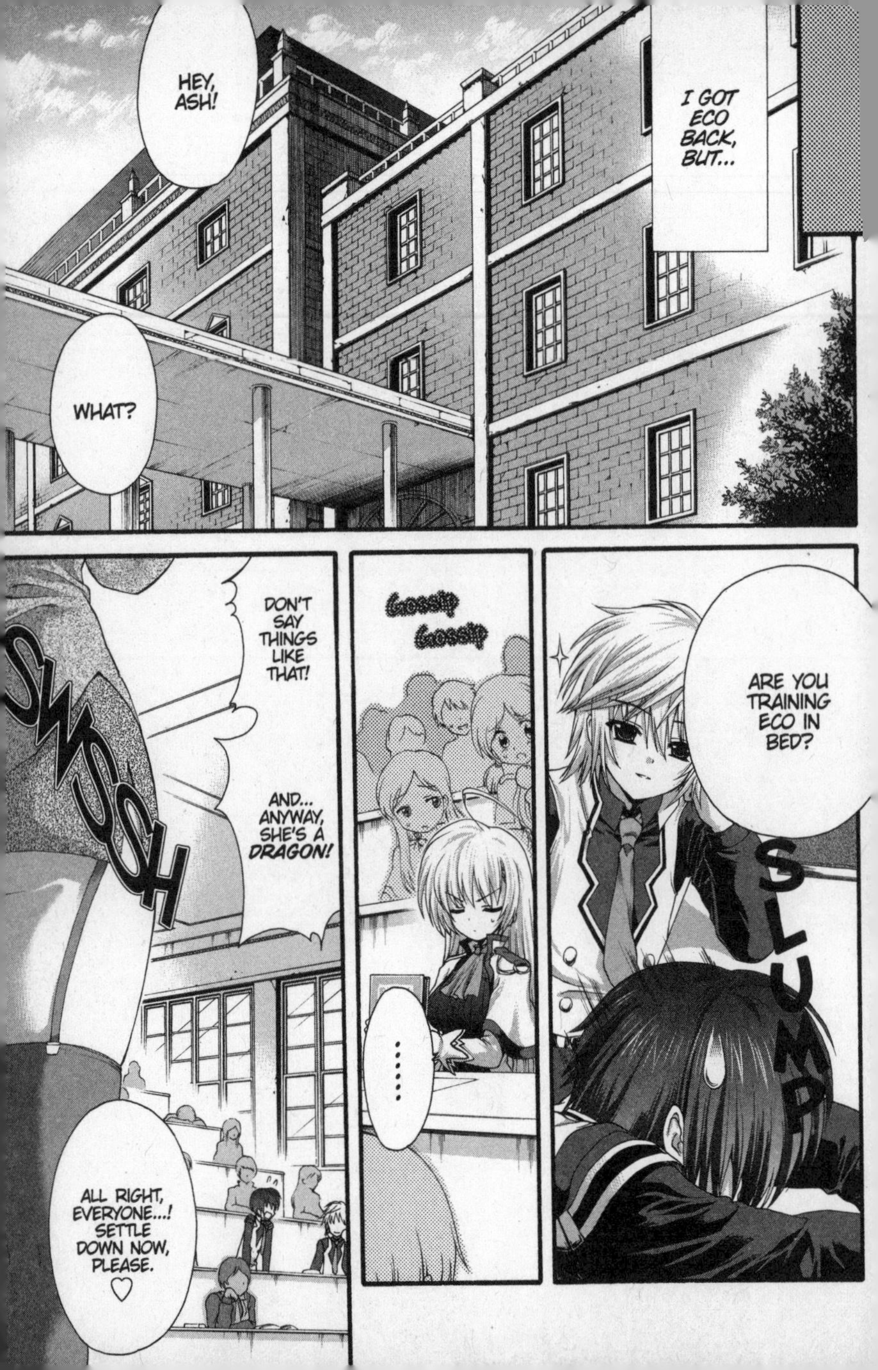
I GOT ECO BACK, BUT...
HEY, ASH!
WHAT?
ARE YOU TRAINING ECO IN BED?
SLUMP
Gossip Gossip
......
DON'T SAY THINGS LIKE THAT!
AND... ANYWAY, SHE'S A DRAGON!
SWOSH
ALL RIGHT, EVERYONE...! SETTLE DOWN NOW, PLEASE. ♡

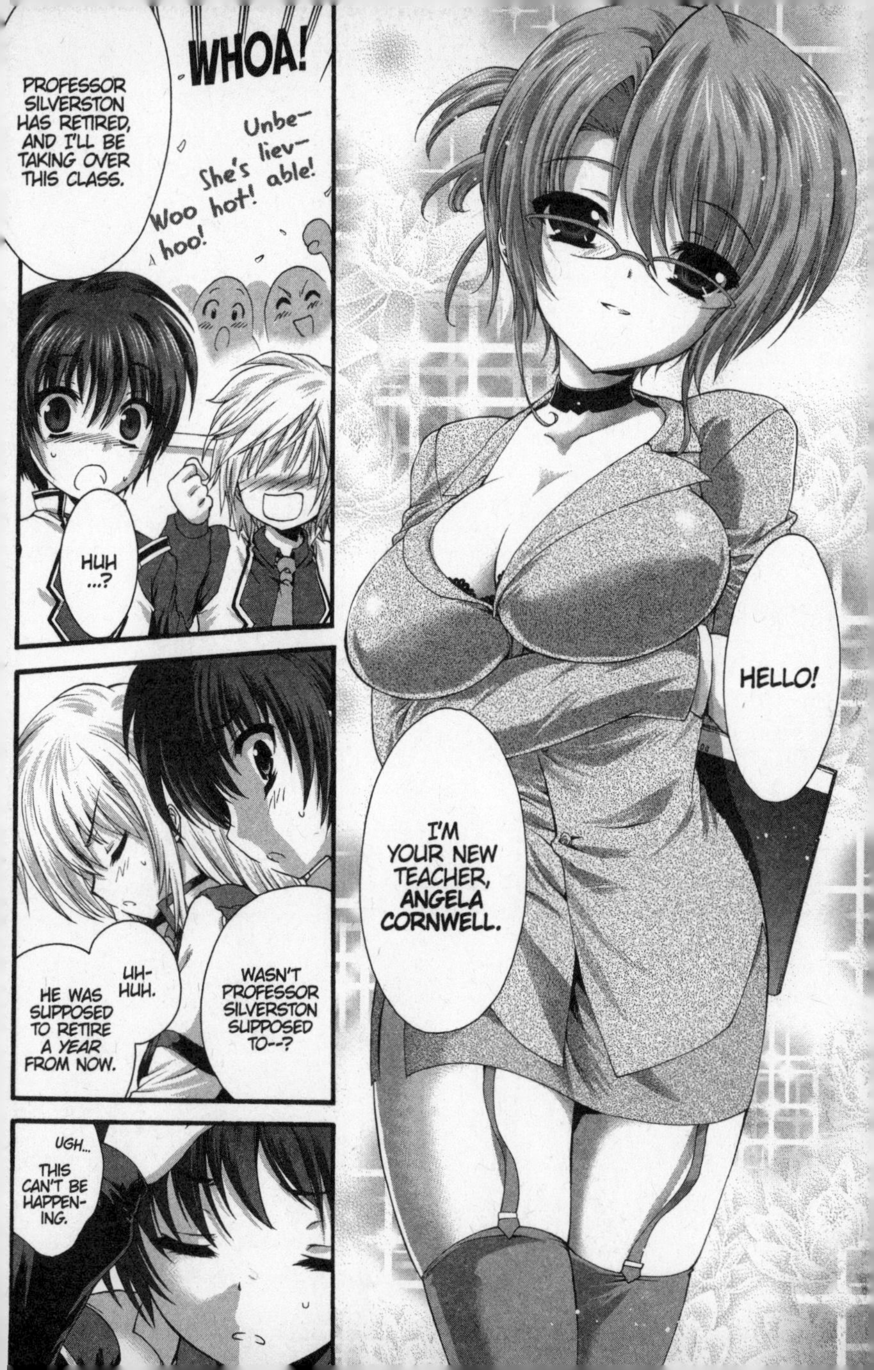
HELLO!
I'M YOUR NEW TEACHER, ANGELA CORNWELL.
PROFESSOR SILVERSTON HAS RETIRED, AND I'LL BE TAKING OVER THIS CLASS.
WHOA!
Unbe-lievable!
She's hot!
Woo hoo!
HUH ...?
WASN'T PROFESSOR SILVERSTON SUPPOSED TO--?
UH-HUH.
HE WAS SUPPOSED TO RETIRE A YEAR FROM NOW.
UGH... THIS CAN'T BE HAPPEN-ING.

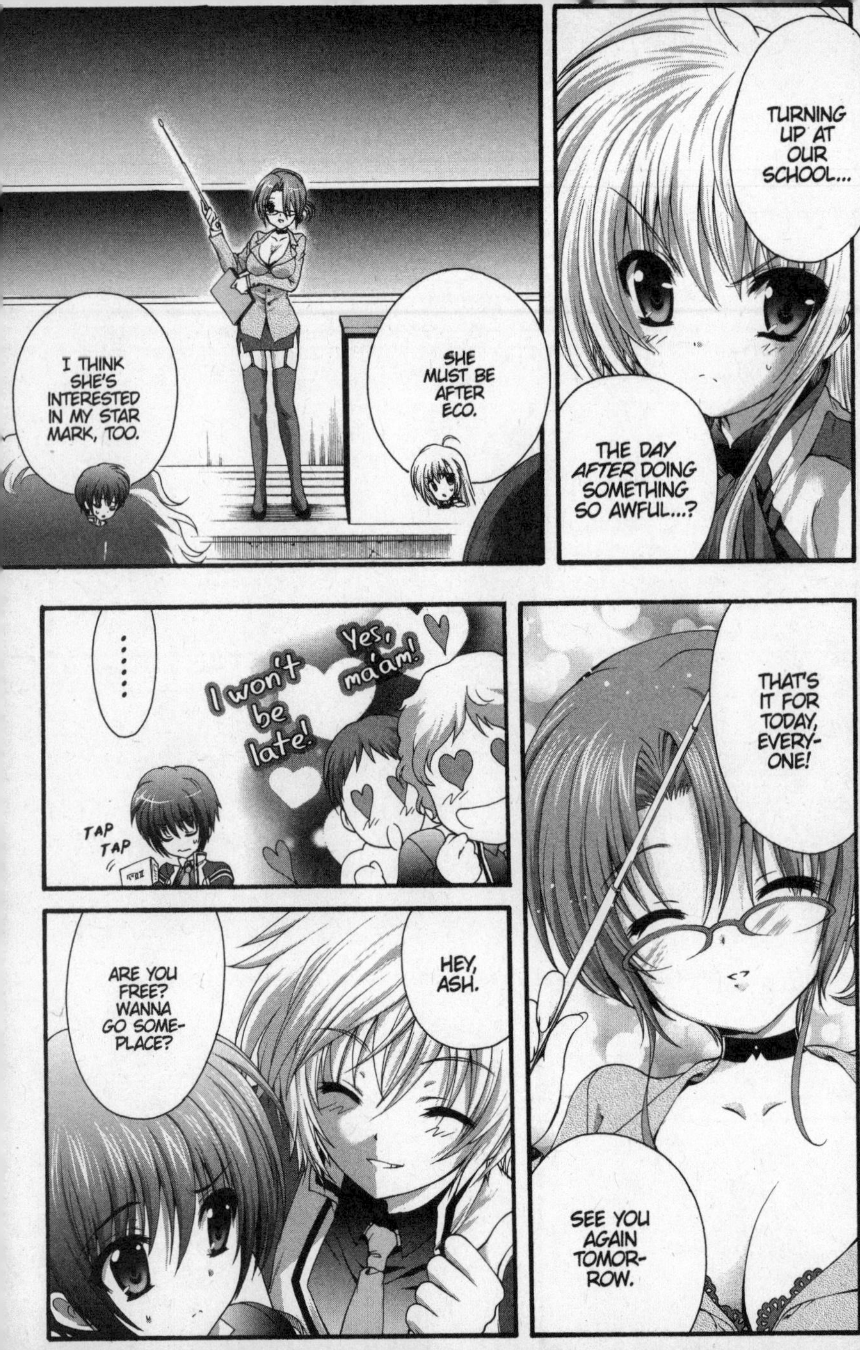
TURNING UP AT OUR SCHOOL...
THE DAY AFTER DOING SOMETHING SO AWFUL...?
SHE MUST BE AFTER ECO.
I THINK SHE'S INTERESTED IN MY STAR MARK, TOO.
THAT'S IT FOR TODAY, EVERY-ONE!
SEE YOU AGAIN TOMOR-ROW.
Yes, ma'am!
I won't be late!
......
TAP TAP
HEY, ASH.
ARE YOU FREE? WANNA GO SOME-PLACE?

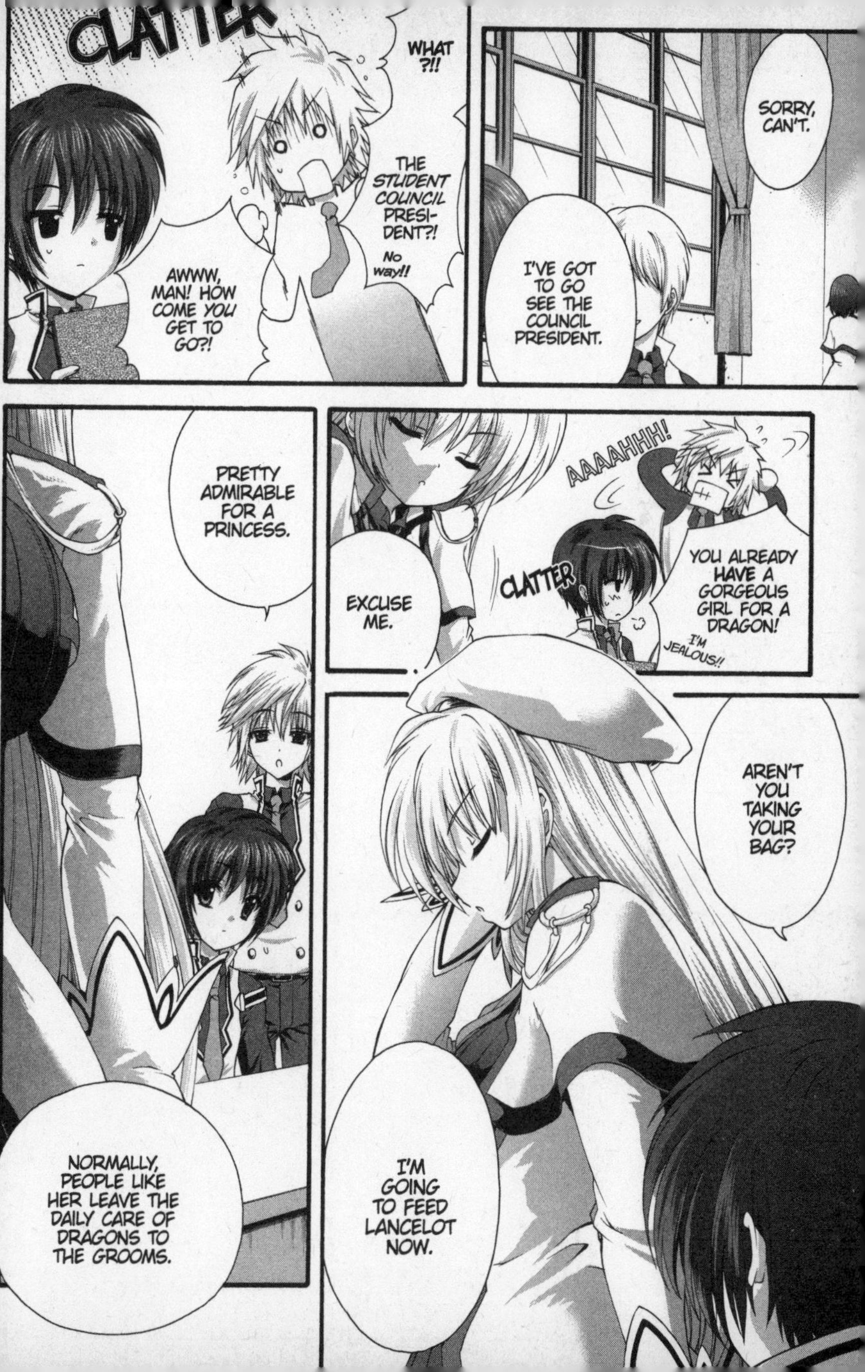
SORRY, CAN'T.
I'VE GOT TO GO SEE THE COUNCIL PRESIDENT.
CLATTER
WHAT?!!
THE STUDENT COUNCIL PRESI-DENT?!
No way!!
AWWW, MAN! HOW COME YOU GET TO GO?!
AAAAHHH!
YOU ALREADY HAVE A GORGEOUS GIRL FOR A DRAGON!
I'M JEALOUS!!
CLATTER
EXCUSE ME.
AREN'T YOU TAKING YOUR BAG?
I'M GOING TO FEED LANCELOT NOW.
PRETTY ADMIRABLE FOR A PRINCESS.
NORMALLY, PEOPLE LIKE HER LEAVE THE DAILY CARE OF DRAGONS TO THE GROOMS.

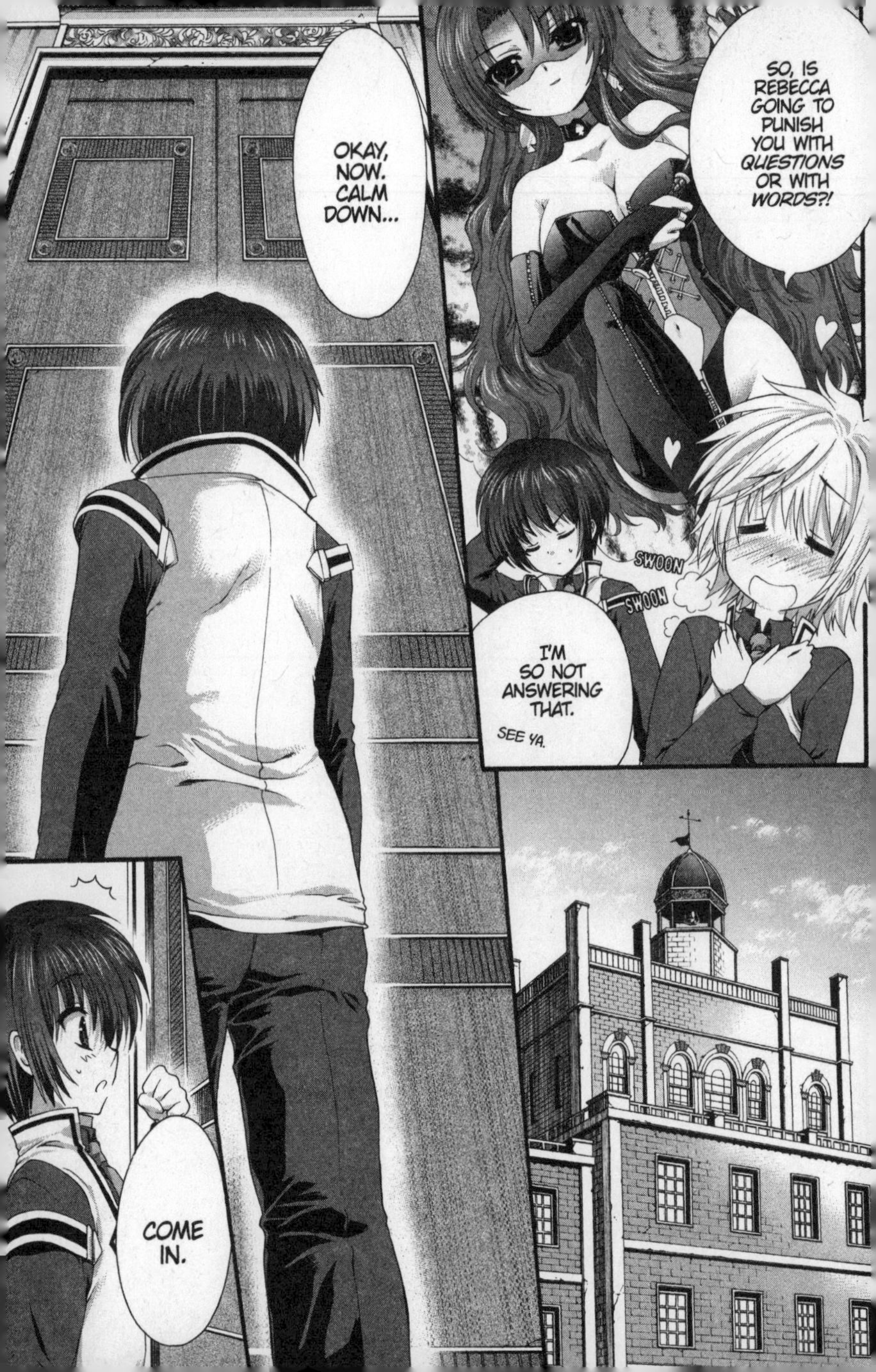
SO, IS REBECCA GOING TO PUNISH YOU WITH QUESTIONS OR WITH WORDS?!
SWOON
SWOON
I'M SO NOT ANSWERING THAT.
SEE YA.
OKAY, NOW. CALM DOWN...
COME IN.

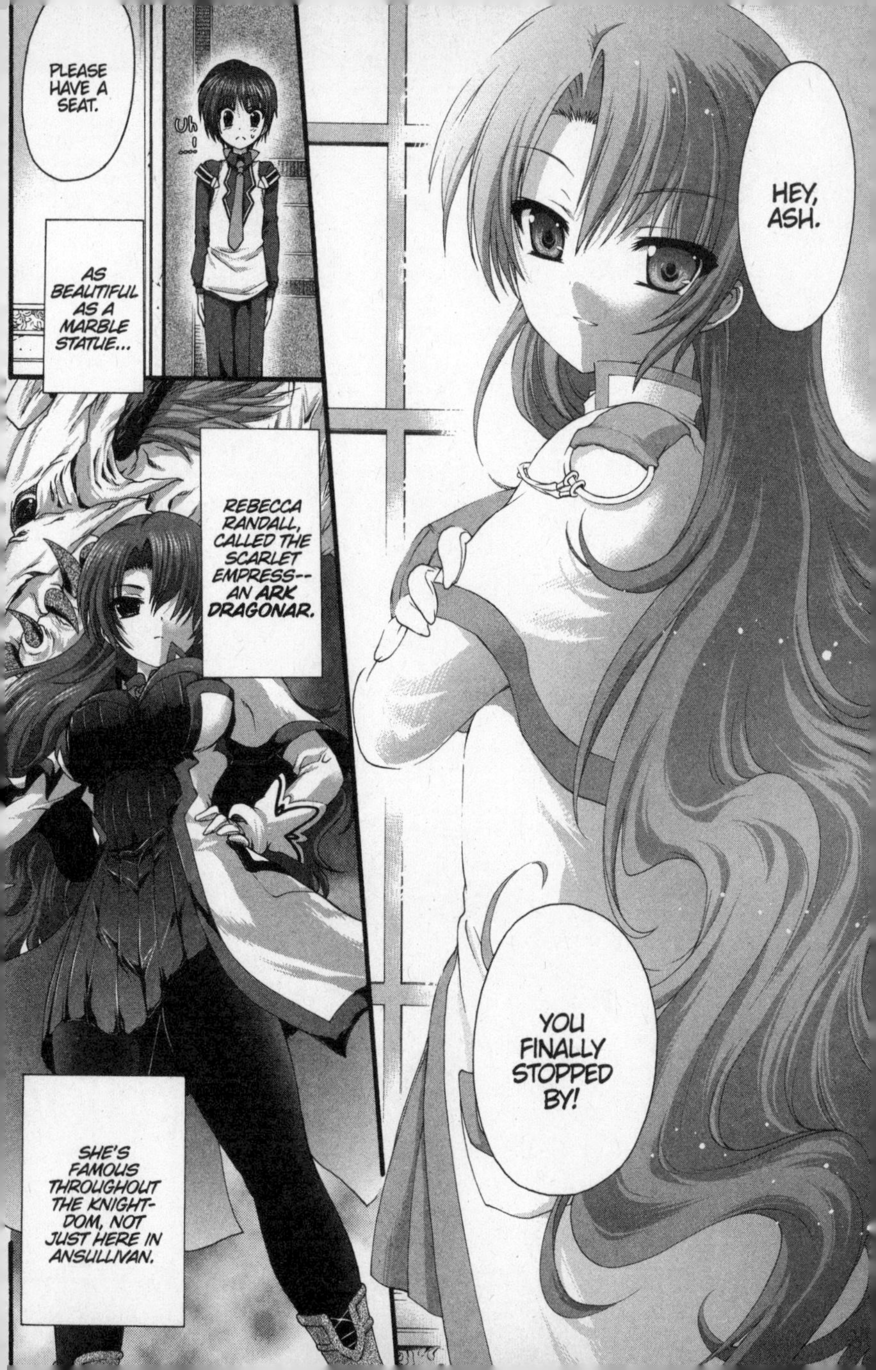
HEY, ASH.
YOU FINALLY STOPPED BY!
PLEASE HAVE A SEAT.
Uh!...
AS BEAUTIFUL AS A MARBLE STATUE...
REBECCA RANDALL, CALLED THE SCARLET EMPRESS-- AN ARK DRAGONAR.
SHE'S FAMOUS THROUGHOUT THE KNIGHT-DOM, NOT JUST HERE IN ANSULLIVAN.

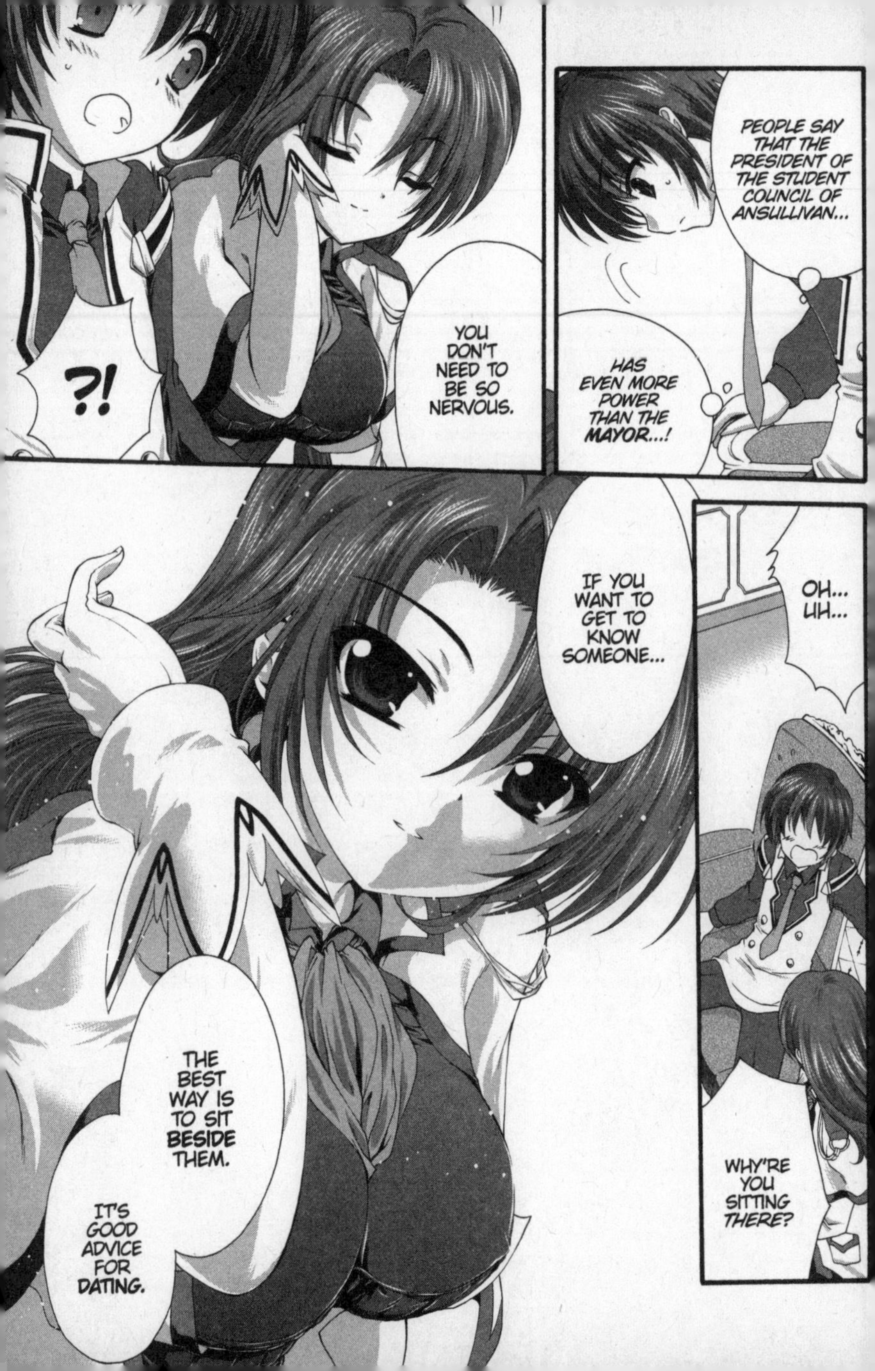
PEOPLE SAY THAT THE PRESIDENT OF THE STUDENT COUNCIL OF ANSULLIVAN...
HAS EVEN MORE POWER THAN THE MAYOR...!
YOU DON'T NEED TO BE SO NERVOUS.
?!
OH... UH...
WHY'RE YOU SITTING THERE?
IF YOU WANT TO GET TO KNOW SOMEONE...
THE BEST WAY IS TO SIT BESIDE THEM.
IT'S GOOD ADVICE FOR DATING.

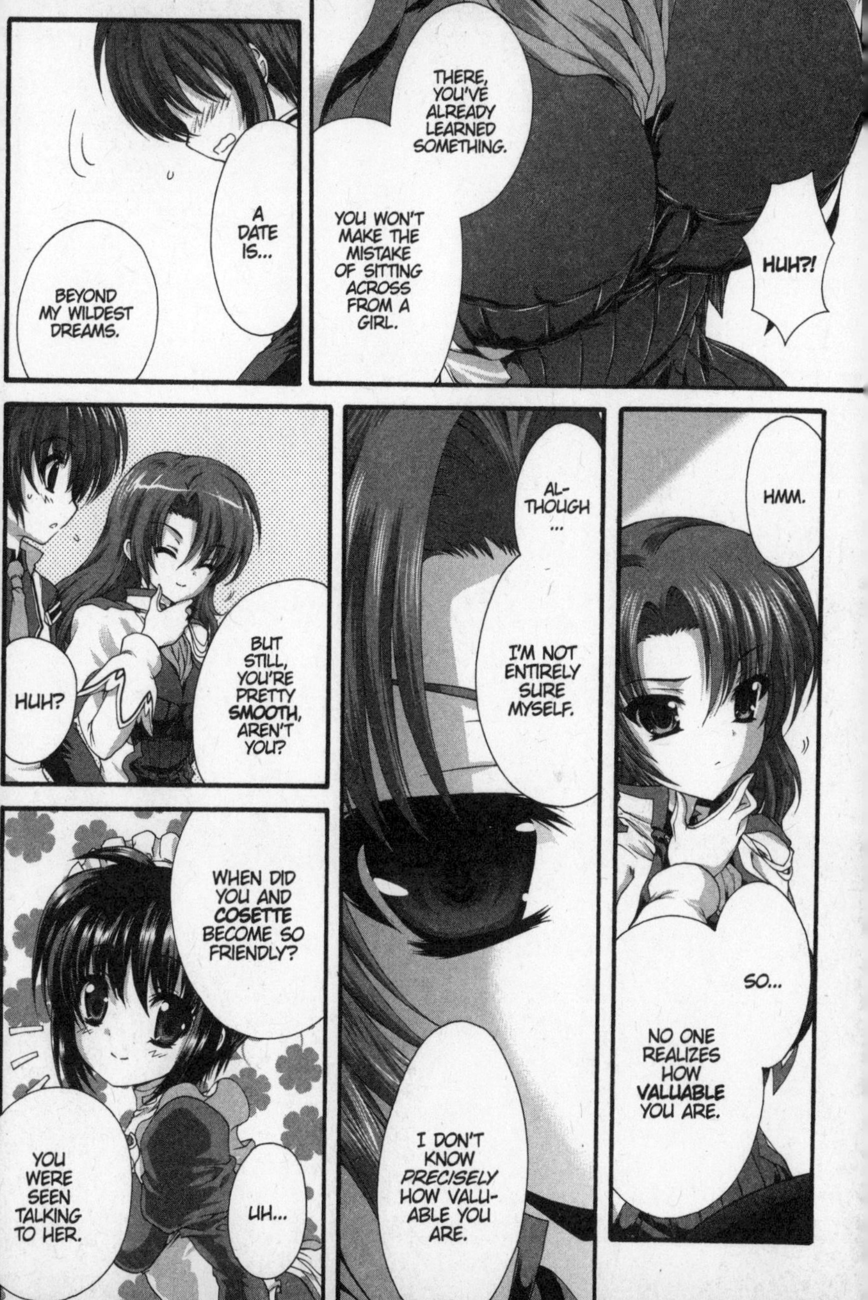

THERE, YOU'VE ALREADY LEARNED SOMETHING.
YOU WON'T MAKE THE MISTAKE OF SITTING ACROSS FROM A GIRL.
HUH?!
A DATE IS...
BEYOND MY WILDEST DREAMS.
HMM.
SO...
NO ONE REALIZES HOW **VALUABLE** YOU ARE.
AL-THOUGH...
I'M NOT ENTIRELY SURE MYSELF.
I DON'T KNOW *PRECISELY* HOW VALU-ABLE YOU ARE.
BUT STILL, YOU'RE PRETTY **SMOOTH**, AREN'T YOU?
HUH?
WHEN DID YOU AND **COSETTE** BECOME SO FRIENDLY?
UH...
YOU WERE SEEN TALKING TO HER.

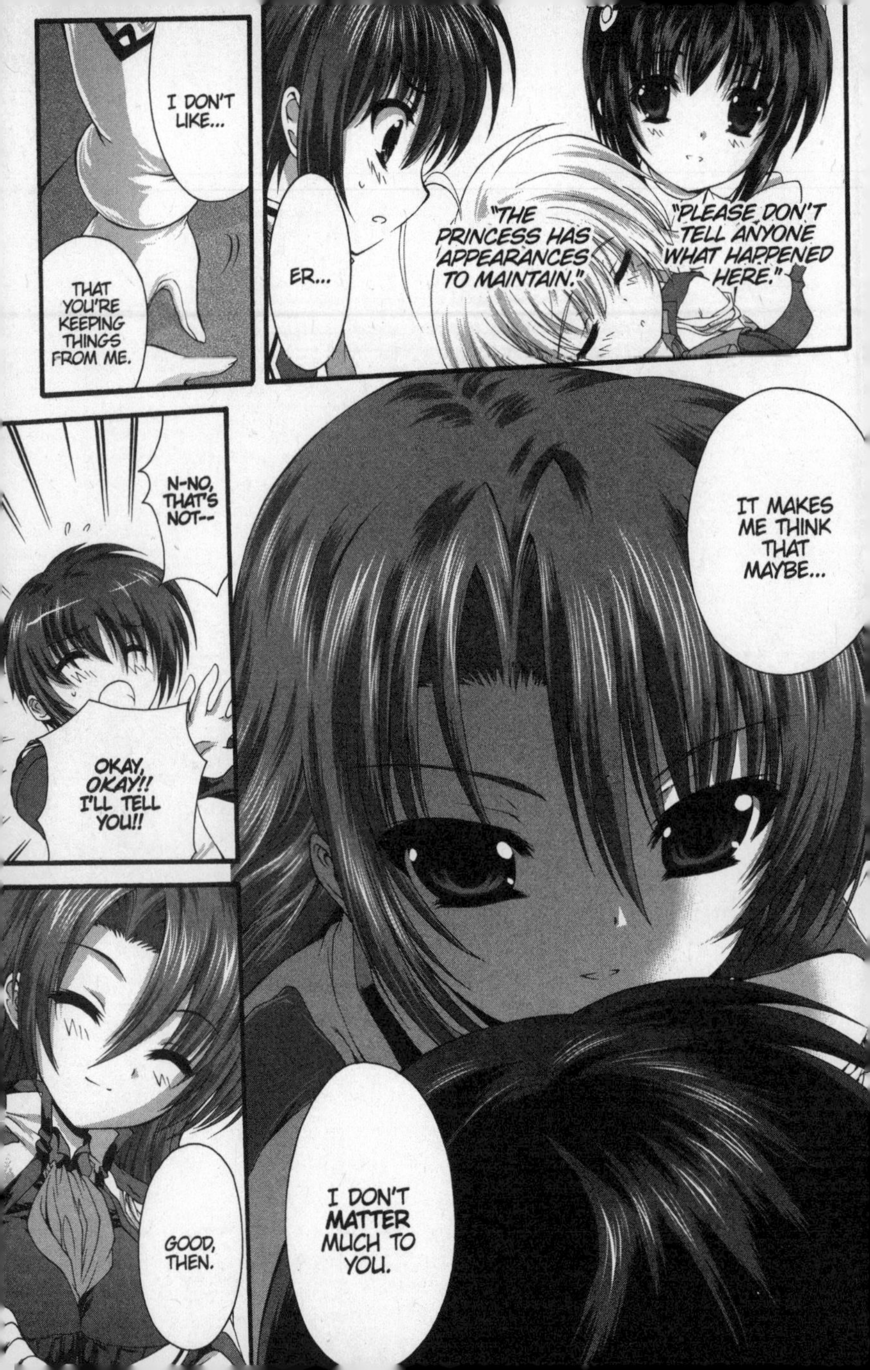
"PLEASE DON'T TELL ANYONE WHAT HAPPENED HERE."
"THE PRINCESS HAS APPEARANCES TO MAINTAIN."
ER...
I DON'T LIKE...
THAT YOU'RE KEEPING THINGS FROM ME.
IT MAKES ME THINK THAT MAYBE...
I DON'T MATTER MUCH TO YOU.
N-NO, THAT'S NOT--
OKAY, OKAY!! I'LL TELL YOU!!
GOOD, THEN.

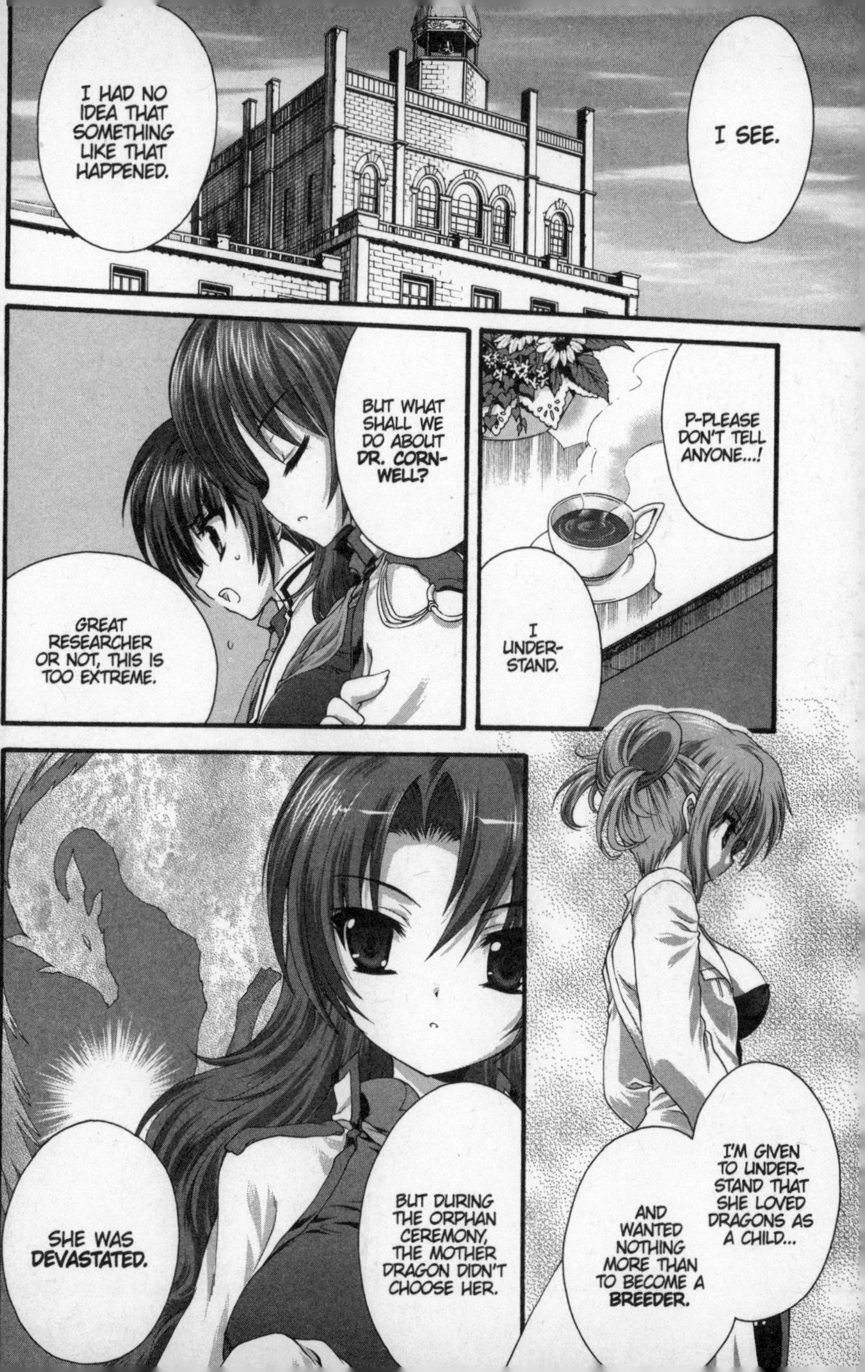
I SEE.
I HAD NO IDEA THAT SOMETHING LIKE THAT HAPPENED.
P-PLEASE DON'T TELL ANYONE...!
I UNDER-STAND.
BUT WHAT SHALL WE DO ABOUT DR. CORN-WELL?
GREAT RESEARCHER OR NOT, THIS IS TOO EXTREME.
I'M GIVEN TO UNDER-STAND THAT SHE LOVED DRAGONS AS A CHILD...
AND WANTED NOTHING MORE THAN TO BECOME A **BREEDER.**
BUT DURING THE ORPHAN CEREMONY, THE MOTHER DRAGON DIDN'T CHOOSE HER.
SHE WAS **DEVASTATED.**

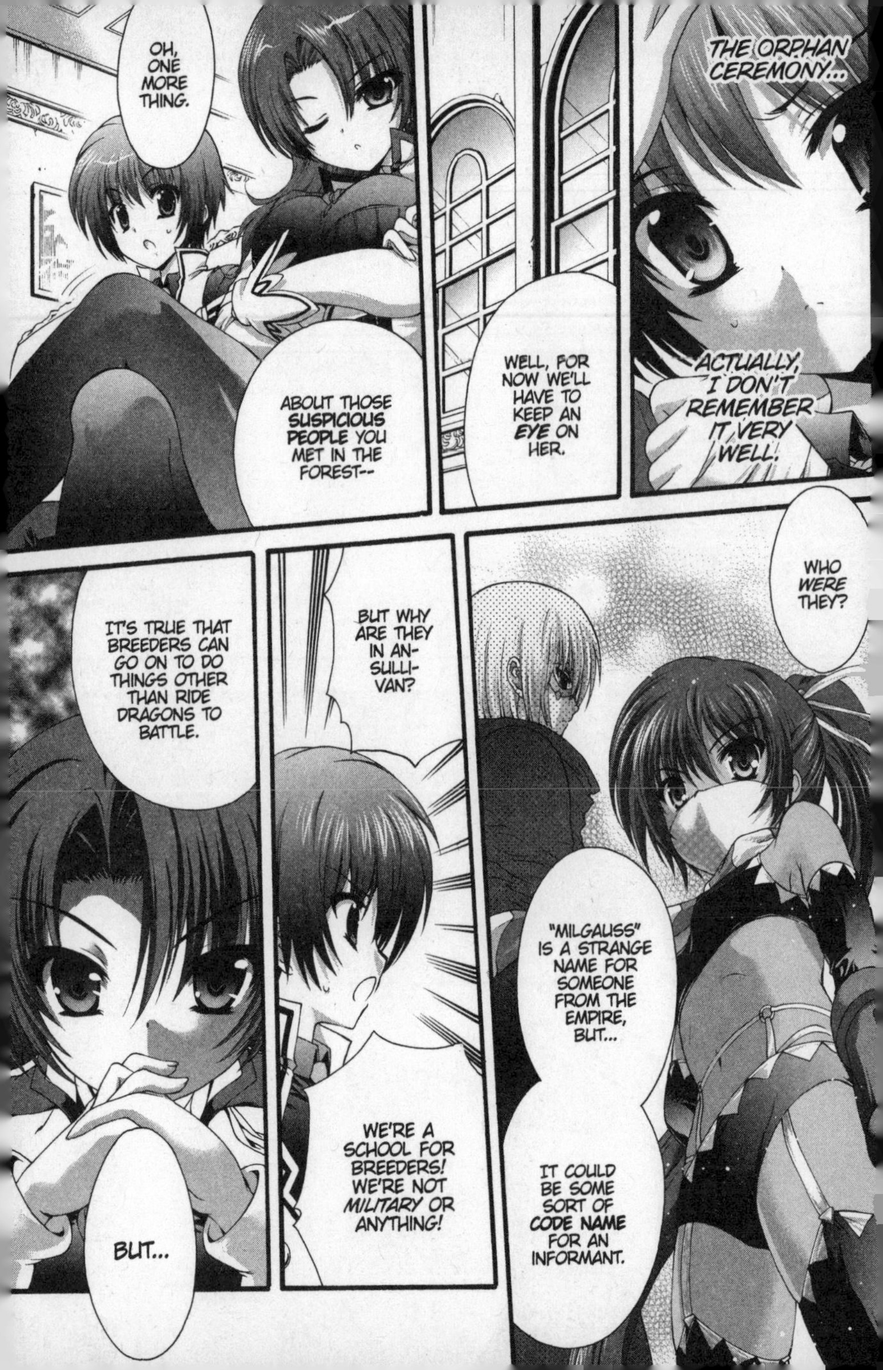
THE ORPHAN CEREMONY...
ACTUALLY, I DON'T REMEMBER IT VERY WELL.
WELL, FOR NOW WE'LL HAVE TO KEEP AN EYE ON HER.
OH, ONE MORE THING.
ABOUT THOSE SUSPICIOUS PEOPLE YOU MET IN THE FOREST--
WHO WERE THEY?
"MILGAUSS" IS A STRANGE NAME FOR SOMEONE FROM THE EMPIRE, BUT...
IT COULD BE SOME SORT OF CODE NAME FOR AN INFORMANT.
BUT WHY ARE THEY IN AN-SULLI-VAN?
WE'RE A SCHOOL FOR BREEDERS! WE'RE NOT MILITARY OR ANYTHING!
IT'S TRUE THAT BREEDERS CAN GO ON TO DO THINGS OTHER THAN RIDE DRAGONS TO BATTLE.
BUT...

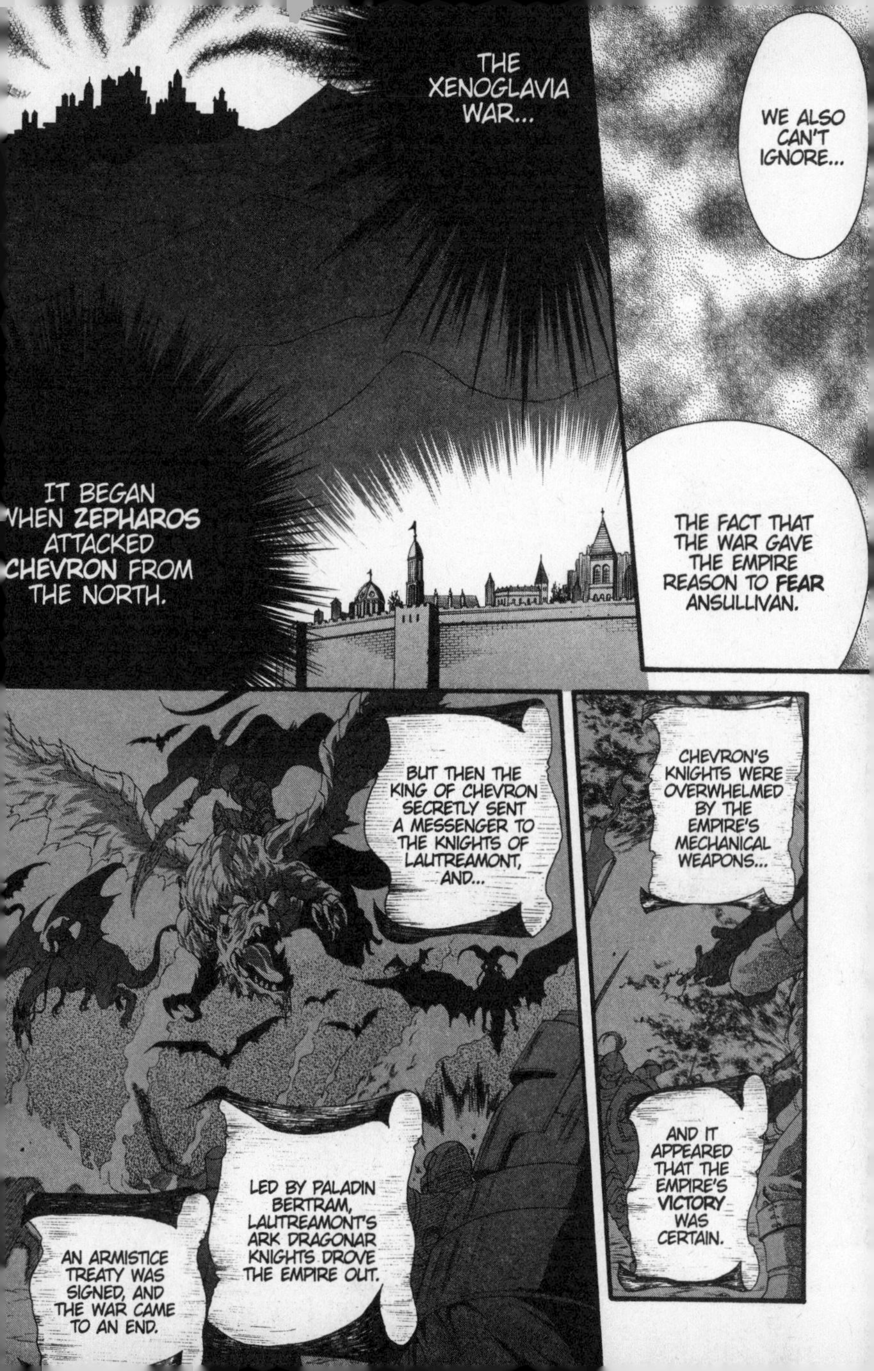
WE ALSO CAN'T IGNORE...
THE FACT THAT THE WAR GAVE THE EMPIRE REASON TO FEAR ANSULLIVAN.
THE XENOGLAVIA WAR...
IT BEGAN WHEN ZEPHAROS ATTACKED CHEVRON FROM THE NORTH.
CHEVRON'S KNIGHTS WERE OVERWHELMED BY THE EMPIRE'S MECHANICAL WEAPONS...
AND IT APPEARED THAT THE EMPIRE'S VICTORY WAS CERTAIN.
BUT THEN THE KING OF CHEVRON SECRETLY SENT A MESSENGER TO THE KNIGHTS OF LAUTREAMONT, AND...
LED BY PALADIN BERTRAM, LAUTREAMONT'S ARK DRAGONAR KNIGHTS DROVE THE EMPIRE OUT.
AN ARMISTICE TREATY WAS SIGNED, AND THE WAR CAME TO AN END.

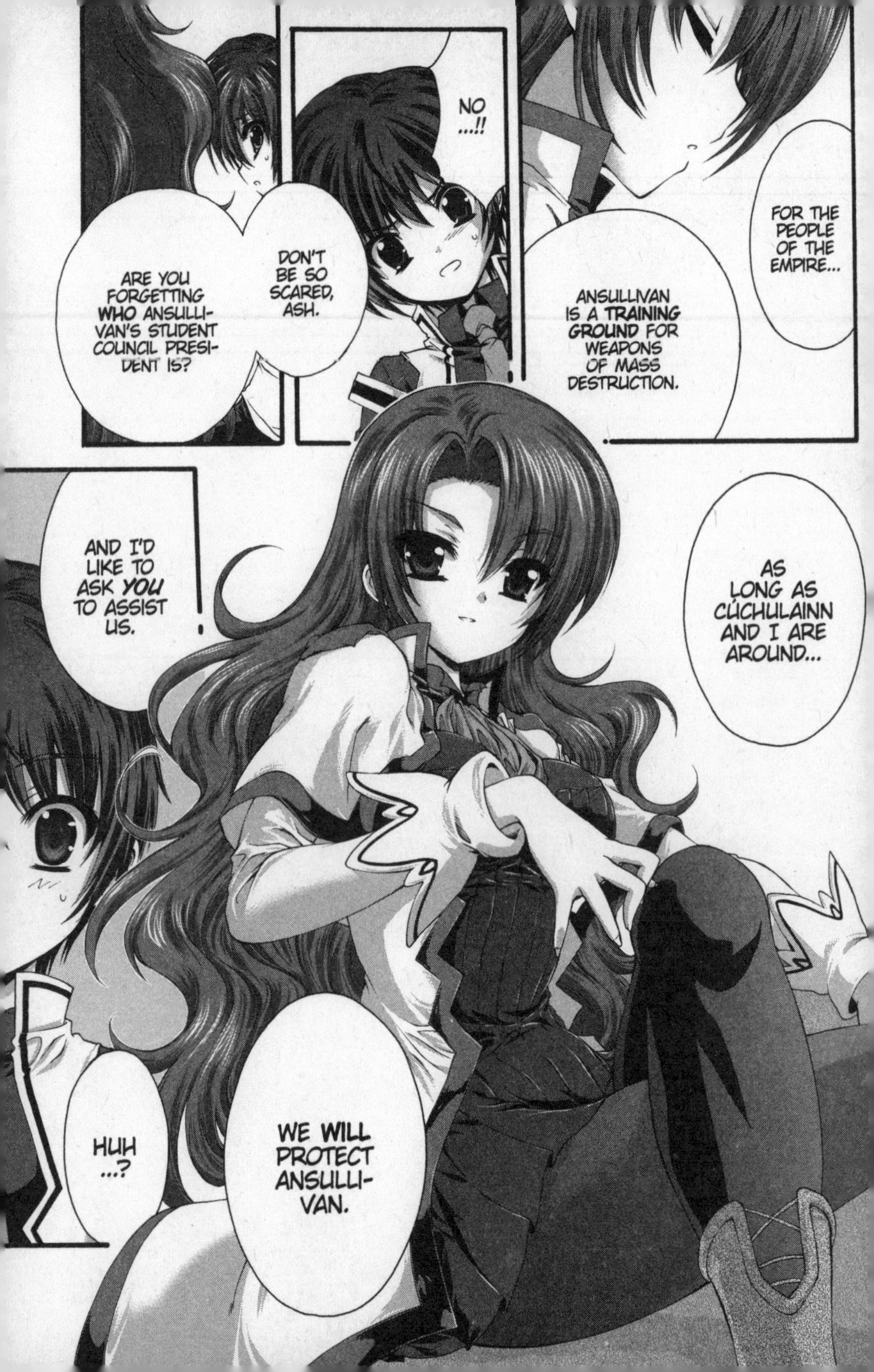
FOR THE PEOPLE OF THE EMPIRE...
ANSULLIVAN IS A TRAINING GROUND FOR WEAPONS OF MASS DESTRUCTION.
NO ...!!
DON'T BE SO SCARED, ASH.
ARE YOU FORGETTING WHO ANSULLI-VAN'S STUDENT COUNCIL PRESI-DENT IS?
AS LONG AS CÚCHULAINN AND I ARE AROUND...
WE WILL PROTECT ANSULLI-VAN.
AND I'D LIKE TO ASK YOU TO ASSIST US.
HUH ...?

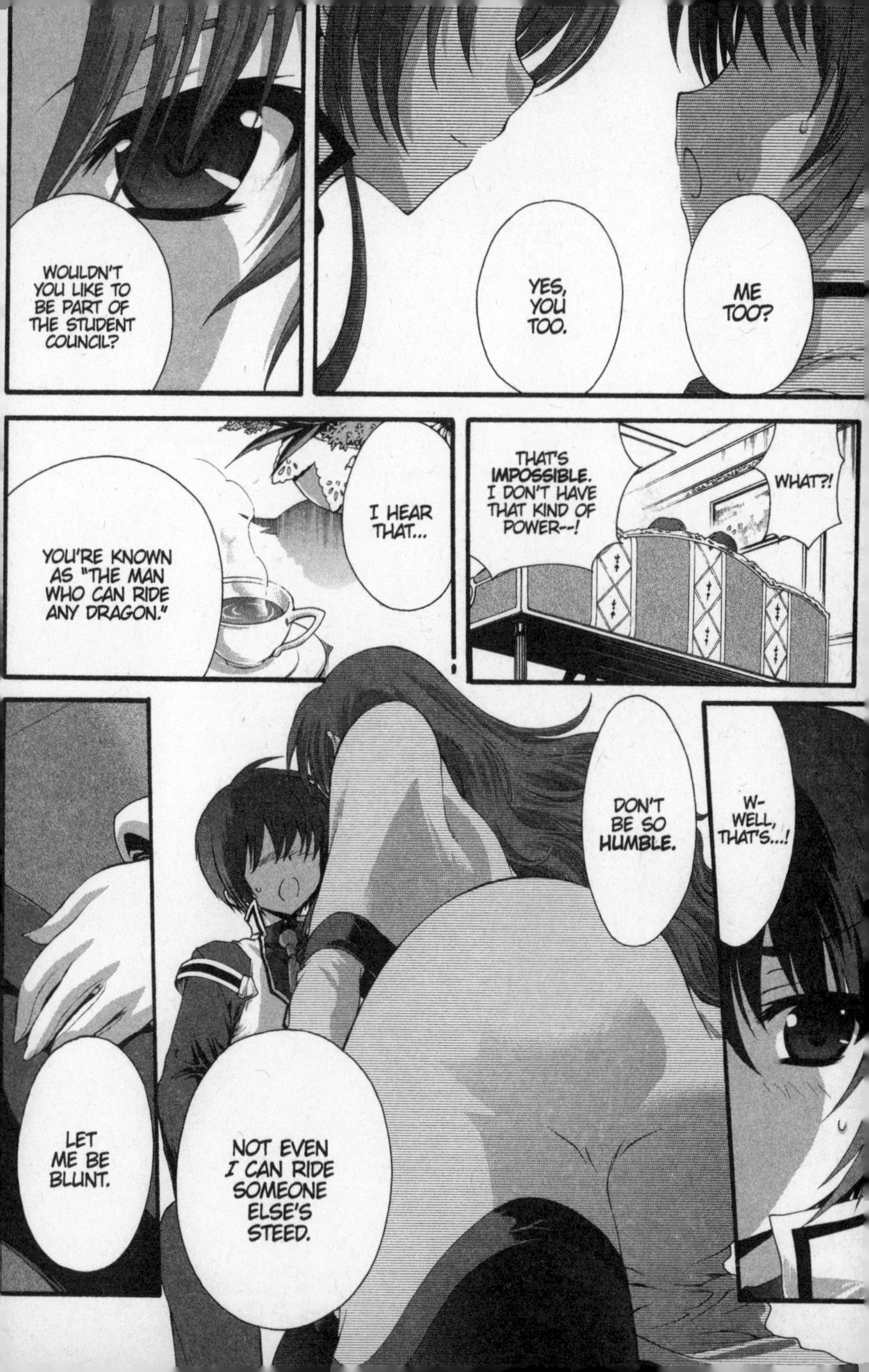
WOULDN'T YOU LIKE TO BE PART OF THE STUDENT COUNCIL?
ME TOO?
YES, YOU TOO.
I HEAR THAT...
YOU'RE KNOWN AS "THE MAN WHO CAN RIDE ANY DRAGON."
WHAT?!
THAT'S IMPOSSIBLE. I DON'T HAVE THAT KIND OF POWER--!
DON'T BE SO HUMBLE.
W-WELL, THAT'S...!
LET ME BE BLUNT.
NOT EVEN I CAN RIDE SOMEONE ELSE'S STEED.

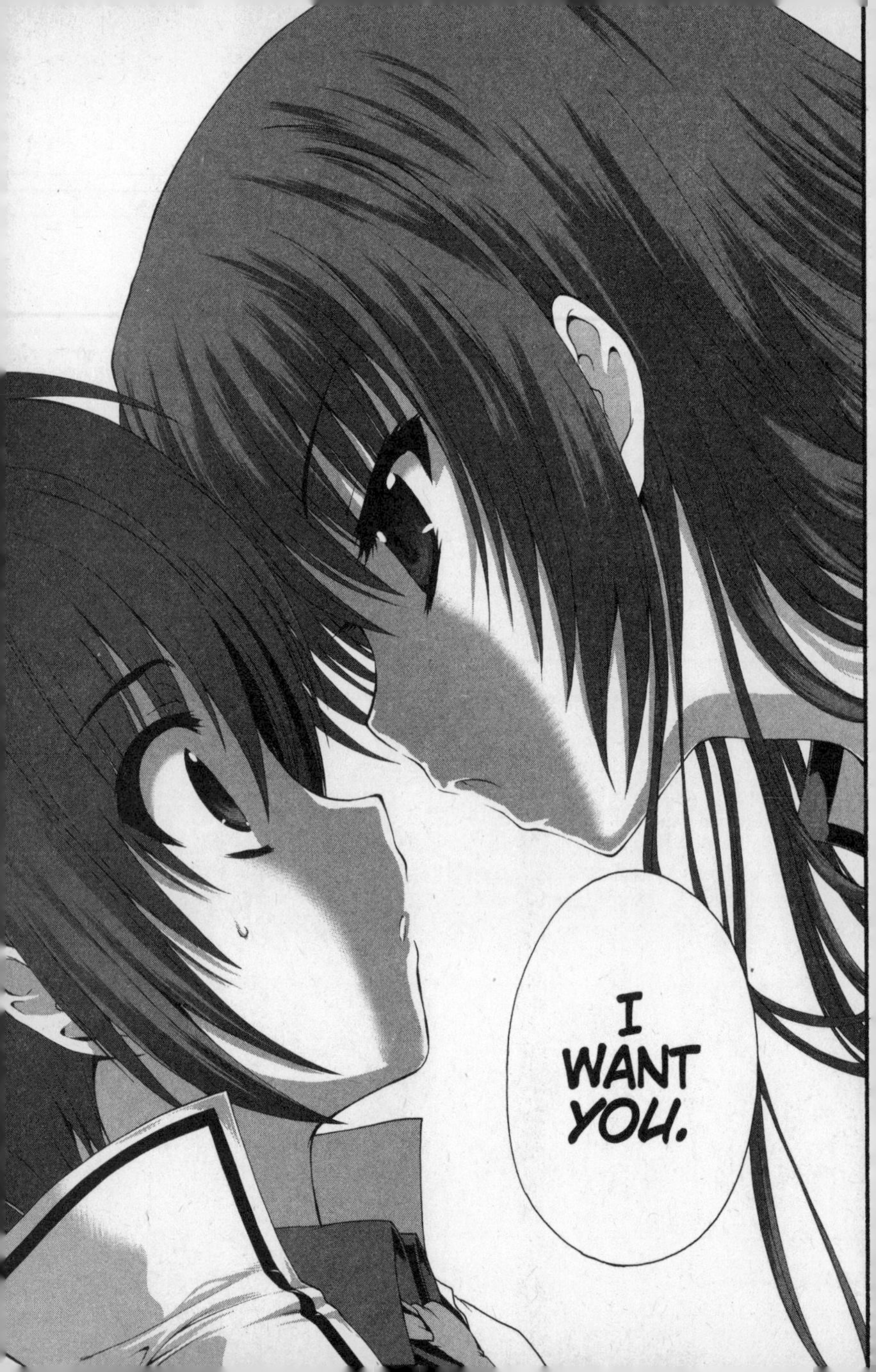
I WANT YOU.

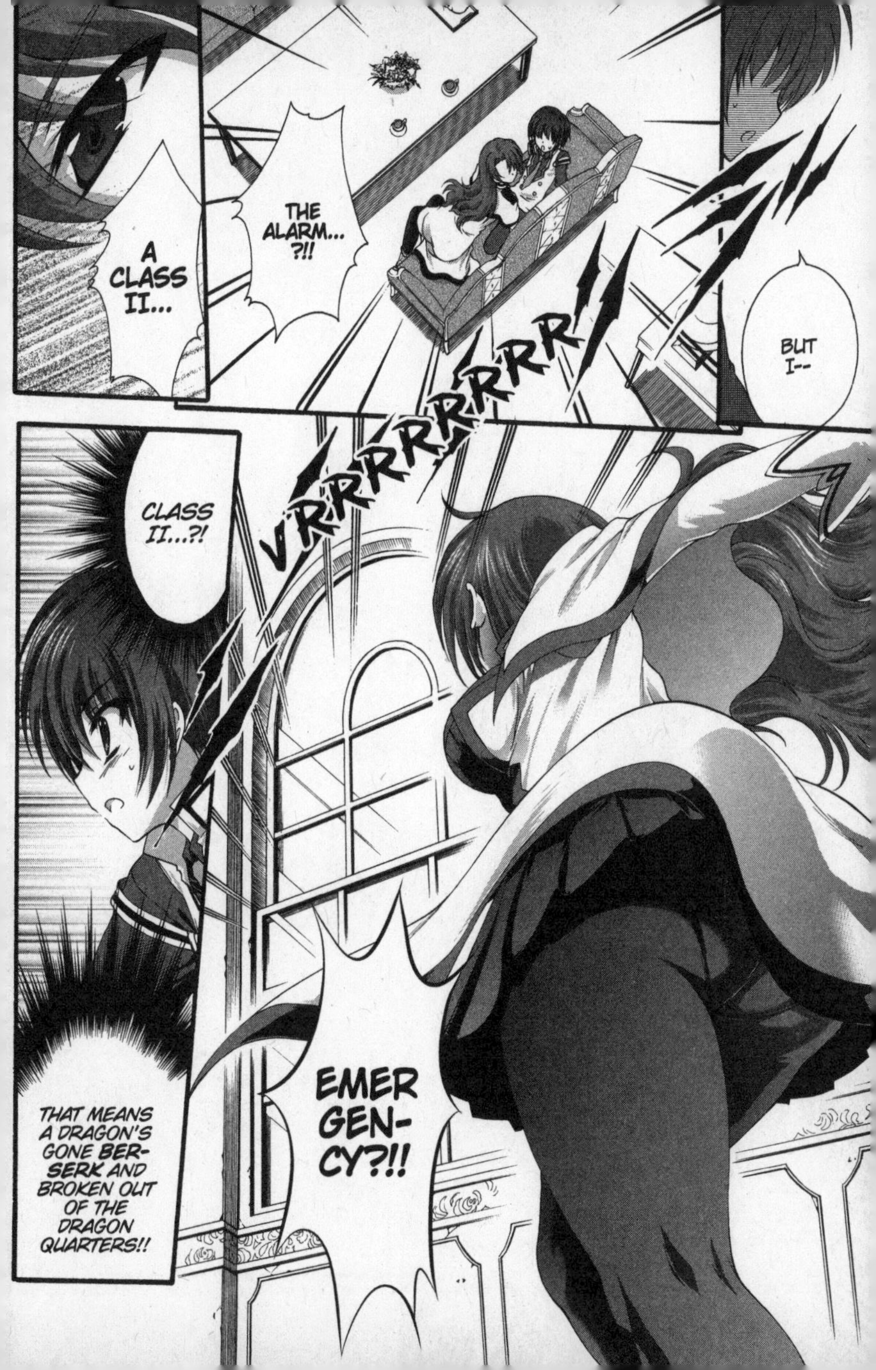
BUT I--
VRRRRRRRRR
THE ALARM...?!!
A CLASS II...
EMERGENCY?!!
CLASS II...?!
THAT MEANS A DRAGON'S GONE BERSERK AND BROKEN OUT OF THE DRAGON QUARTERS!!

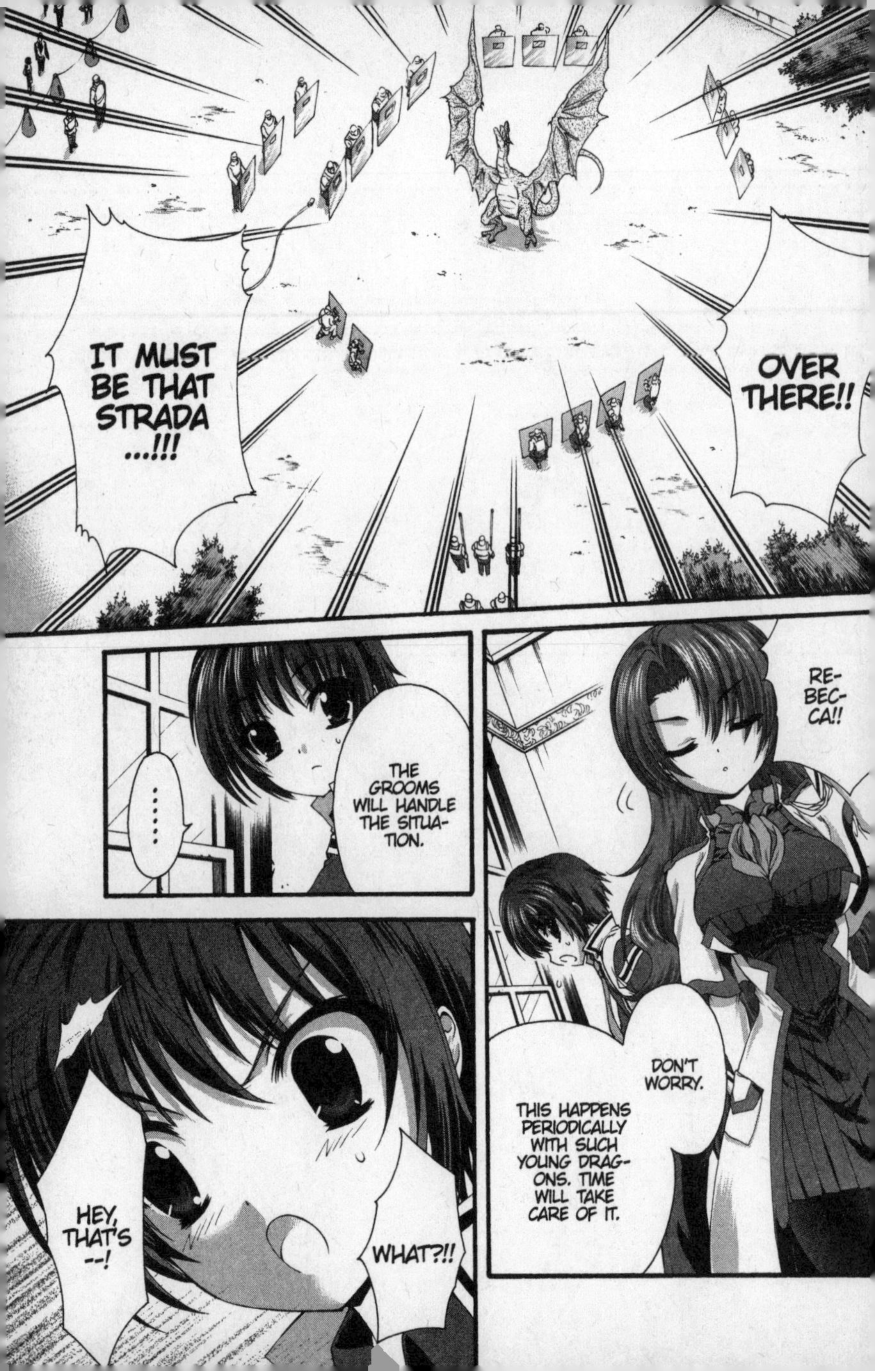
OVER THERE!!
IT MUST BE THAT STRADA ...!!!
RE-BEC-CA!!
DON'T WORRY.
THIS HAPPENS PERIODICALLY WITH SUCH YOUNG DRAG-ONS. TIME WILL TAKE CARE OF IT.
THE GROOMS WILL HANDLE THE SITUA-TION.
......
WHAT?!!
HEY, THAT'S --!

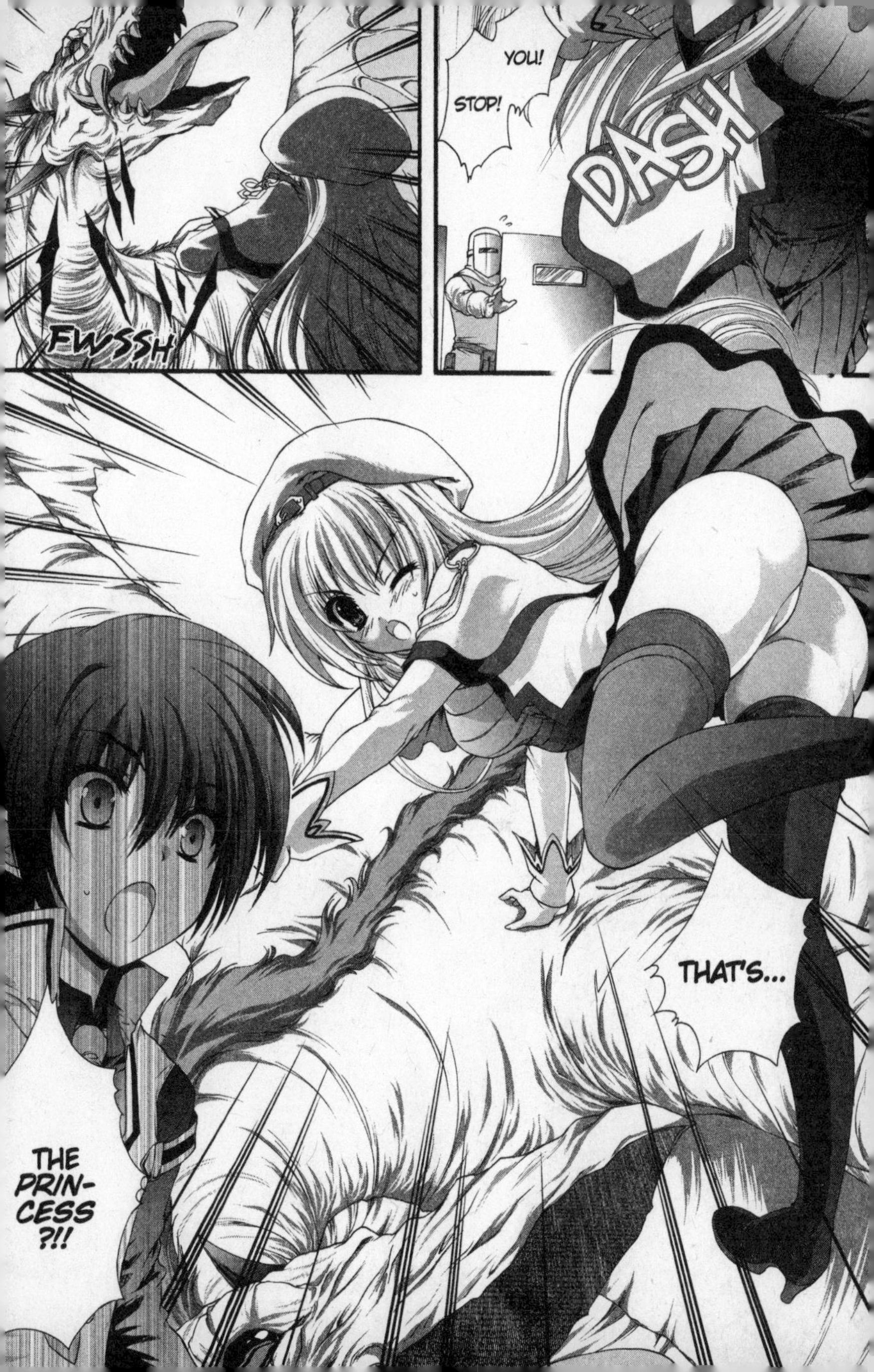
YOU!
STOP!
DASH
FWSSH
THAT'S...
THE PRIN-CESS?!!

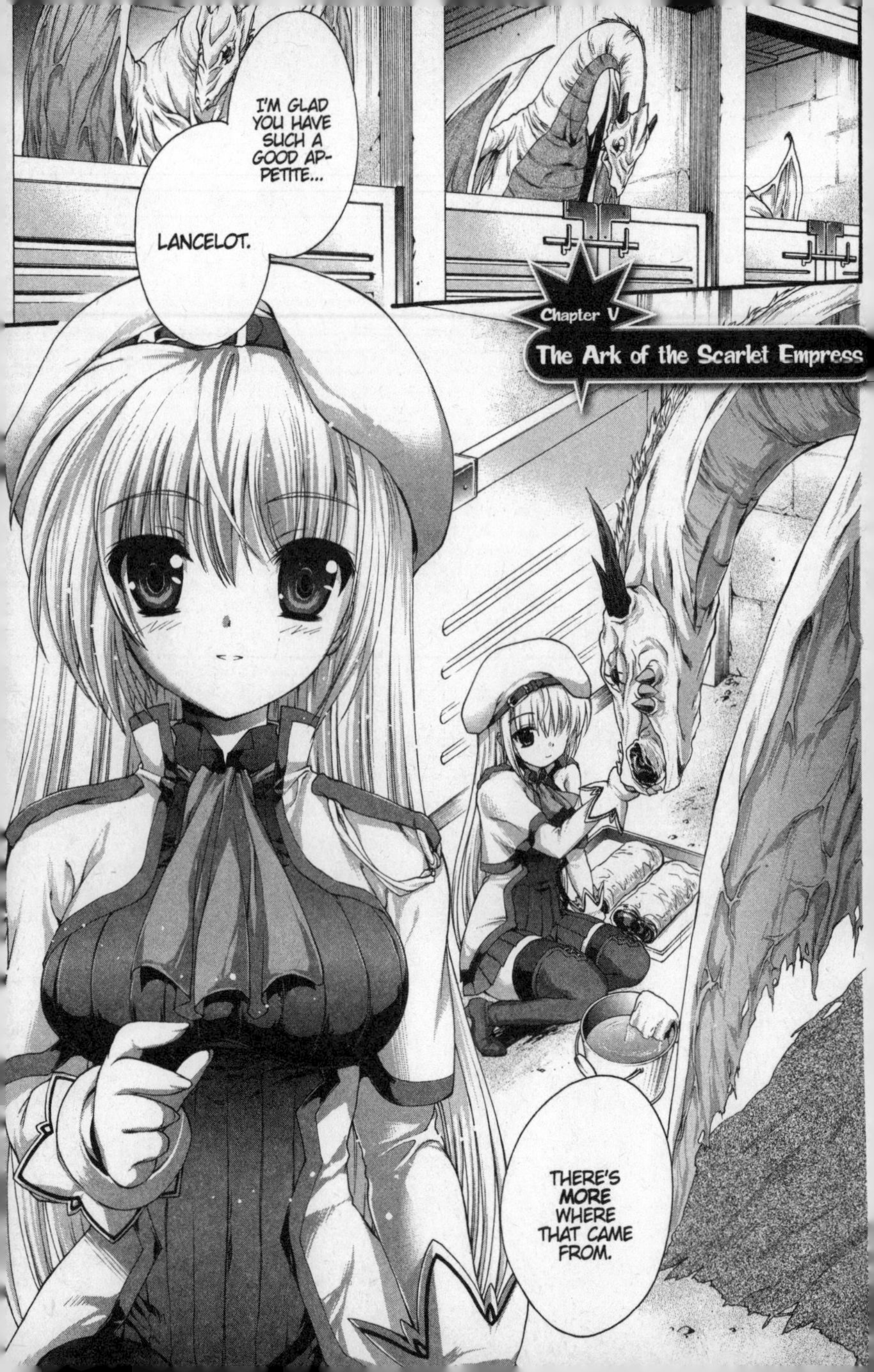
I'M GLAD YOU HAVE SUCH A GOOD AP-PETITE... LANCELOT.
Chapter V
The Ark of the Scarlet Empress
THERE'S MORE WHERE THAT CAME FROM.

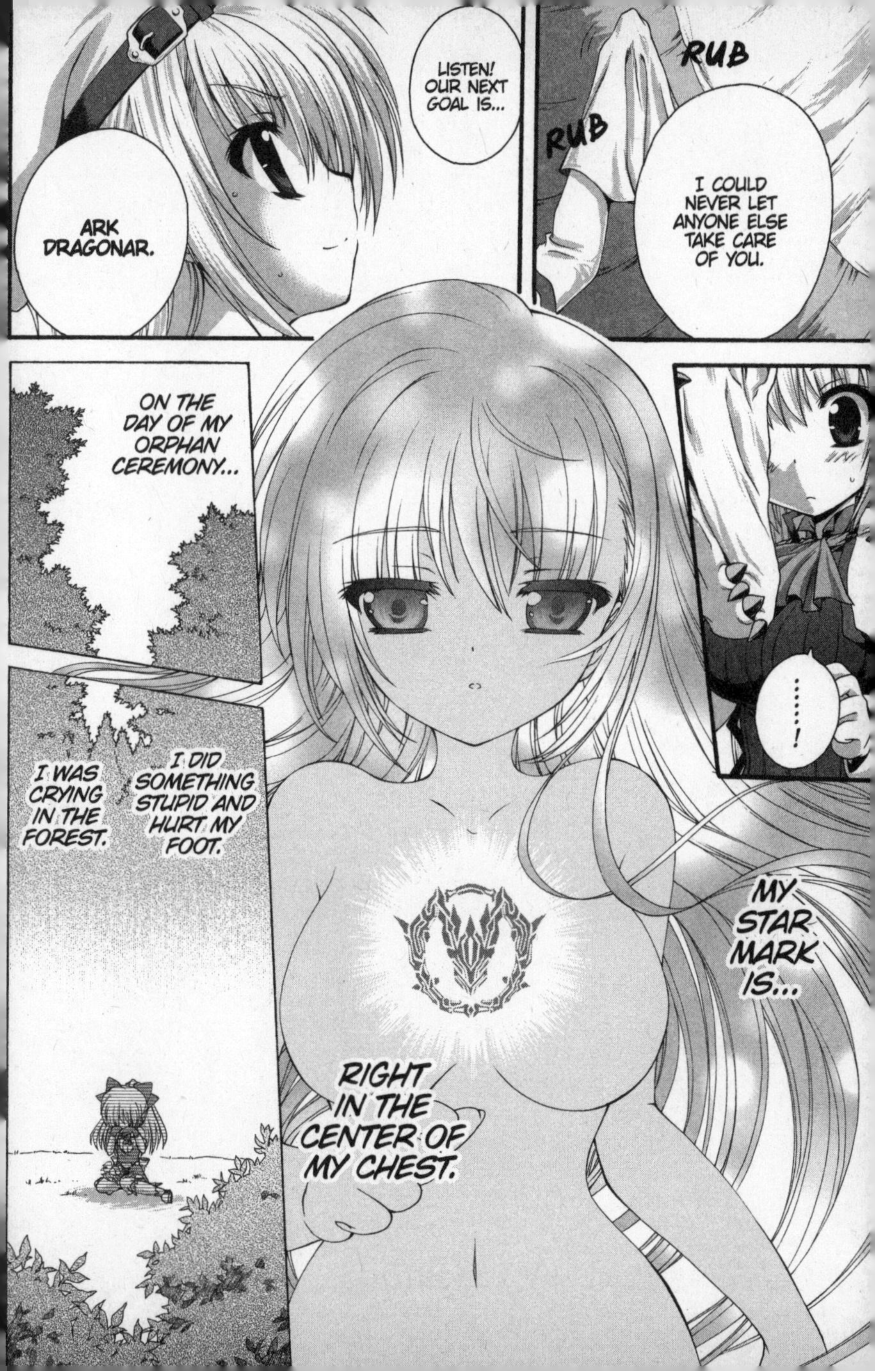
RUB
RUB
I COULD NEVER LET ANYONE ELSE TAKE CARE OF YOU.
LISTEN! OUR NEXT GOAL IS...
ARK DRAGONAR.
......!
MY STAR MARK IS...
RIGHT IN THE CENTER OF MY CHEST.
ON THE DAY OF MY ORPHAN CEREMONY...
I DID SOMETHING STUPID AND HURT MY FOOT.
I WAS CRYING IN THE FOREST.

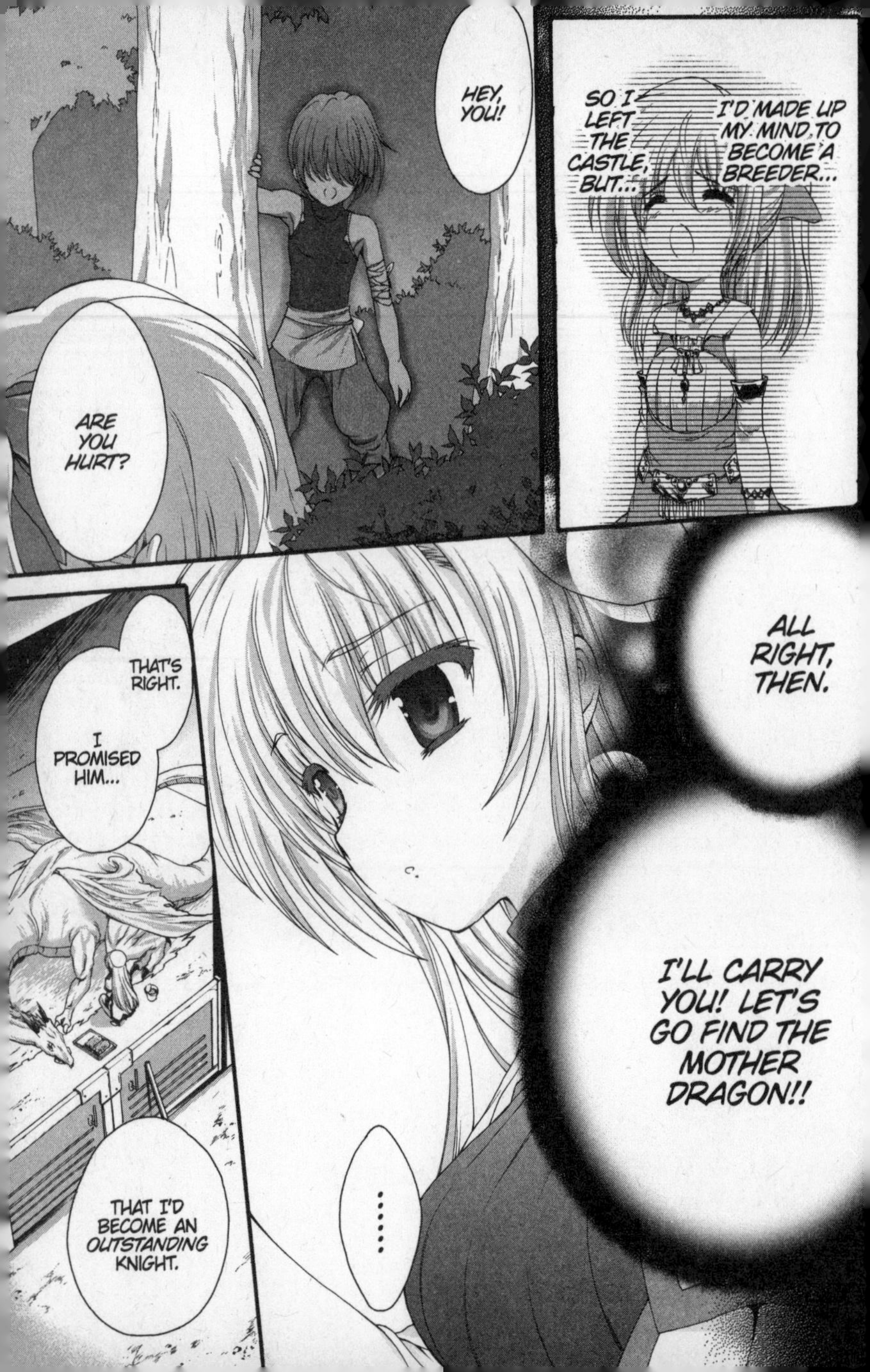
I'D MADE UP MY MIND TO BECOME A BREEDER...
SO I LEFT THE CASTLE, BUT...
HEY, YOU!
ARE YOU HURT?
ALL RIGHT, THEN.
I'LL CARRY YOU! LET'S GO FIND THE MOTHER DRAGON!!
......
THAT'S RIGHT.
I PROMISED HIM...
THAT I'D BECOME AN OUTSTANDING KNIGHT.

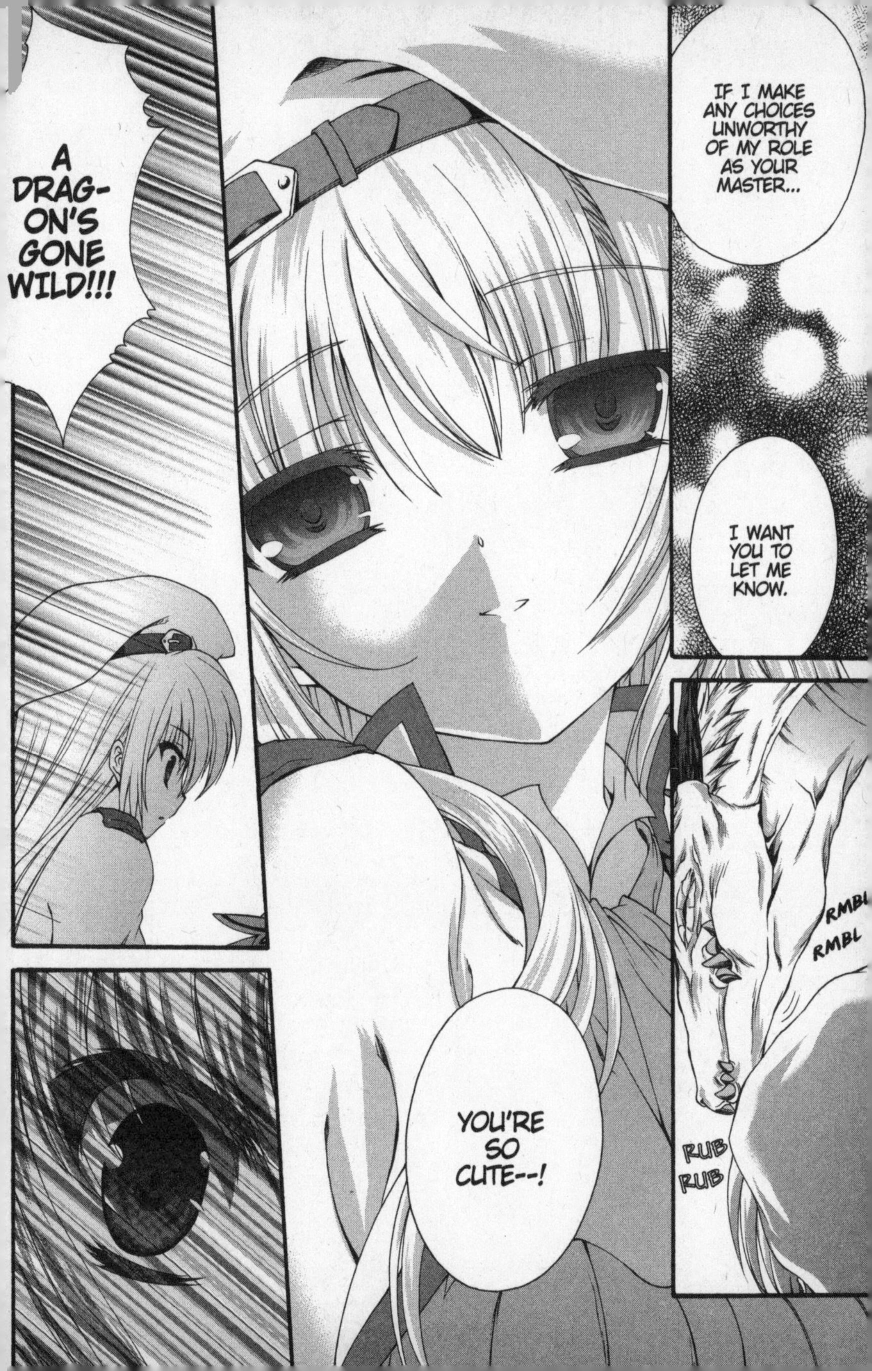
IF I MAKE ANY CHOICES UNWORTHY OF MY ROLE AS YOUR MASTER...
I WANT YOU TO LET ME KNOW.
RMBL
RMBL
RUB
RUB
YOU'RE SO CUTE--!
A DRAG-ON'S GONE WILD!!!

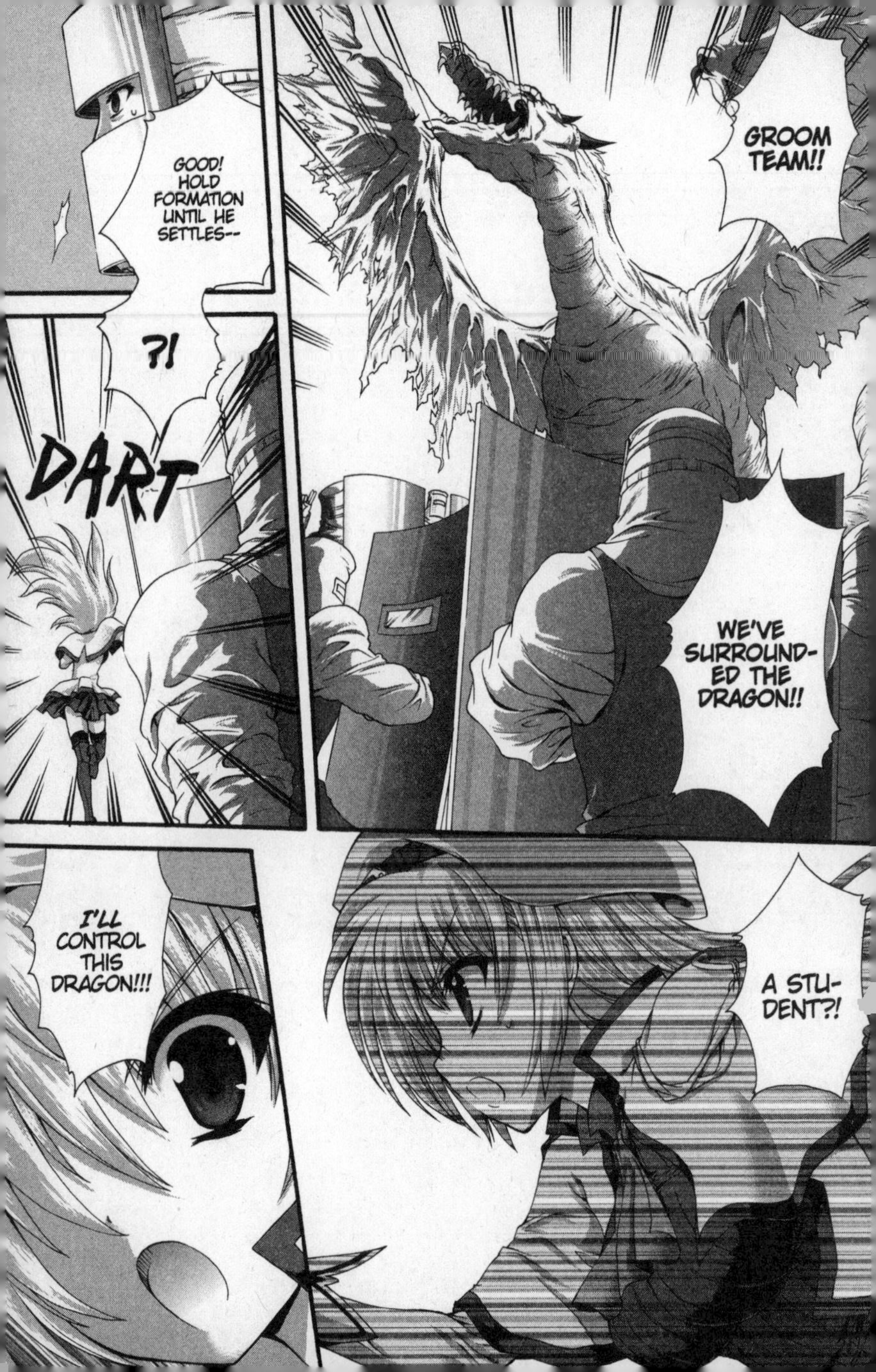
GROOM TEAM!!
WE'VE SURROUND-ED THE DRAGON!!
GOOD! HOLD FORMATION UNTIL HE SETTLES--
?!
DART
A STU-DENT?!
I'LL CONTROL THIS DRAGON!!!

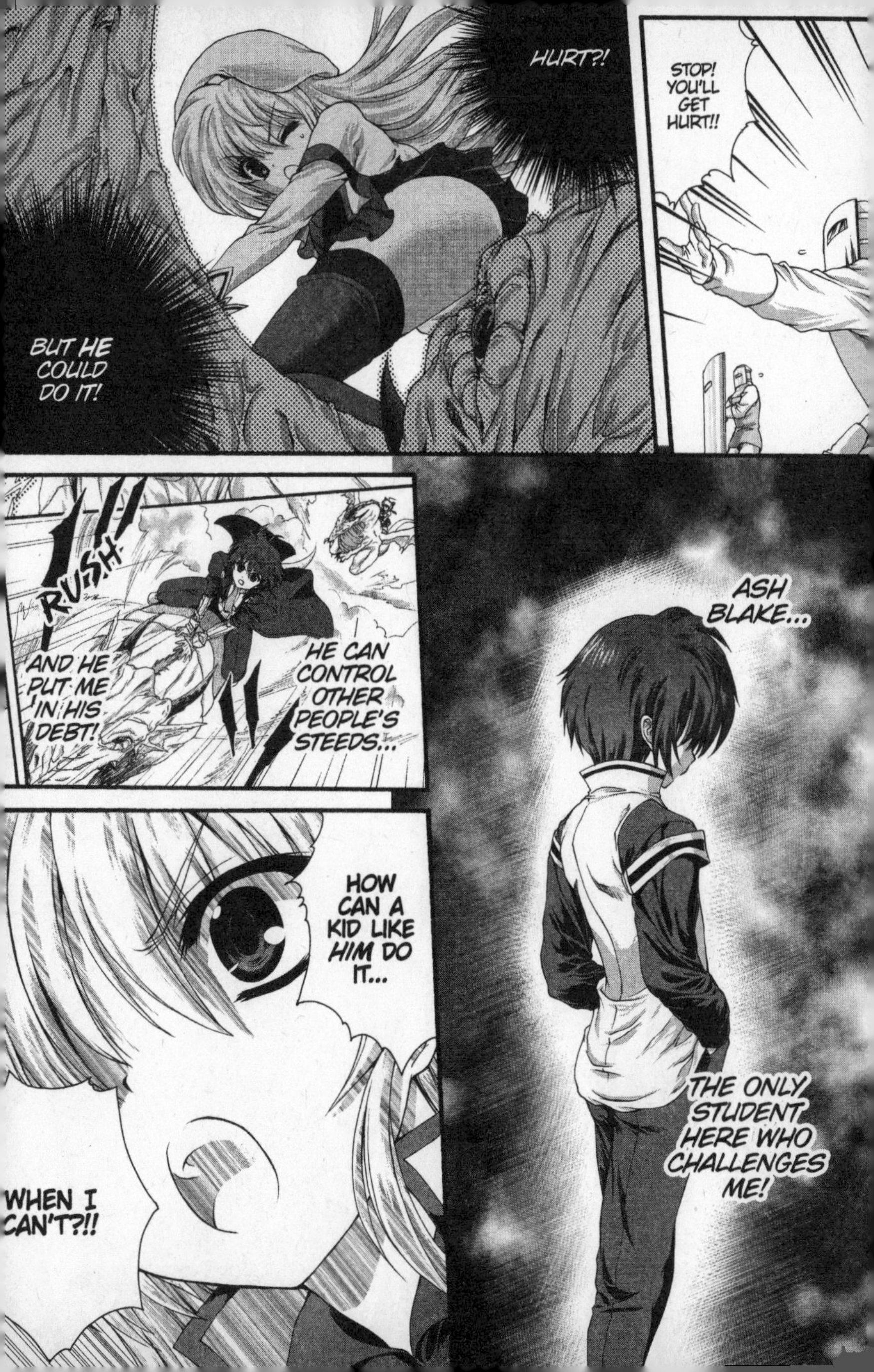
STOP! YOU'LL GET HURT!!
HURT?!
BUT HE COULD DO IT!
ASH BLAKE...
THE ONLY STUDENT HERE WHO CHALLENGES ME!
RUSH
HE CAN CONTROL OTHER PEOPLE'S STEEDS...
AND HE PUT ME IN HIS DEBT!
HOW CAN A KID LIKE HIM DO IT...
WHEN I CAN'T?!!

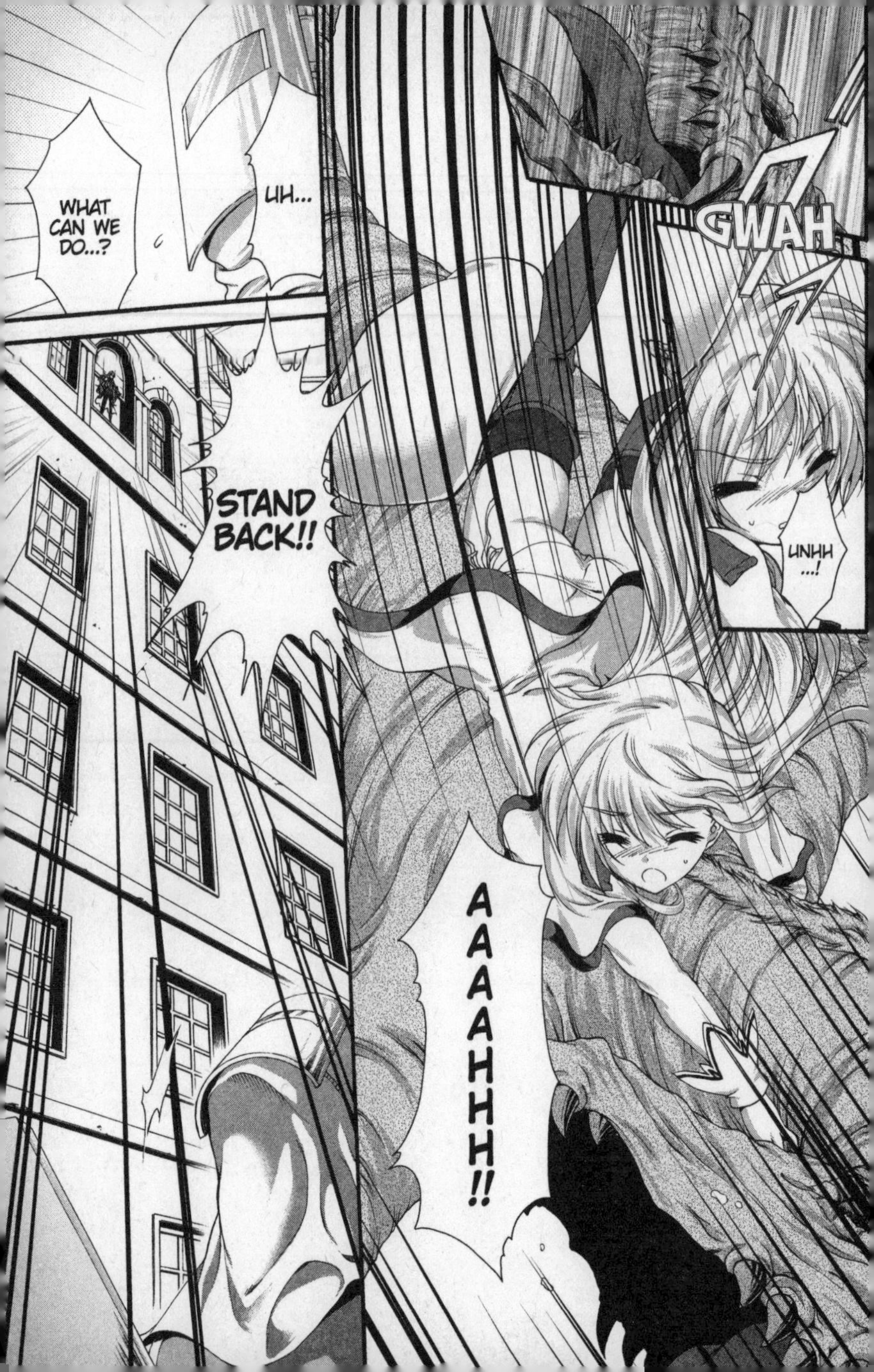
GWAH
UNHH ...!
UH...
WHAT CAN WE DO...?
STAND BACK!!
AAAAHHH!!

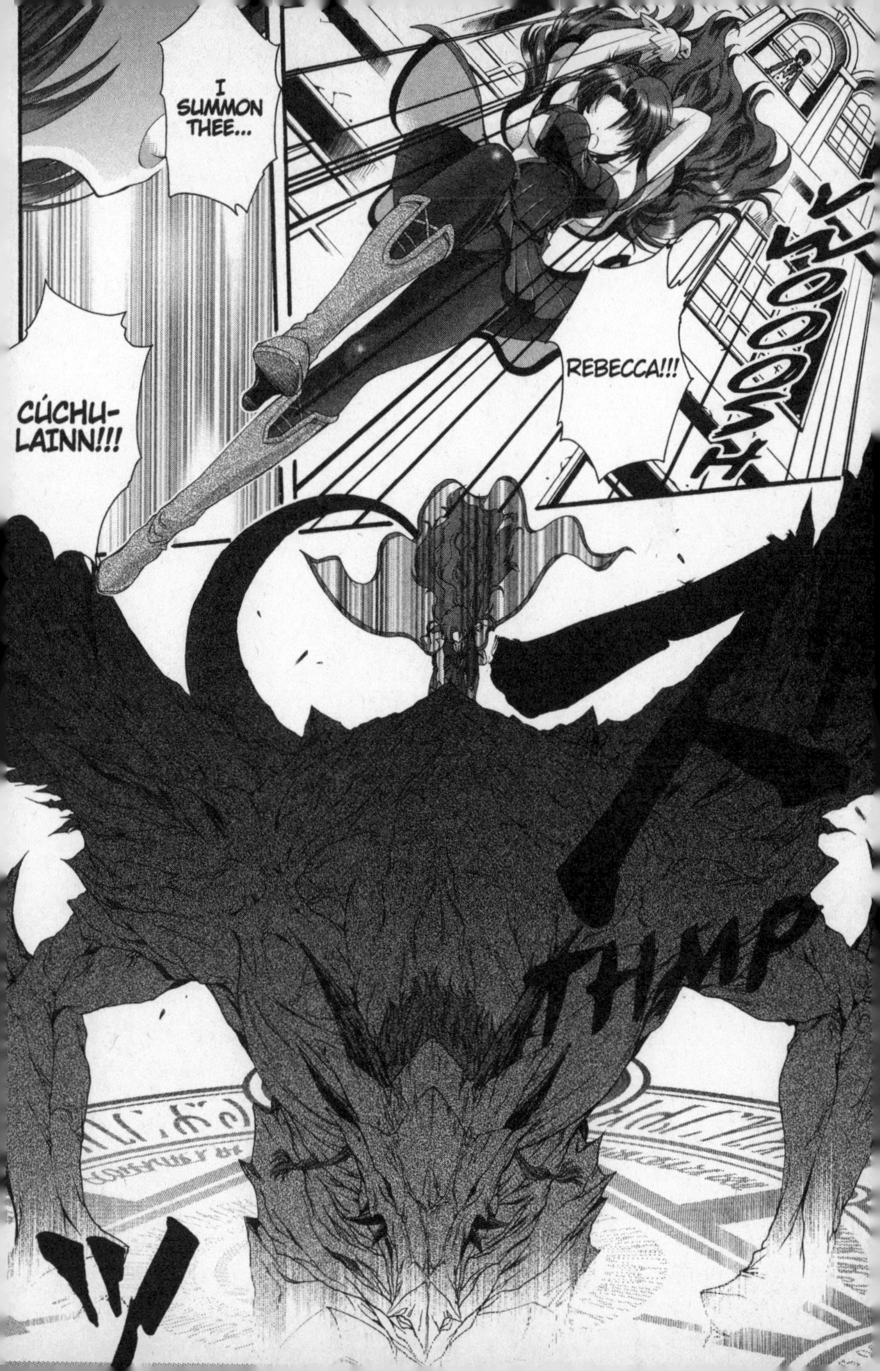
WOOOOSH
REBECCA!!!
I SUMMON THEE...
CÚCHU-
LAINN!!!
THUMP

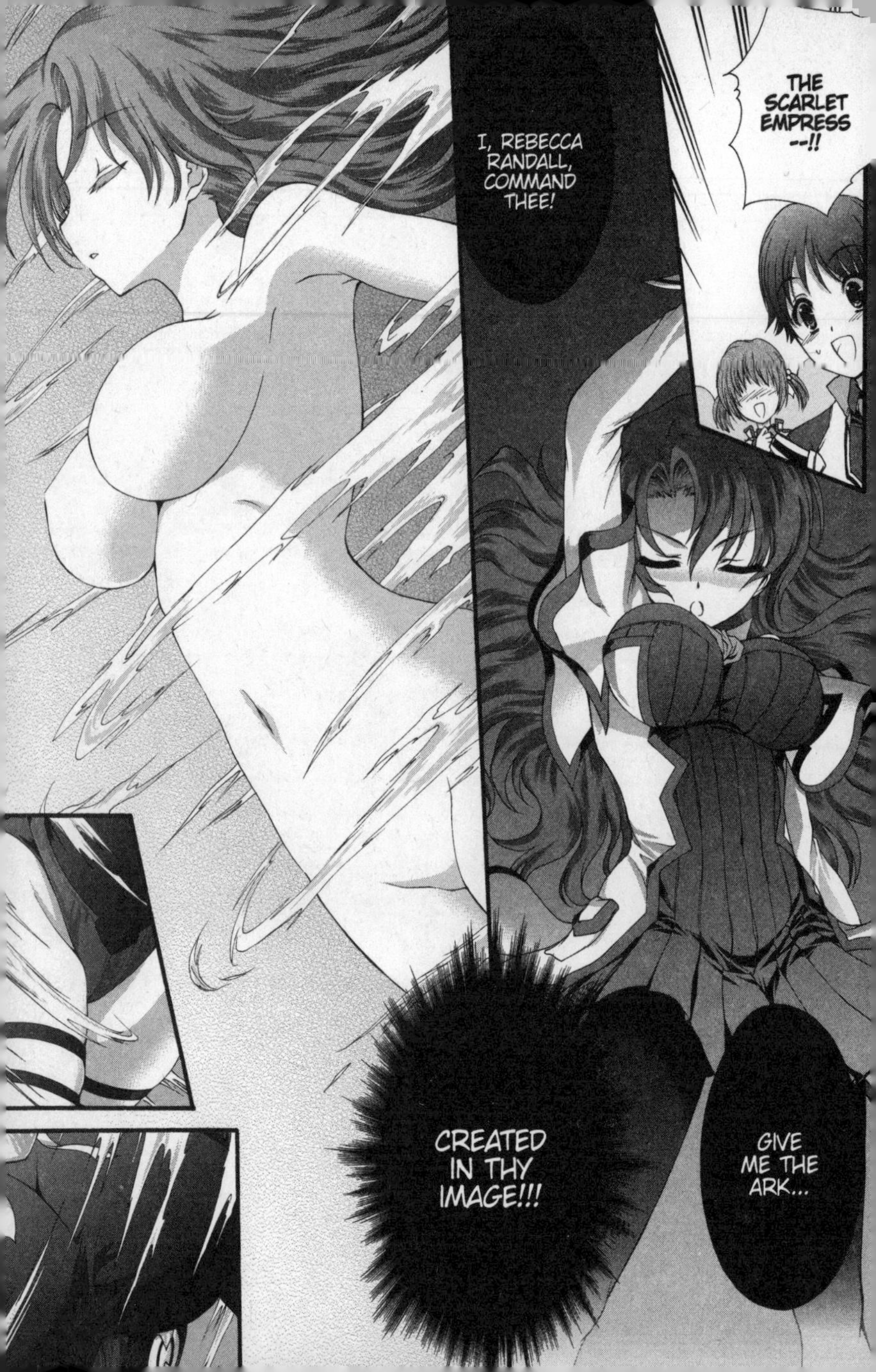
THE SCARLET EMPRESS --!!
I, REBECCA RANDALL, COMMAND THEE!
GIVE ME THE ARK...
CREATED IN THY IMAGE!!!

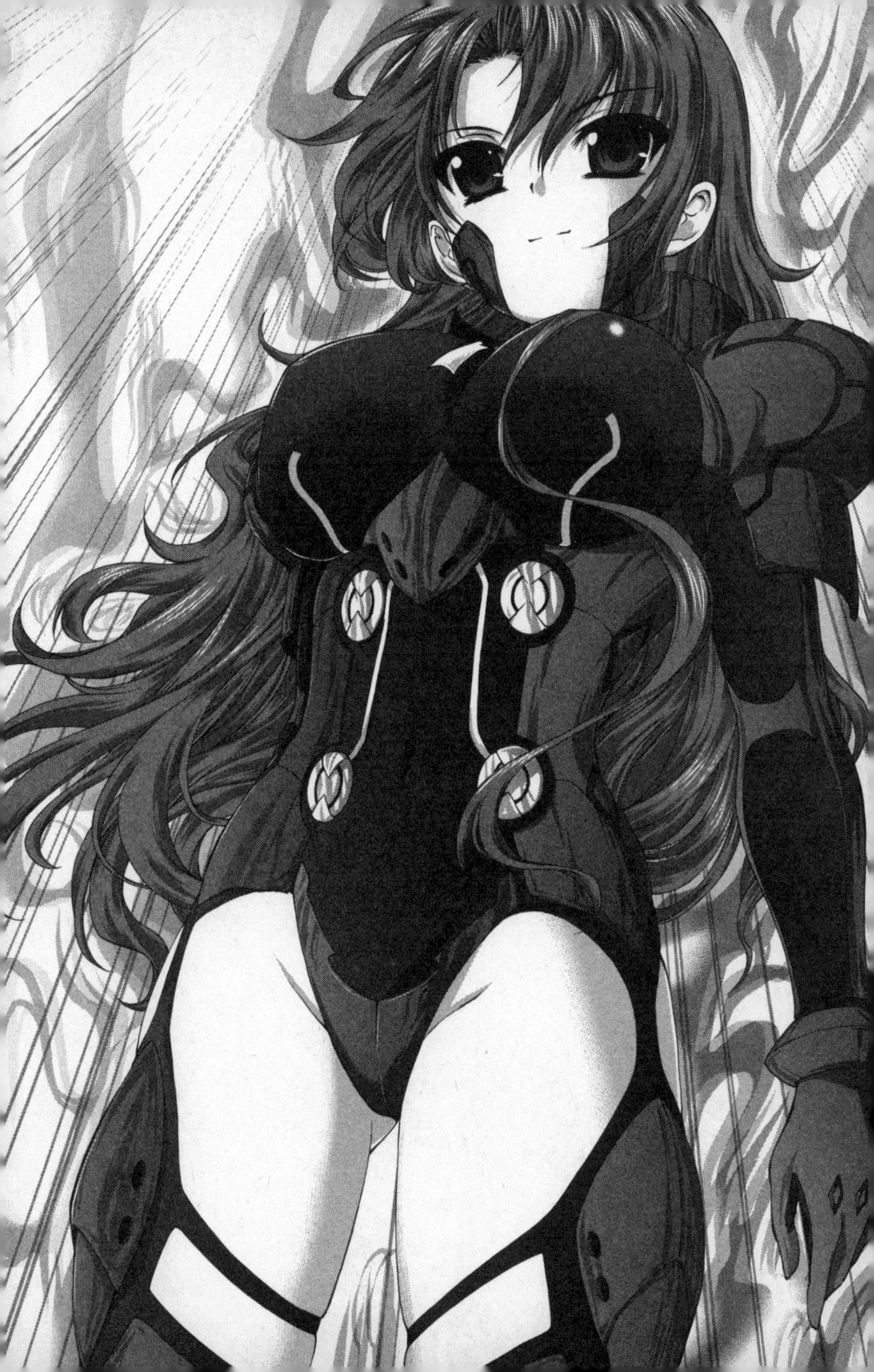

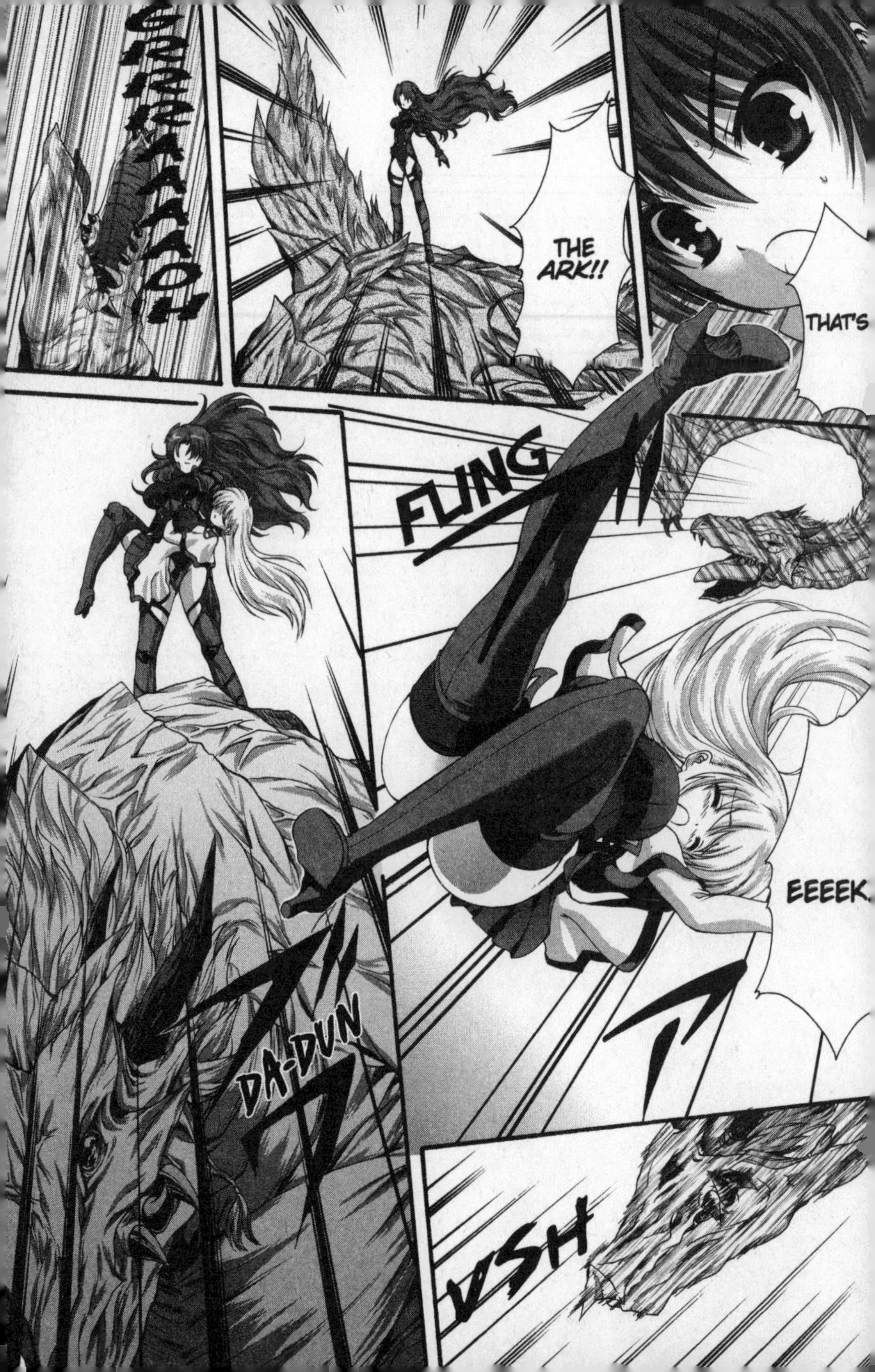
THAT'S
THE ARK!!
GRRRAAAAOH
FLUNG
EEEEK.
DA-DUN
VSH

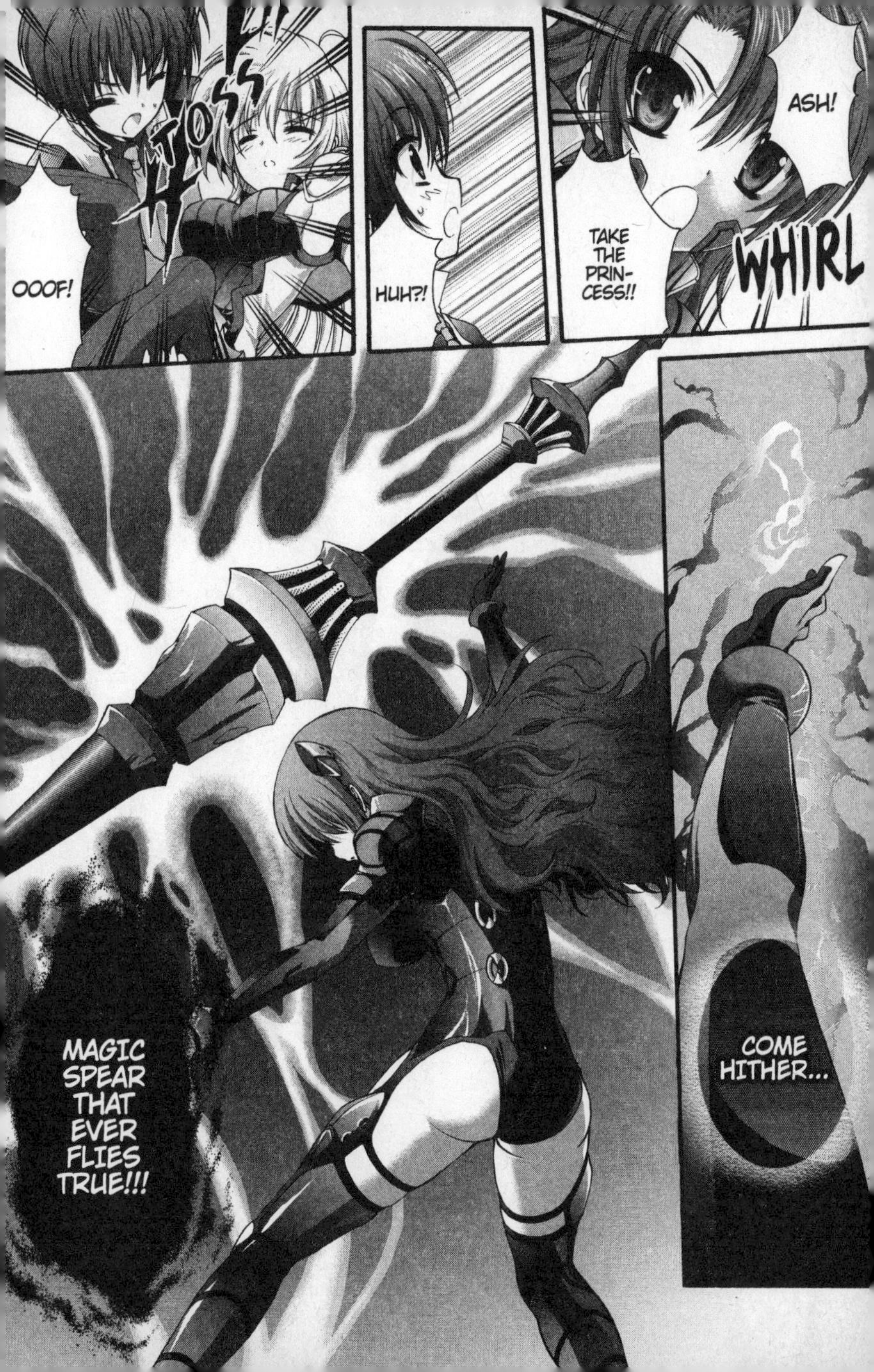
ASH!
TAKE THE PRIN-CESS!!
WHIRL
HUH?!
TOSS
OOOF!
COME HITHER...
MAGIC SPEAR THAT EVER FLIES TRUE!!!

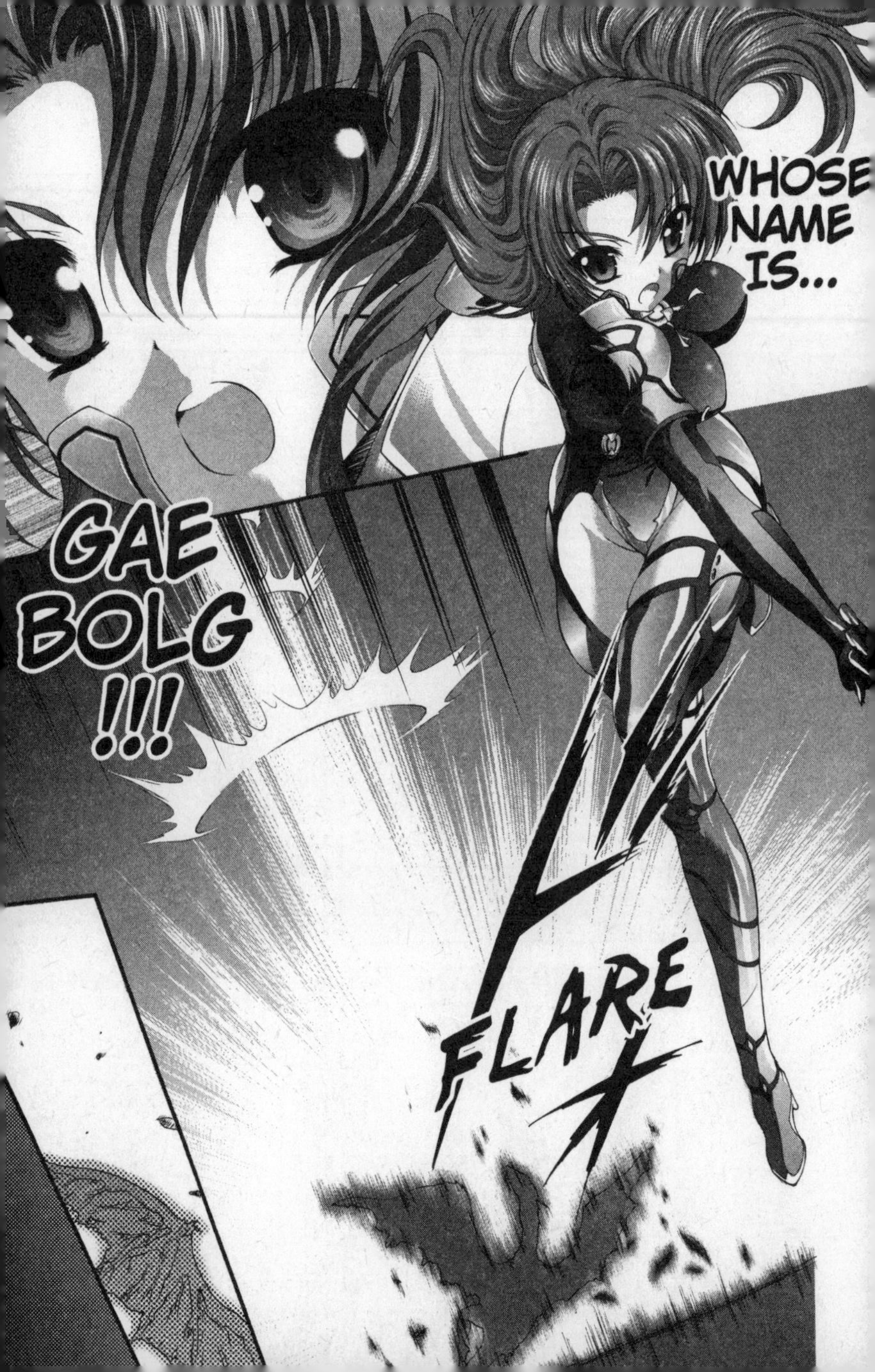
WHOSE NAME IS...
GAE BOLG !!!
FLARE

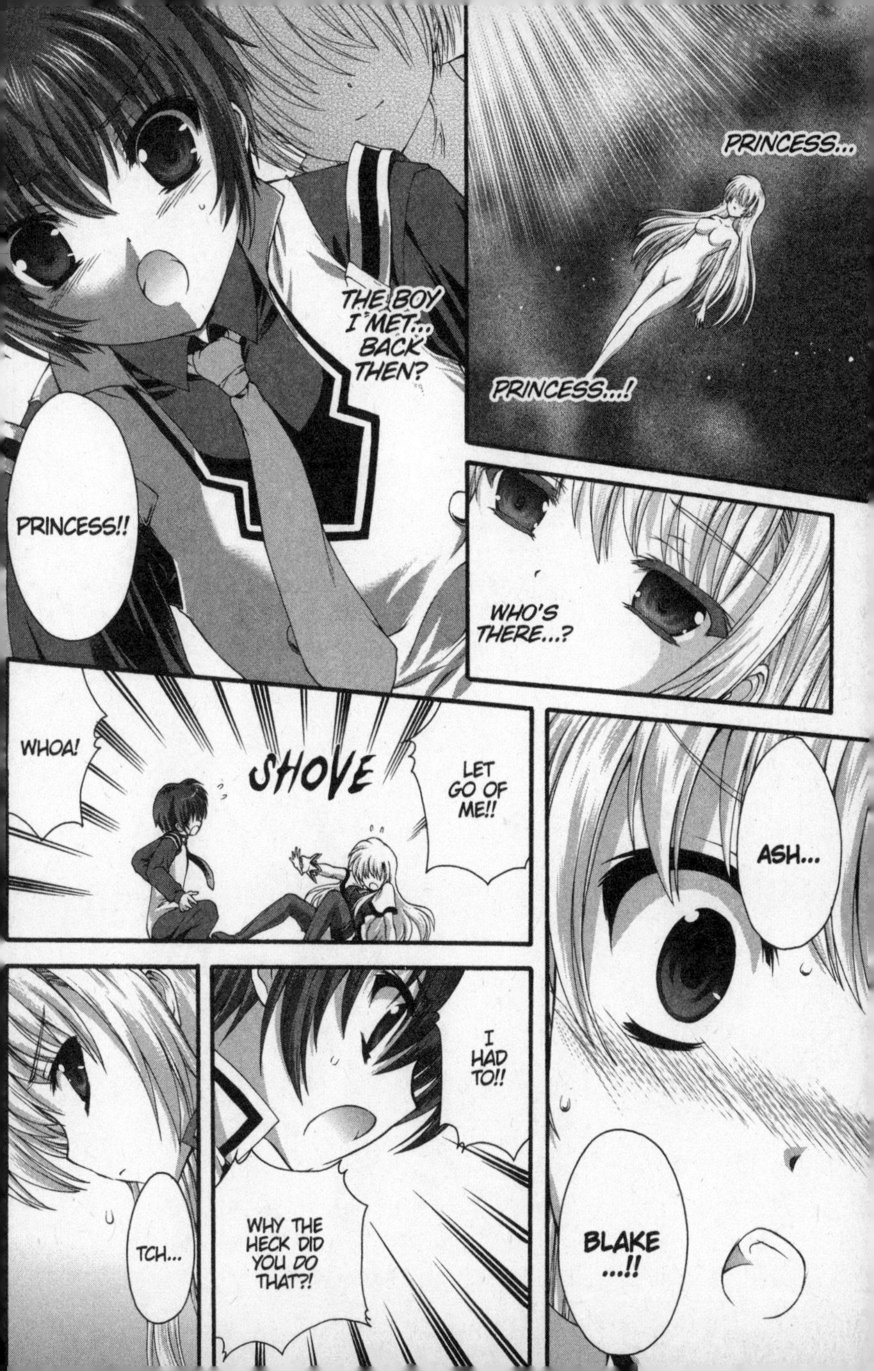
PRINCESS...
PRINCESS...!
WHO'S THERE...?
THE BOY I MET... BACK THEN?
PRINCESS!!
ASH...
BLAKE ...!!
LET GO OF ME!!
SHOVE
WHOA!
I HAD TO!!
WHY THE HECK DID YOU DO THAT?!
TCH...

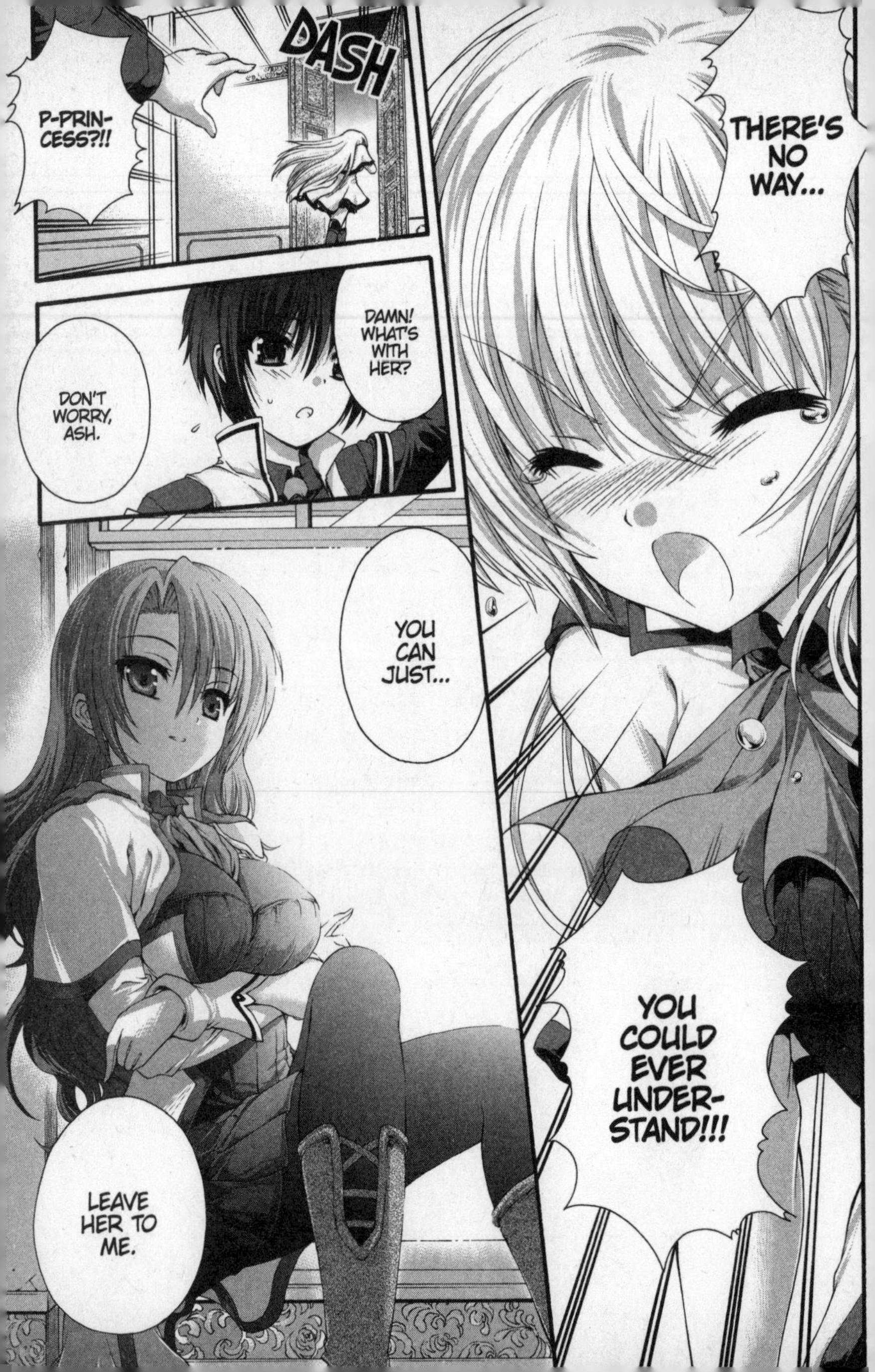
THERE'S NO WAY...
YOU COULD EVER UNDER-STAND!!!
DASH
P-PRIN-CESS?!!
DAMN! WHAT'S WITH HER?
DON'T WORRY, ASH.
YOU CAN JUST...
LEAVE HER TO ME.

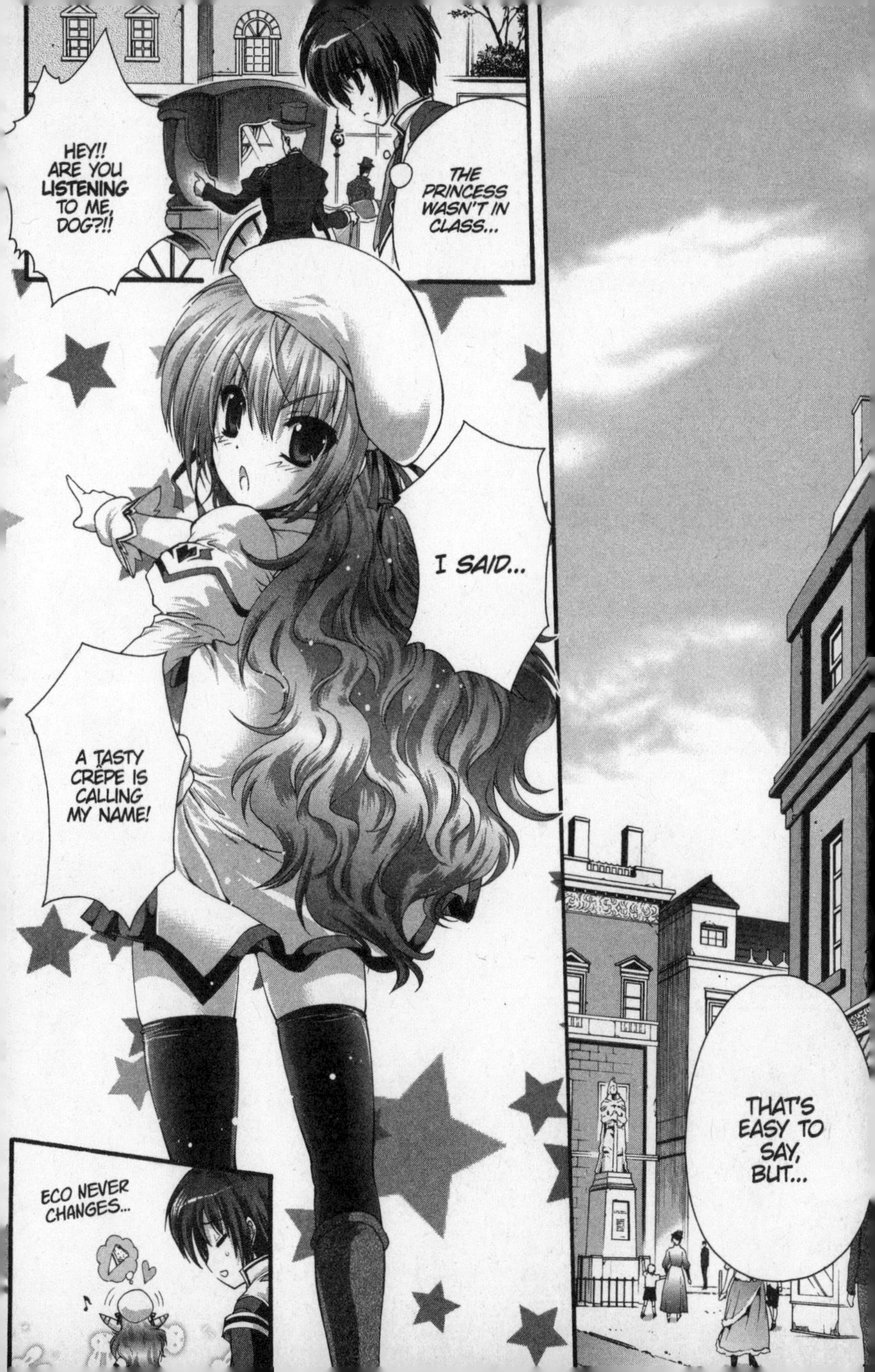
THAT'S EASY TO SAY, BUT...
THE PRINCESS WASN'T IN CLASS...
HEY!! ARE YOU LISTENING TO ME, DOG?!!
I SAID...
A TASTY CRÊPE IS CALLING MY NAME!
ECO NEVER CHANGES...

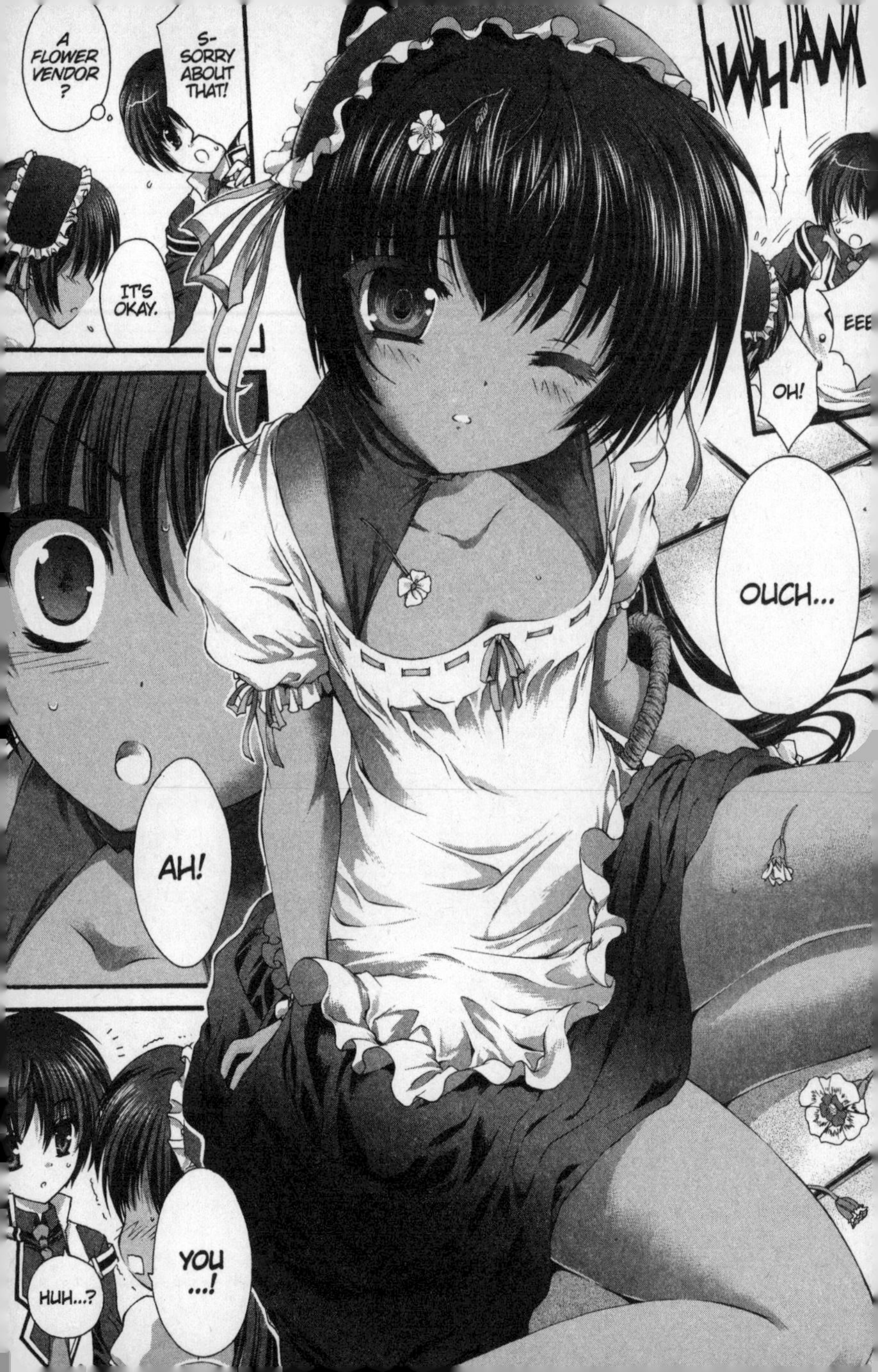
WHAM
EEE
OH!
OUCH...
S-SORRY ABOUT THAT!
A FLOWER VENDOR?
IT'S OKAY.
AH!
YOU...!
HUH...?

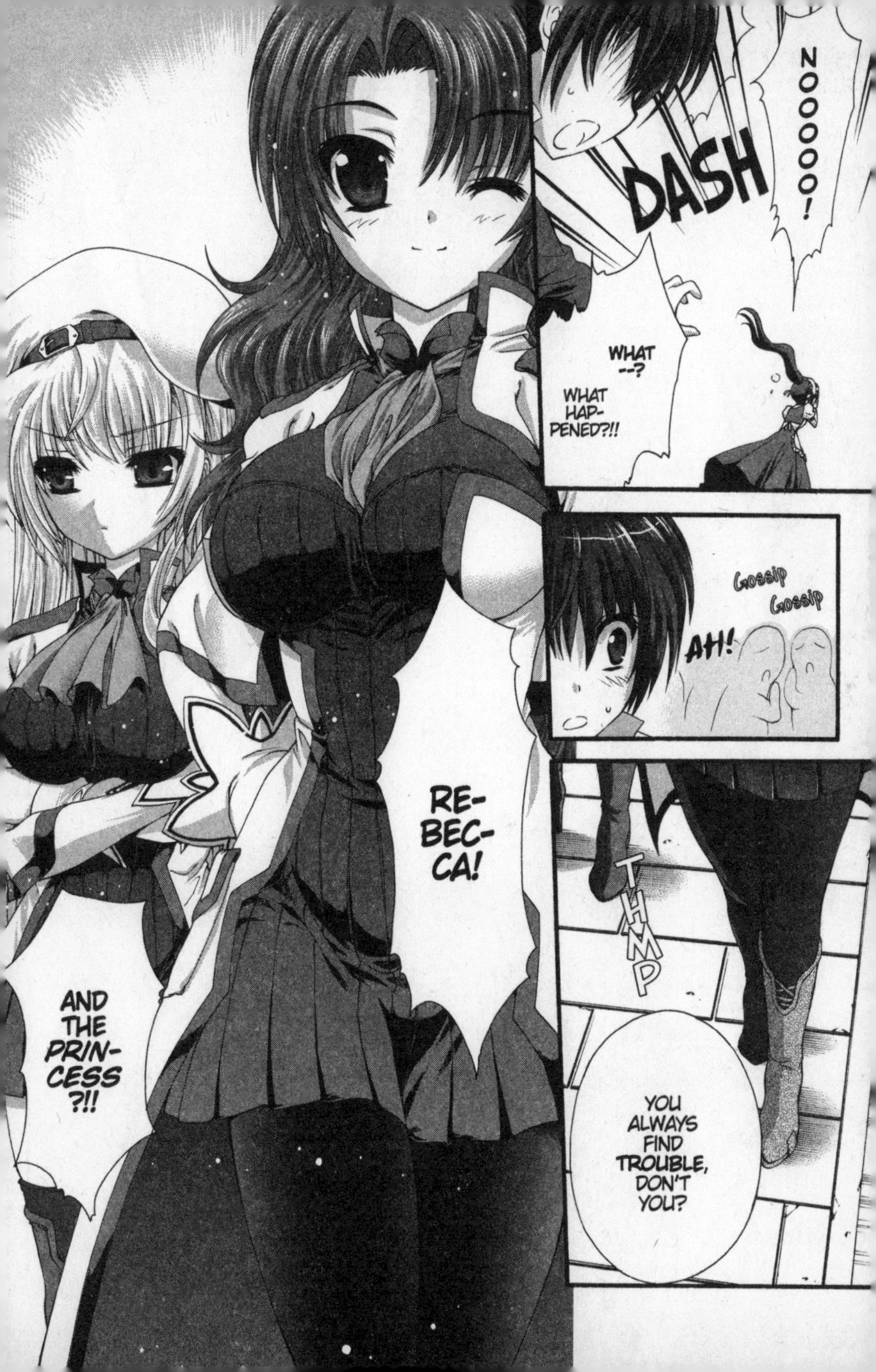
NOOOOOO!
DASH
WHAT --?
WHAT HAPPENED?!!
Gossip Gossip
AH!
THUMP
YOU ALWAYS FIND TROUBLE, DON'T YOU?
REBECCA!
AND THE PRINCESS?!!

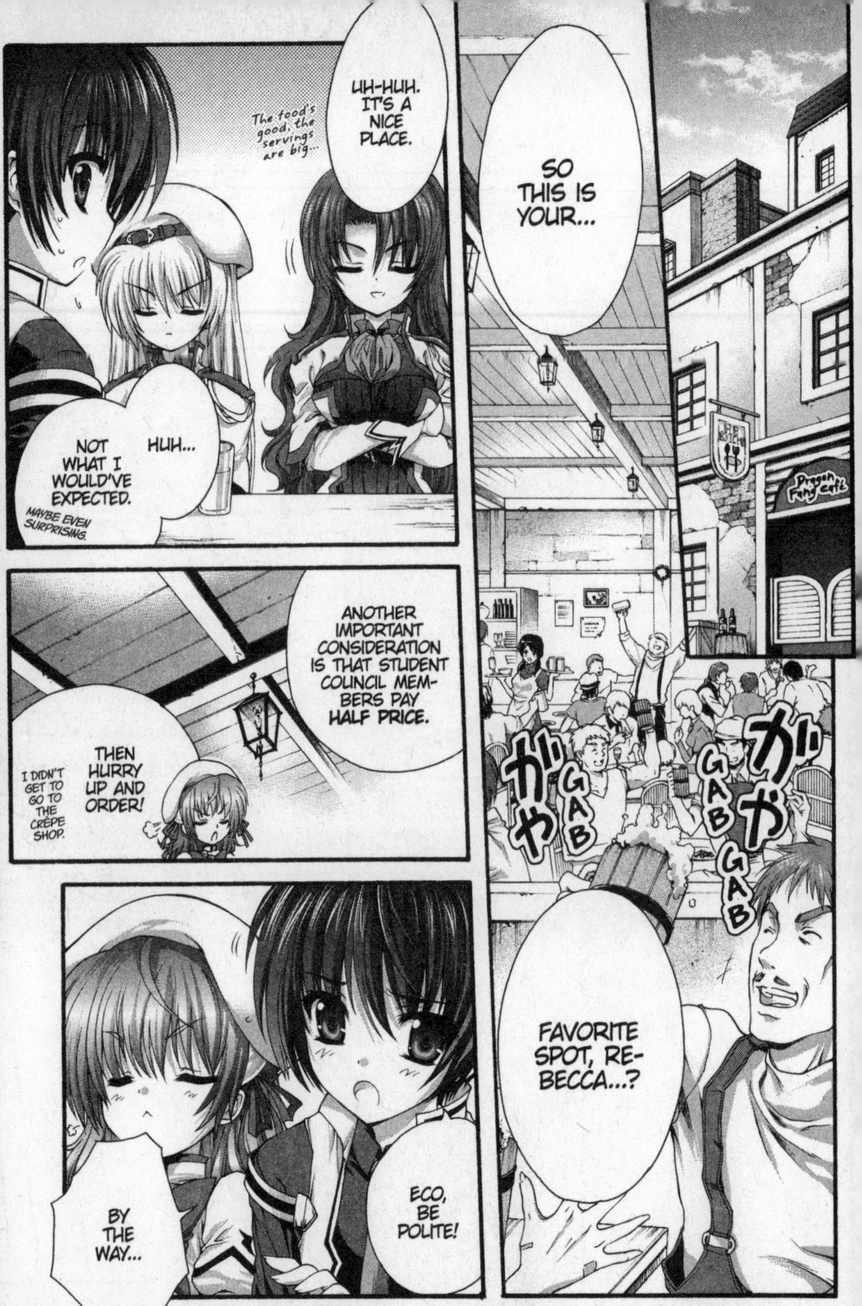
SO THIS IS YOUR...
Dragon Fang Café
がやがや
GAB GAB
がやがや
GAB GAB
FAVORITE SPOT, REBECCA...?
UH-HUH. IT'S A NICE PLACE.
The food's good, the servings are big...
HUH...
NOT WHAT I WOULD'VE EXPECTED.
MAYBE EVEN SURPRISING.
ANOTHER IMPORTANT CONSIDERATION IS THAT STUDENT COUNCIL MEMBERS PAY HALF PRICE.
THEN HURRY UP AND ORDER!
I DIDN'T GET TO GO TO THE CRÊPE SHOP.
ECO, BE POLITE!
BY THE WAY...

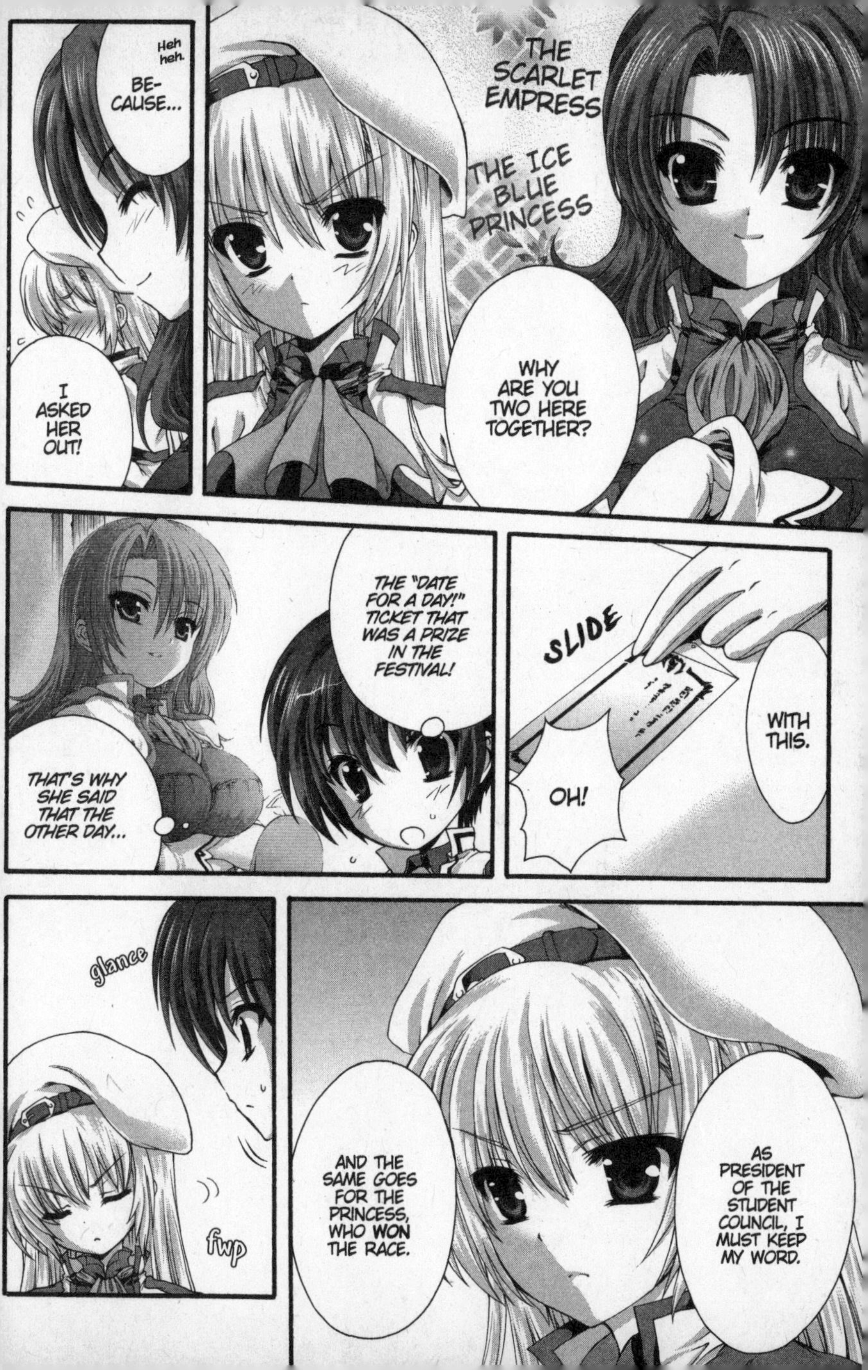
THE SCARLET EMPRESS
THE ICE BLUE PRINCESS
WHY ARE YOU TWO HERE TOGETHER?
Heh heh.
BE-CAUSE...
I ASKED HER OUT!
WITH THIS.
SLIDE
OH!
THE "DATE FOR A DAY!" TICKET THAT WAS A PRIZE IN THE FESTIVAL!
THAT'S WHY SHE SAID THAT THE OTHER DAY...
AS PRESIDENT OF THE STUDENT COUNCIL, I MUST KEEP MY WORD.
AND THE SAME GOES FOR THE PRINCESS, WHO WON THE RACE.
glance
fwp

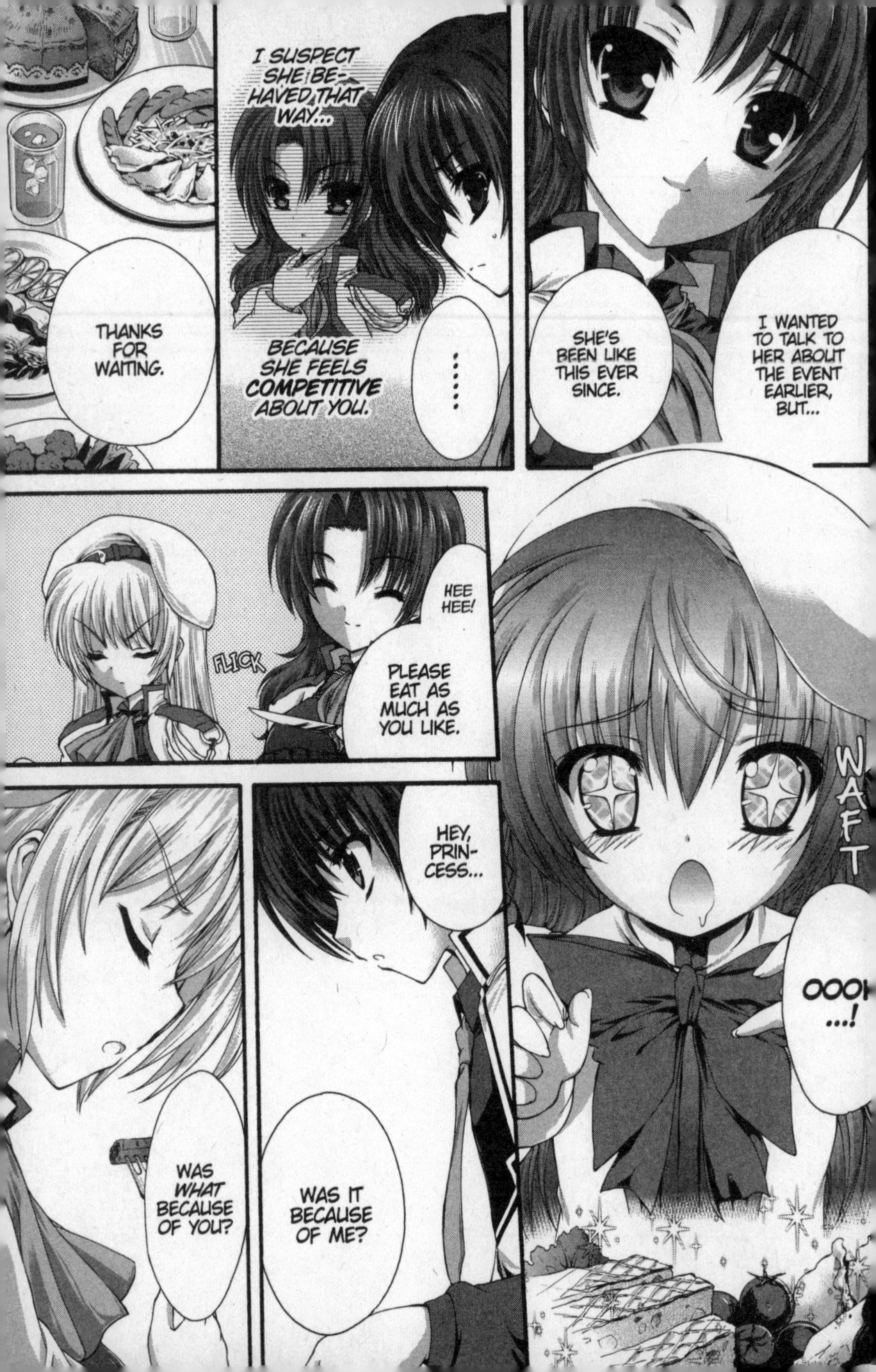
I WANTED TO TALK TO HER ABOUT THE EVENT EARLIER, BUT...
SHE'S BEEN LIKE THIS EVER SINCE.
I SUSPECT SHE BE-HAVED THAT WAY...
BECAUSE SHE FEELS COMPETITIVE ABOUT YOU.
......
THANKS FOR WAITING.
WAFT
OOOH ...!
HEE HEE!
PLEASE EAT AS MUCH AS YOU LIKE.
FLICK
HEY, PRINCESS...
WAS IT BECAUSE OF ME?
WAS WHAT BECAUSE OF YOU?

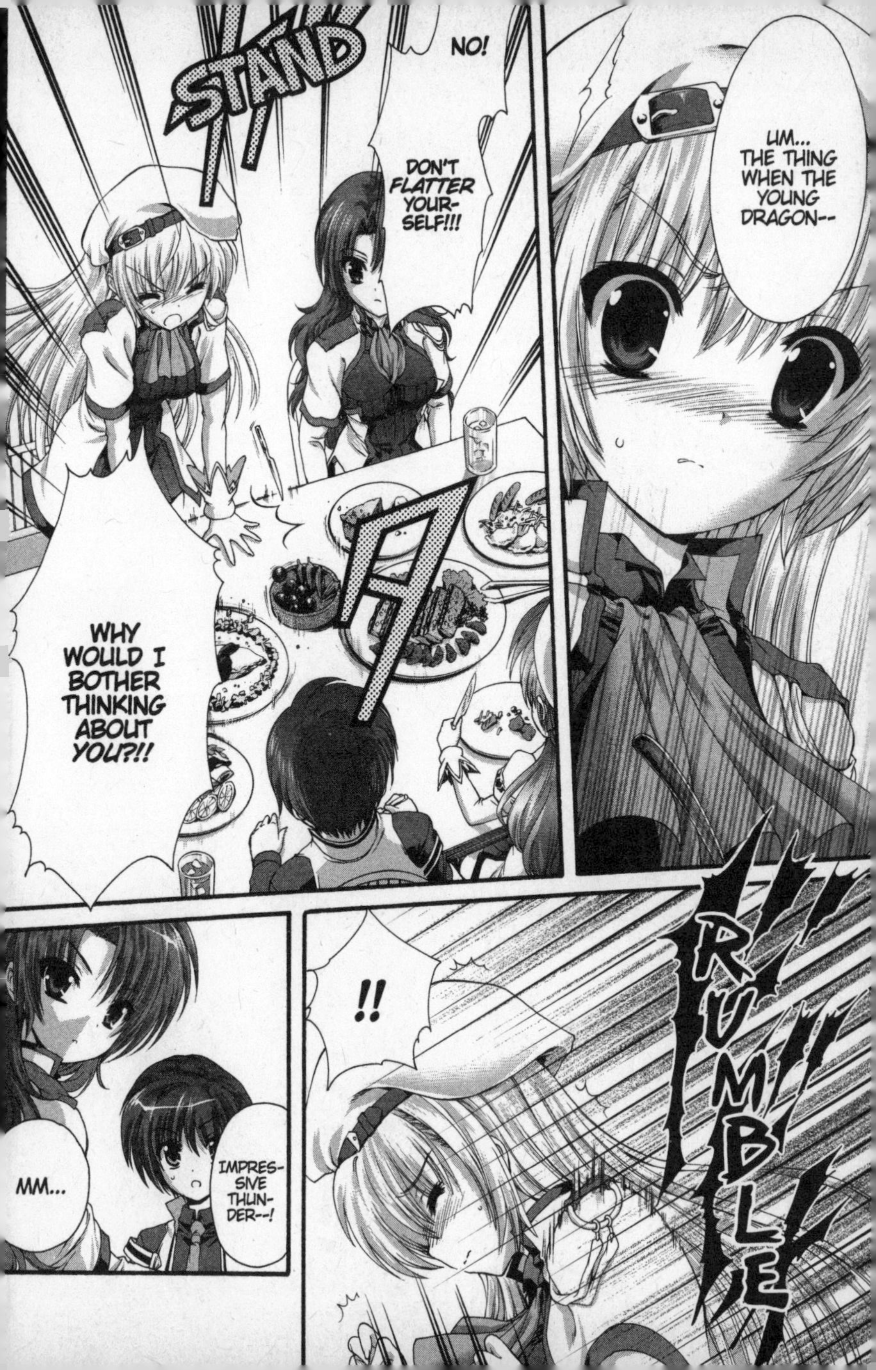
UM... THE THING WHEN THE YOUNG DRAGON--
NO!
STAND
DON'T FLATTER YOUR-SELF!!!
WHY WOULD I BOTHER THINKING ABOUT YOU?!!
RUMBLE
!!
IMPRES-SIVE THUN-DER--!
MM...

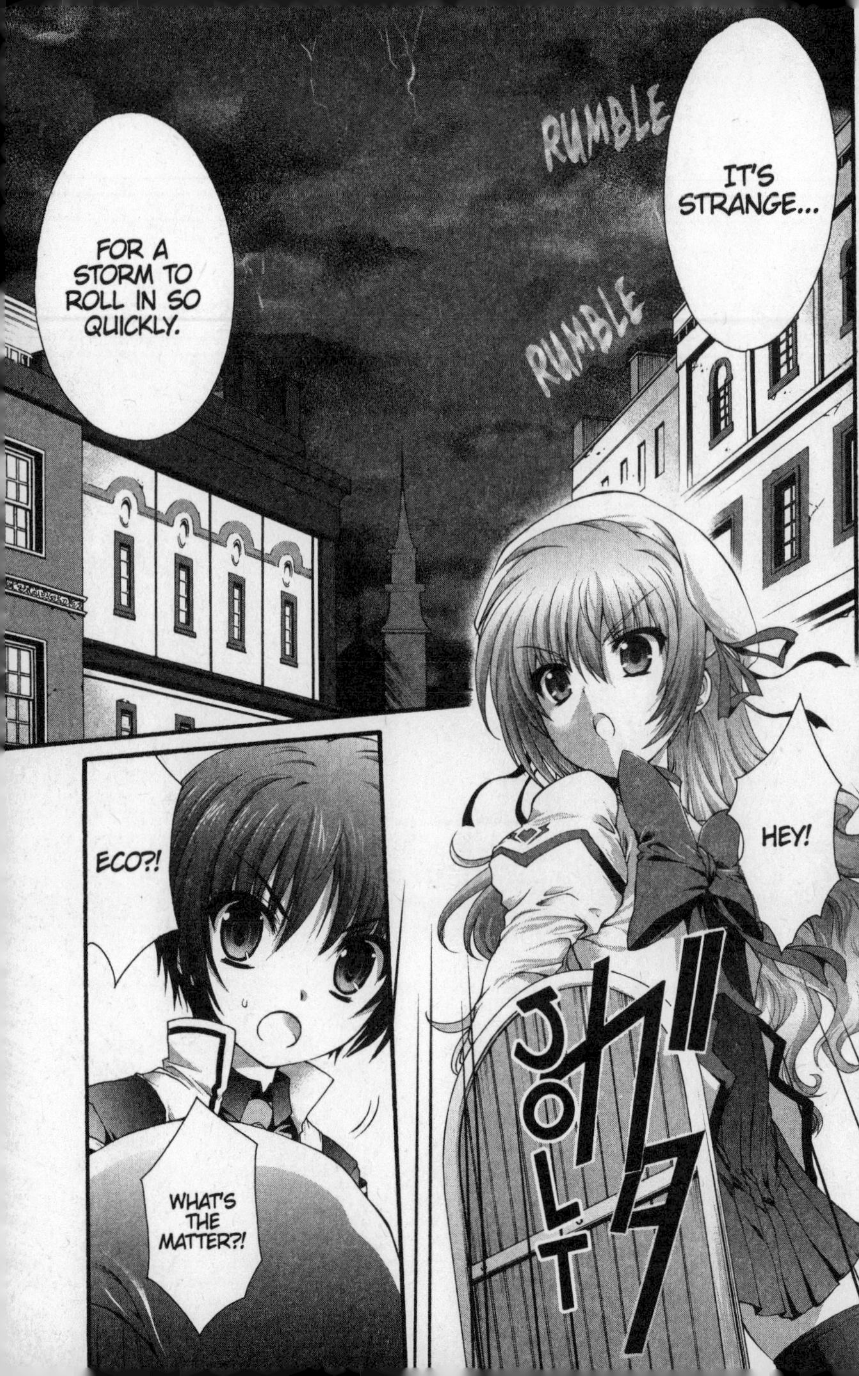
IT'S STRANGE...
RUMBLE
RUMBLE
FOR A STORM TO ROLL IN SO QUICKLY.
HEY!
JOLT
ECO?!
WHAT'S THE MATTER?!

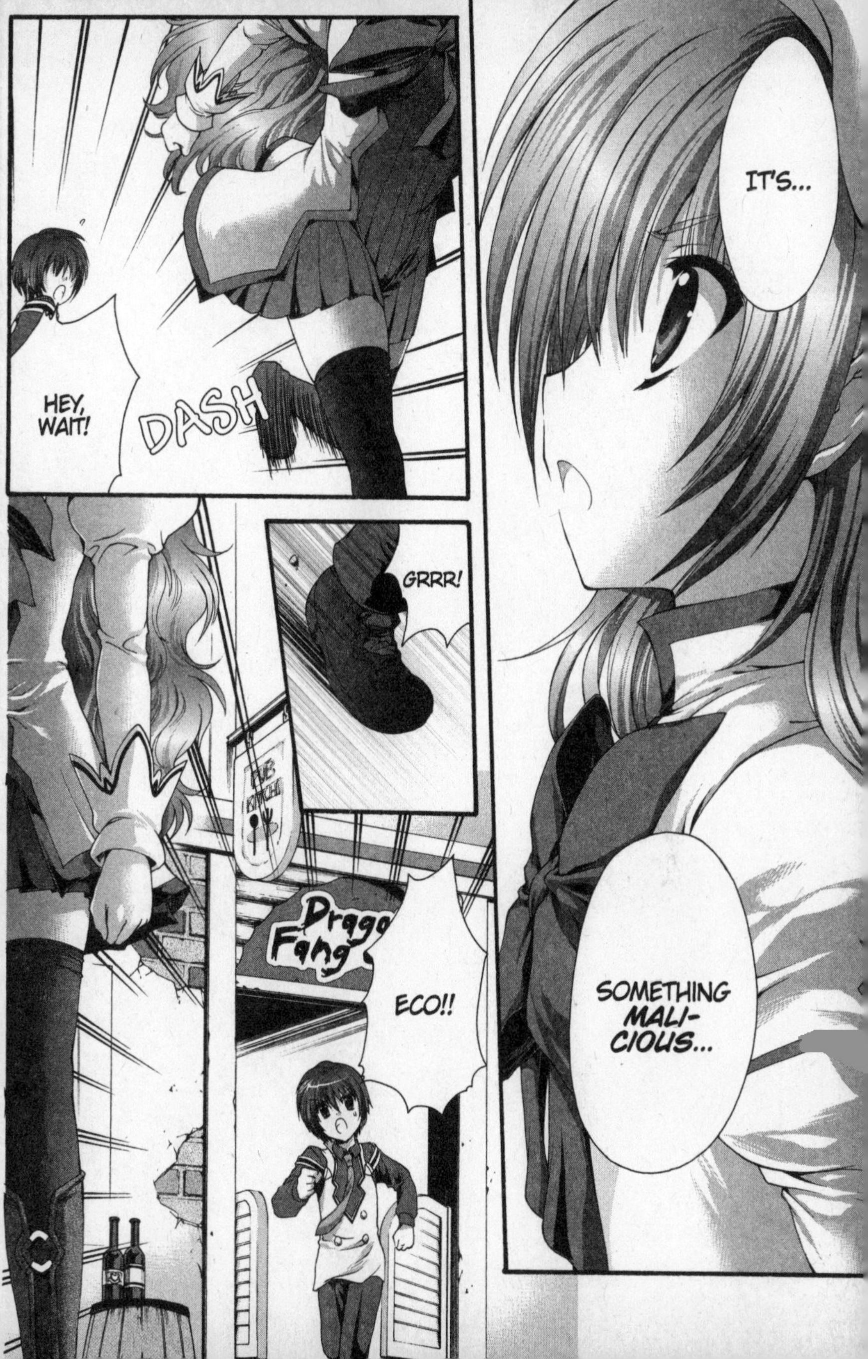
IT'S...
SOMETHING MALI-CIOUS...
DASH
HEY, WAIT!
GRRR!
ECO!!

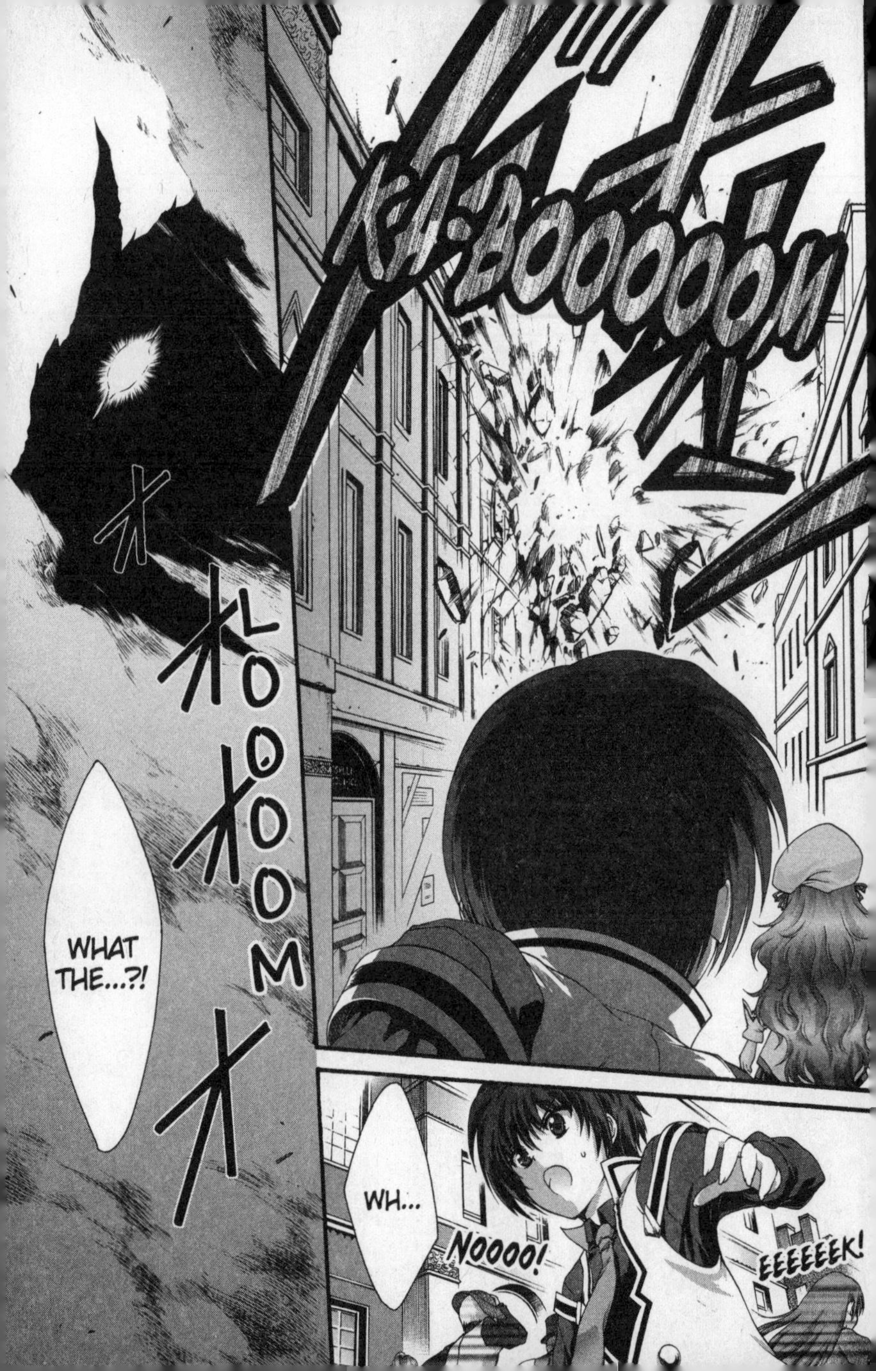
KA-BOOOOOM
LOOOOM
WHAT THE...?!
EEEEEEK!
NOOOO!
WH...

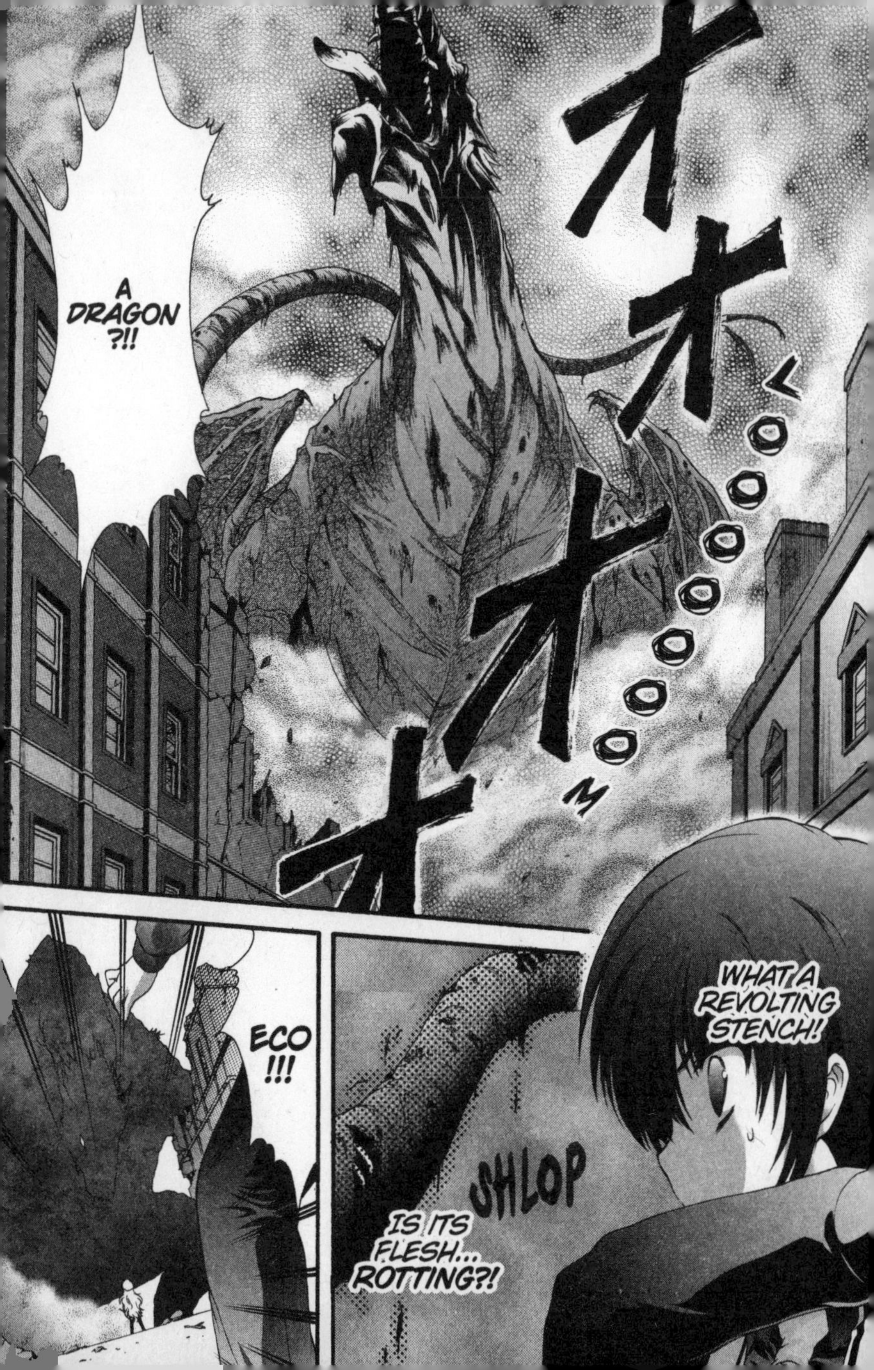
オオオオ
A DRAGON ?!!
WHAT A REVOLTING STENCH!
SHLOP
IS ITS FLESH... ROTTING?!
ECO !!!

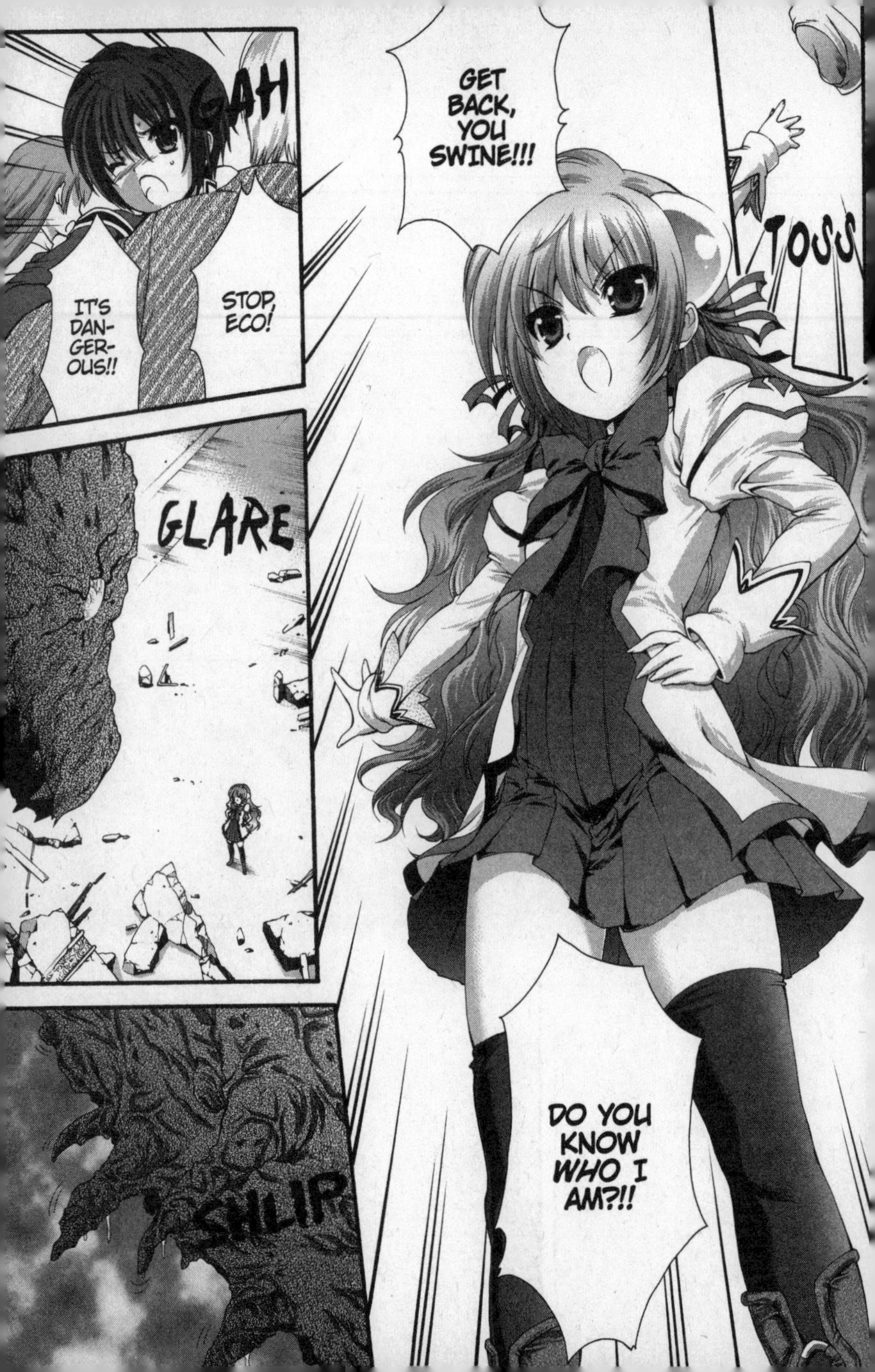
TOSS
GET BACK, YOU SWINE!!!
DO YOU KNOW WHO I AM?!!
GAH
STOP, ECO!
IT'S DAN-GER-OUS!!
GLARE
SHLIP

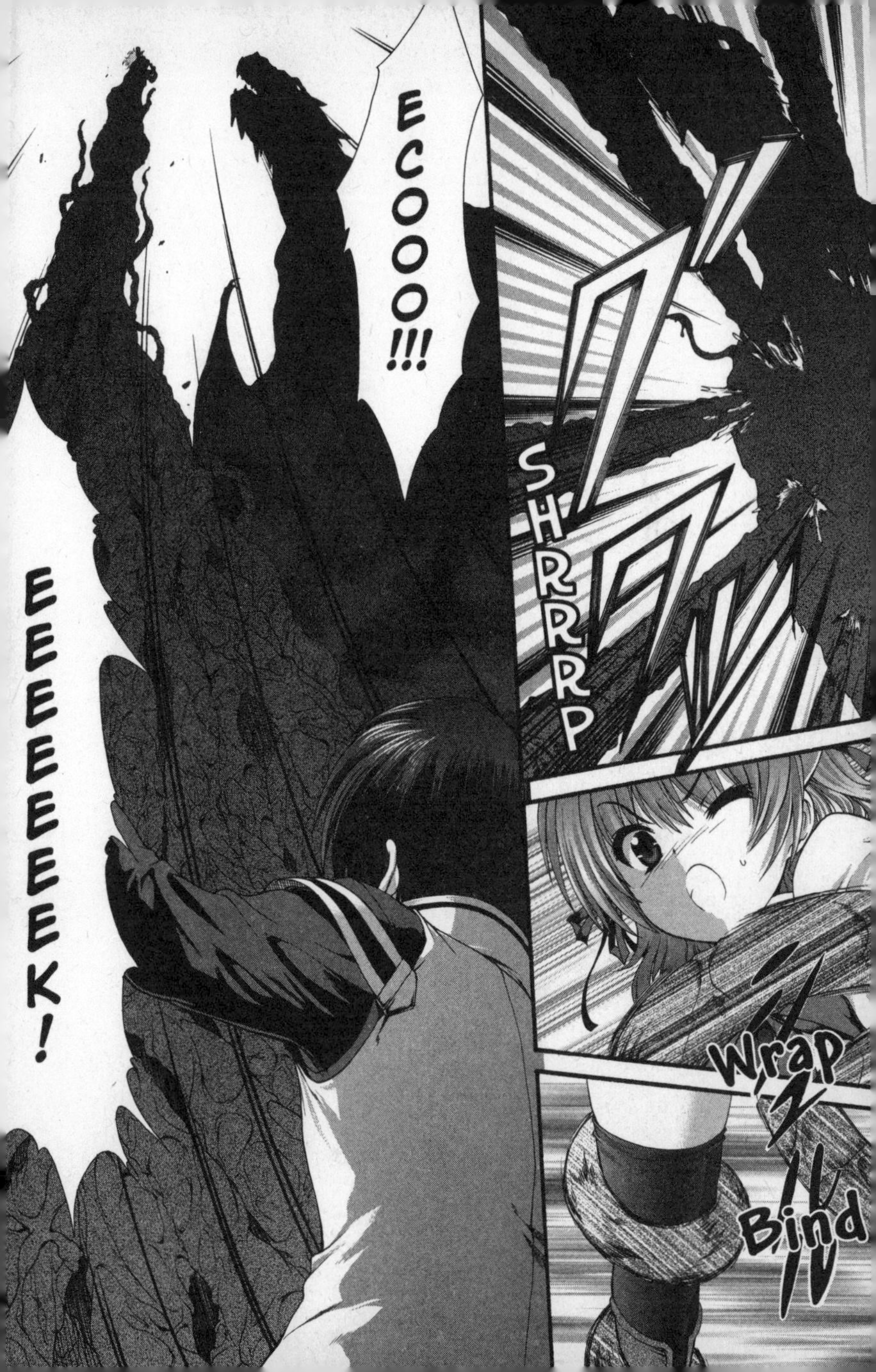
SHRRRP
Wrap
Bind
ECOOOO!!!
EEEEEEEEEK!

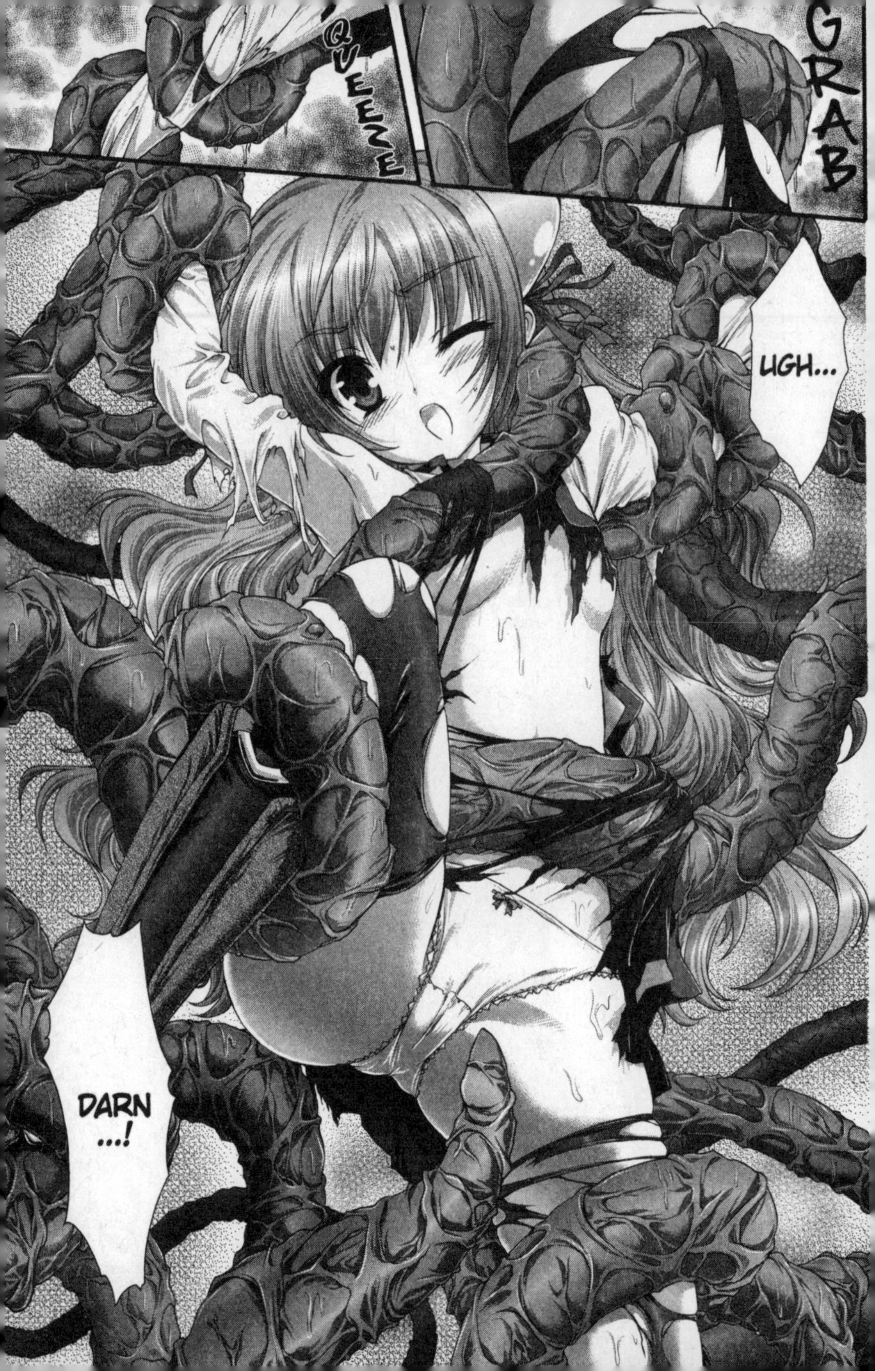
GRAB
QUEEZE
UGH...
DARN ...!

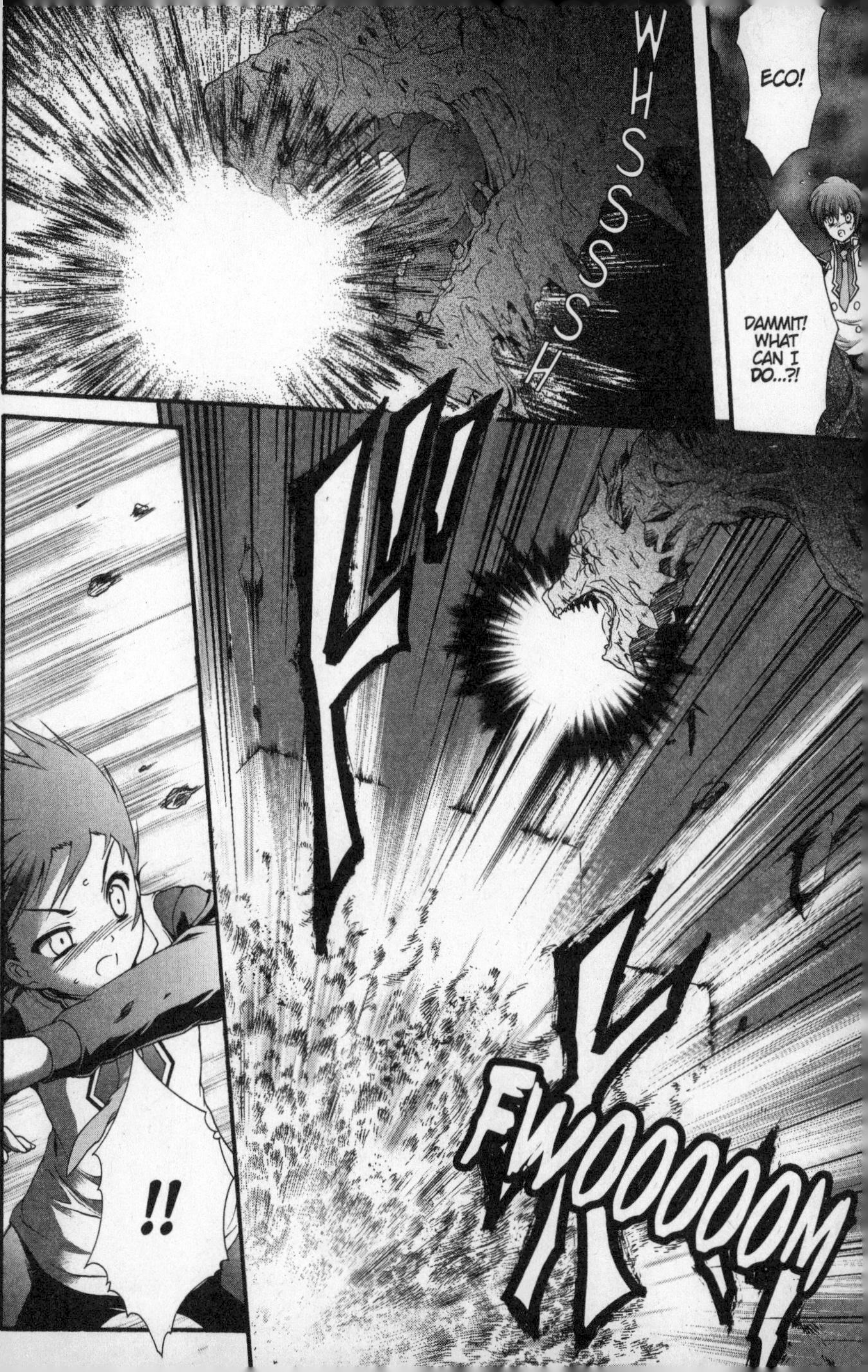
ECO!
DAMMIT! WHAT CAN I DO...?!
WHSSSSSH
FWOOOOOM
!!

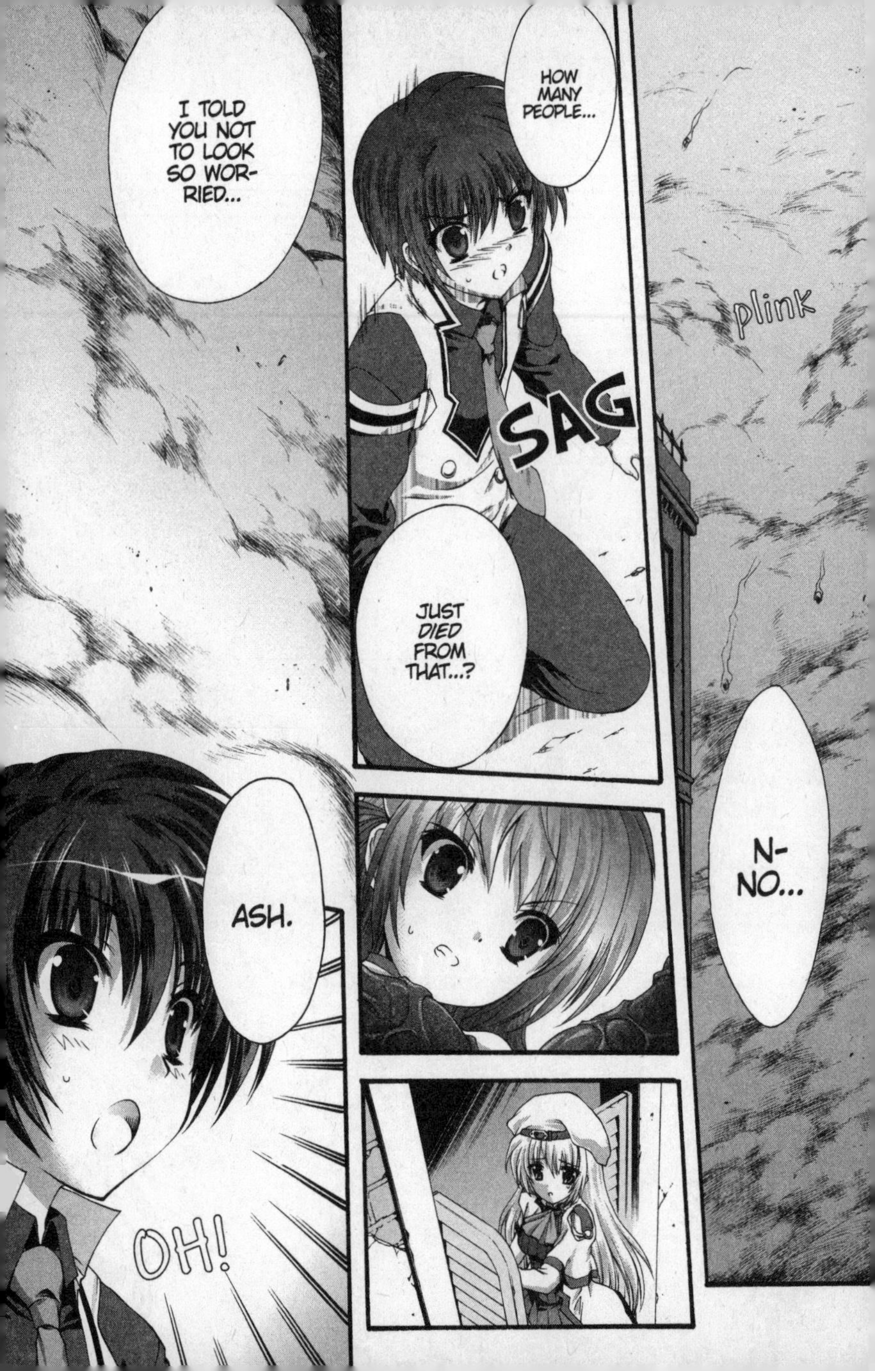
HOW MANY PEOPLE...
SAG
JUST DIED FROM THAT...?
plink
I TOLD YOU NOT TO LOOK SO WOR-RIED...
N-NO...
ASH.
OH!

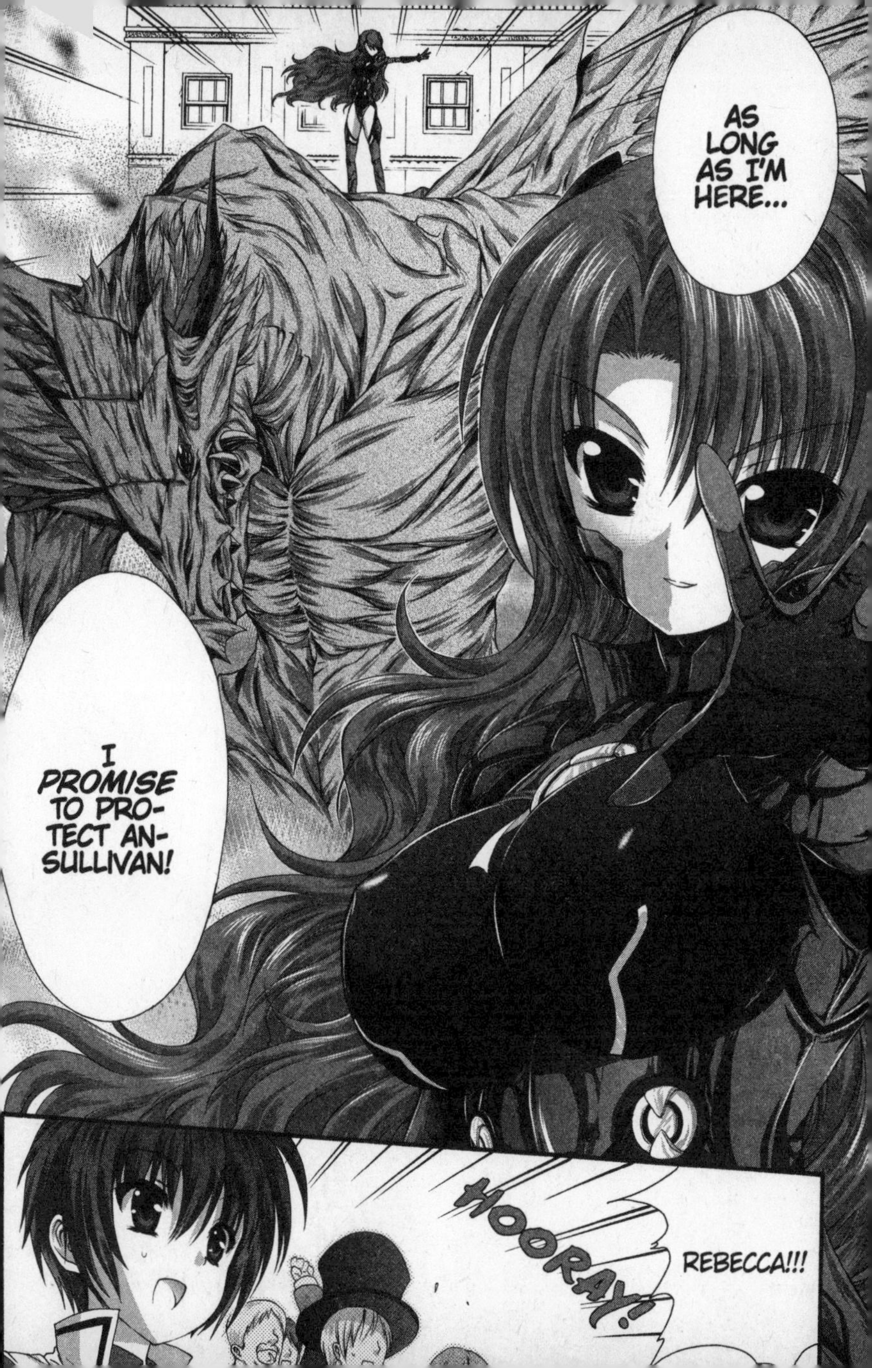
AS LONG AS I'M HERE...
I PROMISE TO PROTECT AN-SULLIVAN!
HOORAY!
REBECCA!!!

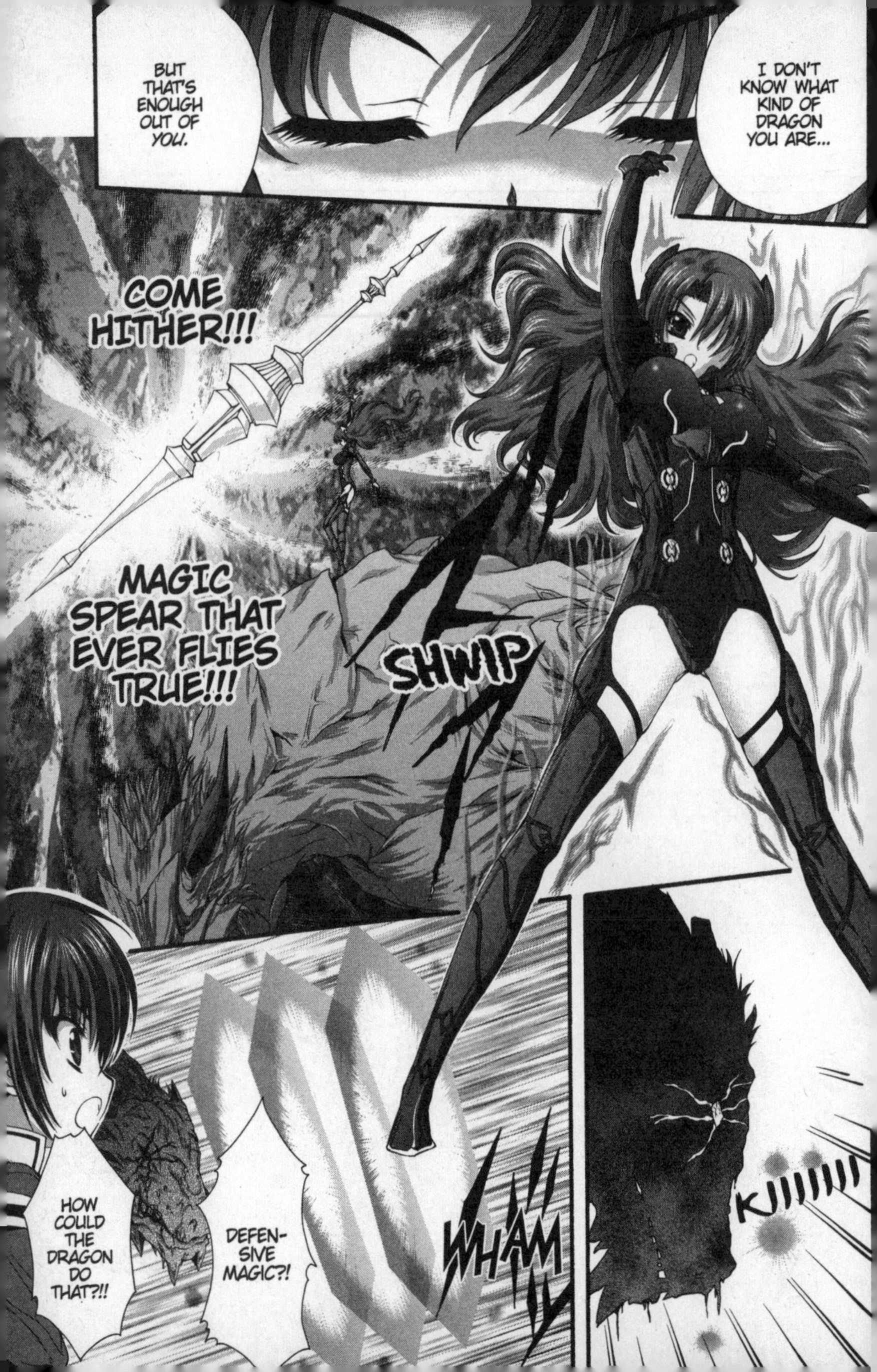
I DON'T KNOW WHAT KIND OF DRAGON YOU ARE...
BUT THAT'S ENOUGH OUT OF YOU.
COME HITHER!!!
MAGIC SPEAR THAT EVER FLIES TRUE!!!
SHWIP
KIIIIIII
WHAM
DEFEN-SIVE MAGIC?!
HOW COULD THE DRAGON DO THAT?!!

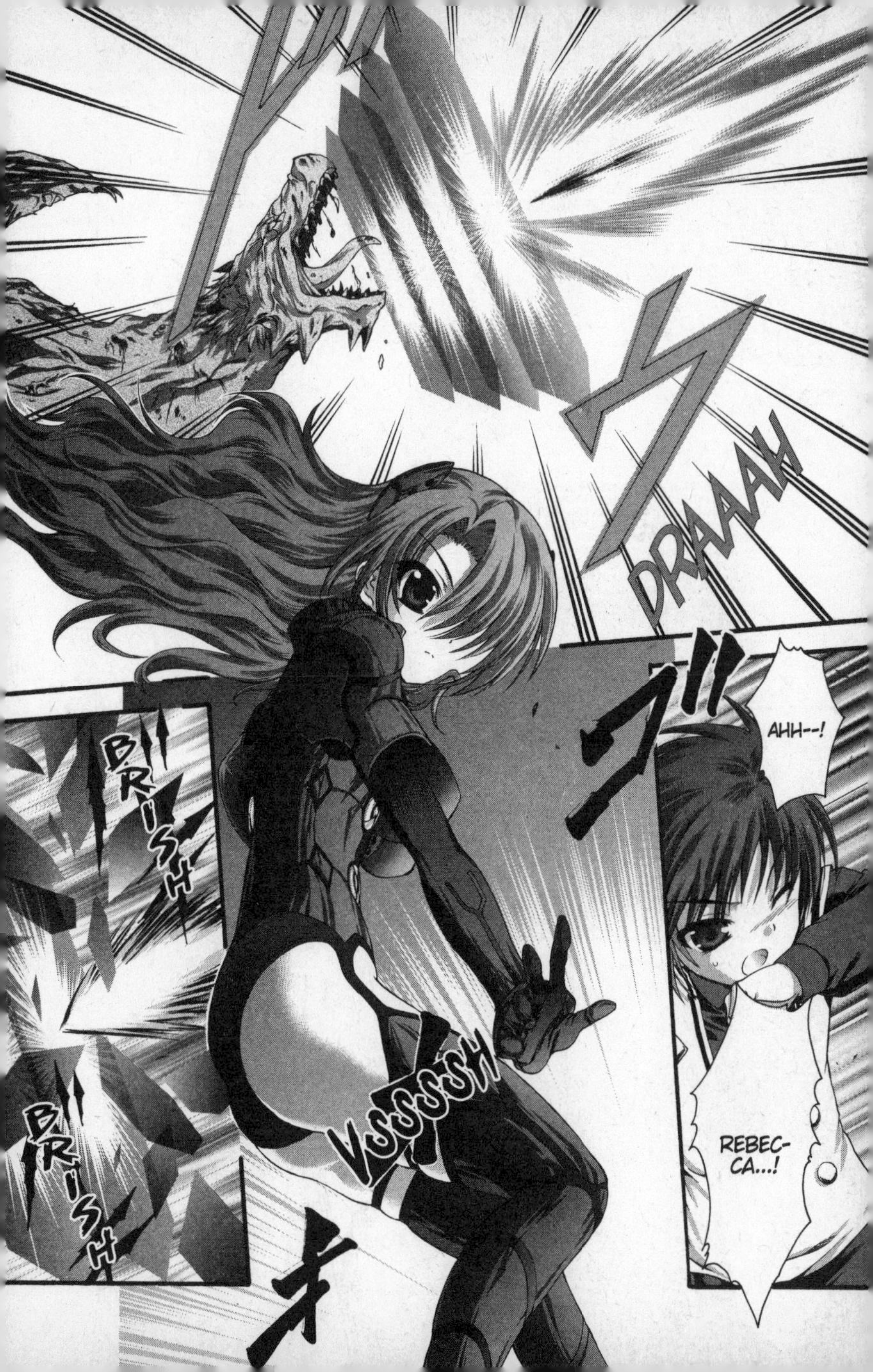
DRAAAH
AHH--!
REBEC-
CA...!
VSSSSH
BRISH
BRISH

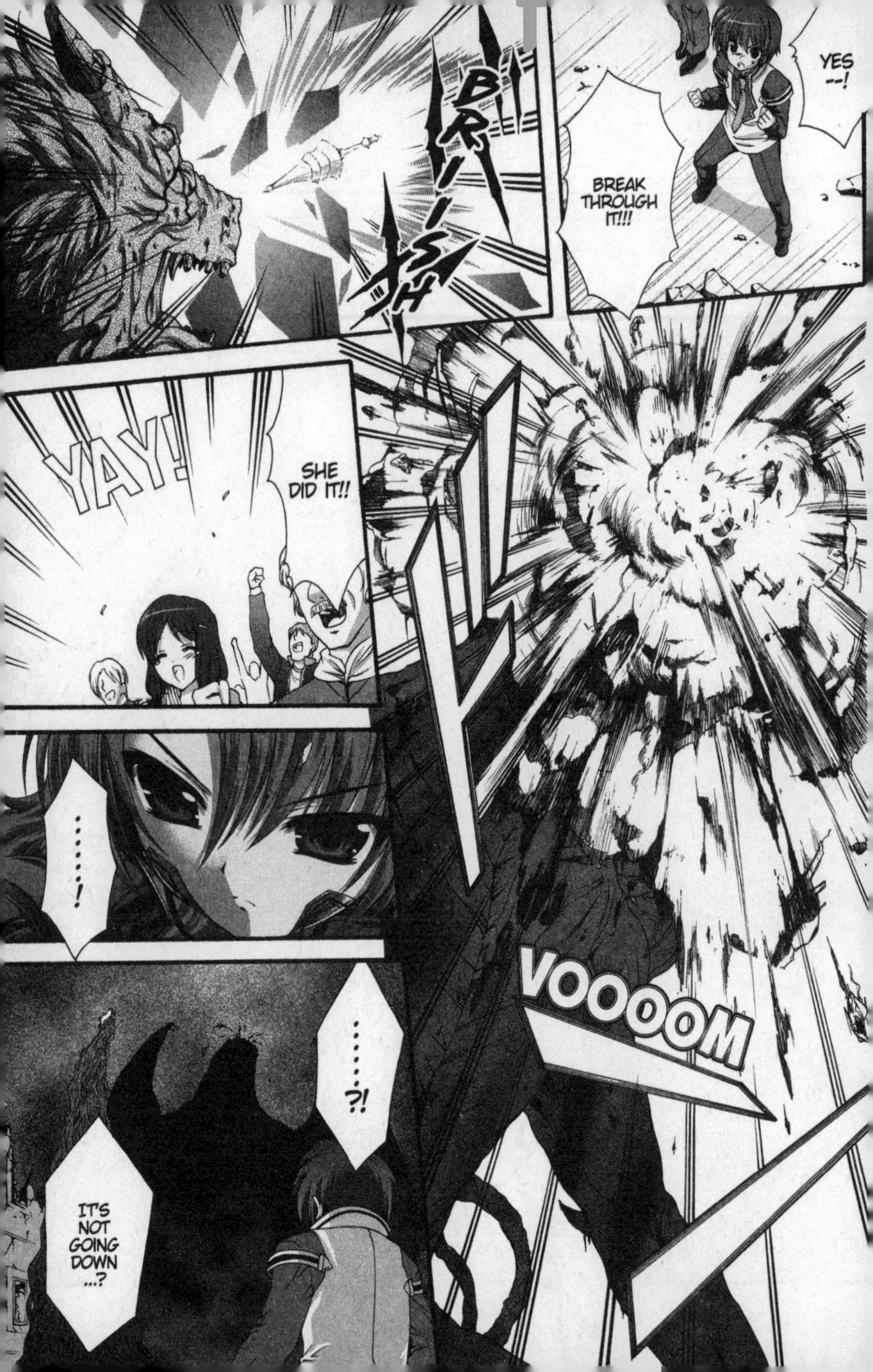
YES --!
BREAK THROUGH IT!!!
BRIISH
VOOOOM
YAY!
SHE DID IT!!
......!
......?!
IT'S NOT GOING DOWN ...?

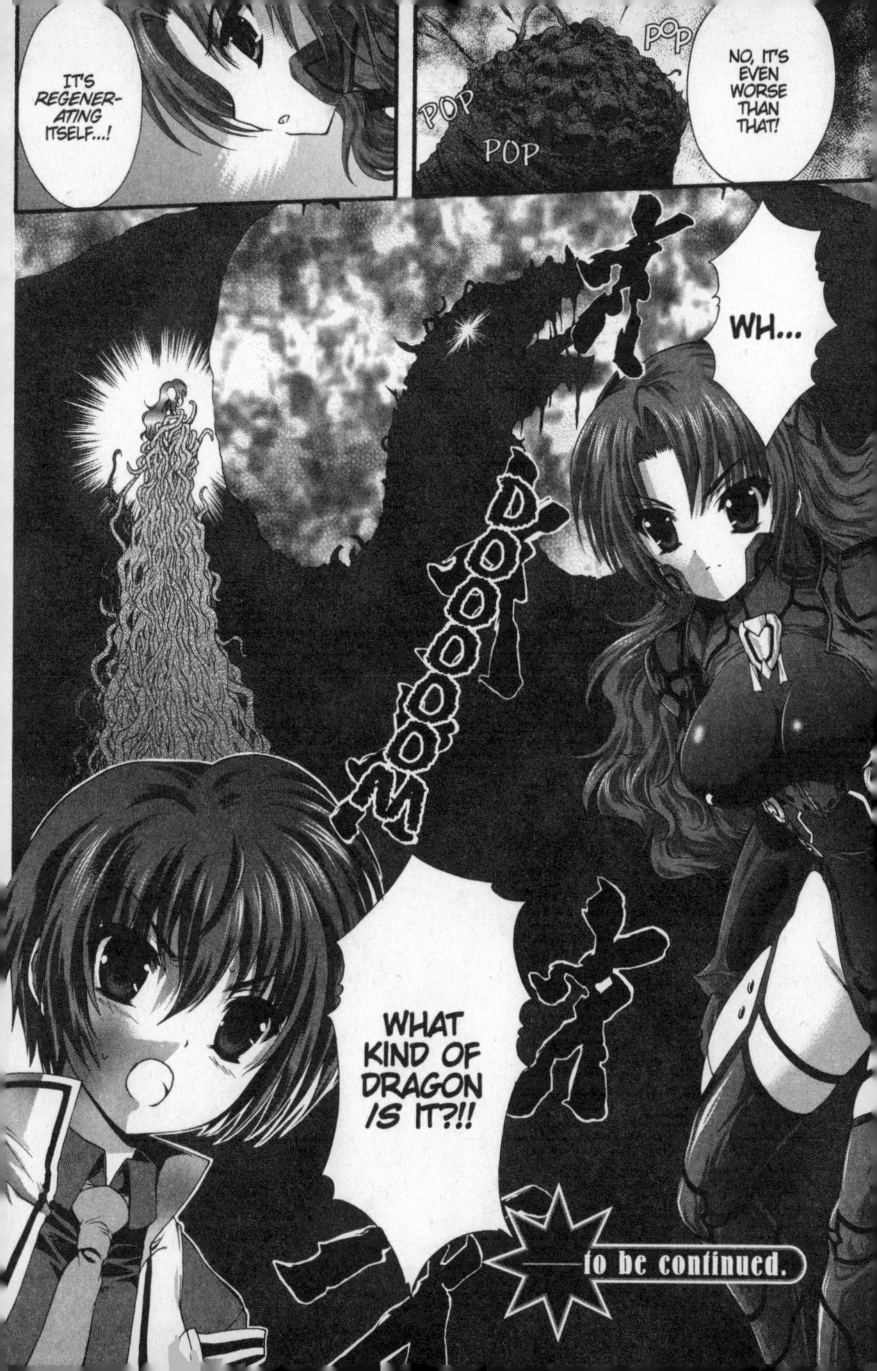
POP
NO, IT'S EVEN WORSE THAN THAT!
POP
POP
IT'S REGENER-ATING ITSELF...!
WH...
DOOOOOOM
WHAT KIND OF DRAGON IS IT?!!
—to be continued.

About the *Dragonar Academy* Character Designs!

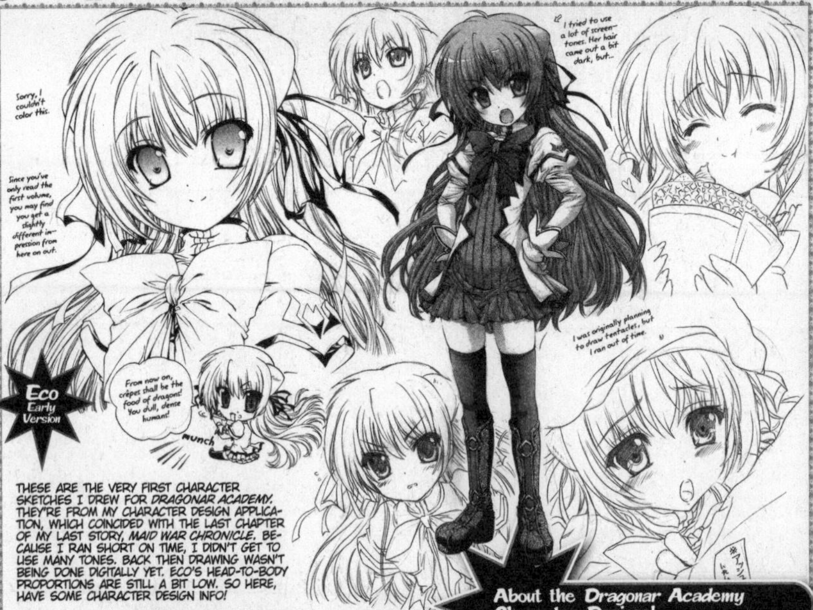
I tried to use a lot of screen-tones. Her hair came out a bit dark, but...
Sorry, I couldn't color this.
Since you've only read the first volume, you may find you get a slightly different impression from here on out.
I was originally planning to draw tentacles, but I ran out of time.
From now on, crêpes shall be the food of dragons! You dull, dense human!
MUNCH
Eco Early Version

THESE ARE THE VERY FIRST CHARACTER SKETCHES I DREW FOR *DRAGONAR ACADEMY*. THEY'RE FROM MY CHARACTER DESIGN APPLICATION, WHICH COINCIDED WITH THE LAST CHAPTER OF MY LAST STORY, *MAID WAR CHRONICLE*. BECAUSE I RAN SHORT ON TIME, I DIDN'T GET TO USE MANY TONES. BACK THEN DRAWING WASN'T BEING DONE DIGITALLY YET. ECO'S HEAD-TO-BODY PROPORTIONS ARE STILL A BIT LOW. SO HERE, HAVE SOME CHARACTER DESIGN INFO!

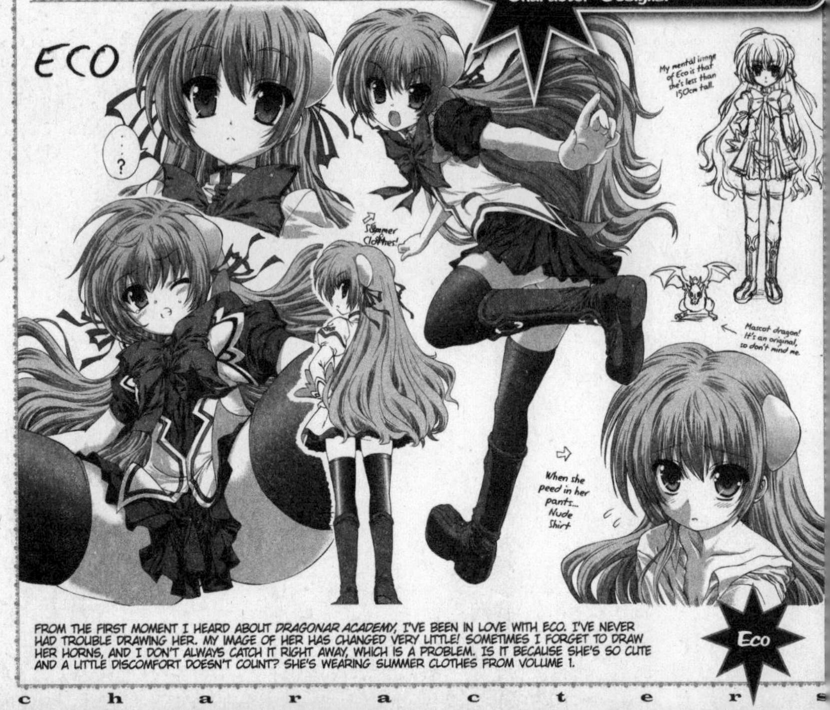
ECO
...?
My mental image of Eco is that she's less than 150cm tall.
Summer Clothes!
Mascot dragon! It's an original, so don't mind me.
When she peed in her pants... Nude Shirt
Eco

FROM THE FIRST MOMENT I HEARD ABOUT *DRAGONAR ACADEMY*, I'VE BEEN IN LOVE WITH ECO. I'VE NEVER HAD TROUBLE DRAWING HER. MY IMAGE OF HER HAS CHANGED VERY LITTLE! SOMETIMES I FORGET TO DRAW HER HORNS, AND I DON'T ALWAYS CATCH IT RIGHT AWAY, WHICH IS A PROBLEM. IS IT BECAUSE SHE'S SO CUTE AND A LITTLE DISCOMFORT DOESN'T COUNT? SHE'S WEARING SUMMER CLOTHES FROM VOLUME 1.

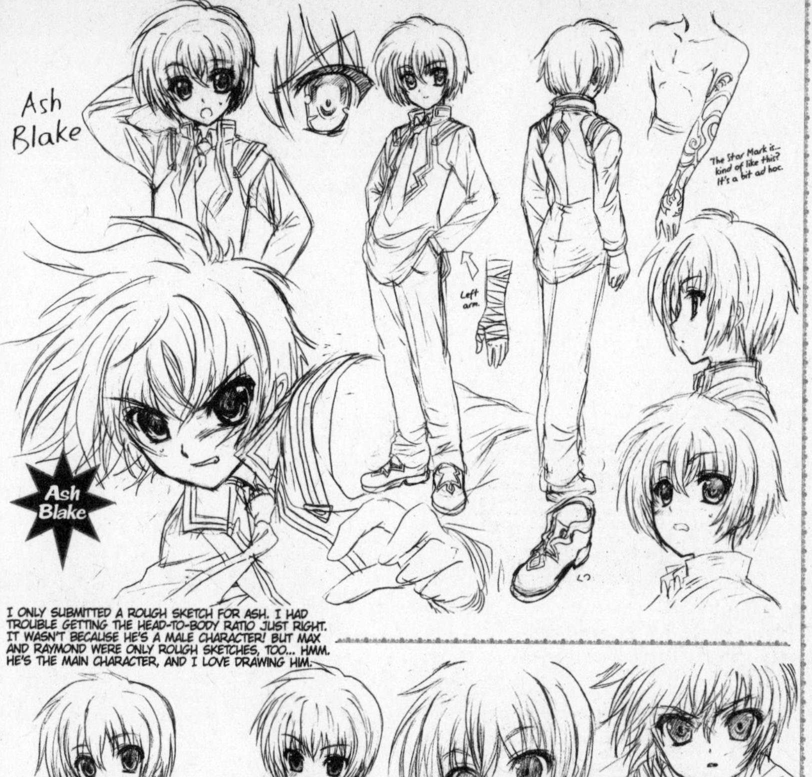
Ash Blake
The Star Mark is... kind of like this? It's a bit ad hoc.
Left arm.
Ash Blake

I ONLY SUBMITTED A ROUGH SKETCH FOR ASH. I HAD TROUBLE GETTING THE HEAD-TO-BODY RATIO JUST RIGHT. IT WASN'T BECAUSE HE'S A MALE CHARACTER! BUT MAX AND RAYMOND WERE ONLY ROUGH SKETCHES, TOO... HMM. HE'S THE MAIN CHARACTER, AND I LOVE DRAWING HIM.

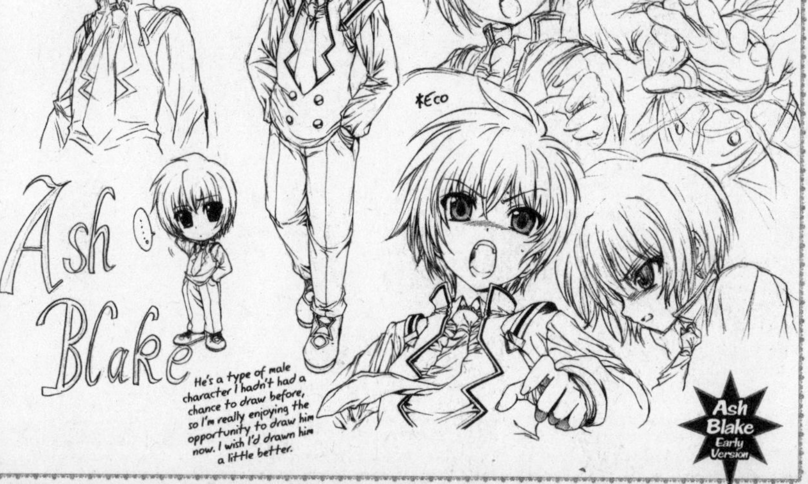
*Eco
Ash Blake
He's a type of male character I hadn't had a chance to draw before, so I'm really enjoying the opportunity to draw him now. I wish I'd drawn him a little better.
Ash Blake Early Version

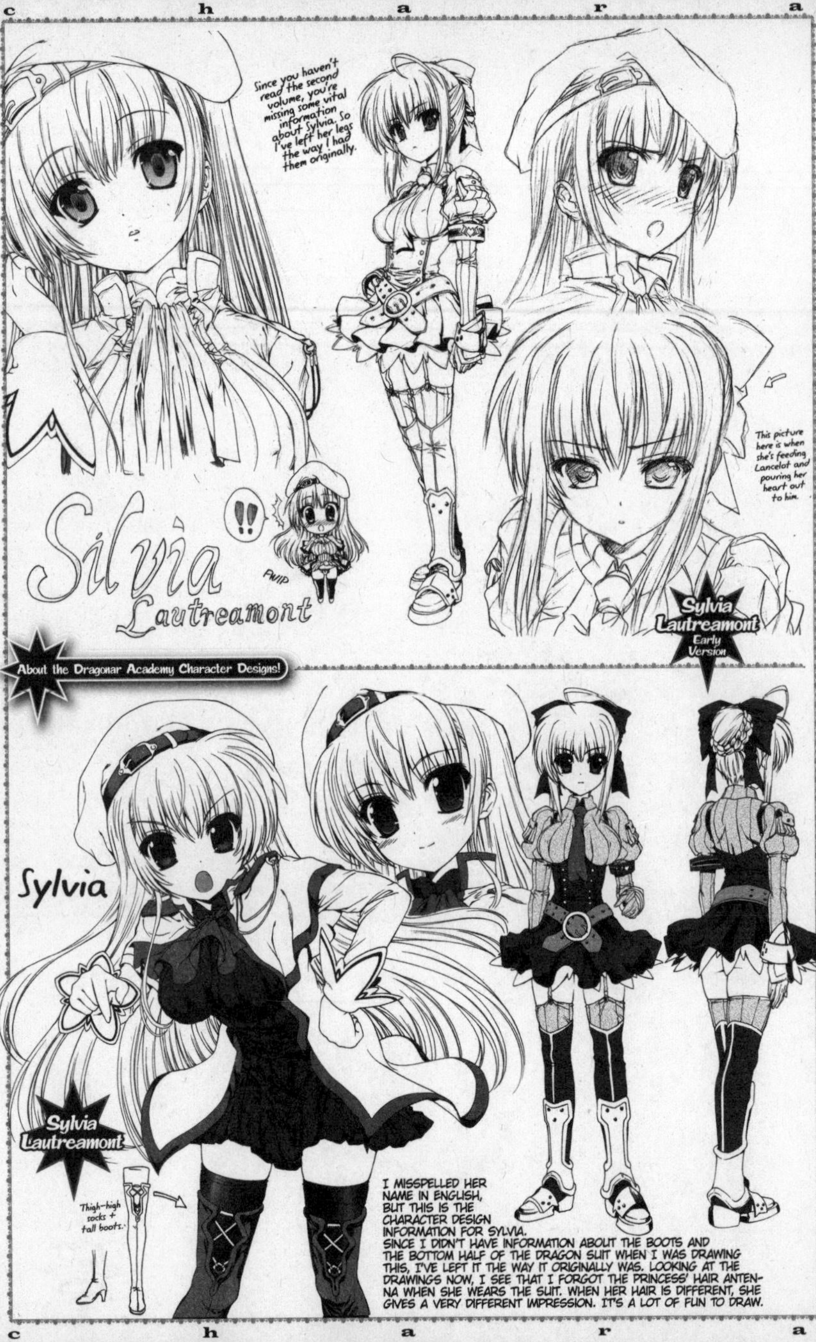
Since you haven't read the second volume, you're missing some vital information about Sylvia. So I've left her legs the way I had them originally.
This picture here is when she's feeding Lancelot and pouring her heart out to him.
!!
FWIP
Silvia Lautreamont
Sylvia Lautreamont Early Version
About the Dragonar Academy Character Designs!
Sylvia
Sylvia Lautreamont
Thigh-high socks + tall boots.
I MISSPELLED HER NAME IN ENGLISH, BUT THIS IS THE CHARACTER DESIGN INFORMATION FOR SYLVIA.
SINCE I DIDN'T HAVE INFORMATION ABOUT THE BOOTS AND THE BOTTOM HALF OF THE DRAGON SUIT WHEN I WAS DRAWING THIS, I'VE LEFT IT THE WAY IT ORIGINALLY WAS. LOOKING AT THE DRAWINGS NOW, I SEE THAT I FORGOT THE PRINCESS' HAIR ANTENNA WHEN SHE WEARS THE SUIT. WHEN HER HAIR IS DIFFERENT, SHE GIVES A VERY DIFFERENT IMPRESSION. IT'S A LOT OF FUN TO DRAW.

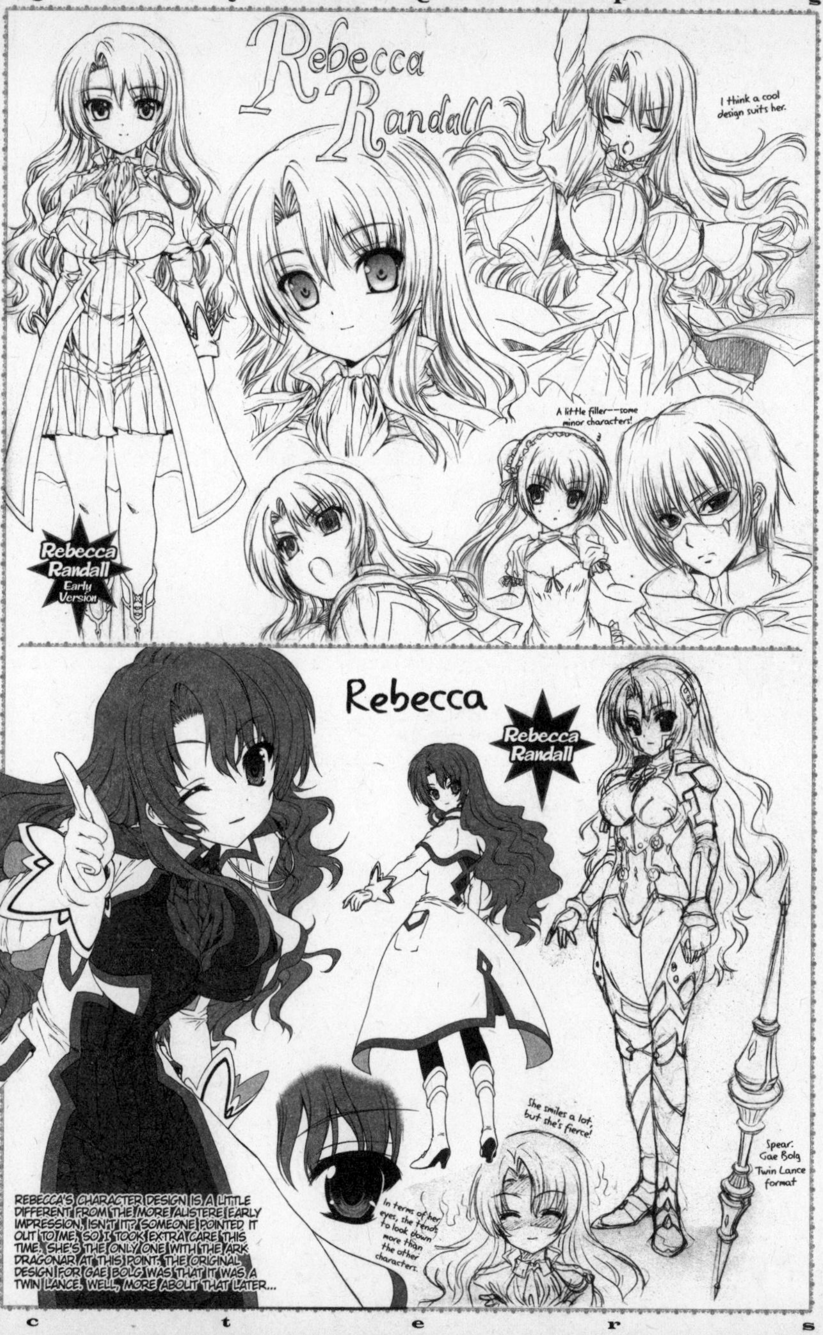
Rebecca Randall
I think a cool design suits her.
A little filler--some minor characters!
Rebecca Randall Early Version
Rebecca
Rebecca Randall
Spear: Gae Bolg Twin Lance format
She smiles a lot, but she's fierce!
In terms of her eyes, she tends to look down more than the other characters.
REBECCA'S CHARACTER DESIGN IS A LITTLE DIFFERENT FROM THE MORE AUSTERE EARLY IMPRESSION, ISN'T IT? SOMEONE POINTED IT OUT TO ME, SO I TOOK EXTRA CARE THIS TIME. SHE'S THE ONLY ONE WITH THE ARK DRAGONAR AT THIS POINT. THE ORIGINAL DESIGN FOR GAE BOLG WAS THAT IT WAS A TWIN LANCE. WELL, MORE ABOUT THAT LATER...

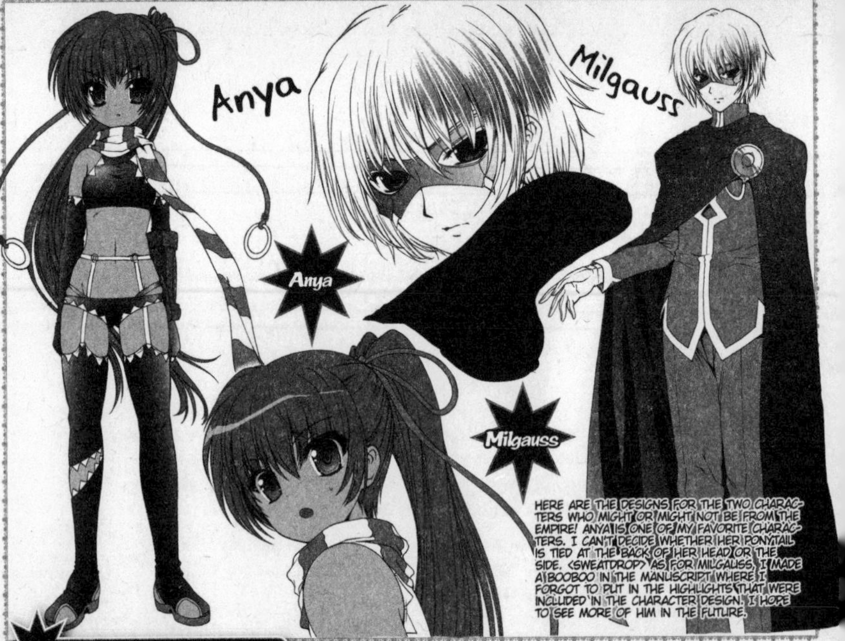
Anya
Milgauss
Anya
Milgauss
HERE ARE THE DESIGNS FOR THE TWO CHARACTERS WHO MIGHT OR MIGHT NOT BE FROM THE EMPIRE! ANYA IS ONE OF MY FAVORITE CHARACTERS. I CAN'T DECIDE WHETHER HER PONYTAIL IS TIED AT THE BACK OF HER HEAD OR THE SIDE. <SWEATDROP> AS FOR MILGAUSS, I MADE A BOOBOO IN THE MANUSCRIPT WHERE I FORGOT TO PUT IN THE HIGHLIGHTS THAT WERE INCLUDED IN THE CHARACTER DESIGN. I HOPE TO SEE MORE OF HIM IN THE FUTURE.

About the Dragonar Academy Character Designs!

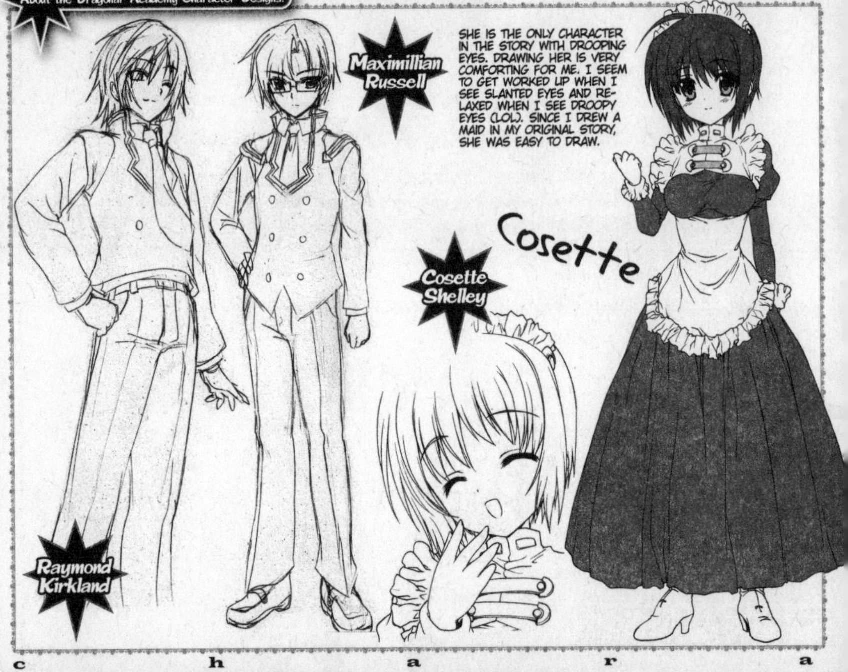
SHE IS THE ONLY CHARACTER IN THE STORY WITH DROOPING EYES. DRAWING HER IS VERY COMFORTING FOR ME. I SEEM TO GET WORKED UP WHEN I SEE SLANTED EYES AND RELAXED WHEN I SEE DROOPY EYES (LOL). SINCE I DREW A MAID IN MY ORIGINAL STORY, SHE WAS EASY TO DRAW.
Maximillian Russell
Cosette
Cosette Shelley
Raymond Kirkland

Comments from the original author for the light novel version of *Dragonar Academy*.

Original Story by Shiki Mizuchi

Meeting Ran-sensei was the greatest moment for this story--and the greatest moment for me, the author of the original.

Since April 2011, every time the latest issue of *Monthly Comic Alive* magazine comes out, I get lost in the manga version of *Dragonar Academy*--so lost that I forget that I was the author of the original story!

The manga version gives Ran-sensei's particular soft touch and liveliness to the characters, while remaining faithful to the character designs that Kohada Shimesaba created. Together, they portray a world with majestic dragons that run and fly in a fantastic European setting which is drawn down to the most minute detail.

While I send cheers and applause to Ran-sensei, I'm also inspired! As the original story author, I have to work to not be overshadowed.

I hope more people come to love *Dragonar Academy* through this manga version. It really is a lucky story!

Humbly,
Shiki Mizuchi

Character Design by Kohada Shimesaba

Hello! This is Kohada Shimesaba. Seeing characters I designed come alive so vividly is such a nice surprise! (LOL) I'm sure everyone will enjoy it!!

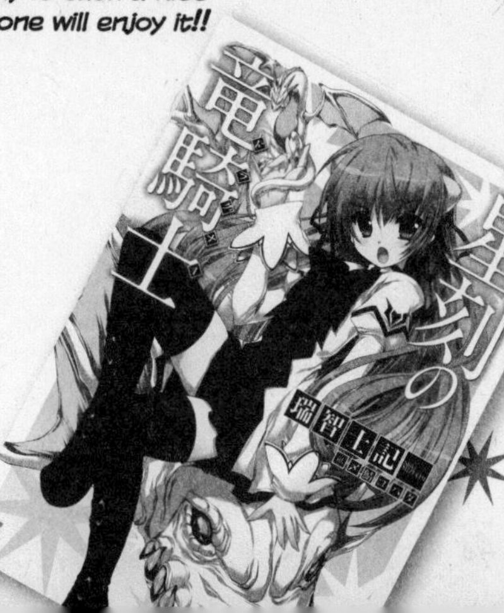
星刻の竜騎士

Postscript

Hi, this is RAN. How did you like the manga version of *Dragonar Academy*? I'm still learning, but I'll do my best to convey the wonderful, beautiful world created by Shiki Mizuchi-sensei... not to mention the adorable Eco and the others.

BTW, I like Eco's expression when she's not mad.

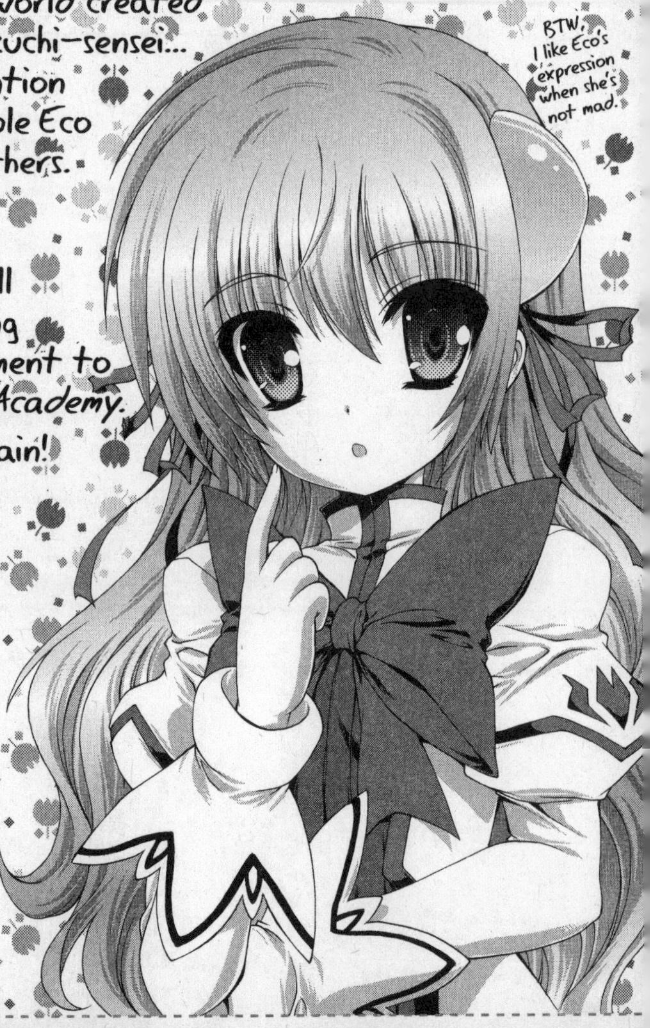

I hope you'll keep sending encouragement to *Dragonar Academy*.

See you again!

RAN

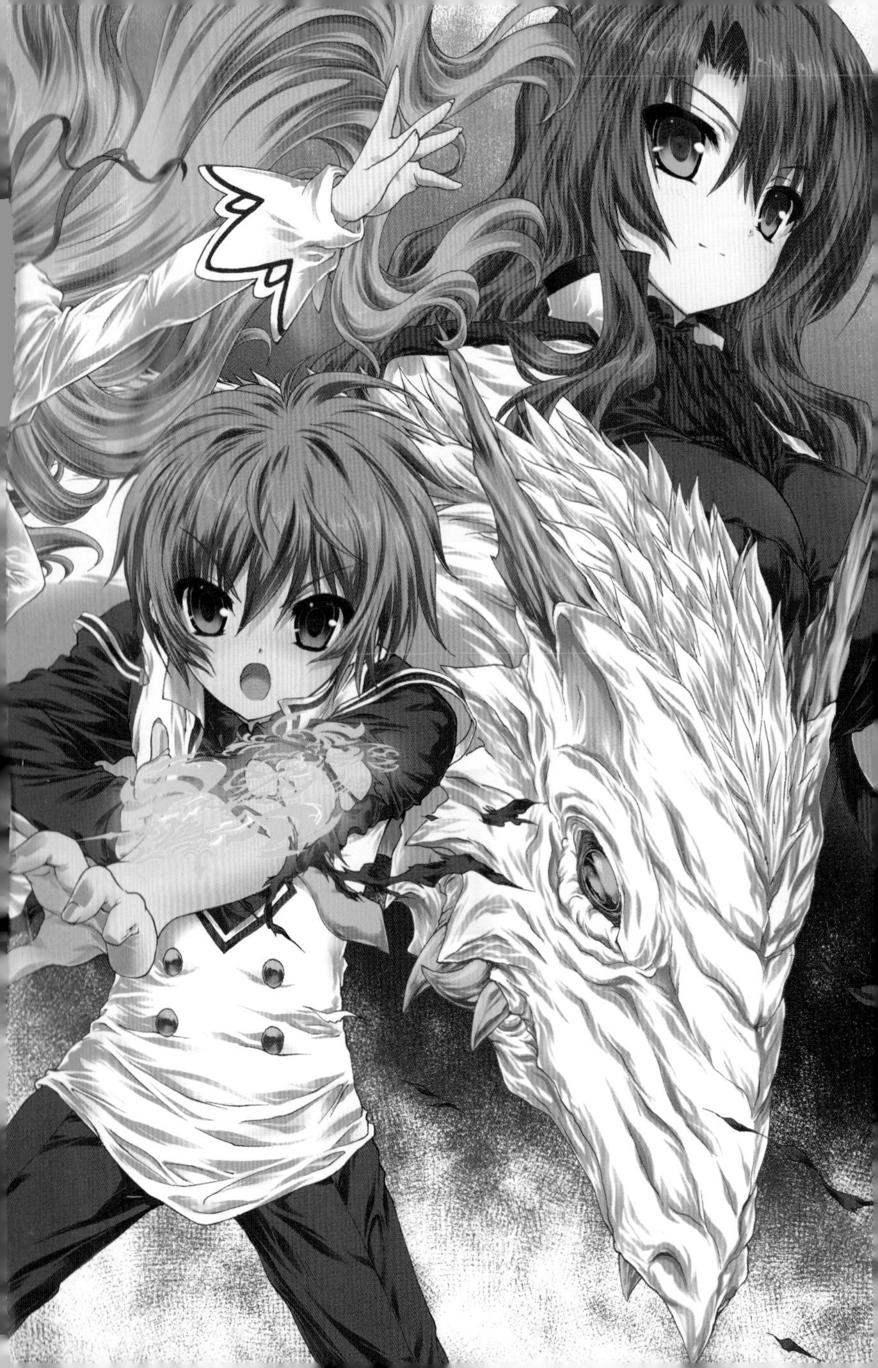

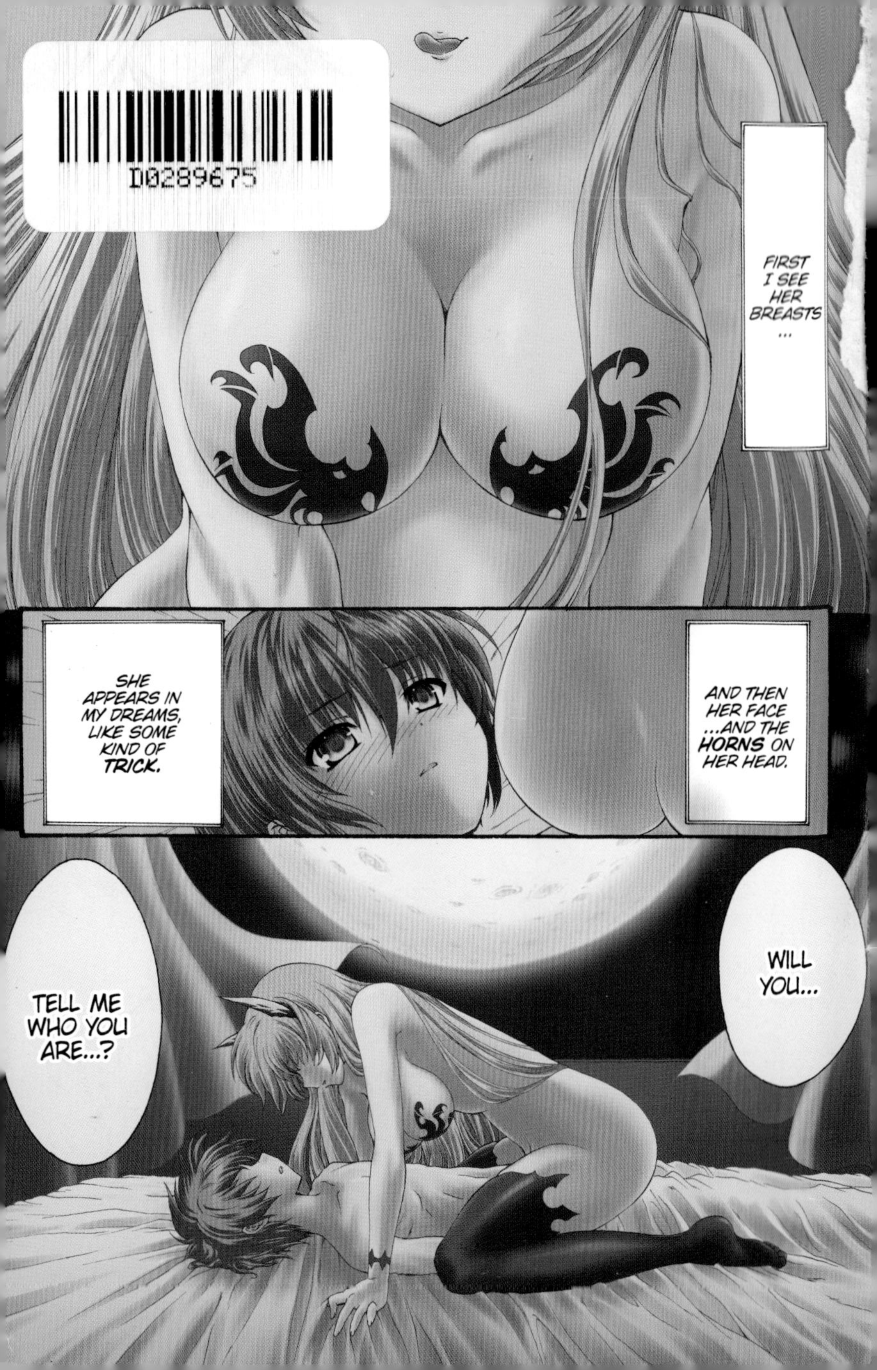

FIRST I SEE HER BREASTS ...
AND THEN HER FACE ...AND THE **HORNS** ON HER HEAD.
SHE APPEARS IN MY DREAMS, LIKE SOME KIND OF **TRICK.**
WILL YOU...
TELL ME WHO YOU ARE...?